12/03

A Companion to the Works of Franz Kafka

Studies in German Literature, Linguistics, and Culture

Edited by James Hardin
(*South Carolina*)

Camden House Companion volumes

The Camden House Companions provide well-informed and up-to-date critical commentary on the most significant aspects of major literary works, periods, or figures. The Companions may be read profitably by the reader with a general interest in the subject. For the benefit of student and scholar, quotations are provided in the original language.

A COMPANION TO THE WORKS OF

Franz Kafka

Edited by
James Rolleston

CAMDEN HOUSE

First published 2002 by Camden House

Camden House is an imprint of Boydell & Brewer Inc.
PO Box 41026, Rochester, NY 14604–4126 USA
and of Boydell & Brewer Limited
PO Box 9, Woodbridge, Suffolk IP12 3DF, UK

ISBN: 1–57113–180–9

Library of Congress Cataloging-in-Publication Data

A companion to the works of Franz Kafka / edited by James Rolleston.
p. cm. — (Studies in German literature, linguistics, and culture)
Includes bibliographical references and index.
ISBN 1–57113–180–9 (alk. paper)
1. Kafka, Franz, 1883–1924 — Criticism and interpretation.
I. Rolleston, James, 1939–   II. Studies in German literature, linguistics, and
culture (Unnumbered)

PT2621 .A26 Z6629 2002
833'.912—dc21

2002022298

A catalogue record for this title is available from the British Library.

This publication is printed on acid-free paper.
Printed in the United States of America

The publisher wishes to thank Schocken Books, New York, a Division of Random House, for permission to reprint quotations from the following works by Franz Kafka in the world excluding the United Kingdom and Commonwealth (but including Canada): *The Complete Stories*, edited by Nahum N. Glatzer, translated by Willa and Edwin Muir, copyright 1946, 1947, 1948, 1949, 1954, 1958, 1971 by Schocken Books; *The Trial, Definitive Edition*, translated by Willa and Edwin Muir, copyright 1925, 1935, 1946 and renewed 1952, 1963, 1974 by Schocken Books; *The Castle, Definitive Edition*, translated by Willa and Edwin Muir, copyright 1930, 1941, 1954 and renewed 1958 by Alfred A. Knopf, Inc.; *The Collected Stories*, edited and introduced by Gabriel Jospovici and published by Knopf/Everyman's Library; *Letters to Friends, Family, and Editors*, translated by Richard and Clara Winston and published by Schocken Books; and *The Diaries of Franz Kafka*, translated by Joseph Kresh, edited by Max Brod, and published by Schocken Books.

The publisher also wishes to thank the Random House Group, London, for permission to reprint quotations from the following works by Franz Kafka in the United Kingdom and Commonwealth (excluding Canada): *The Complete Stories*, edited by Nahum N. Glatzer, translated by Willa and Edwin Muir; *The Trial*, translated by Willa and Edwin Muir; *The Castle*, translated by Willa and Edwin Muir; *The Diaries of Franz Kafka 1910–1913*, translated by Joseph Kresh, edited by Max Brod, all published in the UK and Commonwealth by Martin Secker and Warburg.

For Rosalind

Contents

Preface

THIS VOLUME HAS COME into being at the initiative of James Hardin, whose vision for his Series is compelling: the best possible scholars are to be invited to write original essays that advance literary scholarship, while at the same time asking the broad questions that interest readers who are not scholars. With a single author, such as Franz Kafka, it is also essential to offer an overall account of his career, bringing all major texts into view. I have been fortunate indeed that such an eminent group of Kafka scholars accepted my invitation. And Kafka himself makes it easy to embrace Dr. Hardin's multiple goals: no critical issue concerning Kafka's work stays obscure for long, since his sentences have a way of addressing, directly and disconcertingly, the daily lives of subsequent generations.

We are particularly fortunate to have Walter Sokel's meditation on his "life of reading Kafka," which has also meant reading a half century of Kafka criticism — the ever renewed struggle to make "sense" of Kafka's potent enigmas. With slight modifications Sokel's essay also introduces his new collection of Kafka-essays, *The Myth of Power and the Self* (2002); I am grateful to Arthur Evans, director of the Wayne State University Press, for facilitating this dual event.

The present book has benefited from the close critical reading of James Walker, senior editor at Camden House: his probing queries were widely welcomed by the contributors. Finally I want to thank my outstanding assistant, Eleanor Johnson, whose command of both technology and style have been indispensable.

James L. Rolleston
Durham, N.C.
March 2002

Kafka's Works by Year of First Appearance, With Date of First English Translation

1908   Eight stories and sketches, among those later collected in the volume *Betrachtung*, published in the journal *Hyperion:*

"Der Kaufmann" ("The Tradesman," 1948)

"Zerstreutes Hinausschaun" ("Absent-Minded Window-Gazing," 1945)

"Der Nachhauseweg" ("The Way Home," 1945)

"Die Vorüberlaufenden" ("Passers-By," 1945)

"Kleider" ("Clothes," 1948)

"Der Fahrgast," ("On the Tram," 1948)

"Die Abweisung" ("Rejection," 1948)

"Die Bäume" ("The Trees," 1945)

1909   "Gespräch mit dem Beter" ("Conversation with the Supplicant"), "Gespräch mit dem Betrunkenen" ("Conversation with the Drunk"), from the manuscript of *Beschreibung eines Kampfes* (*Description of a Struggle*, 1958)

"Die Aeroplane in Brescia" ("The Aeroplanes at Brescia," 1947)

1910   Five stories from *Betrachtung* published in *Bohemia* as "Betrachtungen" (Meditations): includes four of the 1908 group (two temporarily retitled) plus "Zum Nachdenken für Herrenreiter" ("Reflections for Gentlemen-Jockeys," 1948)

1913   *Betrachtung* (*Meditation*, included in *The Penal Colony*, 1948). Collection includes nine stories beyond the nine previously published in 1908 and 1910:

"Kinder auf der Landstraße" ("Children on a Country Road," 1945)

"Entlarvung eines Bauernfängers" ("Unmasking a Confidence Trickster," 1948)

"Der plötzliche Spaziergang" ("The Sudden Walk," 1948)

"Entschlüße" ("Resolutions," 1948)

"Der Ausflug ins Gebirge," ("Excursion into the Mountains," 1948)

"Das Unglück des Junggesellen" ("Bachelor's Ill Luck," 1948)

"Das Gassenfenster," ("The Street Window," 1948)

"Wunsch, Indianer zu Werden" ("The Wish to Be a Red Indian," 1945)

"Unglücklichsein" ("Unhappiness," 1945)

"Das Urteil" ("The Judgment," 1945), written 1912

"Der Heizer. Ein Fragment" ("The Stoker," first chapter of *Amerika,* 1946), written 1911–12

1915   "Die Verwandlung" ("The Metamorphosis," 1937), written 1912

1916   "Vor dem Gesetz" ("Before the Law," 1948), written 1914

1917   "Schakale und Araber" ("Jackals and Arabs," 1942) and "Ein Bericht für eine Akademie" ("A Report to an Academy," 1934), published together as "Zwei Tiergeschichten" ("Two Animal Stories")

1918   "Ein Landarzt" ("A Country Doctor," 1945)

1919   "In der Strafkolonie" ("In the Penal Colony," 1941), written 1914

Ein Landarzt (*A Country Doctor,* 1948), collection of stories written 1917 except where noted:

"Der neue Advokat" ("The New Advocate")

"Ein Landarzt" ("A Country Doctor")

"Auf der Galerie" ("Up in the Gallery")

"Ein altes Blatt" ("An Old Manuscript," 1940)

"Vor dem Gesetz" ("Before the Law," 1948), written 1914

"Schakale und Araber" ("Jackals and Arabs," 1942)

"Ein Besuch im Bergwerk" ("A Visit to the Mine")

"Das nächste Dorf" ("The Next Village")

"Eine kaiserliche Botschaft" ("An Imperial Message")

"Die Sorge des Hausvaters" ("The Cares of a Family Man")

"Elf Söhne" ("Eleven Sons")

"Ein Brudermord" ("A Fratricide")

"Ein Traum" ("A Dream"), written 1914–15

"Ein Bericht für eine Akademie" ("A Report to an Academy," 1934)

1921   "Der Kübelreiter" ("The Bucket Rider," 1938), written 1916–17

1922   "Erstes Leid" ("First Sorrow," 1937)

"Ein Hungerkünstler" ("A Hunger Artist," 1938)

1924   *Ein Hungerkünstler* (*A Hunger Artist*, 1948), collection includes:
"Erstes Leid"
"Eine kleine Frau" ("A Little Woman," 1943)
"Ein Hungerkünstler"
"Josefine, die Sängerin oder Das Volk der Mäuse"
    ("Josephine the Singer, or the Mouse Folk," 1942)

1925   *Der Prozess* (*The Trial*, 1935), written 1914–15

1926   *Das Schloß* (*The Castle*, 1930), written 1921–22

1927   *Amerika* (*Amerika*, 1938), written 1911–12

1931   *Beim Bau der chinesischen Mauer* (*The Great Wall of China*, 1946).
First posthumous collection of stories, includes:
"Der Dorfschullehrer / Der Riesenmaulwurf" ("The Village
    Schoolmaster / The Giant Mole"), written 1914–15
"Die Brücke" ("The Bridge"), written 1916
"Der Jäger Gracchus" ("The Hunter Gracchus"), written 1917
"Beim Bau der Chinesischen Mauer," written 1917
"Der Schlag ans Hoftor" ("The Knock at the Manor Gate"),
    written 1917
"Der Nachbar" ("My Neighbor"), written 1917
"Eine Kreuzung" ("A Crossbreed / A Sport"), written 1917
"Eine alltägliche Verwirrung" ("A Common Confusion"),
    written 1917
"Die Wahrheit über Sancho Pansa" ("The Truth About Sancho
    Pansa"), written 1917
"Das Schweigen der Sirenen" ("The Silence of the Sirens),
written 1917
"Zur Frage der Gesetze" ("The Problem of Our Laws"),
    written 1920
"Prometheus," written 1918
"Das Stadtwappen" ("The City Coat of Arms"), written 1920
"Kleine Fabel" ("A Little Fable"), written 1920
"Die Abweisung" ("The Refusal"), written 1920
"Das Ehepaar" ("The Married Couple"), written 1922
"Von den Gleichnissen" ("On Parables"), written 1922
"Forschungen eines Hundes" ("Investigations of a Dog"),
    written 1922
"Der Bau" ("The Burrow"), written 1923–24

1936   *Beschreibung eines Kampfes: Novellen, Skizzen, Aphorismen aus dem Nachlass* (*Description of a Struggle,* 1958). Second posthumous collection, includes:

      "Beschreibung eines Kampfes," written 1904–9

      "Blumfeld, ein älterer Junggeselle" ("Blumfeld, an Elderly Bachelor," 1938), written 1915

      "Der Gruftwächter" ("The Warden of the Tomb," 1958), dramatic fragment, written 1916–17

      "Heimkehr" ("Homecoming"), written 1920

      "Nachts" ("At Night"), written 1920

      "Die Truppenaushebung" ("The Conscription of Troops," 1945), written 1920

      "Gemeinschaft" ("Fellowship"), written 1920

      "Die Prüfung" ("The Test"), written 1920

      "Poseidon" (1946), written 1920

      "Der Geier" ("The Vulture," 1938), written 1920

      "Der Steuermann" ("The Helmsman"), written 1920

      "Der Kreisel" ("The Top"), written 1920

      "Gibs auf!" ("Give it up!"), written 1922

      "Der Aufbruch" ("The Departure"), written 1922

1951   *Hochzeitsvorbereitungen auf dem Lande* (*Wedding Preparations in the Country,* 1954), written 1907–8

Abbreviations of Kafka's Works

B *Briefe 1902–1924.* Ed. Max Brod. Frankfurt am Main: S. Fischer; New York: Schocken, 1958.

BB *Beim Bau der chinesischen Mauer.* Ed. Hans-Gerd Koch. Frankfurt am Main: S. Fischer, 1994.

BK *Beschreibung eines Kampfes: Novellen, Skizzen, Aphorismen aus dem Nachlass.* New York: Schocken, 1946.

BV *Brief an den Vater.* Faksimile Edition mit einem Nachwort von Joachim Unseld. 1952. Frankfurt am Main: Fischer Taschenbuch Verlag, 1994.

BV/ZF "Brief an den Vater." *Zur Frage der Gesetze.* Ed. Hans-Gerd Koch. Frankfurt am Main: S. Fischer, 1994.

C *The Castle: A New Translation, Based on the Restored Text.* Trans. Mark Harman. New York: Schocken Books: 1998. Paperback: 1999.

CS *The Complete Stories.* Ed. Nahum N. Glatzer. New York: Schocken, 1971, 1983.

CollS *Collected Stories,* ed. Gabriel Josipovici, New York: Knopf/Everyman's Library, 1993

D *Drucke zu Lebzeiten.* Ed. Wolf Kittler, Hans-Gerd Koch, and Gerhard Neumann. Frankfurt am Main: S. Fischer, 1994.

EP *Das Ehepaar und andere Schriften aus dem Nachlaß.* Ed. Hans-Gerd Koch. Frankfurt am Main: S. Fischer, 1994.

F *Briefe an Felice und andere Korrespondenz aus der Verlobungszeit.* Ed. Erich Heller and Jürgen Born. Frankfurt am Main: S. Fischer, 1967.

H *Hochzeitsvorbereitungen auf dem Lande und andere Prosa aus dem Nachlaß.* Ed. Max Brod. Frankfurt am Main: S. Fischer, 1953.

L *Ein Landarzt und andere Drucke zu Lebzeiten.* Ed. Hans-Gerd Koch. Frankfurt am Main: S. Fischer, 1994.

LF   *Letters to Felice.* Trans. James Stern and Elisabeth Duckworth. Ed.
        Erich Heller and Jürgen Born. New York: Schocken Books, 1973.

LF/BV   *Letter to His Father/Brief an den Vater* (bilingual edition). Trans.
        Ernst Kaiser and Eithne Wilkins. New York: Schocken, 1966.

LFFE   *Letters to Friends, Family, and Editors.* Trans. Richard and Clara
        Winston. New York: Schocken, 1977.

M   *Briefe an Milena.* Ed. Jürgen Born and Michael Müller. Frankfurt
        am Main: S. Fischer, 1983.

NS I   *Nachgelassene Schriften und Fragmente I.* Ed. Malcolm Pasley.
        Frankfurt am Main: S. Fischer; New York: Schocken, 1993.

NS II   *Nachgelassene Schriften und Fragmente II.* Ed. Jost Schillemeit.
        Frankfurt am Main: S. Fischer; New York: Schocken, 1992.

P   *Der Proceß.* Ed. Malcolm Pasley. Frankfurt am Main: S. Fischer,
        1990.

S   *Das Schloß.* Ed. Malcolm Pasley. Frankfurt am Main: S. Fischer,
        1982.

SA   *Das Schloß, Apparatband.* Ed. Malcolm Pasley. Frankfurt am Main:
        S. Fischer, 1982.

SE   *Sämtliche Erzählungen.* Ed. Paul Raabe. Frankfurt am Main:
        S. Fischer, 1981.

T   *Tagebücher.* Ed. Hans-Gerd Koch, Michael Müller, and Malcolm
        Pasley. Frankfurt am Main: S. Fischer, 1990.

Tr   *The Trial.* Trans. Breon Mitchell. New York: Schocken, 1998.

U   *Das Urteil und andere Erzählungen.* Frankfurt am Main: Fischer
        Taschenbuch Verlag, 1997. (Based on: Franz Kafka, *Drucke zu
        Lebzeiten.* Kritische Ausgabe. Ed. Wolf Kittler, Hans-Gerd Koch,
        and Gerhard Neumann. Frankfurt am Main: S. Fischer, 1994.)

Introduction: Kafka Begins

James Rolleston

FRANZ KAFKA REMAINS the most widely read German author of the twentieth century, and it is worth seeking some precision as to why this is so. W. H. Auden famously called him "the author who comes nearest to bearing the same kind of relation to our age as Dante, Shakespeare, and Goethe bore to theirs" — yet he is an improbable Shakespeare: in his slender authorized corpus (he completed none of his three novels) there is no grand vision, no narrative culminating in usable meaning. Indeed it is the absence of these totalities that is the key to Kafka's enduring actuality. The century he uncannily anticipated was defined by the crisis of secular modernity: unable to maintain the guarantees of universal scientific and social progress, modernity has been convulsed by totalizing world views, such as fascism and religious fundamentalism, offering the very psychological stabilization that modernity resists. Kafka's spare, lucid, yet ultimately enigmatic texts confront, from countless different perspectives, the vulnerability of a modern psyche seeking refuge in the materiality and conventional assumptions of the present.

Because Kafka's best friend Max Brod possessed special authority as his literary executor, Brod's view of Kafka's stories as existentially religious gained canonical status in the 1920s and 1930s. But the more closely these texts were read, the less religious coherence they seemed to offer. They were perhaps definable as allegories or parables — but what did they allegorize, how could their "truth" be translated? Gradually it became evident that whatever worldview came to dominate the Western intellectual scene — existentialist, structuralist, postmodern — Kafka's writing seemed to respond eagerly, as if pioneering the new trend. To be sure, the "religious" reading could never become obsolete; Kafka's strategic use of Christian and Jewish motifs is unmistakable. But religious "truth," even one accessible only by negation of the world as presented, became ever less plausible. The decisive turn in twentieth-century Kafka studies, to which the present volume is obviously indebted, was the inversion of the modernist purification of language, so important to Kafka himself — the reactivation of the biographical dimension he had so rigorously excluded. This turn does not imply a new positivism (art "explained" by life), but is frankly heuristic: if Kafka's literary texts, diaries, letters, dreams are read in the context of the historical upheavals occurring all around him, what new points of entry to his achievement may we expect? We have learned a great deal about books he read, also about verbal choices he made when writing fiction; does all this material give us insight into the suggestiveness and durability of Kafka's works, including the fragmentary ones? The answer is a conditional yes, the condition being that a reader start by responding unreservedly to the intensity of Kafka's achieved stories.

Franz Kafka was born in Prague on 3 July 1883, eldest son of Hermann and Julie (née Löwy); two younger brothers died in infancy and his three sisters, Elli, Valli, and Ottla, were born in 1889, 1890, and 1892 respectively. This family constellation was decisive for Franz: he never really left Prague until near the end of his life (1923), and he became close to his sisters, particularly Ottla, in whose house in Zürau he convalesced in 1917–18 after the diagnosis of tuberculosis. His relations with his father were extremely difficult, being resolved (if at all) far too late, in the soberly accusatory "Brief an den Vater" (Letter to His Father) of 1919. He himself commented about the letter that it contained "Advokatenstreiche" (lawyer's tricks). Kafka trained as a lawyer, gaining his degree in 1906, and from 1908 until his formal retirement in 1922 worked for the semi-governmental Worker's Accident Insurance Company. He was a highly regarded official, but his work troubled him on two levels: he could not evade emotional involvement in the suits he tried, becoming interested in the socialist causes of the day; and he came to grudge the hours he spent at work, as his literary vocation became all-consuming — yet had to be pursued primarily at night.

Two particular experiences shaped Kafka, the best known being his "Heiratsversuche," or attempts to get married. He became engaged to marry three times, twice to a Berlin businesswoman, Felice Bauer, whom he met in August 1912, just over a month before he wrote his "break-through" story "Das Urteil" (The Judgment) in the single night of September 22–23. The tortuous, self-lacerating letters he wrote Felice were eventually published (1967) and render the dissolution of the engagements (1914, 1917) understandable; the diary entries from July 1914 convey his obsessive sense of being "on trial" for his own inadequacies — and contain the first sketches for *Der Process* (The Trial), which was then produced in its (incomplete) entirety in the fall and winter of 1914–15. The third engagement, to Julie Wohryzek in 1919, was, he felt (and contended in the "Brief an den Vater"), predestined to fail.

Kafka's second shaping experience was that of anti-semitism and its cultural impact on Jews, and it framed his life. His biographer Ernst Pawel reminds us of the frequent anti-semitic incidents in Bohemia, the Austro-Hungarian province where Kafka grew up, in the late nineteenth century (39–44). While Kafka's family were not particularly observant Jews, the conspicuous "identity" of Prague Jewry was inescapable. Kafka became increasingly interested in Jewish issues; in 1923, when he was already seriously ill (he died on 3 June 1924), he began studying Hebrew with a view toward emigration to Palestine. And his three sisters, as well as his close friend and Czech translator Milena Jesenská, all died in Nazi concentration camps between 1942 and 1944. Kafka spent the last year of his life in Berlin, his only "escape" from the multiple enclosures of his Prague-centered lifetime; his companion was an "Ostjüdin" (East European Jew), Dora Dymant. His heightened interest in the full range of Jewish experience gains its significance only in retrospect, but it offers yet another dimension to the symbiosis of his stories with the darkness and upheavals of the twentieth century.

Kafka's stories begin in the middle; or rather, near the end, as the very specific situational details seize hold of the hero's mind (sometimes his body too) and propel him forward. Indeed, as Henry Sussman reminds us below, the French critic Maurice Blanchot contended that Kafka's protagonists have in a sense already died; in the case of "Die Verwandlung" (The Metamorphosis, 1915) this thought probably occurs to most readers. Yet one can plausibly reverse this perspective and argue that the protagonists are "given birth" by the story, that, despite Kafka's deceptively "realistic," often quasi-conversational style, their prior existence as individuals lacks all specificity (here, of course, "Die Verwandlung" constitutes an elaborate exception). They seem to lack memory: when K. in *Das Schloß* (The Castle, 1926) "remembers" a past, his words appear contradictory, strategic, disingenuous. And Kafka himself lends support to the notion that birth is to be understood as a literary event. Famously he compared his story "Das Urteil" (The Judgment, 1913) to "eine regelrechte Geburt" (a regular birth, *T* 491). The contrasting status of non-literature, that is, his own life, is evoked in his diary for 24 January 1922: "Das Zögern vor der Geburt. Gibt es eine Seelenwanderung, dann bin ich noch nicht auf der untersten Stufe. Mein Leben ist das Zögern vor der Geburt" (Hesitation before birth. If there is a migration of souls, then I haven't yet reached the lowest level. My life is hesitation before birth, *T* 888, my translations).

My word for evoking this strange fusion of birth- and death-perspectives in a narrative would be hierarchy. The instant Kafka's characters come into existence, each moment is lived vertically, in relation to some "higher" dimension from which a process of judgment continually emanates. In the opening chapter of *Das Schloß* this is extremely obvious: verbal exchanges and physical movements are subjected to instant analysis in K.'s "mind," an analysis that often seems unconnected to conventional notions of character or motivation. Clearly such a fusion of behavior and judgment corresponds to a religious view of the world, an assumption of some ultimate "external" validity, and the initial "religious" interpretation of Kafka can never become irrelevant, as several essays in this volume emphasize: Kafka's explicit religious interests (Judaism, Kierkegaard, etc.) were intense and ongoing. Yet religion presumes a doctrinal consistency in the "external" perspective from which worldly behavior is judged, and that is what we never find in Kafka. The protagonists' mental language is imbued with ethical and spiritual values, but these "higher" words emanate from and immediately return to the worldly struggle that has, as it were, given birth to these characters, and that, by virtue of its ceaseless temporality, destabilizes all striving toward wisdom or detachment. "Noch war er frei" (He was still free, *P* 13), thinks Josef K. in the opening chapter of *Der Proceß* (The Trial, 1925): freedom as a higher value, freedom as something tactical, a quasi-authorial awareness of the whole story to come (Stanley Corngold stresses the near-simultaneous production of the book's first and last chapters) — all these elements are indissolubly present in K.'s language. It is time itself, being-in-the-world, that precludes all stable understanding. When K.'s lawyer, in a later chapter, evokes at tedious length the Court's strange customs, we read his words (with K.) either as a mythical production receding uselessly into the past, or as a text encoding tips for K.'s future behavior. The one thing we do not perceive is a stable description of a coherent world-structure.

Another way of describing this vertical-temporal quality of Kafka's fictional language is suggested by Saussurean linguistics, which were being formulated precisely during Kafka's lifetime. The key words are synchrony and diachrony: a language exists as a closed system in which words are defined through their difference from each other, not through any innate bond with material things. In speaking we construct sentences in time, diachronically, by ceaselessly making synchronic choices from the coherent dictionary of individual words that not only subsist in our minds but fundamentally structure the possibilities and parameters of our "thinking." All thinking is operational, in other words, and its operations synthesize, moment by moment, ancient "wisdom" embedded in the language, the urge to describe the material world — and of course the current motivations of the "self." In this model the synchronic dimension, the embeddedness of all sentences in a coherent language system, would correspond to the "judging" hierarchy of religion; but where religion would situate, a priori, the singular eye of God, the linguistic model precludes all singularity or higher value — its totalizing quality is definable solely through difference, the infinite potentiality of verbal combination. In practice, of course, the one version of hierarchy is quite compatible with the other, since religious constructions of the world pervade all language systems. What Kafka's protagonists do is to provoke these "systemic" reactions in the reader because of their uncanny closeness to their author: they let us see the synchronic word-choices Kafka is making, even as they struggle to assert their own perspectives on a fictional landscape. This mutual dependence of author and protagonist is something Kafka was very much aware of, becoming explicit in his well-known diary entry of 6 August 1914: "Der Sinn für die Darstellung meines traumhaft inneren Lebens hat alles andere ins Nebensächliche gerückt, und es ist in einer schrecklichen Weise verkümmert und hört nicht auf, zu verkümmern" (The project of portraying my dreamlike inner life has thrust everything else into irrelevance, where it atrophies terrifyingly and never ceases becoming atrophied, *T* 546).

Can one be more specific about how Kafka achieves this unique "self-portrayal"? Malcolm Pasley, one of the chief editors of the critical edition of Kafka's works, has written illuminatingly about the genesis of Kafka's texts. In "The Act of Writing and the Text" he stresses the immediacy of Kafka's sources, the way writing instruments and writing pads affect the fictional outcome far more than any preconceived plan. Indeed, in an early diary entry (15 November 1911) Kafka says that everything he writes according to such a plan turns out be "trocken, verkehrt, unbeweglich" (dry, wrong, inflexible, *T* 251); wonderful ideas come to him, but in the gap between experience and execution they sink into a kind of stream — he tries to grab at them but their fullness flows away from him, leaving him with something merely bad and disturbing. Pasley argues that this imagery of fullness sinking is constant in Kafka's self-description; for it to be recovered, total immersion is required, a writing that doesn't even exist until the image-flow is entered. Certainly that is how Kafka expressed himself on 23 September 1912, immediately after finishing "Das Urteil": "Die fürchterliche Anstrengung und Freude, wie sich die Geschichte vor mir entwickelte, wie ich in einem Gewässer vorwärtskam" (the fearful striving and joy as the story unfolded before me, as I advanced as if wading through water, *T* 460). The "dreamlike inner life" cannot be articulated any other way; obviously Kafka's mind is not empty when he sits down to write, but such pre-existing "experience" has no particular relevance to the process of fiction. Indeed, in a remarkable letter to Felice Bauer about "Das Urteil" (2 June 1913), Kafka remembers what he had been thinking: "[ich wollte] einen Krieg beschreiben, ein junger Mann sollte aus seinem Fenster eine Menschenmenge über die Brücke herankommen sehn, dann aber drehte sich mir alles unter den Händen" (I meant to describe a war; from his window a young man was to see a vast crowd advancing across the bridge, but the whole thing turned in my hands into something else, *F* 394). For Pasley the most remarkable thing is that Kafka then hardly revises at all: the story's own impulse drives it unerringly forward, and if its self-certainty falters, the evidence of the diaries is that Kafka simply stopped, drew a line underneath, and began something new. This is not always so, of course: Kafka struggled to complete certain stories ("Die Verwandlung" [The Metamorphosis], "In der Strafkolonie" [In the Penal Colony]) that were tantalizingly close to their "inner" perfection. But his core writing pattern certainly suggests why he was unable to complete any of his three novels.

Crucial as it is to understand Kafka's compositional method, attempting to do so raises more questions than it answers. The water imagery certainly evokes the Unconscious: was Kafka practicing a kind of "automatic writing" such as was to become popular among the surrealists? If, as he seems to say, he enters a "stream of consciousness," a style very well established in his youth (by Schnitzler and others), where does the drive to structural perfection come from? How are we to understand the intensely aware, self-reflexive, un-dreamlike quality of his prose? Pasley's thesis of the "gradual completion of the story as it is being written" (209) is unsatisfyingly circular. Certainly one can stress Kafka's modernism, his commitment to the potentially redemptive goals of an aesthetic language that we find also in contemporaries such as Rilke and Musil. But we still confront the apparent oxymoron of "unconscious perfection."

The concept of hierarchy can help us here. In a letter to Max Brod in April 1918 Kafka elaborates a spatial image of writing; Pasley cites the letter (202) but views it merely as a type of modernist depersonalization:

> wenn wir etwas schreiben . . . sind wir mit allem, was wir haben, auf den Mond übersiedelt, es hat sich nichts geändert, wir sind dort, was wir hier waren, im Tempo der Reise sind tausend Unterschiede möglich, in der Tatsache selbst keine, die Erde, die den Mond abgeschüttelt hat, hält sich selbst seitdem fester, wir aber haben uns einer Mondheimat halber verloren, nicht endgültig, hier gibt es nichts Endgültiges, aber verloren. (*B* 240–41)

[when we write something . . . we have moved to the moon with everything we have, nothing has changed, we are there what we were here,
a thousand differences are possible in the tempo for the journey, but
not in the fact of the journey itself; the earth, having shaken off the
moon, holds more firmly to its own identity, we however have lost our
identities for the sake of a home on the moon, not definitively, nothing
here is definitive, but lost nonetheless.]

In Kafka's image the moon of literature is inherently (but not definitively) other, yet it is striking how many details of his whimsical image
maintain the earth-moon linkage: there is a journey involved, with varied
pacing; once the writers are gone, the earth breathes more easily — but
of course it is the writers who discern this fact, who can view the earth
as a whole from their lunar perspective. This is the privileged standpoint
of the writer, the standpoint for which Kafka's characters yearn in vain,
the view from the moon. Through the medium of the character's situation, one inexorably embedded in the moving earth, the "vertical" image
of the world (defined for the protagonist by the world's systems) can be
opened upward, purified, given a literary value utterly unavailable to
earth's denizens imprisoned in their stories. There is nothing mystical,
or even aesthetic, about this perspective: Kafka's lunar view is fundamentally analytical, a probing of mundane events "as if" freedom from
the earth were possible. To be sure, no "identity" is available on the
moon, the writer has "lost" any such figuration. But such loss is prereq-
uisite to any truth. And it is this vertical relationship, between a diachronic story claiming total autonomy, and an analytical, synchronic view
of the world as radically Other, that constitutes the texture of Kafka's
storytelling.

Kafka's view from the moon can be updated technologically as a
camera focused on a particular earthly spot: based in outer space, the
camera both captures the world as a whole and moves in steadily, closer
and closer, to an unvarying place on the earth's surface. The perspective
is unchanging yet what is seen appears utterly different, indeed cannot
be recognized, depending on the distance from which the point on the
surface is viewed. The image of the camera eye might seem fanciful,
except that Kafka provides us with striking corroboration in the "Brief
an den Vater": "Manchmal stelle ich mir die Erdkarte ausgespannt und
Dich quer über sie hin ausgestreckt vor. Und es ist mir dann, als kämen
für mein Leben nur die Gegenden in Betracht, die Du entweder nicht
bedeckst oder die nicht in Deiner Reichweite liegen" (Sometimes I
imagine the earth spread out like an atlas and you covering its whole
expanse. And it seems then as though, for my life, only those regions can

have relevance that either you don't actually cover or that lie outside your domain, *BV/ZF* 60). In this perspective from above, Kafka's relation to his father becomes a single, synchronic system that defines the events of their lives a priori. But of course this moment is one of the most purely metaphorical, that is, fictive, in the entire "Brief." For whole stretches the vertical perspective is radically reversed, with Franz viewing his father from underneath: "Du stießest mich, so als wäre ich dazu bestimmt, mit paar offenen Worten in diesen Schmutz hinunter. Bestand die Welt also nur aus mir und Dir, eine Vorstellung, die mir sehr nahe-lag, dann endete also mit Dir diese Reinheit der Welt, und mit mir be-gann kraft Deines Rates der Schmutz" (With a few frank words you thus thrust me down into this dirt, as if I were destined to it. If the world consisted solely of you and me — an image to which I was much at-tracted — then this purity of the world ended with you and, by virtue of your advice, dirt began with me, *BV/ZF* 56). The "advice" involved the father's view that Franz should visit a prostitute; but the word "purity" signifies far beyond the context. Essentially Franz is denying the father's arrogation to himself of purity *in the letter* he is writing, that is, in the domain of his creativity. In life he has been in the position of one of his characters, looking upwards at a world of Value that is a priori and eludes his comprehension, let alone his reach. He could see his father's hypoc-risy in life, but that perception certainly did not cancel the claim to pu-rity. For one thing purity is a highly charged positive attribute in all language systems, even if only *ex negativo,* as antithesis to "impurity." Moreover, the word is particularly powerful in Kafka's cultural system, because of its association with modernism, with the pure/purified work of art. So Franz cannot escape the "synchronic" hierarchy that frames every "diachronic" move he makes in life. Attaining the "pure" comprehensiveness of the lunar perspective necessarily thrusts him back down into a daily world where purity belongs irrevocably to the Other, to the system embodied, however grotesquely, in his father. Through sheer analytical power Franz can gain an overview, but only momentarily: This is the moment of art, and it is indeed achieved through a "purifica-tion" of life — but it offers no escape from life, indeed it absolutely mandates a plunging in, an entering of the psychic water so that the process of emerging into art can be enacted yet again.

This hierarchy and its aporias conditioned everything Kafka wrote. In 1917, two years before the "Brief an den Vater," Kafka drafted the relig-ious (or anti-religious) aphorisms that Ritchie Robertson discusses in the present volume. No. 54, in particular, is relevant here, because its two paragraphs, often cited separately, evoke the hierarchical extremes we have seen operating in the "Letter":

> Es gibt nichts anderes als eine geistige Welt; was wir sinnliche Welt nennen ist das Böse in der geistigen und was wir böse nennen ist nur eine Notwendigkeit eines Augenblicks unserer ewigen Entwicklung.
> Mit stärkstem Licht kann man die Welt auflösen. Vor schwachen Augen wird sie fest, vor noch schwächeren bekommt sie Fäuste, vor noch schwächeren wird sie schamhaft und zerschmettert den, der sie anzuschauen wagt. (*BB* 236–37)

> [There exists nothing but a spiritual world; what we call the material world is the evil within the spiritual and what we call evil is but a necessary event in a single moment of our eternal unfolding.
> With the most powerful possible light one can dissolve the world. Faced by a weak gaze, the world becomes firm, faced by a weaker gaze it acquires fists, faced by an even weaker gaze it becomes bashful and shatters whoever dares to look directly at it.]

The first section evokes the top of the perceptual hierarchy in its purest form, with irrefutable (albeit circular) logic. For the word spiritual to have meaning, as Kafka sees it, it must be all-inclusive, must be the perspective that renders coherent such antitheses as time and space, good and evil. To apprehend the spiritual is like going to the moon, with the accompanying "loss" of which Kafka speaks in his letter to Brod: what is lost is the actual experience of evil, that is, material and temporal identity as such. From this distance time can be evoked quasi-spatially, as "eternal unfolding," but it cannot be lived. The second section slides down the hierarchy and conveys what living in time actually means. The first version of life, "dissolving" the world by focusing all one's energy, is the only viable one. To accept the world is to be defeated by it; to affirm conventional categories (good and bad) *within* the apparent ("material") framework of the world is to lose all access to the spiritual. The parable "Vor dem Gesetz" (Before the Law, 1914) spells this out. By seeking access to the law the "man from the country" empties his life of meaning. Only at the moment of death does he glimpse the "Glanz der unverlöschlich aus der Türe des Gesetzes bricht" (*L* 212; "radiance that streams inextinguishably from the gateway of the law," *CS* 4). The image of powerful light connects this phrase to Kafka's aphorism; one must generate one's own (creative) light in order to "dissolve" the world and become at one with the spiritual. If one accepts the world's categories, that is, "lives," one will never see the spiritual light, even though it shines all the time, "inextinguishably."

Kafka's aphorisms may seem to conduct the reader into an arcane, speculative universe. But it is crucial to remember that, as the imagery of the "Brief an den Vater" shows, Kafka is always struggling with the same cosmic issue; writing is always potentially "sacred," the only knowable embodiment of "the most powerful possible light," which is why virtually all Kafka's stories begin their life as diary entries. To begin a story is an act of "dissolution" (dissolving the everyday, cf. the images of water Kafka uses to evoke the genesis of "Das Urteil"), even when it ultimately looks like "construction." If we turn now to some actual beginnings, it is worth reviewing briefly Kafka's relationship to Gustave Flaubert, one of his central models throughout his life (the first diary reference to Flaubert is in 1904, the last in 1921). Flaubert, an originator of what became known as modernism, also moves his authorial "camera" freely in relation to his characters, sometimes viewing Emma Bovary as a rather trivial bourgeois woman, sometimes virtually identifying with her ("Mme. Bovary, c'est moi"), communicating her pain with enormous intensity. Flaubert has this freedom because it is language itself that counts for him, the stable top of his hierarchy. Literary language does not have to convey any "truth"; in fact, at the end of his career Flaubert became fascinated with stupidity and emotional emptiness, as in the "Dictionary of Received Ideas." His posture outside the bourgeois world, dedicated to the purification of language into style, appears unshakable.

This stability, as we have seen, is unavailable to Kafka. Fascinated, as Flaubert was, by the sheer ordinariness of life, Kafka could not exempt himself from it. He had to inhabit its darkest spaces and concentrate the "light" of his vision on dissolving it as a totality: it is only the achieved dissolution, the shattered world that can count, for Kafka, as modernist counter-totality. That is why he can hold so fast to words like "true" and "spiritual" while refusing them analytical content: these words stand for the perspective at the top of the hierarchy, a perspective that Kafka as author can only glimpse and never authentically occupy.

The first sentence of *Madame Bovary,* in Francis Steegmuller's translation, reads as follows: "We were in the study hall when the headmaster entered, followed by a new boy not yet in school uniform and by the handyman carrying a large desk." The "new boy" is of course Charles Bovary; the novel begins and ends with him. But the "camera" of the sentence is placed at a distance. The "we" play no special role, they only enable the narrator to enter the schoolroom and simply, delightedly, *describe.* The text's ambitions are to construct, and simultaneously to compress, an era in a provincial place: details are self-contained, they may or may not refer "symbolically" to a character's emotions (some clearly do), but their key mission is to be authentic while conveying the author's irony. Thus the large desk evokes the pomposity and rigidity of the bourgeois school environment — without dwelling on such points. The novel's claim to truth derives from conveying both the intricacy and the *closure* of this provincial world. It begins in the school because that is where "values" are inculcated, where the triviality that drives Emma crazy (and by which she has been shaped herself) becomes the norm. The opening sentence points to a "constructive" texture, a simultaneous proliferation and deconstruction of details that have meaning only as microelements in an emerging fusion of world and style.

The opening sentence of "Das Urteil" also situates its protagonist with seeming precision: "Es war an einem Sonntagvormittag im schönsten Frühjahr" (*L* 39; "It was a Sunday morning in the very height of spring," *CS* 77). Actually the standard English translation misleads, missing the "fairy-tale" tonality that darkens the morning light: "It was *on* a Sunday morning. . . ." What is the "it"? We don't know yet, because the hero, Georg Bendemann, doesn't know: his perceptions are producing the "most beautiful" spring morning, the illusion of harmony on which the "it" intervenes. If we think back to the aphorism we recognize that Georg has the "even weaker gaze" (as the paragraph continues, it stresses how little he actually notices) that characterizes one whom the world will "shatter." In terms of Kafka's hierarchical vision, the "it" is the sinking below the surface of life that will constitute this "breakthrough" story. The special quality of "Das Urteil" is that the dissolving of Georg's world occurs *through* his construction of it as meaningful: what the reader gradually sees through his eyes is the radical *inauthenticity* of the construction. The contrast with Flaubert could not be starker: where Flaubert's details accumulate in their empty authenticity, Kafka's details are there to be shattered — and are indeed shattered, one by one, by the father who, for this one "moment" in humanity's "infinite unfolding," is entitled to the voice of the spiritual.

We have seen how Kafka returned repeatedly to the meaning of "Das Urteil" for his art, to the almost involuntary "dissolving" power of its opening. Later he became more conscious of the role of beginnings, of the power of certain sentences to open onto the depths, while so many others (in the Diaries) lead only to a faltering, a non-dissolution and hence a non-world. The late stories usher us into the protagonist's various obsessions with a virtuosity that is to be savored. "Der Bau" (The Burrow, 1923–24) opens: "Ich habe den Bau eingerichtet und er scheint wohlgelungen" (*EP* 165; "I have completed the construction of my burrow and it seems to be successful," *CS* 325). With this character, Kafka transposes the "downward" movement of the hierarchy onto a real underground creature; the earth will do as well as water to convey the indispensable dissolving/crumbling premise of creativity. First to go, obviously, is the dream of completion as such: the burrow is "completed," yet the entire (incomplete) story is devoted to its incompletion, or rather, to the oxymoronic quality of "a complete burrow." Indeed the projection of something "complete" becomes ever more fantastic, as in the almost free-floating image of the ideal "Burgplatz" (castle keep). Moreover, the perfect tense of the opening sentence ushers in the entire struggle of the protagonist with temporality. The burrow is literally a life's work; it embodies the various intensities of past years. But it is precisely not a work of art, the protagonist cannot stand back from it, much though he would like to. It is a structure in the world, a structure for living, and as such it mocks the use of the perfect tense. As the protagonist strives to shape past and present into a continuum, his memory taunts him with the various physical actions he used to be able to execute but can no longer. To speak in the perfect tense is to envision one's death; moreover, even the work of art cannot justify its author's "life" (as Kafka tells us so plainly in the "Brief an den Vater") — and the burrow is not a work of art. The word "scheint" (seems) anticipates the debate between Martin Heidegger and Emil Staiger in the early 1950's about a Mörike poem and the double meaning of "scheinen": to seem/to shine. If we deploy the hierarchical metaphor, Kafka's usage permits just such ambivalence. Certainly the "seeming" of the burrow's completion literally crumbles away; but that very process, in its comprehensive exploration of possible motivations, dreams, obsessions, generates the not-quite-complete (but magisterial) story that we have. On this meta-level of a story about itself, the burrow indeed "shines" with the light of the spirit.

In Kafka's very last story, about Josephine the singing mouse, the stakes involved in art-creation are raised still further. "Unsere Sängerin heißt Josefine" (*L* 274; "Our singer is called Josephine," *CS* 360). The hierarchical ambivalence of the first two words is extreme: Josephine is our *singer,* she is the very embodiment of the mouse-folk's need for collective meaning; when she sings, it is as if the history and legends of the people are compressed into pure sound and "realized" in the moments of performance. But she is also *our* singer, little more than an artisan, a worker whose artistry is non-transferable to everyday life: prophetic leader and near-slave in a single appellation. The verb "heißt" (is called) is also suggestive: the naming would seem to be a kind of privilege, the assignment of singular status; but the naming also projects forward to the very end of the story, when we hear that Josephine will be "vergessen . . . wie alle ihre Brüder" (forgotten like all her brothers). The naming will be essentially revoked, rendered meaningless, "da wir keine Geschichte treiben" (since we do not practice history); moreover, since the story plays out entirely in the present tense, the simple verb "heißt" is gradually but irrevocably dissolved. Yet even as the story puts every aspect of Josephine's "art" in question, it strives to re-base that art through a kind of reception theory: the audience re-generates her singing as a collective memory, a strictly momentary vision of the whole story of mousedom.

In reassigning the lunar perspective, the glimpse of the whole, from Josephine to the mouse-folk, Kafka is clearly thinking of his readers, of the reception process that his particular aesthetics cannot do without. Several essays in this volume culminate in the posing of the core hermeneutic question of translation from text back to world, notably Walter Sokel's citing of Kafka's seemingly bewildered question to Felice about the meaning of "Das Urteil": he, Kafka, professes now not to "understand" it at all. In a sense such non-understanding is structurally mandated by Kafka's hierarchy. The very categories of earthly understanding *must* be dissolved in order for a work of art to come into being that formally cannot be translated back into the world of the partial, the experiential, the temporal. Kafka may well have been terrified by the purity of his own aesthetics; for the concept of autonomous art, an article of faith for Flaubert and so many modernists, was ultimately unavailable to him. The "spiritual" telos of his stories simply cannot be circumscribed by the categories of aesthetics. As Clayton Koelb has it, Kafka must imagine his readers, must somehow integrate the process of dissolution with the potential of reception.

Among Kafka's early readers it was Walter Benjamin who saw most clearly that interpretation is not just a secondary activity provoked by the enigma of the primary texts. Interpretation is integral to Kafka's modernism in a special sense. Since he has no Flaubertian aesthetic perch from which to view the disintegration of modern experience, he must plunge down into the maelstrom himself, with language as his only tool — and it cannot be a language of description: lacking a fixed vantage point, everything, including (indeed especially) his own body, becomes alien territory for Kafka. Benjamin reminds us that the collapse into fragmentation had already occurred, articulated by Hofmannsthal in the famous "Chandos Letter" of 1901 as a collapse of language. And Benjamin suggests, in a late letter to his friend Theodor Adorno written in 1940, that

Kafka began to speak at that very moment of silence, of the ruin of tradition: "Perhaps the language which escaped Hofmannsthal was the very language which was given to Kafka at around the same time. For Kafka took on the task which Hofmannsthal had failed morally, and therefore also poetically, to fulfil" (329).

Interpretation thus becomes a primal activity: as the tradition of bourgeois norms disintegrates, the modern big city dweller (so Benjamin argues) becomes indistinguishable from the prehistoric consciousness, released by the collapse of restraints on memory into the domain of the everyday. And the impossibility of individual identity is underlined by the insights of modern physics; Benjamin cites at length a passage from the physicist Arthur Eddington, written in 1929, about the hazards of entering a room: "In the first place I must shove against an atmosphere pressing with a force of fourteen pounds on every square inch of my body. I must make sure of landing on a plank traveling at twenty miles a second around the sun — a fraction of a second too early or too late, the plank would be miles away" (*Illuminations* 142). With the implosion of "civilized" norms, interpretation becomes the first stage of consciousness, and is utterly without ontological ground: one can (must) associate one experiential fragment with another. But, as the quotation from Eddington emphasizes, one must also tear apart apparent fixity. Silence and paralysis would seem inevitable. Yet Kafka, as Benjamin shows, persisted in functioning, in reconstructing the processes of consciousness, within this primal fragmentation. Interpretation links the flashes of perception; but consciousness also *organizes*, projects temporal sequences into a mask of coherence. Kafka's work is full of organizations; Benjamin stresses the constant interplay, particularly in evocations of the law, between exaggerated precision and ceaseless flux: "None [of the law's messengers] has a firm place in the world, firm, inalienable outlines. There is not one that is not either rising or falling, none that is not deeply exhausted and yet is only at the beginning of a long existence. To speak of any order or hierarchy is impossible here" (117). For Benjamin, Kafka essentially defines "organization as destiny" (123), and provides the mythical figure for that destiny in the building of the Great Wall of China: infinitely detailed, infinitely pointless, "organizing" time to the stage where both origins and goals recede into enigma.

Perhaps Benjamin's best known insight into Kafka is his articulation of the importance of *gesture:* "Kafka's world is a world theater. For him, man is on the stage from the very beginning" (124). This may be the step that radically differentiates Kafka from other modernists: he does not claim the "identity" of observer or anthologist (like, say, Joyce) because he cannot, his plunge into the fragmentation of modernity is accompanied at every stage by *other* consciousnesses, by interested parties who may or may not be from his own time. The importance of gesture is totally traditional, and in a stable epic world the gestures of the players certify the symbolic framework. In Kafka, the impact of gesture is even greater, precisely because the interpreting consciousness is desperate for understanding — but the gestures remain undecidable, whether or not they "confirm" the spoken words that may accompany them: in the present volume Corngold and Theisen in particular explore this anguished confluence of interpretation and gesture. Interpreting, organizing, gesturing (and being gestured at): these are the primal processes of consciousness, processes that used to indicate outcomes and frameworks, but that in Kafka's world are forever in motion, enveloped in opacity, the more certainly endangered the more they appear stable.

Walter Benjamin knew little of the "facts" of Kafka's life, facts that Kafka famously excluded from his work; but he did read Max Brod's biography when it was published in 1938 — and was thoroughly skeptical about it. In his letter to Gerhard Scholem of 12 June 1938 (excerpted in *Illuminations* without the Brod discussion), Benjamin finds the temperamental incompatibility between Kafka and his friend to be extreme, concluding: "His friendship with Brod is for me above all a question mark, one that he wished to erect at the margin of his life" (*Briefe* 764, my translation). This sentence of Benjamin's resonates throughout the enormous accumulation of biographical data about Kafka entering the public realm in the 1970s. The work of Binder, Wagenbach, Stölzl, Robertson, and others has enduring validity; but this radical inversion of the "timeless" Kafka undoubtedly tempted some critics to reductiveness, to the sense that the "Kafka problem" could be solved by history. But Benjamin reminds us that for Kafka, who indeed asserted that he was "nothing but literature," life circles back towards work in an endless series of loops.

If we are now in a very productive era of Kafka scholarship, benefiting from linguistic theory and cultural studies, it is because Benjamin's resolute skepticism towards historicism frames the new explorations of Kafka's situatedness. Indeed the integration of biographical material with contemporary theory enables critics to renew the intensity of Benjamin's modernist reading. Benjamin writes: "Kafka's work presents a sickness of tradition. . . . We can no longer speak of wisdom. Only the products of its decay remain" (*Illuminations* 143–44). Today we might rephrase this world-historical process as a decentering of the Western tradition — and a quest for the counter-traditions, the "subaltern voices" that speak from underneath the Eurocentric surface. It is precisely Kafka's combination of experiential fragmentation with stylistic rigor that opens his texts to new kinds of historical understanding. It is the thinking of difference in every sense that enables cultural studies to locate new vocabularies in the moment of bourgeois disintegration. With uncompromising honesty Kafka pulverizes seeming continuities into gestures and fragments of myth and habit. And precisely because Saussurean linguistics has led to our understanding of the arbitrary constructedness of thought and feeling, cultural studies can articulate codes and assumptions in Kafka's texts without in any way imposing some new rigidity or claim to truth. As Elizabeth Boa argues, for example: "Kafka portrays relations between the sexes as power relations, but not as a simple timeless melodrama between male and female principles. In his work gender, class, generational, and ethnic tensions constantly interact" (21). The contested nature of cultural codes means that the flux and fragmentation outlined by Benjamin in Kafka's writing is made even more legible by close attention to both the prejudices and the "commonsense" that infused the world he confronted daily.

This applies *a fortiori* to the overtly "cultural" world inhabited by a man of Kafka's status and education. Mark Anderson's book *Kafka's Clothes* explores the many meanings of aestheticism, as ideology and as fashion, in Kafka's cultural perspective; it is the very rigor with which Kafka sought to exclude such motifs from his fictions that makes them perceptible. Uncompromising negation, as Benjamin stresses, is the defining gesture of Kafka's relation to traditions and ideologies, one that he sought to work out in detail in his 1917 aphorisms (explored here by Ritchie Robertson). But this negativity necessarily contains what is being negated; and in our era after modernism, indeed after many other isms, our "organizational" need to restructure the past can gain new sustenance from Kafka. As Anderson argues:

> Kafka's negative relation to history is itself subject to historical analysis — specifically, it developed as a particular phase in the history of West European Judaism. . . . There is a necessity to Kafka's negativity which historical reconstruction should not attempt to deny. But nor should one confuse cause and effect by arguing from the vantage point of what Kafka's texts have come to mean for later generations. For Kafka and his contemporaries, negativity had a precise historical content, quite different from that of French Existentialism, Surrealism, the Second World War, or deconstructive theories of language. Negative does not mean nothing; it exists in relation to something. (*Reading Kafka*, 21)

Anderson's evocation of past Kafka-readings reminds us that a continuum of intense arguments exists between Benjamin's modernism and cultural studies. This continuum is what Walter Sokel magisterially explores in the opening essay of this book, as he reflects on his sixty years of reading and writing about Kafka. The immense variety of the other contributions evokes the heuristic scope of cultural studies. In a potential analogy to the two poles of Kafka's own creative hierarchy (as I have outlined it), cultural studies dissolves the hermeneutic center (the circle of author, work, and reader) in two opposite directions. On the one hand the interpretive camera focuses down into the key words of Kafka's fictions, textual movement and self-reflection at the micro-level: Stanley Corngold's study of the opening pages of *Der Proceß* exemplifies this quest. His restless dissection of the "verhaftet/gefangen" (arrested/taken captive) diptych can be linked to Russell Berman's probing of "urteilen" (judging) and Bianca Theisen's reassessment of the spectator's "weeping" in "Auf der Galerie" (Up in the Gallery, 1917). The very formalization of events in language opens onto the depths where concepts twist and turn, both enabling and undermining the flux of human "intentions."

At the other extreme cultural studies opens Kafka's stories to the popular, legal, even literary texts that were swirling about him in his daily life, sometimes reaching the status of reference in his diaries or letters. Given the very special creative process we have been discussing — the dissolving of a formal individual perspective into a psychic "world" that is then to be shattered and transcended — intertextual readings of Kafka have the potential to be extremely fruitful. And so it is with the essays here by Goebel and Zilcosky, linking Kafka's works to colonialist and orientalist writing of the era, with which he was demonstrably familiar. Such discussions by no means purport to explain the inexplicable; the wealth of biographical material now available has on occasion tempted readers to "translate" literary events into documented moments in Kafka's personal experience. Such interpretation violates two key elements of Kafka's creativity: the continuum of subjective events (certainly including his reading) in the psychic depths, that is, the meaninglessness of singling out what is "personal"; and the fundamental Otherness of literature, its emergence through a drastic pulverizing of subjectivity. What Goebel and Zilcosky do, in contrast, is to suggest dimensions of Kafka's uniquely hierarchical shaping of his characters' experience, such as the colonialist trope of "overseeing" (or "surveying") native territory, both aestheticizing it and defining it in relation to a metropolitan center. Does this critical opening to the norms and fashions of Kafka's world conflict with his modernist vision of a purified literature? Fidelity to Kafka's dream is certainly difficult for a critic, precisely because we now know how much is going on above and beneath every phrase. But Richard Gray shows that it is not impossible: by fusing specific close readings of passages from "In der Strafkolonie" (particularly the opening) with an ongoing review of the interpretive traditions, Gray offers a very full perspective on what has been said and can still be said about Kafka's great story. Such an essay amounts to a kind of archive about a given Kafka text, ordering the history of past thinking for a reader to explore, taking a strong position (it could not be otherwise; a critic is not a librarian) but showing how that position has emerged in history and how it might develop in the future.

This collection of essays aims to interest all Kafka readers, hence quotations are given in English as well as German. The ongoing Critical Edition of Kafka is the textual base for most (but not all) of the contributors. Some use published translations, but many essayists, including myself, prefer to do our own translations. However, the *Complete Stories* (Schocken 1971, 1983) is generally referenced, since most readers of Kafka in English know it. In the case of *Der Proceß* and *Das Schloß*, very recent re-translations (by Breon Mitchell and Mark Harman) have quickly established themselves as normative. In this volume Mark Harman explores what is involved in translating the new Critical Edition. Kafka may not have revised his texts much, but he certainly cut a lot out; by exploring these "variants" (deleted passages in the manuscript of *Das Schloß*) Harman opens yet another window onto the invention and production of Kafka's characters.

Works Cited

Anderson, Mark, ed. *Reading Kafka: Prague, Politics and the Fin de Siècle*. New York: Schocken, 1989.

——, *Kafka's Clothes: Ornament and Aestheticism in the Habsburg Fin-de-Siècle*. New York: Oxford UP, 1992.

Benjamin, Walter. *Illuminations*. Ed. Hannah Arendt. Trans. Harry Zohn. New York: Schocken, 1968.

——. *Briefe*. Ed. Gershom Scholem and Theodor W. Adorno. Frankfurt am Main: Suhrkamp, 1978.

——, and Theodor W. Adorno. *The Complete Correspondence 1928–1940*. Ed. Henri Lonitz. Trans. Nicholas Walker. Cambridge: Harvard UP, 1999.

Binder, Hartmut. *Motiv und Gestaltung bei Kafka*. Bonn: Bouvier, 1966.

——. *Kafka in neuer Sicht*. Stuttgart: Kröner, 1976.

———, ed. *Kafka-Handbuch*. Stuttgart: Kröner, 1979.

Kafka, Franz. *Briefe 1902–1924*. Ed. Max Brod. Frankfurt am Main: S. Fischer; New York: Schocken, 1958. (*B*)

———. *Briefe an Felice*. Ed. Erich Heller, Jürgen Born. Frankfurt am Main: S. Fischer; New York: Schocken, 1967. (*F*)

———. *The Complete Stories*. Ed. Nahum N. Glatzer. New York: Schocken, 1983. (*CS*)

———. *Tagebücher*. Ed. Hans-Gerd Koch, Michael Müller, Malcolm Pasley. Frankfurt am Main: S. Fischer, 1990. (*T*)

———. "Aphorismen." *Beim Bau der chinesischen Mauer*. Ed. Hans-Gerd Koch. Frankfurt am Main: S. Fischer, 1994. (*BB*)

———. "Brief an den Vater." *Zur Frage der Gesetze*. Ed. Hans-Gerd Koch. Frankfurt am Main: S. Fischer, 1994. (*BV/ZF*)

———. "Der Bau." *Das Ehepaar*. Ed. Hans-Gerd Koch. Frankfurt am Main: S. Fischer, 1994. (*EP*)

———. *Der Proceß*. Ed. Hans-Gerd Koch. Frankfurt am Main: S. Fischer, 1994. (*P*)

———. *Ein Landarzt und andere Drucke zu Lebzeiten*. Ed. Hans-Gerd Koch. Frankfurt am Main: S. Fischer, 1994. (*L*)

Pasley, Malcolm. "The Act of Writing and the Text: The Genesis of Kafka's Manuscripts." *Reading Kafka: Prague, Politics and the Fin de Siècle*. Ed. Mark Anderson. New York: Schocken, 1989. 201–14.

Pawel, Ernst. *The Nightmare of Reason: A Life of Franz Kafka*. New York: Farrar, Straus, Giroux, 1984.

Robertson, Ritchie. *Kafka: Judaism, Literature and Politics*. New York: Oxford UP, 1987.

Stölzl, Christoph. *Kafkas böses Böhmen*. Munich: Text und Kritik, 1975.

Wagenbach, Klaus. *Franz Kafka: Eine Biographie seiner Jugend*. Bern: Francke, 1958.

Critical Editions I:
The 1994 Paperback Edition

James Rolleston

APART FROM THE STORIES Kafka published in his lifetime, his most influential works were edited and published by Max Brod, his close friend and executor, in the years following his death in 1924. Central to his reputation were the three novels: *Der Proceß* (The Trial, published 1925), *Das Schloß* (The Castle, 1926), and *Der Verschollene* (The Missing Person, originally titled *Amerika* by Brod, 1927). Since many of Kafka's other stories were more or less fragmentary and sometimes embedded in diary entries, editorial decisions were always many and difficult. Brod acknowledged that he made compromises: for example, Kafka's first story "Beschreibung eines Kampfes" (Description of a Struggle) exists in two versions; Brod initially published a "blended" text (1936), but later endorsed the special publication of the two versions on facing pages (1969).

With the importance of establishing reliable, scholarly versions of Kafka's texts becoming self-evident, a critical edition of all of them was projected by the S. Fischer Verlag of Frankfurt am Main, and the first two volumes, one containing *Das Schloß* and the other being an *Apparatband* to that novel, that is, an exhaustive presentation of variants and crossed out phrases, appeared in 1982. (This *Apparatband* is the focus of Mark Harman's essay in the present volume.) The other stories and novels were published in hard covers in the same way; then, in 1994, Fischer published a paperback edition of all the fictional texts, compiled by Hans-Gerd Koch without the variants but with some necessary annotation and cross-referencing. This version of the Critical Edition is both convenient and widely used by scholars. A brief description of this edition follows:

Volume One: *Ein Landarzt und andere Drucke zu Lebzeiten* (A Country Doctor and Other Publications During His Lifetime).

Contains all the texts Kafka published himself, including those not collected in book form:

Betrachtung (Meditation, 1912), a collection of short fictions, some written as early as 1904, several previously published in magazines. A group of five had appeared in 1910 in the Prague journal *Bohemia,* under the title *Betrachtungen.*

"Der Heizer" (The Stoker, 1913), separate publicaton of the opening chapter of the unfinished novel *Der Verschollene.*

"Das Urteil" (The Judgment), written September 1912, first published in 1913 in the journal *Arkadia,* then in 1916 as a separate volume in Kurt Wolff's series *Der jüngste Tag.*

"Die Verwandlung" (The Metamorphosis), written fall 1912, published 1915 in the journal *Die weißen Blätter.*

"In der Strafkolonie" (In the Penal Colony), written fall 1914, published 1919.

Ein Landarzt (A Country Doctor), a collection of short stories written in 1916–17, published 1919. Includes the following texts discussed in the present volume: "Auf der Galerie" (Up in the Gallery), "Vor dem Gesetz" (Before the Law), "Schakale und Araber" (Jackals and Arabs), "Die Sorge des Hausvaters" (The Cares of a Family Man), and "Ein Bericht für eine Akademie" (A Report to an Academy), as well as the title story.

Ein Hungerkünstler (A Hunger Artist), a collection proofread by Kafka and published posthumously in 1924. Includes "Erstes Leid" (First Sorrow) and "Ein Hungerkünstler" (1922), "Eine kleine Frau" (A Little Woman, 1923), and "Josefine, die Sängerin oder Das Volk der Mäuse" (Josephine the Singer, or the Mouse Folk, 1924).

The most interesting of the uncollected texts are "Die Aeroplane in Brescia" (The Airplanes in Brescia, 1909), about the visit of Kafka and Brod to an air-show; and "Der Kübelreiter" (The Bucket Rider, 1917), a wild vision of the wartime coal shortage.

Volume Two: *Der Verschollene* (The Missing Person, written 1911–13), includes six numbered chapters, two lengthy additional texts, and three fragments.

Volume Three: *Der Proceß,* written 1914–15, includes ten "canonical" chapters and six fragments.

Volume Four: *Das Schloß,* written 1922–23, includes twenty-five chapters, many clearly incomplete.

Volume Five: *Beschreibung eines Kampfes und andere Schriften aus dem Nachlaß* (Description of a Struggle and Other Writings from the Literary Remains).

This and the following three volumes mark the decisive step forward in the Critical Edition: all Kafka's unpublished fictions are included, in chronological order, with the many, often striking "beginnings" interspersed with more familiar "completed" texts — from which, however, all subsequent editorial additions have been removed (provisional titles, concluding punctuation, etc.). Again, these volumes lack the variants and crossouts of the hardback Critical Edition; but the resultant, totally readable sequencing of Kafka's texts offers innumerable fresh glimpses into his world.

Both versions of Kafka's first full-length fiction, *Beschreibung eines Kampfes* are here: he worked on the first from 1904 to 1907, the second from 1909 to 1911, and, while never completing the project, Kafka reworked several passages for publication, in *Betrachtung* and elsewhere. The other early project, the novel fragment *Hochzeitsvorbereitungen auf dem Lande* (Wedding Preparations in the Country), is printed in three versions, each briefer than the one before: the first version dates from 1906–7, the other two from 1909.

The volume concludes with "incomplete" but highly significant fictions from the time of Kafka's work on *Der Proceß:* "Der Dorfschullehrer" (The Village Schoolteacher) and "Der Unterstaatsanwalt" (The Assistant Public Prosecutor) were begun in December 1914, while *Der Proceß* was still in progress; Kafka then drafted "Blumfeld ein älterer Junggeselle" (Blumfeld, an elderly Bachelor), shortly after stopping work on *Der Proceß* on 20 January 1915.

Volume Six: *Beim Bau der chinesischen Mauer und andere Schriften aus dem Nachlaß* (The Great Wall of China and Other Writings from the Literary Remains).

The extremely varied texts date from autumn 1916 to spring 1918. They include Kafka's only substantial effort in dramatic form: the fragment "Der Gruftwächter" (The Warden of the Tomb); and the famous sequence of aphorisms that he wrote while convalescing, after the diagnosis of tuberculosis in 1917, at his sister Ottla's house in the country (the aphorisms are the particular focus of Ritchie Robertson's essay in the present volume).

Many of the fictions from this time were collected in *Ein Landarzt*. But there are also some very significant ones that Kafka did not finalize for publication: the various fragments of "Der Jäger Gracchus" (The Hunter Gracchus, analyzed by Ruth Gross in the present volume), "Beim Bau der chinesischen Mauer" (The Great Wall of China), "Jeder Mensch ist eigentümlich" (Every Human is Peculiar), and the retrospective essay "Vom Jüdischen Theater" (On the Yiddish Theater).

Volume Seven: *Zur Frage der Gesetze und andere Schriften aus dem Nachlaß* (On the Question of the Laws and Other Writings from the Literary Remains).

The texts here date from the winter of 1917–18 to summer 1922 and include the unique "Brief an den Vater" (Letter to His Father, 1919); its blend of autobiography and "lawyer's tricks" make it indispensable for understanding Kafka. The other texts, all fragmentary but some substantial, are very little known. They include "Ich war bei den Toten zu Gast" (I was a Guest of the Dead), "Ein regnerischer Tag" (A rainy Day), "Unser Städtchen liegt nicht etwa an der Grenze" (Our Town doesn't lie on the Border), "Poseidon saß an seinem Arbeitstisch und rechnete" (Poseidon sat at his Worktable and figured), "Anfangs war beim babylonischen Turmbau alles in leidlicher Ordnung" (In the Beginning of the Babylonian Tower-Building all was in tolerable Order), "In der Karawanserei war niemals Schlaf" (In the Caravanserai there was no Sleep)

Volume Eight: *Das Ehepaar und andere Schriften aus dem Nachlaß* (The Married Couple and Other Writings from the Literary Remains).

Very substantial texts from Kafka's last two years are here. Apart from the four stories collected in *Ein Hungerkünstler* (vol. 1), there is the long text to which Brod gave the title "Forschungen eines Hundes" (Investigations of a Dog), beginning "Wie sich mein Leben verändert hat . . ." and concluding "Aber immerhin Freiheit, immerhin ein Besitz." Unsatisfied, Kafka then began a second version, stopping in midsentence after four pages. And Kafka's final long fragment, "Ich habe den Bau eingerichtet und er scheint wohlgelungen" (discussed by Clayton Koelb under Brod's familiar title, "Der Bau"), follows immediately upon a paragraph in which K. from *Das Schloß* is named.

By the end of his writing life, virtually all of Kafka's beginnings have the power to fascinate. Particularly intriguing are "Es war sehr unsicher, ob ich Fürsprecher hatte" (It was very uncertain, whether I had Advocates), "In unserer Synagoge lebt ein Tier in der Größe etwa eines Marders" (In our Synagogue lives an Animal of about the Size of a Marten), "Bilder von der Verteidigung eines Hofes" (Pictures from the Defense of a Manor House), "In der Stadt wird immerfort gebaut" (In the City Building goes on constantly), "Die allgemeine Geschäftslage ist so schlecht" (Business in general is so bad [which in a second version receives the title "Das Ehepaar"]), and "Ein Sarg war fertiggestellt worden" (A Coffin had been made ready). While the decision about what is complete and what is fragmentary in Kafka may never be final, the Critical Edition gathers all his fictional efforts in chronological order. New questions arise concerning the status of beginnings, endings, aphorisms, fragments, traditions: questions without end.

Critical Editions II: Will the Real Franz Kafka Please Stand Up?

Clayton Koelb

IT WILL BE HELPFUL, as a preliminary step in considering the various texts of Kafka currently available, to divide his writings into two principal categories: (A) works published by Kafka during his lifetime; and (B) everything else he wrote.

The total contents of (A) is surprisingly sparse, comprising all in all under five hundred pages printed in large format. It includes the following:

(1) Seven publications in book form

    (a) *Betrachtung* (a collection of eighteen short pieces)

    (b) *Das Urteil*

    (c) *Der Heizer* (part of a manuscript fragment Brod would later publish as the novel *Amerika*)

    (d) *Die Verwandlung*

    (e) *In der Strafkolonie*

    (f) *Ein Landarzt* (fourteen stories, including the one from which the volume takes its title)

    (g) *Ein Hungerkünstler* (four stories, including the one named in the title)

(2) Ten items, all relatively brief, that appeared in various periodicals (among these are such things as the "Gespräch mit dem Beter" and the "Gespräch mit dem Betrunkenen," excepted from larger projects that Kafka never completed to his satisfaction).

The works belonging to this (A) category are relatively unproblematic and require little discussion, since we can safely assume that Kafka meant these works to be read in the form in which he published them. Like the works of any important and widely studied writer, these texts can be compared to the manuscript materials available to us, and we can make note of changes and occasional errors. In some cases, the materials from Kafka's literary estate offer a larger context in which these published texts can perhaps be better understood. But the texts as published set a safe norm against which we can read the variants revealed by study of archival materials and can reasonably be taken to represent a firm authorial intention. A thoroughly reliable critical edition is available in Fischer Verlag's two-volume *Drucke zu Lebzeiten.*

The (B) category presents a very different picture, though some of it presents fewer problems than the rest. We can divide this "unpublished" material into three broad areas:

(1) Business reports, memos, letters, and so on, produced as part of Kafka's career in insurance (published *post mortem* as the "amtliche Schriften");

(2) Letters to diverse friends, associates, lovers, and relatives (edited and published after Kafka's death by various hands);

(3) The literary *Nachlaß,* placed in the care of Max Brod by Kafka's will and containing a large variety of material, some of it clearly drafts of fictional works-in-progress, some of it diary-like notes, some of it of an indeterminate kind.

Only specialists and the extraordinary Kafka enthusiast take the trouble to look at the business writings; they are of considerable interest to this group, but they play no role in Kafka's reputation as a giant of modern literature. The letters, on the other hand, have come to have a wide readership and have taken a special place of their own in the Kafka canon. Their relation to Kafka's body of fictional work is a complex and interesting one, and they reward the attention of both the general reader and the literary scholar. Though there are numerous practical problems in making such material public, and though some material has been withheld from publication for reasons best known to the letters' recipients and editors, the editorial and textual difficulties of this material are relatively straightforward and create no particular dilemmas for the reader.

The same cannot be said for the large body of work left to Max Brod in Kafka's literary estate. It has only recently become clear to the community of Kafka scholarship just how complex, disorganized, and downright confusing this mass of manuscript pages really was when Brod got possession of it, and how much of that complexity, disorganization, and confusion remain as an essential element of its nature.

Brod himself did everything he could to transform the difficulty and obscurity of the material he had inherited into clarity and simplicity. This was unquestionably a well-intentioned and perhaps even a laudable misrepresentation. Brod's goal, after all, was to make a place in the world for his dead friend's work, a place that was by no means assured by the enthusiastic but very limited readership Kafka had acquired for himself in his lifetime. Brod's own view was that the relatively obscure Franz Kafka was a literary giant of unmatched technical brilliance and intellectual subtlety, and that his own duty lay in bringing this giant into the full public appreciation such brilliance deserved. In this endeavor he was stunningly successful. It is entirely probable that without Brod's efforts, Kafka's reputation would never have spread as far as it did, or as fast.

It was Brod's Kafka that everyone read, and Brod's Kafka that became an international literary phenomenon. So we must, no matter how reluctantly, accept Brod's editions as the baseline from which one must begin. We must do so in spite of the fact that we now know how heavily Brod intervened in some of this material. Nowhere is this more evident than in the Brod edition of *Der Prozeß* (I cite the title here as he published it), one of the clearest examples of Brod's willingness to recast the materials he found in his friend's legacy. An examination of the materials Kafka actually wrote shows that the projected novel had never reached a form even remotely ready for publication; that Kafka had not yet formed a clearly discernible conception of the narrative as a whole; and that much of what he had been working on had been produced as disjointed fragments, each having only the sketchiest relation to the others. The only clear elements were the beginning and the end, which Kafka had evidently produced in the first hot enthusiasm of his inspiration.

Brod took this unwieldy and often obscure pile of papers and turned it into one of the most important novels of the twentieth century. It was in reality a collaboration between a living novelist and a dead one, with Brod supplying the narrative line missing in the manuscript by a quite intelligent paste-up job. All the words, all the sentences were Kafka's, but the actual story those sentences told was largely created by Brod's arrangement. So what are we to do with this distinctly impure text? The first impulse of the literary scholar is to reject the enterprise as an impermissible intervention by Brod, since it is Kafka's work we want to read, Kafka's work we thought we were reading before we realized how far Brod's hand had reached into the text.

Let me suggest, however, that this would be an unfortunate and ultimately pointless rejection. The Brod version of *Der Prozeß* is the one that was translated and read around the world, the one that influenced several generations of writers and readers, and indeed the one that changed the course of modern literary history. It is now an indisputable part of that history that no scholarly denunciation, no matter how loud and no matter how well documented, can expect to dislodge. It is possible that future generations of readers will come to know this text in the form Kafka left it — though it remains uncertain that such readers will really wish to do so — but the past will not be changed. Literary historians will always have to use the Brod editions of this and other major texts as the basis on which to understand the Kafka of the twentieth century.

It does not follow from this that the Brod editions should be considered only as historical artifacts. If we accept the fact that a book like *The Trial* was indeed a collaborative effort, we might accept further that it is actually quite a good book indeed. And it may not even be the terrible twisting of Kafka's real intentions that we might surmise. After all, Kafka had wanted to collaborate with Brod — not on this project, to be sure, but on others we know about. And he did give the materials to Brod in a very deliberate act of sharing his most intimate artistic self with another. The Kafka-Brod collaboration needs not only to be acknowledged; it needs to be given our informed consent.

That said, however, it remains necessary for us to look elsewhere for a better sense of what Kafka actually wrote and left behind in the papers entrusted to Brod. We should do this, not necessarily in the hope of getting a better text to read, but rather out of a desire to understand the precise origins of the texts we have read and have come to care about. There are two important critical projects that can help us in that effort.

The first is the "kritische Ausgabe" published over the past several years by S. Fischer Verlag and edited by a team of distinguished Kafka scholars including Jürgen Born, Gerhard Neumann, Malcolm Pasley, and Jost Schillemeit. This is by far the most complete critical edition currently available, and it is an enormously useful tool for the Kafka scholar. On the whole these volumes present reliable texts with carefully prepared apparatus, which both scholars and general readers will find useful. No serious student of Kafka can afford to ignore this edition.

But it has to be conceded that the editors of the Fischer volumes have not necessarily broken with the precedent set by Brod in his first editorial interventions. Again, the example of *Der Process* (the form of the title used in Kafka's MS) is instructive. The Fischer volume, edited by Malcolm Pasley, presents some material not present in the Brod edition, and it slightly rearranges the order of some of it. But the basic narrative framework proposed by the Brod edition remains unaltered.

A stark contrast is offered by another critical edition, the "historisch-kritische Ausgabe" now being offered by Stroemfeld/Roter Stern. Here we have what must be considered the absolute bottom line: Kafka's manuscript in facsimile form with a printed transcription on facing pages. Here there is as little editorial intervention as one can possibly imagine, to such an extent that the "novel" does not even appear as a single book. Each fragmentary piece of the MS is presented in a separately bound folio, and all are boxed together in no particular order. The editor,

Roland Reuß, makes a very strong case in his introductory essay that there is in fact no sound editorial principle for ordering these fragments.

Unless one is a fan of the (now old) *nouveau roman,* it is extremely difficult to read the Stroemfeld edition as a novel. One can only read it as a bundle of loosely related fragments that might, with a good deal of work, be made into a novel. This is both the great strength and the great weakness of this entirely fascinating editorial enterprise. For a scholar with a deep and perhaps even obsessive interest in the minutiae of Kafka's life and work, Reuß's edition is a treasure, offering a clear, unretouched picture of the messy bunch of mainly uncompleted chapters that the author actually left behind. One look at this edition changes forever one's idea of what this "novel" really was when Brod found it. But readers who love Kafka as a storyteller, as the writer Hermann Broch called the great mythographer of the twentieth century, will find little here to satisfy them.

If the Stroemfeld edition is a fair representation of the *Process* that Kafka really wrote — and there is good reason to think it is — then the story the book wishes to tell turns into a kind of "imperial message" from an impossibly distant authority. It can never reach us. We can only sit and dream it to ourselves. Or we can do as Malcolm Pasley and the other Fischer editors have done, as indeed readers have been doing for decades, and let Max Brod dream it for us.

It should be evident, then, that none of the three major editorial enterprises (Brod, Fischer, Stroemfeld) can serve alone to give us a clear picture of the Kafka who looms so large in modern literature. There are just too many Kafkas to be encompassed in a single editorial perspective. The "real" Franz Kafka is never going to stand up.

Beyond Self-Assertion:
A Life of Reading Kafka

Walter H. Sokel

THE INTENT OF THIS NARRATIVE is to give, through one individual reader's response, a view of the kind of impact Kafka's unique and epochal achievement has had, and thus to contribute toward an understanding of its nature and significance.

Fantastic Mimesis

The work that opened my access to Kafka was "Die Verwandlung" (The Metamorphosis), which I first read as a refugee in New York in 1941. As I have learned since then, it is the text by Kafka that has opened his world to many other readers. Its impact was overwhelming. It changed my life and determined my choice of profession, since I embarked upon the study of literature, and German literature in particular, to get to know the secret of Kafka's power and to have the opportunity to preoccupy myself with his writings. Through the study of the literature to which he belonged, at least linguistically, I hoped to acquire a key to the enigma of his work.

The enormous effect "Die Verwandlung" had on me was first of all based on identification with its main character's situation. The text literally captivated me, in the sense that it kept me emotionally glued to the deplorable position of its protagonist. I suffered and agonized in Gregor's place. Suppose, I asked myself, an analogous fate should happen to me? Empirically it was inconceivable, but the persuasive magic of Kafka's story made it appear by no means certain that something like it could not happen to myself, or to anyone for that matter. Even if I would not turn literally into a bug, could I not get into the same kind of absolute isolation, turn into an object of horrendous disgust, beneath even the contempt reserved for human beings? The Second World War was raging. Couldn't I be transformed by mutilation into a thing like Gregor? And, if not by war, by some accident, or by the disfiguring effects of disease?

And even if the cause of quarantining might not be physical, could it not be some mental or moral lapse, or any stroke of outrageous fortune, that might make me exactly like Gregor? Horrifying uniqueness was not limited to individuals. The horror of it was its being potentially a universal condition without, however, losing, for those unfortunate enough to fall its victims, the sting of absolute aloneness. And was it not the fate of each one of us eventually to find herself or himself cut off forever from all fellowship in the transition from life to death? Tolstoy's *The Death of Ivan Ilyich* seemed to me to be the only other narrative that came near to producing something comparable to Kafka's metamorphosis effect.

Like *The Death of Ivan Ilyich*, "Die Verwandlung" also achieved, through the reader's identification with a single victim, an enormous enlargement of the scope of empathetic sensitivity toward all human beings. Going beyond *Ivan Ilyich*, however, Kafka's text had the effect upon me of extending sympathy and solidarity in suffering to life beyond the human species. A human being had been changed into a specimen of vermin. Might not the huge cockroach I chanced upon in an upper Manhattan bathroom be a creature with some feeling, some sensibility, might it not by some inexplicable fluke be sheltering another traveling salesman or former clerk, another Gregor Samsa? Or at least a being not totally unlike myself? Kafka's fiction gave such horrendously persuasive testimony to these possibilities that it took quite a while after the reading of his story for me to gather enough insensitivity to get rid of cockroaches again.

For Northrop Frye, as I was to learn not too long thereafter, identification with a fictional character was the distinguishing sign of the effect of mimesis in literature. For Aristotle mimesis was the essence of art. Teaching Aristotle's *Poetics* several years after my first soul-shaking encounter with Kafka's story made me better understand that experience and allowed me to place it in a cultural context. Kafka's tale seemed to me a prime example of mimetic art, and it produced the effect of tragedy. For more than any other, it was the text that had made me identify with the abysmal suffering depicted in it, engendering in me the emotions ascribed by Aristotle to tragedy — fear and pity, pity of poor lonely Gregor and fear for myself if somehow his fate should also become mine. Despite the grotesque singularity of this fate, there radiated a deeply disquieting universality from the life Kafka portrayed. What went on in his work concerned me with terrifying urgency, and I felt that it would equally concern anyone else who allowed himself to be opened and drawn by its magnetic power.

Kafka's tale seemed to encompass the whole spectrum of mimesis, combining what Northrop Frye was to distinguish as high and low mimesis. It was mimesis at its highest because it moved on a level of identification that Aristotle understood as tragic, and it was low mimesis because it presented tragedy in a modern petty-bourgeois milieu peopled by banal characters. Its hero one could pity, but not admire, and the supporting cast of characters aroused one's indignation by their callous and brutal self-centeredness in the face of their family member's unimaginable plight. Yet their behavior was quite understandable if one's expectations of human beings were correspondingly low.

Yet while it was the consummation of mimetic art, "Die Verwandlung" was also its opposite. Its plot derived from and was predicated on an utterly improbable, indeed a fantastic event. Tzvetan Todorov employs "Die Verwandlung" as his prototypal instance of fantastic literature, distinguishing it from the marvelous. The marvelous, the realm of fairy tale and mythology, is set completely apart from everyday empirical reality and consistently deviates from its rule. The fantastic, by contrast, presents the penetration of empirical reality by an enigmatic event, which remains unexplained, but might eventually find either a natural or a supernatural explanation. A text remains fantastic as long as the case remains undecided and the explanation is withheld (Todorov 26). That, I felt, was precisely the case in "Die Verwandlung." The text began with an eruption of the fantastic — Todorov's definition of the term was, of course, unknown to me at the time — into an everyday world; the mysterious event remained unexplained in the story, and continued to puzzle and haunt the reader forever. Todorov speaks of a naturalization of the fantastic in Kafka's story as the realistic representation of the hero's psyche, and the behavior of the other characters makes us tend to lose sight of the fantastic nature of the whole (171). Yet that never happened in my reading. I could not cease to be perplexed, to wonder, and to speculate on the possible causes of Gregor's miraculous transformation, and I never, while reading, gave up entirely the hope that an explanation might be forthcoming. Whatever it might be, enlightenment would bring consolation and, in a sense, redemption. But enlightenment, of course, never came. The story remains, in our ordinary as well as in Todorov's sense of the term, fantastic. I saw, however, that it was not the fantastic event as such, but the response of the characters to it, their total failure to ask the questions and marshal the emotions appropriate to the mystery that had entered their lives; it was their refusal to venture mentally beyond the "natural" world — in other words, it was the naturalistic, the mimetic elements of the story that left the reader with that overwhelming sadness, that feeling of irredeemable loss and final defeat of life that we call tragic. By contrast, the fantastic, even though it sets the sad fate in motion, provides a glimmer of unrealized hope. It invites the hope for a counter-metamorphosis, for a repeal of the disastrous eruption, or at least for an insight into the enigma. The fantastic provides the constant incentive, so strangely absent from the narrative scene itself, to continue the search, to question, to wonder, and to reflect. The fantastic activates. It functions as a counter-effect to the mimetic aspect, a utopian — in the original sense of not appearing in any actual place — alternative to the saddening and depressing reality that the story depicts.

The uplifting effect of the fantastic showed itself in my initial response to the beginning of the story. It was neither terror nor commiseration but humorous amusement. I subsequently realized that the humor in Gregor's initial situation derives from the reader's still looking at him from outside or above, as he or she follows with amused detachment Gregor's bravely absurd attempts to adjust to his altered shape and go on with his life, trying to minimize what has happened to him, to "naturalize" the transnatural. The initially humorous effect of the fantastic expresses the superiority of writing to its subject, the elevated perspective writing automatically assumes toward what it writes. This enables the reader to smile at the character. In Northrop Frye's terminology, it produces irony, a mode opposed to mimesis (Frye 33–34). Instead of making him identify with the world represented in the work, irony enables the reader to feel superior to it. This humorous effect vanishes, the smile is wiped off the face, as Kafka's text turns radically mimetic, immersing the reader into the internal perspective of the narrative, the protagonist's consciousness. The effect of "freezing the laughter" by abruptly ending the reader's detachment I later found characteristic also of *Der Proceß* (The Trial). Yet, by continuing to keep alive the urge to understand, to search for the illuminating answer, the fantastic in Kafka's work continues to counterbalance the tragic effect of mimetic identification. It represents the tonic nature of the writing process, creation as distinct from its content.

I became consciously aware of the liberating function of Kafka's fantastic mode when, inspired by my discovery of "Die Verwandlung," I voraciously read all the works of Kafka on which I could lay my hands. The very short pieces especially acted upon me as a transfiguring experience, expanding, to an incredible degree, my emotional and mental horizons, pushing out of sight the boundaries of literature that had hitherto confined me to mimetic representation. The usual response of other readers of Kafka — there were not too many at that time — who found him depressing baffled me. Yes, to be sure, sad and horrific events

occurred in his stories, frustrating, defeating, and destroying his characters. Yet the effect of the whole was tonic, as exciting and invigorating
as the discovery of new worlds.

I found Kafka liberating because he seemed to free us from the
shackles of mimesis, the dictate that bound art to the portrayal of nature.
Kafka's writing opened for me another dimension of reality in which the
rules of waking life were overthrown without, however, letting us escape
into the wish-fulfilling conventions of daydreaming and fairy tale. Kafka
simply pushed back the walls that had until now imprisoned experience
transmitted in and through literature. In Kafka banal everyday bourgeois
reality and the miraculous interpenetrated each other and formed a unity
that mystified and gave rise to incessant emotional and mental activity.
As Kafka himself had noted after having written the text of his "breakthrough," "Das Urteil" (The Judgment), his writing expanded immeas-
urably the scope of what was sayable, and thus significant (T 460). For
that reason, Kafka appeared to be a revolutionary force of the greatest
potency.

My discovery of Kafka led me to, and subsequently coalesced with, my
discovery of surrealism, expressionism, and avant-garde art in general. Kafka
thus appeared in the context of a revolution of the most encompassing
ambitions, ranging from the aesthetic to the psychological, the social, and
even the political realm, and collapsing their traditional distinctions. It was
a revolt against human submission to any established reality. Even though
it had failed in historical actuality and been superseded by world-wide
reaction and the relapse into bourgeois "normality," or even worse, had to
see its aspirations perverted into the "anti-bourgeois" tyrannies of Fascism,
Nazism, and Stalinism, it nonetheless retained for me, its sadly belated
convert, the promise of a resurrection and rebirth. The attempt to explore
and to understand Kafka, and the avant-garde expressionism in which I saw
him situated, formed for me an access to this promise.

Kafka's initial effect upon my life was activating in a twofold way. He
acted upon me as a writer as well as a reader. Under Kafka's immediate
spell, I produced a flood of short stories and novellas, each based on a
dream of the preceding night. I jotted them down rapidly and spontane-
ously, writing without plan and outline, as Kafka himself had written
"Das Urteil," as he reports in his diary, in one uninterrupted sitting. I
too used my few spare hours of late evenings and nights to write these
stories, and titled the volume they eventually formed "Out of the World
Night," alluding with the title to their source in my dreams, to the noc-
turnal hours of their composition, and to the nightmarish look history
had assumed at the time — the middle of the Second World War —

when the fate of civilization hung in the balance. Contemporary reality seemed bent on imitating Kafka in a gruesome way.

Kafka's effect upon me as reader was more lasting in my life, however, since the compulsive need to seek to understand him led to my choice of profession. It was one that would give me the opportunity to pursue this need. In my interpretive quest the dreamlike or oneiric element in his writing provided my point of departure.

Oneiric Functionalism

As a native of the city of Freud, I found it natural to use the author of the classic text of dream interpretation as the first guide in my quest to understand and interpret Kafka's work, which fascinated me on account of its dreamlike quality. Kafka himself, as I read in his diary, had found thinking of Freud quite "natural" when composing the work of his breakthrough (*T* 461). Thus Freud offered himself as the first key in trying to unlock the "secret doors" to Kafka's texts. They seemed to me structured according to principles analogous to dreams as analyzed by Freud. I saw the manifest text as a disguised *expression* or projection of the protagonist's feelings, tendencies, and desires that were never admitted to the consciousness presented in the text. As in dreams, events appeared to occur in the external world, even though they were the dreamer's own projections. Thus they seemed bewildering and mystifying to the reader, who remained dependent on the explicit consciousness of the narrative, which like a dream kept the forces that produced and moved the action concealed.

This view of Kafka's writing seemed to receive strong support from Friedrich Beissner's theory of the "uni-mental" (einsinnige) perspective that he saw as characteristic of Kafka's narrative art (Beissner 28). "Uni-mental perspective" implies that the entire content of a narrative, all events, actions, characters, and scenes represented in it, are perceived by a single consciousness, that of the protagonist. There is no omniscient narrator who allows the reader to enter the mind of any other character or who intrudes with information and opinions of his own. It is through the protagonist's consciousness alone that the reader gains access to the story. The uni-mental perspective is also the perspective of the dreaming mind. Beissner's notion of the uni-mental perspective of Kafka's works seemed to me an ideal corroboration of the dreamlike or oneiric principle that I saw structuring Kafka's fiction. In dreams, too, a single mind, the dreamer's, perceives and produces all the events and scenes that appear.

All that happens is the projection of one mind. Yet it appears to be occurring in a world external to that mind. Something closely analogous seemed to me to occur in Kafka's narratives. The fantastic and distorting element in them indicated that the narrated events were expressions of movements and forces in the protagonist's psyche. Yet, as in dreams, the narrative consciousness was never allowed to become explicitly aware of that. Like dreams Kafka's narratives signified the self-alienation of the human mind. The oneiric analogy accounted for the weird distortions and fantastic happenings in Kafka's stories that mingled with and penetrated their mimetic and realistic aspects.

Kafka's narrative creations appeared to share with the oneiric text, as interpreted by Freud, a fundamental feature of all works of literary art as approached by the work-immanent school of the New Critics, then, in the fifties, at the height of their influence. I should like to term that common element textual functionalism, by which I understand a view of textual creations that sees the meaning of a text emerging from its structure, as the interplay and interconnectedness of all its elements. The Freudian method of interpreting dreams and the work-immanent approach of the New Critics together led me back to Aristotle's *Poetics*, which sees the meaning of an epic or drama to lie in its mythos, in the entire action, and not in any individual part, such as the speeches of characters, considered in isolation. No matter how great the general significance of their content might appear to be, only the role they play in the action as a whole determines their meaning. Thus I began to look at Kafka as the creator of narrative textures whose meaning would have to be looked for in the functions of their details.

The critic who helped me most in this task was Theodor Adorno with his pioneering essay on Kafka, published in his volume *Prismen* (Prisms). Adorno turned against the view, initiated by Max Brod, of Kafka's works as religious allegories, which had been the principal approach to Kafka until then. It equated over-arching figures in his works, such as the father in "Das Urteil," the Court in *Der Proceß*, the Castle bureaucracy in *Das Schloß*, with divinity. This view of Kafka had always disappointed me. I felt that its facile subordinating of Kafka to traditionally received patterns of thinking cheated us of the fascinating novelty and strange power of his work. Adorno rejected this cultural "domestication" of Kafka, which reduced the unknown to the known. He rejected it on grounds that seemed to me related to the work-immanent approach to literature. Adorno held the basic mistake of Brod's school in its search for the meaning of Kafka's work to lie in the arbitrary equation of a part of the work, such as the Court or the Castle, with an idea external to the work — such as God — which gets no mention in the text. Kafka's reader, Adorno maintained, should not rush to look for the "meaning" of over-arching images by translating them into cultural concepts ready at hand but external to the text. The web between Leni's fingers in the *Der Proceß* might prove much more important to the understanding of this novel than the question of the meaning of the Court. For Adorno meaning was not to be found in a referentiality to something outside the text. Meaning could be looked for only in the details that together formed the narrative (Adorno 248). With that Adorno appeared to point toward the only promising approach to understanding Kafka.

The functionalist approach to which Freud's theory of dreams, the Aristotelian New Critics, and Adorno had led me was to receive the most powerful confirmation from Kafka himself. In trying to interpret "Das Urteil" for Felice, Kafka explains the figure of the protagonist's friend in Russia not as an independent, three-dimensional, mimetically conceived character, but as a function in the protagonist's relationship with his father. The friend, Kafka says, is what father and son have in common. He goes on to say that the whole story is a "tour" (Rundgang) around this relationship (*F* 397). Kafka's own reading of his work thus seems to endorse a functionalist approach, which sees characters and scenes not as mimetic representation, but as functions in the dreamlike narrative, which in turn is the projection into apparently external scenes and characters of forces and problems in the protagonist's existence.

Thus Kafka's own reading of his work tends to support an "intrinsic" against the religious school's "extrinsic" interpretation. The intrinsic approach does not look for what a narrative text "means," but for what it tells and does. It looks for its *mythos* not as a synopsis that can be abstracted from the work and recounted as its "gist," but as the structure that forms a work and makes it cohere, as the entity that all textual details together produce by implicitly referring to each other. What was to be considered in seeking to understand a text was the part each textual element — character, event, scene, gesture, image, spatial and temporal reference, simile and metaphor, etc. — played in relation to all other elements that together made the texture as which a text manifests itself. That was for me the intrinsic meaning of a work.

In my first publication on Kafka, "Kafka's 'Metamorphosis': Rebellion and Punishment," (1956), I inquired into the function of Gregor's narrated monologue near the beginning of the story, which conveyed his feelings toward his job and its connection with his father's debt to Gregor's firm. I concluded that Gregor's metamorphosis functions as the accommodation and union of two contradictory impulses in a single event and image — rebellion and simultaneous punishment for it.

Through the investigation of the narrative function of a central detail of the text, the representation of ambivalence emerged for me as a basic meaning of Kafka's writing that also accounted for its dreamlike effect.

Kafka's works shared with dreams, as Freud had taught us to see them, a dual nature. Like dreams they had a liberating function, as they gave expression to socially forbidden feelings and thoughts. However, again like dreams, they also had a censoring, concealing, and thus repressive side that made the rebellion they tried to express unrecognizable to consciousness. By the same expressive activity through which they sought to give shape to revolt against patriarchal authority, they sought to cancel this revolt, camouflaging its meaning and compromising its rebellious impulse with the gesture of submission. By the same signifying act with which Kafka's writing assaulted and provoked authority, it reinstated it and restored it to its ruling place. The very nature of the fantastic in Kafka which before, in the context of the avant-garde cultural revolution, I had seen only as emancipating, I now recognized as consisting, to an equal degree, of self-censoring repression. Self-subjection to patriarchal power would become an extremely important factor in my further reflections on Kafka.

Kafka's life-documents, his diaries, and especially his "Brief an den Vater" (Letter to His Father, 1919), contained the most profound ambivalence toward authority in general and paternal authority in particular. They also gave voice to the most severe self-doubts and the most bitter self-accusations and condemnations, rarely rivaled in the literature of autobiography. Worship of his father, the prototypal authority figure of his life, alternated with a deeply rebellious and ironically, and even satirically, critical stance. Kafka appeared to me to be understandable only if these two opposite sides were equally taken into account. Thus, years later, I could not agree with Deleuze's influential reading of Kafka, which, in the spirit of '68, extols Kafka as a master of rebellious subversion, while ignoring or downplaying the self-punishing and worshipfully submissive aspect of his life as well as his art. Omitting that side of his work could not, I felt, do justice to its fundamental complexity.

Oneiric functionalism and close attention to ambivalence and ambiguity, especially toward the patriarchal power figure that, as the antagonistic force in it, dominates Kafka's work, guided me through the writing of *Tragik und Ironie* (Tragedy and Irony, 1964).

The Myth

Tragik und Ironie emerged from an inquiry into the narrative function of women in Kafka's total oeuvre. What brought me to it was the crucial role I saw women play in Kafka's life documents — diaries and letters. His letters to two women, Felice Bauer and Milena Jesenská, fill volumes that rank among the most remarkable epistolary literature of all time. That is only one example attesting to the decided importance of woman in Kafka's world.

With the question of the function of Kafka's fictional women in mind, I proceeded to investigate all relevant fictional texts, comparing them with each other. In the course of this undertaking I came to realize the amazing degree of inner unity, interconnectedness, and dense cross-referentiality of all his works. They seemed to form a kind of mega- or meta-text that I began to see as a kind of myth, or rather a *mythos* or super-narrative, with numerous fascinating variations and a decided development. Kafka's myth appeared as a developing unity in rich diversity.

The content of Kafka's myth coincided with the title of his earliest extensive narrative, "Beschreibung eines Kampfes" (1904–5). I saw the myth describing or enacting a threefold conflict — a combat within the self, the protagonist-persona of Kafka's fiction, and a struggle of each half of the divided self with the supreme antagonist of Kafka's myth, a patriarchal power figure.

In my realization of the fundamental oneness of Kafka's work, in which its character as a myth resided, Wilhelm Emrich's monumental *Franz Kafka* (1958) inspired me. The basic thesis of Emrich's work, to be sure, I found freighted with the baggage of German Idealism and much too abstractly philosophical to be relevant to Kafka. Emrich's metaphysical preoccupation completely ignored the biographical and psychological roots of Kafka's work as well as its, in the broadest sense, political dimension, bound up with the essential part power and power struggles played in it. Emrich ignored the close relation of Kafka's work to everyday existence, on the one hand, and, on the other, to the realm of the unconscious and the dream. Emrich's Kafka was too theoretical, in a German Idealist way, to be recognizable as the author I had experienced. Kafka's life documents told a story that had nothing to do with Emrich's construction of him as the hidden prophet of Hegel's Universal, which was fragmented and lost in a modern world aware only of the particular. The complete omission of the text Kafka considered his most important, "Das Urteil," from Emrich's discussion of Kafka's *opus* appeared to me symptomatic of his tendency to miss what was essential in

Kafka. Emrich seemed to me to substitute the Idea of German Idealism for the God that Brod's school had, albeit with considerably greater justification, imported into Kafka's fictional universe.

Emrich, however, was extremely helpful in making a mythos appear as the unifier of Kafka's bewildering work. He superbly showed the interconnectedness of Kafka's texts, and the need to approach his opus intertextually within its own parameters. He succeeded in attuning Kafka's reader to the teeming and often extremely subtle cross-references among Kafka's texts that made them into a meta-text. The links among the texts are objects, characters, actions, gestures, spatial references, and images occurring in them, which function not like allegories or symbols pointing to domains extrinsic to the text, but as allusive signs with special meanings largely restricted to Kafka's work. They make for a coherence of Kafka's total *opus* that is both structural and thematic.

Through the examination of the narrative function of women figures in Kafka's works, the fundamental conflicts that I have mentioned came into view as the theme of Kafka's myth. The struggle between the ascetic bachelor and the worldly self appears, in its earliest version, "Beschreibung eines Kampfes," initially at least, to occur between two independent characters. However, by the oddness and fantastic nature of their behavior and discourse, the text soon hints at their actually emanating from a single self divided within itself. In this earliest phase of the struggle, the ascetic bachelor self is the first-person narrator of the story. For that reason, I called this prototype of an ever-recurring figure in Kafka's myth the "pure self" (*Tragik* 40, 48, 72–73), with the dual meaning of "pure" in mind signifying both the chastity and the fundamental authenticity of that aspect of the self. The action shows the pure self's effort to undermine the self-confidence of the worldly, "engaged" self and win him over to his own withdrawn and solitary way of life. He finally drives the other to an act of symbolic self-destruction.

In the text of what Kafka called his "breakthrough," "Das Urteil," the paternal power figure enters the struggle of the selves. The power figure is here literally the father of the — likewise literally — engaged self, which is the son as the father's ostensibly successful rival and successor, about to marry and found a household of his own. In this second phase of the struggle between the pure and the engaged self described by Kafka's myth, the role of protagonist and perceiving consciousness of the story has shifted from the pure self figure to the engaged self. The latter has entered a second struggle, which it wages against the paternal power figure. The protagonist, in the literal sense of the hero fighting in an agon of wills, seeks to take the father's place in a conflict that has the

features of a classical Freudian Oedipal struggle. In it, the pure self figure, Georg Bendemann's estranged childhood friend who has exiled
himself to Russia, functions as the father's ally against the hero — according to the father's version of events, which is the only one the reader
gets. With the friend's help, the father defeats the worldly self and drives
it to self-destruction.

In "Das Urteil," the bachelor self still seems to be an independent,
apparently mimetically conceived character. Upon close reading, however, it appears to embody a repressed aspect of the protagonist, as I
showed in my 1977 article "Perspectives and Truth in 'The Judgment'"
(205). The combined attack of father and pure self figure functions as
the projection of an internal conflict in the protagonist's self, a self-
repudiation of the self's engagement and adulthood. This actual nature
of the conflict, however, never becomes explicit and articulated. It reveals
itself only in the strange dreamlike sequence of actions and events. The
father's surprising and puzzling verbal assault upon his son only apparently triggers the latter's self-liquidation. It is the hero himself who
indirectly, by action, gesture, and subtext of the discourse, asks for the
father's judgment of his engagement, which represents his maturing and
emancipation. And in the end, it is the self alone that carries out its
"punishment."

This internalization of the three-cornered battle between worldly self,
paternal power figure, and pure self is complete in the two tales of punishment following "Das Urteil" — "Die Verwandlung" and *Der Proceß*.
In these texts the struggle between the two selves appears totally inter-
nalized. It is a ferocious battle within a single character between self-
assertion and humiliating self-destruction, the latter winning out over the
former.

In the destruction of the self-assertive hero in Kafka's tales of punishment, the repressed truth of the hero plays the decisive role. There is
in the protagonist a hidden longing to be rid of the adult self, to return
to a childlike "innocence," to surrender to and be reunited with the
power figure as the self's origin. As that is impossible, non-being is preferable to being. It is because this tendency, which in *Tragik und Ironie* I
saw as the "true self" (53, 82–83), operates so powerfully on the deepest
level of the protagonist's being, never acknowledged by his consciousness,
that his apparently worldly self so readily cooperates and brings about, or
helps in bringing about, its own destruction. The deepest, long-repressed,
but ultimately effective wish of the protagonists of Kafka's tales of direct
and indirect self-destruction is, as in Nietzsche's view of Dionysian tragedy, the repeal of the individuated self.

This deepest and "true," that is, ultimately effective and prevailing, tendency in the protagonist remains excluded from articulated acknowledgment. It erupts, as a "return of the repressed," against the protagonist's consciousness, which it subverts and destroys. Since these texts are structured on a uni-mental perspective, namely the protagonist's consciousness, the reader has no other possibility but to identify with it. Thus the turn of events perplexes and dumbfounds the reader, who shares in the protagonist's defeat. The seemingly groundless, unjust, and irrational attack upon and final destruction of the protagonist also assault, shake, and utterly bewilder the reader's rationality and assail his or her self-confidence. In that way, the text undermines and subverts the principles of reason, consciousness, and selfhood as such, in the reader as well as in the character.

According to another passage in the same document, however, writing for Kafka has a purpose exactly opposite to the one just described. Writing, Kafka maintains here, is his flight from his father, the refuge and sole hiding place on earth where his father's power cannot reach. In the writer as one fleeing from the patriarchal sphere, I saw the prototype of what I called the ascetic or pure self figure of Kafka's myth, most strikingly exemplified by Georg Bendemann's childhood "friend" who had "virtually fled" ("sich förmlich geflüchtet," *U* 7) their common place of origin to a bachelor's existence in distant Russia. As the father figure becomes broadened and universalized in Kafka's work into patriarchal authority in general, and finally collectivized as family, community, people, species, and, ultimately, procreative life, nature, indeed physical reality as a whole, the pure self figure's flight from paternal power turns into a flight from life, nature, and empirical reality.

Flight, too, is a kind of self-assertion, as it seeks to save the self from the reach of paternal power. In this self-preserving movement, the self discovers a power of its own, totally different, to be sure, from the nature-given power of the father figure, and potentially superior to it. In the poetics of flight, writing is not a mourning over absence and loss, but the base for a defiant self-aggrandizement. Self-elevation and -aggrandizement mark the pure self figure of Kafka's myth, from the Ego's exercise of magical capabilities in "Beschreibung eines Kampfes," to the "singing" mouse Josefine's insistence on her special status that should exempt her from the communal duties all members of the people have to assume. Unlike the worldly self, the pure self does not seek to supplant the father figure in its own domain. Instead it asserts its apartness, its absolute uniqueness, its difference from and superiority to that domain. Thus an arena of enormous conflict opens up, the combat of the absolute self against the power of natural and collective life.

However, this struggle involves no violence, since, unlike the worldly self, the pure self does not aim at displacing the power figure. In consequence there is in this combat no destruction of the self. The pure self is frustrated and denied in its ambition, but it is not killed. Irony replaces tragedy in the later phase of Kafka's work. The pure self protagonists of Kafka's late fiction are not internally divided. They are fanatically unified, merged with the quest they single-mindedly and doggedly pursue. (One of their number is indeed a canine investigator.) Their identity is one with the claim they tenaciously uphold.

This claim or demand might have as its content recognition for a unique achievement or an extraordinary talent such as indefinite fasting ("Ein Hungerkünstler" [A Hunger Artist]) or producing music in a species in which such a capacity is deemed unique ("Josefine"). Or it might consist of a professional call for doing some special work (*Das Schloß*). Or it might be a unique distinction supposedly conferred upon them ("Forschungen eines Hundes" [Investigations of a Dog]). It might be the possession of the correct interpretation of a societal procedure ("In der Strafkolonie" [In the Penal Colony]) or a "right" they believe is theirs ("Vor dem Gesetz" [Before the Law]). The claim sets the pure self apart and pits it against the world that surrounds it, and, in that sense, the pure self protagonists of Kafka's myth resemble, or rather caricature, the "absolute individual" of Kierkegaard's *Fear and Trembling*. They are Quixotic versions of Kierkegaard's Abraham. The demand of the pure self figures usually relates to some form of "art," as in "Ein Hungerkünstler" and "Josefine," or to a mission based on a skill and a calling, as in the case of the surveyor in *Das Schloß*, or to some magical power with which the protagonist believes himself endowed, as in "Beschreibung eines Kampfes" and "Forschungen eines Hundes." These very special "abilities" claimed by Kafka's protagonists point to their function as metaphoric significations of Kafka's self-image as a writer with very special powers and consequently very special requirements, which his *Briefe an Felice* (Letters to Felice) as well as his diaries make vividly clear. The pure self figures also share with the image of their author as represented in his life documents a certain fussiness, a compulsive concern with dietary "purity," as in "Schakale und Araber" (Jackals and Arabs), or unending fasting, as in "Ein Hungerkünstler" and "Forschungen eines Hundes."

The striking parallels between Kafka's self-representation as a very special kind of writer, fanatically devoted to and consisting of nothing but literature, and the pure self figures' claimed or demonstrated extra-human achievements and magical powers, which make them creatures *sui generis*, reveal the close kinship of the protagonists of Kafka's late works to their creator.

The self figure's claim receives no validation. The power figure, which comes to coincide with the fictional reality prevailing in Kafka's texts, persists in denying or ignoring the self's claim. The claimant stays forever cheated of fulfillment. Sharing the pure self figure's perspective, the reader, at least initially, also shares the protagonist's feeling of being wronged. She or he sympathizes with the claimant when his strenuous attempts to have his claim recognized fail. The reader does not at first experience the irony of the situation, but only its pathos, inhering in the subject's view. The protagonist appears a victim of injustice. That, at least, was my own first response upon reading Kafka's tales, and I found it confirmed by most other readers. With Kafka's protagonists we too felt aggrieved and driven to protest a flagrantly unfair social and world order.

However, upon continued close re-readings, the irony in the claim, albeit unacknowledged by the protagonist, became apparent. The claim turned out to be invalid. It was founded on false premises, on wrong assumptions and deceptions, which either remained unconscious, that is, unarticulated in the text, or are so fleetingly mentioned that the reader tends to stay unaware of them. If the reader detects this deception, she or he does so in spite of the narrative perspective.

The irony of Kafka's late texts resides in the discrepancy between the ostensible and the actual. Ostensibly the protagonist's claim appears to be justified, but actually it is absurd, or at any rate, at sharp variance with the fictional reality represented in the text. Beneath this irony, however, lurks another, deeper irony, the contradiction between a claim that expresses an absolute subjectivity of inner conviction and its need to have an external agency confirm it. The contradiction between the subjective arrogance of the claim and the desperate appeal for its "objective" validation constitutes the fundamental irony permeating the last phase of Kafka's writing. Now the struggle enacted in Kafka's myth is the self's insistent appeal to the power figure for recognition and confirmation of its unique status and special being summed up in its claim. The self seeks to impose itself upon the power figure — which might extend to include the community, the species, or the world — that blocks its cause. Insistence upon admission into a specific space, seat, and domain of the power figure ("Vor dem Gesetz," *Das Schloß*), most aptly expresses the self's demand.

The irony in Kafka's myth ultimately inheres in the nature of self-assertion, which paradoxically is forever in need of an Other's recognition and acquiescence to attain its triumphant fulfillment. The appeal to have the self's specialness validated ironically reconfirms the Other's power as the force that, by bestowing or withholding recognition, decides the subject's fate. In the very quest to realize itself, selfhood reveals its utter dependence on the Other. Kafka's writing describes a project that pursues a self-contradictory and thus unrealizable goal — the creation of the absolutely sovereign self through the administration of external power.

This self-contradiction in the pure self's quest continues the self-division of the protagonists of Kafka's earlier narratives of self-destruction. Now, however, the division does not lie in the repression of one part of the self by another, leading eventually to a "return of the repressed" that, erupting, explodes the self. Now it lies in the self's embodiment of a conceptual self-contradiction.

This difference entails a markedly different narrative structure. In the tales of punishment where the hero's destruction was built into the narrative from the beginning, the action moves with a more or less dramatic momentum toward the fatal ending. The end inheres in the narrative as its *telos*. In composing *Der Proceß*, for instance, Kafka wrote the last scene of the novel, Josef K.'s execution, immediately after the opening chapter, which describes his arrest. In the later works, where the self's refutation proceeds by ironizing rather than destroying the self, this change of narrative objective requires a new form. Now the text does not enact a drama, but demonstrates an object lesson on the problematic nature of the self. Narrative becomes parabolic exposition and requires no conclusion. Either these late narratives are fragments like *Das Schloß* or the ending is an arbitrary cut-off point, the hero's death from natural causes terminating a condition that could go on indefinitely ("Vor dem Gesetz," "Ein Hungerkünstler," "Josefine"). Only in the transitional text, "In der Strafkolonie," is the violent end of the Officer intrinsic to the plot, since here claim and self-destruction coincide.

Apart from a very small group of texts, foremost among them "Ein Bericht für eine Akademie" (A Report to an Academy), in which the ego becomes an at least partially positive force, Kafka's myth appears, in *Tragik und Ironie*, as a severe critique and refutation of selfhood — first in a violent and tragic, then in an ironic and parabolic mode. I saw the ultimate "truth" of Kafka's narratives, resting in the power figure of his work, become co-extensive with collective life and reality itself. I did not see Kafka worshipping power uncritically. Far from it — a great portion of the satirizing irony of his texts I saw aimed at the authority figures in them, from the fathers in his projected volume *Die Söhne* (Sons) to Josef K.'s Court, K.'s Castle bureaucracy, and the empire of China. Yet, in the main, the power figure serves as the catalyst that reveals the falsity and nullity of the self. The refutation of self-assertion formed for me the unifying theme of the myth told by Kafka's works.

Since I saw this myth developing in two principal phases or modes — one tragic, the other ironic — I chose, emphasizing this development, *Tragedy and Irony* to be the title of my book. If the unity of Kafka's myth had been my overriding concern, the title would have been *The Myth of Power and the Self.*

Beyond Tragedy and Irony

Since the experience of poststructuralism directed me toward the overarching role of poetics, explicit and implied, in Kafka, it led me to see the attack upon the self, which Kafka's myth describes, as enacted by the process and activity of writing. The tragic dissolution or ironic refutation of the self is thus not purely a thematic occurrence in the content of Kafka's narratives. It is enacted in and through Kafka's writing. The "truth of the self" of Kafka's myth can be equated with the writing process. The conflict between writing as an activity and the writer as a person, as an ego, underlies and forms the contrast between the truth of the self and the pure self figures in Kafka's myth. Writing, not merely as thematic representation, but as narrative process, undoes selfhood, not only in the story, but in the activity that makes the story.

In *Tragik und Ironie* the dissolution or refutation of the self appeared in negative terms, as the negation of the self, the longing for its disappearance in reunion with its origin, as analogous to Freud's death instinct. Writing would thus have a purely negating function. It was to serve the undoing of the ego, of individuated being. However, re-reading Kafka, particularly his diaries, has shown me an affirmative mission of writing. It came with the discovery of the enormous significance his dreamlike, visionary inner world possessed for Kafka. He viewed the lifting of this haunting inner world to the light of day as the mission of his writing. Writing as giving expression to the pressing multitudes of oneiric visions of his mind was thus quite literally an evocation of the truth of the self. This truth I came to see as the source of Kafka's art. This inner world of dreams and visions was precisely the world forever beyond the reach of the paternal power figure. Its truthfulness, however, depended on immediacy, on the abolition of the writer's ego as medium of the writing. The ultimate impossibility of such immediacy doomed the writer to self-despair (Sokel, "Kafka's Poetics," 19).

Since both self and power figure manifest themselves in and as language, the consideration of Kafka's thinking on language made both acquire a new aspect. Since language is a realm shared by both contestants of Kafka's myth, their contest appears as one of competing notions of language. However, since language is what both antagonists have in common, can it also provide the ground on which power and self could be reunited?

Attention to language as the medium of Kafka's art also made me aware of the super-personal character of the oneiric. Dreams are metaphors that, as linguistic formations, partake of the socio-cultural realm. Thus, taking up a suggestion made by Günther Anders in the 1930s, I extended consideration of the oneiric structure of Kafka's writing to an examination of the part played in it by the metaphors buried in language (*Franz Kafka* 4–5). Poststructuralist and deconstructionist emphasis on the self-reflexivity of writing made me see Kafka's fiction as the arena of conflicting and alternative poetologies implied in it.

In *Tragik und Ironie,* I had fully accepted Friedrich Beissner's theory of the protagonists' uni-mental perspective as the sole narrative perspective of Kafka's works. I failed to look into the problem posed by the contradiction between a strictly uni-mental perspective and the overwhelming evidence of irony in Kafka's writing. For irony is not possible without at least a duality of points of view. I felt that the co-existence of irony and singleness of narrative perspective had to be addressed. By examining the relationship of narrative perspective to narrated action in works of Kafka's middle period, I was able to put the distinction between what I had seen as the tragically dramatic and the ironically expository forms of Kafka's writing into terms of narrative point of view. In the dramatic subgenre, the bearer of the point of view is identical with the subject of the narrative action. The ironically and parabolically expository texts by contrast distance the bearer of the narrative point of view from the action that the narrative represents. The introduction of an observer figure at some distance from the action, who assumes the reader's role within the text, accomplishes this shift. Thus while the uni-mental perspective is preserved, it moves from the agonist of the struggle to a detached character who, within the text, represents the reader called upon to interpret and judge what he perceives. The narrated action lays the structural foundation for the possibility of irony. However, subsequent re-examination of a text of the tragically dramatic type, *Der Proceß,* caused me to realize that even in what I had termed the "tragic" phase of Kafka's writing, the very presence of a narrating voice distinct from the agent of the narrative action makes for a duality of perspectives, and, with it, irony ("Franz Kafka: *Der Prozess*," 110). Irony emerged as ubiquitous in Kafka's oeuvre. Thus I have been led not only to modify the strict polarity between a tragic and ironic phase in the development of Kafka's work, but also to qualify the notion of the uni-mental perspective as applying to Kafka's total work. The notion of the uni-mental perspective is valid, to be sure, in regard to the absence of an omniscient narrator in Kafka's work. It is not valid, however, if it implies the lack of narrative point of view that markedly differs from and, with subtle irony, undermines the protagonist's point of view. In that sense, all of Kafka's works are based on a duality of perspectives, and irony is one of the foundations not only of Kafka's late works, but of his entire output.

Contexts

In *Tragik und Ironie* I had, despite heavy reliance on Freudian psycho-analytic concepts and on Nietzsche's *Geburt der Tragödie* and his attack upon ascetic values, mainly resorted to intertextuality within Kafka's works. From close text-immanent examination of Kafka's texts and the numerous interconnections and cross-references between them, which included his life documents, I had gained the idea of Kafka's myth as the description of a number of intertangled struggles — within the self, and between the self and variants of patriarchal power.

Stimulated by critical developments in intertextuality and the placement of literature in interdisciplinary cultural studies, I began to re-read Kafka's texts in the light of other texts from literary, intellectual, social, and cultural history. I have continued to rely on close textual reading, but have also allowed contexts to help cast additional light on Kafka's texts. I have not been primarily interested in a study of "influences," rather in analogies widening the horizons of the reading of Kafka's texts. Analogies and relationships were to help me to place Kafka's myth in a broader framework of significance and historical-cultural relevance, transcending biographical and psychological referentiality.

Intertextuality has aided me in discovering added dimensions of individual texts as well as Kafka's myth as a whole. To begin with, I went beyond using Freud merely as an explanatory model in the thematic analysis of Kafka's works, and investigated through close intertextual readings the structural parallelism between Freudian thinking and Kafka's way of writing. I also tried to make specific Freudian concepts, such as narcissism and the Ego, as well as particular case studies, shed light on individual texts by Kafka in essays such as "Freud and the Magic of Kafka's Writing," "Kafka's Beginnings," and "The Wolfman and the Castle."

Paying attention to the metonymic relationship between bourgeois patriarchal family and capitalist business hierarchy in "Die Verwandlung" led me to see striking analogies between Kafka's representation of human self-alienation and corresponding notions crucial to Marxist theory. Those analogies do not by any means imply that Kafka was influenced by Marxism. They are rather meant to highlight the historical and socio-cultural relevance of the struggle between patriarchal power and the self depicted in Kafka's story. Bringing out the anthropological implications of Kafka's myth enabled me to show how the bourgeois nuclear family, depicted in "Das Urteil" and "Die Verwandlung," contains the seeds of the cultic community of "In der Strafkolonie" and the bureaucratic feudalism of *Das Schloß*. It also showed how Kafka's representation of the son figure in the patriarchal bourgeois family tends to make the latter the locus of prominent myths in Frazer's anthropological classic, *The Golden Bough* ("From Marx to Myth," 493).

The contextual approach to Kafka also endowed the individual players in Kafka's myth with broader significance. Connecting Kafka's aphorisms of the Zürau period, with their copious comments on the Book of Genesis, to both Gnosticism and the Hebrew Bible, the pure self figure's conflict with patriarchal power acquired aspects of the historic struggle between two great strains of Western religious traditions ("Between Gnosticism and Jehovah"). The split self of Kafka's tales of punishment gains an important additional dimension when associated with Kafka's role in the conflict between Jewish assimilation and the search for roots in Jewish traditions and the Yiddish language ("Kafka as a Jew," 848–50).

The contexts built into Kafka's texts do not merely enrich the understanding of their socio-historical significance, but are also essential to the grasp of their structure and content. Analogies between notions of existential thought and Kafka's K. novels enable us to see the nature of K.'s "call" to be the surveyor of the Castle (*Franz Kafka*, 42–44), and Josef K.'s "trial" as a hermeneutical choice between competing interpretations of and responses to his "arrest" ("The Programme of K.'s Court").

Aspects of Kafka's texts neglected or ignored in previous reading came into prominent view through their contexts, and conversely previously neglected parts of Kafka's texts revealed new contexts for them. In *Tragik und Ironie*, I had read Kafka's story of the humanization of an ape, "Ein Bericht für eine Akademie," to use an example, by exclusively focusing on the problems faced by the simian narrator and the solutions found by him (*Tragik* 369–98). Read in that light, the "report" appeared in Freudian terms as the account of the formation of an Ego through adaptation to and partial identification with violently Oedipal father figures. Dwelling, in re-reading, upon the richly described human environment of the ape and the crucial role played by it in his transformation, the narrative came to reveal, in addition, an extremely significant cultural-historical and political referentiality. Kafka's short text emerged as an important contribution to the "grand narrative" (Lyotard 15) of the twentieth century, the Westernization of the globe from its colonialist-imperialist to its "postmodern" phase.

It became clear to me, however, that a single context could never do justice to the complexity of any text by Kafka. Each context can illuminate only one of the numerous aspects and positions that the struggles described in Kafka's mythos present. The richness of Kafka's texts demands that each context be illuminated by other contexts. For instance, in the text of "Die Verwandlung," the context of Marxist notions of human self-alienation and reification shifts to the anthropological-cultic context of the scapegoat-savior myth ("From Marx to Myth" 493–94). However, even two such widely differing contexts do not contain the spectrum of Kafka's story. Following the example of Marthe Robert's reading of *Das Schloß* as a kind of history or compendium of the subgenres of the European novel, I found a rich variety and sequence of discourses, each of central import to Kafka's and our century, forming together the contextual referentiality of the story of Gregor Samsa's transformation ("Kafka and the Twentieth Century").

"Die Verwandlung" begins with a comic discourse describing Gregor Samsa's initial reaction to his transformation. One can easily read this opening scene in terms of Henri Bergson's view of the comic as a human being's inappropriately routinized, automaton-like behavior. However, as the reader gets absorbed into the point of view of the protagonist, experiencing the latter's fate from within the character's consciousness, the comic discourse gives way to a quasi-Marxist and quasi-Freudian discourse that presents human self-alienation as the individual's victimization by the hierarchical orders of capitalist business and patriarchal family. This discourse of human self-reification, familiar from Georg Lukács's *History and Class Consciousness* (83–109), goes over into a proto-existential discourse in which self-alienation results from the individual's "bad faith," the lack of courage to make authentic decisions in shaping one's life — a discourse subsequently made familiar by Martin Heidegger and Jean-Paul Sartre. In the concluding parts of Kafka's text, this existential view of Gregor's mode of being gives way to a discourse with echoes from Kierkegaard's *Fear and Trembling,* in which the "absolute individual" — which Gregor has literally turned into because of his totally unique, unprecedented form of being that transcends all species — is thrown beyond the confines of speech, into an inability to be understood by others because an utterly unique fate eludes the generalizing nature of language. Here speechlessness hints at a realm of transcendence alluded to through music — his sister's violin playing and its effect upon Gregor. Finally this discourse in turn cedes place to the discourse of myth — the myth of the scapegoat-hero, the rain king sacrificed to the survival of the group, a discourse prominent in turn-of-the-century anthropology. "Die Verwandlung" thus can serve as an example illustrating Kafka's writing as the scene in which prominent discourses of the late nineteenth and twentieth century converge. In the at times strikingly anticipatory relationship of Kafka's text to subsequently emerging discourses lies what has often been felt as the "prophetic" power of Kafka's writing. No single one of these contexts illuminates the whole text. Only their sequence and interplay provides something approximating a "meaning" of the tale.

As he confessed to his publisher, Kurt Wolff, Kafka felt very attuned to the "embarrassing" nature of his age, and he confronted it again in his work (*B* 150). To a degree that his writings and life documents would not let one suspect at first, the conflicts represented in his work strangely and markedly converge with the conflicts that formed our century. However, his writing corresponds to the age on a level far below explicit articulation. It relates to the age as dreams do to waking life. Life permeates dreams in a manner not conceptualized and articulated, but allusive and concealing. In the same estranging and mystifying way, Kafka's mythos alludes to and expresses historical reality.

Emancipation, Myth, and the Reader

In *Tragik und Ironie,* a divided or self-contradicting protagonist confronted a triumphantly monolithic power figure. Subsequent re-readings of "Die städtische Welt" (The Urban World, 1911), a proto-version of "Das Urteil" (*T* 151–58), "Ein Bericht für eine Akademie," and the short parables of the Emperor and China complex caused me to look at Kafka's power figure in a new light. The power figure, too, appeared divided — into two aspects: one hostile and oppressively menacing, the other benign but unattainable. While the former conforms to the Oedipal violator and aggressor, the latter embodies the origin and source of being to which the self longs to return. In "Ein Bericht für eine Akademie," the two aspects of the power figure appear distributed over two species — simian and human, corresponding to the two identities of the protagonist who evolves from ape to man. This division between the power figure's two aspects or ways of being extends through Kafka's entire work. It finds its historical-religious context in the division within the divinity as envisioned by the Gnostics.

In the late phase of his writing, however, Kafka deconstructs this split. It is not the power figure that is divided into two aspects or two natures. Both are projections of the self's dependence. Power does not exist and rule by itself. It exists only as the hold it has on the subject. It is the embodiment of the subject's self-enslavement. This adds a new dimension to the notion of guilt so pervasive in Kafka's work. The self is guilty not only toward its truth, which aims to dissolve it, and not only toward an "objective" reality which its subjective claim misses and contradicts. It bears guilt also toward itself for not developing the independence that would make it an adult autonomous self. It is guilty of an obsessive fixation on the power figure that allows the latter to judge and rule it. Thus a critical and emancipatory view of the self emerges that complements the self-punishing and self-ironizing view I had emphasized in *Tragik und Ironie*.

Yet even where Kafka is most critical of the power figure, the bearer of primary guilt is still the self, for allowing power to obsess and dominate it. Kafka remains a self-reflexive author, differing from the unambiguously subversive producer of "minor literature" whom Deleuze, in the wake of the revolt of 1968, has made so widely fashionable. However, in contrast to the Kafka image of *Tragik und Ironie*, my present view sees Kafka as closer to emancipatory literature. Kafka no longer seems to me to identify "truth" with the power figure. Beyond the voice of power, which I had seen swaying Kafka's work, I now hear the voice of the victimized self protesting it. "Truth," in the sense of a final, "official," evaluative judgment or "message," I now find quite unavailable in Kafka's world. No single player in the contests that are his myth possesses it. No single position provides a longed-for resting point, an ultimate, satisfying closure, for the reader. That is also the reason why no single approach is able to cope with any of Kafka's texts. Kafka does not put forward a particular worldview in his works. He does not advocate any one of the positions he presents. He merely describes ever-varied, ever-shifting conflicts of competing points of view. He does not present a thesis, but he represents a *mythos*. A *mythos* shows, but does not judge. None of its phases, aspects, and forms, which Kafka's individual texts enact, can be reduced to and equated with a single position represented in it. Therefore, there cannot be one single context that could "explain" a Kafka text.

In Kafka's telling of the myth of Prometheus, the narrator views myth as a doomed attempt to explain the inexplicable, to master the irreducible strangeness and groundlessness of fact. Applied to Kafka's own myth, the irreducible fact around which his myth weaves its circles is ambivalence that finds no possibility of a definitive and closing answer to a never-ending, ever-open contest.

Throughout Kafka's work, we encounter the fateful interlocking of two mutually exclusive perspectives in a combat without end. One is condemnatory toward selfhood and the assertiveness to which it has to resort. The other critiques the opposite — the self's dependence on and subjection to the power figure. The unresolvable contradiction between these two perspectives underlies and permeates all of Kafka's work, spawning an irony that is directed at all combatants in the struggles his myth relates. A final evaluative meaning, expressing a definite and defin-able intentionality in his work, is thus impossible. The fundamental am-bivalence of Kafka's writing precludes an ultimate judgment that could be called an "explanation."

Yet Kafka's myth is the ever-renewed attempt to push toward such an explanation. It harbors a profound need to interpret and to "under-stand" that infects the reader. Constantly re-dramatizing and re-enacting the ways that lead to the impasse, the myth presses toward, without ever getting to, its eventual "understanding."

As he confided to his diary, Kafka wrote to lift his inner world, the dreamlike visions that crowded in on and haunted him, into the light of day. That he considered to be his mission ("Kafka's Poetics," 9). Writing was to enact the transformation of his chaotic inner world into a world that could be read, interpreted, and thus possibly, eventually, under-stood. In that way, writing served as the means of transforming the visionary writer into a reader. As a letter to Felice that accompanied the copy of his recently composed story "Das Urteil" makes clear, Kafka sought to understand his writing (*F* 394). He turned into a reader, trying to interpret and make sense of his texts.

However, he had to turn to a second reader, Felice, asking whether she could find any sense in his story. For he himself could find none. This request to his reader, quite astonishing for an author to make, shows that Kafka's writing received its meaning from reading, and not, as we would traditionally expect, the other way around. Kafka, in writing, does not seem to have a preconceived meaning, a fixed intention, in his mind. Writing is merely the means of bringing his inner world to the light of day, into readable form, which makes — perhaps — that further light that is understanding attainable. Reading is to provide what writing by itself cannot give. When the writer fails in his task as a reader, he turns to another reader. Thus the reader is to continue the writer's work of bringing his visionary inner world closer to the light of understanding. Even though, according to Kafka's view of myth, a full "explanation" will, because of the groundless nature of being, never be possible, portions of the way toward understanding can become progressively clearer through the process of interpretive reading.

Note

This essay, with slight changes, constitutes the introductory chapter of my book, *The Myth of Power and the Self* (Detroit: Wayne State UP, 2002). Parts of this essay have appeared in *The Journal of the Kafka Society of America*, 1998.

Works Cited

Adorno, Theodor W. "Notes on Kafka." In *Prisms*. Trans. Samuel and Shierry Weber. 1967. Cambridge, Massachusetts: MIT Press, 1981. 243–71. (Originally published as: "Aufzeichnungen zu Kafka." In *Prismen: Kulturkritik und Gesellschaft*. Berlin and Frankfurt am Main: Suhrkamp Verlag, 1955. 302–42.)

Anders, Günther. *Kafka pro und contra, die Prozess-Unterlagen*. Munich: C. H. Beck, 1951.

Beissner, Friedrich. *Der Erzähler Franz Kafka*. 2nd ed. Stuttgart: W. Kohlhammer, 1952.

Deleuze, Gilles, and Félix Guattari. *Kafka: Toward a Minor Literature*. Trans. Dana Palmer. Theory and History of Literature Vol. 30. Minneapolis: U of Minnesota P, 1986. (Original edition *Kafka: Pour une littérature mineure*. Paris: Les éditions de Minuit, 1975.)

Emrich, Wilhelm. *Franz Kafka*. Bonn: Athenäum Verlag, 1958.

Frye, Northrop. *Anatomy of Criticism: Four Essays*. Princeton: Princeton UP, 1957.

Kafka, Franz. *Briefe an Felice und andere Korrespondenz aus der Verlobungszeit*. Ed. Erich Heller and Jürgen Born. *Gesammelte Werke*. Ed. Max Brod. Frankfurt am Main: S. Fischer, 1967. (*F*).

———. *Briefe 1902–24*. Ed. Max Brod. 1958. Frankfurt am Main: Fischer Taschenbuch Verlag, 1975. (*B*).

———. *Tagebücher*. Ed. Hans-Gerd Koch, Michael Müller, and Malcolm Pasley. Frankfurt am Main: S. Fischer; New York: Schocken Books, 1990. (*T*).

———. *Nachgelassene Schriften und Fragmente*. Ed. Malcolm Pasley. Frankfurt am Main: S. Fischer; New York: Schocken Books, 1992.

————. *Brief an den Vater*. Faksimile edition mit einem Nachwort von Joachim Unseld. 1952. Frankfurt am Main: Fischer Taschenbuch Verlag, 1994. (*BV*).

————. *"Das Urteil" und andere Erzählungen*. Frankfurt am Main: Fischer Taschenbuch Verlag, 1997. (Based on: Franz Kafka, *Drucke zu Lebzeiten*. Kritische Ausgabe. Ed. Wolf Kittler, Hans-Gerd Koch, and Gerhard Neumann. Frankfurt am Main: S. Fischer, 1994. (*U*).

Kierkegaard, Søren. *Fear and Trembling: A Dialectical Lyric by Johannes de Silentio. Fear and Trembling and the Sickness Unto Death*. Trans. Walter Lowrie. Princeton UP, 1968.

Lukács, Georg. *History and Class Consciousness: Studies in Marxist Dialectics*. Trans. Rodney Livingstone. Cambridge, Massachusetts: MIT Press, 1971. (*Geschichte und Klassenbewußtsein: Studien über marxistische Dialektik*. Berlin, Malik Verlag, 1923.)

Lyotard, Jean-Francois. *The Postmodern Condition: A Report on Knowledge*. Trans. Geoff Bennington and Brian Massumi. Theory and History of Literature, vol. 10. Minneapolis: U of Minnesota P, 1984. (Originally published as *La condition postmoderne: rapport sur le savoir*. Les Editions de Minuit, 1979.)

Robert, Marthe. *L'ancien et le nouveau, de Don Quichotte à Franz Kafka*. Paris: R. Grasset, 1963.

Sokel, Walter H. (Works listed chronologically.) "Kafka's 'Metamorphosis': Rebellion and Punishment." *Monatshefte* 48 (1956): 203–14.

————. *Franz Kafka. Tragik und Ironie: Zur Struktur seiner Kunst*. Frankfurt am Main: Fischer Taschenbuch Verlag, 1976. (Original edition: Munich/Vienna: Albert Langen-Georg Müller Verlag, 1964).

————. *Franz Kafka*. Columbia Essays on Modern Writers 19. New York/London: Columbia UP, 1966.

————. "The Programme of K.'s Court: Oedipal and Existential Meanings of *The Trial*." In *On Kafka: Semi-Centenary Perspectives*. Ed. Franz Kuna. London: Paul Elek, 1976. 1–21.

————. "Perspectives and Truth in 'The Judgment.'" In *The Problem of the Judgment: Eleven Approaches to Kafka's Story*. Ed. Angel Flores; with a new translation of "The Judgment" by Malcolm Pasley. New York: Gordian Press, 1977 (1976). 193–237.

————. "The Three Endings of Josef K. and the End of Art in *The Trial*." *The Kafka Debate: New Perspectives for Our Time*. Ed. Angel Flores. New York: Gordian Press, 1977. 335–53.

————. "Kafka's Poetics of the Inner Self." In "From Kafka and Dada to Brecht and Beyond: Five Essays By Peter Demetz, Reinhold Grimm, Egon Schwarz, Walter H. Sokel, and Leslie Willson." Eds. Reinhold Grimm, Peter Spycher, Richard A Zipser. *Modern Austrian Literature. Journal of the International Arthur Schnitzler Research Association.* 11 (1978): 37–58.

————. "Language and Truth in the Two Worlds of Franz Kafka." *German Quarterly* 52 (1979): 364–84.

————. "Freud and the Magic of Kafka's Writing." *The World of Franz Kafka.* Ed. J. P. Stern. New York: Holt, Rinehart, and Winston; London: George Weidenfeld and Nicholson, 1980. 154–58.

————. "Franz Kafka: *Der Prozess* (1925)." In *Deutsche Romane des 20. Jahrhunderts: Neue Interpretationen.* Ed. Paul Michael Lützeler. Königstein/Ts.: Athenäum, 1983. 110–27.

————. "From Marx to Myth: The Structure and Function of Self-Alienation in Kafka's 'Metamorphosis.'" *Literary Review* 26 (1983): 485–96.

————. "Between Gnosticism and Jehovah: The Dilemma in Kafka's Religious Attitude." *Germanic Review* 60 (1985): 69–77.

————. "Frozen Sea and River of Narration: The Poetics behind Kafka's Breakthrough." *New Literary History* 17 (1986): 351–63.

————. "Kafka's Beginnings: Narcissism, Magic and the Function of Narration in 'Description of a Struggle.'" *Kafka and the Contemporary Critical Performance: Centenary Readings.* Ed. Alan Udoff. Bloomington and Indianapolis: Indiana UP, 1987. 98–110.

————. "The Wolfman and the Castle." *Journal of the Kafka Society of America* 12 (1988): 64–68.

————. "Kafka and the Twentieth Century: Its Discourses in His Work." *Journal of the Kafka Society of America* 19 (1995): 4–8.

————. "Kafka as a Jew." *New Literary History* 30 (1999): 837–53.

Todorov, Tzvetan. *The Fantastic: A Structural Approach to a Literary Genre.* Trans. Richard Howard. Cleveland/London: Case Western Reserve UP, 1973.

Kafka before Kafka: The Early Stories

Judith Ryan

KAFKA — AND ALL THE ASSOCIATIONS that name carries with it — has become so much a part of today's culture that it is hard to imagine the course of modern literature without his presence. Yet when Kafka's first stories appeared, many readers thought the name was a pseudonym adopted by the Swiss writer Robert Walser. Walser's short prose texts, which had been appearing sporadically in little magazines since 1899, had a seemingly unmistakable style. In a quietly playful, childlike and yet knowing, sometimes even slyly ironic tone, they presented everyday experiences and familiar human types. While they gently mocked creative genius and the laborious process of narrative composition, they also derived a kind of rapture from noticing small details in the world around the narrator, as he wanders through natural landscapes, engaging in flights of fantasy. The voice that narrates the texts is a personal one, and if it is at times a little eccentric, it is predominantly charming, even captivating. None of this sounds very much like the Kafka we know. Nor is it, in fact, identical with the tone of Kafka's earliest writings; but turn-of-the-century readers can be forgiven if they were inclined to confuse the two authors.

The texts that Kafka's contemporaries found so Walseresque were eight short pieces that appeared in the journal *Hyperion* in 1908 and five pieces that appeared in the Easter supplement of the newspaper *Bohemia* in 1910. They were reprinted, along with five new texts, in Kafka's first book-length volume *Betrachtung* (Meditation), published in December 1912. The brevity of the texts, their often whimsical character, and the way they dwell on minute observations seemed to point in the direction of Robert Walser. So did the fact that several of them depicted a walk or an outing. Yet however much these early prose pieces owe to Walser's writings, they also add their own characteristic twist to the Swiss author's narrative schema. It is of course easier to see this in hindsight than it can have been for contemporary readers. Robert Musil, for example, felt troubled by the way in which Kafka's *Betrachtung* seemed like a "Spezialfall des Typus Walsers, trotzdem es [= das Buch *Betrachtung*] früher erschienen ist als dessen *Geschichten*" (special instance of the Walser type, even though it appeared earlier than Walser's *Stories;* Musil 9:1468). A more recent critic sees the relationship between Walser and Kafka as "near and far at once" (Böschenstein 200–212).

The fact that both Kafka's and Walser's earliest texts appeared in magazines and newspapers is typical of the literary scene at the time. It was the custom for Prague cafés to subscribe to such publications and leave them out for perusal by their clientele. As in Paris, Berlin, and Vienna, the coffeehouses were one of the principal meeting places of artists, writers, and intellectuals. The café Louvre and the café Arco (whose habitués were known as the "Arconauts") were two of those that Kafka and his friends frequented. Not only local publications like *Bohemia, Deutsche Arbeit, Das Prager Tagblatt, Hyperion,* and *Wir* were freely available in the coffeehouses, but also papers and journals from other parts of the German-speaking world, as well as magazines in foreign languages. The newest ideas, the most exciting aesthetic innovations, the hottest tips of the cultural world were quickly disseminated through the coffeehouse milieu.

Kafka read a wide range of literary periodicals, as his diary-notebooks indicate. In addition to the Prague journals and newspapers, he also read the *Neue Rundschau,* the *Inselalmanach, Pan,* and *Die weißen Blätter,* among others. A sketch for his essay on "minor literatures" lists "journals" as one ingredient in what he describes as the "Lebhaftigkeit" (liveliness) of such literatures, which thrive on dispute and the simultaneous existence of multiple schools of thought (*T* 326). Alongside the journals and the coffeehouse groups, German-speaking Prague also had a rich offering of public lectures, not only through the university, but also through organizations devoted to public speaking and discussion. There was, in addition, a lively program of theatrical performances. Speakers and theatrical groups from other parts of Europe, notably Berlin and Vienna, were frequent visitors in Prague. Kafka's diaries register his frequent attendance at and thoughtful response to contemporary lectures, plays, and other cultural events.

This system of production and consumption may have been one of the reasons why brief texts of various kinds came to play such a significant role in literary life during almost three decades beginning in the 1890s. Short stories, personal essays, aphorisms, brief prose reflections, lyric poetry, and prose poems were among the dominant genres of the time. A combination of fashion and convenience (a short text can more readily be read in a café than a full-length novel) led to a proliferation of literary miniatures. Publishing houses, by contrast, still preferred novels or, at the least, collections of poems or stories with a consistent theme that would unify the volume. Walser bowed to his publishers' demands, producing three novels in the period 1906 to 1909, though he continued to compose in miniature genres throughout his career. Rainer Maria Rilke, another contemporary, felt increasingly under pressure from his publishers to produce a novel, although it was not until long after he had left Prague that he succeeded in assembling a mosaic of short texts into his innovative modernist "prose book" *Die Aufzeichnungen des Malte Laurids Brigge* (The Notebooks of Malte Laurids Brigge, 1910). Kafka's struggles to produce full-length novels, also at the insistence of his publishers, began around 1913 and continued for the rest of his life. His friend Max Brod, by contrast, successfully wrote a series of novels beginning with his bizarre Expressionist work *Schloß Nornepygge* (Nornepygge Castle, 1908). Kafka comments at some length on Brod's novel Jüdinnen (Jewish Women, 1911) in his 1911 diary (*T* 161–62). But Brod was also one of the chief instigators of the boom in short texts, as indicated by his yearbook *Arkadia*, which actually only appeared in a single issue in 1913 and included poems, one-act plays, and short stories by several of the key players on the coffeehouse scene, including Kafka.

Although we think of Kafka as a prose author, he also wrote poetry in his early years. Only three of these poems are extant: a couplet inscribed in a friend's autograph album, a short lyric in free verse titled "Kleine Seele" (Little Soul, *NS I* 181), and the five-line verse epigraph to the first version of "Beschreibung eines Kampfes" ("Description of a Struggle," *NS I* 54). There is good reason to believe, however, that Kafka wrote many more poems that have not survived. By the same token, he also produced many more prose texts during his early years than he saw fit to keep. The preservation of several early texts is due to the fact that he gave copies to friends, notably Max Brod. One of Kafka's recent editors notes that, in 1910 alone, the number of texts Kafka threw out appears to have been enormous (Koch 217). Kafka comments in his diary that what he has "weggelegt und weggestrichen" (put aside and crossed out) is "ein Berg, es ist 5 mal soviel als ich überhaupt je geschrieben habe" (a mountain; it is 5 times as much as I've ever written, *T* 133).

It would not be wrong to say that Kafka's greatest talent lay in shorter works rather than the novel. The text he himself described as his creative "breakthrough" is the short story "Das Urteil" (The Judgment), written in 1912 and published in 1913. When he put together a collection of work produced prior to the breakthrough, he selected a set of miniature texts, many of which he extracted from somewhat longer narratives. This was the aforementioned 1912 volume *Betrachtung,* which includes pieces originating as far back as 1903–4. He put aside two early projects: the opening of a novel, *Hochzeitsvorbereitungen auf dem Lande* (Wedding Preparations in the Country, 1906–9), and the first chapter of a novel he had begun to write jointly with Max Brod in 1911, *Richard und Samuel*. The title of Kafka's earliest extant novella, "Beschreibung eines Kampfes" (Description of a Struggle, begun in 1904) might also be applied to the tension in his conception of his writing between a desire to produce full-length novels and a recognition that shorter texts were better suited to his abilities.

It is a pity we do not have copies of Kafka's seminar papers or study notes from his student years. We do, however, have a set of jottings he sent to Max Brod in response to an essay on aesthetics that his friend had published in the journal *Die Gegenwart* in February 1906, a few months before Kafka received his law degree. Significantly, Kafka's responses have mainly to do with questions of imagination and perception. In particular, he subjects to careful analysis Brod's claim that only a new impression excites aesthetic pleasure. In accord with contemporary theories about the discontinuity of self and experience, Kafka points out that in actuality everything is new, "denn da alle Gegenstände in immer wechselnder Zeit und Beleuchtung stehn und wir Zuschauer nicht anders, so müssen wir ihnen immer an einem andern Orte begegnen" (for since all objects are in constantly changing time and perspective, and we viewers likewise, so we always encounter them at a different point, *NS I* 10). Kafka wonders, furthermore, whether Brod is right to use the term "ästhetische Apperzeption" (aesthetic apperception) in connection with the aesthetic experience, and he accuses his friend of clinging to the concept of apperception "wie an ein Geländer" (as if to a railing, *NS I* 11) and thus covering up a basic uncertainty that underlies his entire argument.

Uncertainty is a central theme in Kafka's "Beschreibung eines Kampfes." The nameless narrator of the outer story is beset with questions about the solidity of his person and of things around him, and two main figures of the inset stories, the fat man and the worshiper, only serve to accentuate these concerns. The story begins toward midnight at the end of a party. The narrator and a new acquaintance are weary and more than a little inebriated, and a light snow has fallen, making the roads slippery. Thus it seems at first only natural that the two young men have difficulty walking steadily. Only gradually does it become clear that their wobbly condition is less the result of external circumstances than a fundamental state of being. In the course of the narrator's nighttime excursion through Prague and its surroundings, as well as through his conversations with the fat man and the worshiper, the stability of self and world is called into question in a variety of ways. The two friends' awkward bodily movements not only recall the jerky motion of early films (of which Kafka was a great fan), but also evoke disjointedness on a more metaphorical level. The friends are sometimes distinct persons, at other times they blur together. Bodies sometimes have an all too palpable reality, at other times people appear to be merely tissue paper cutouts.[1] Recurrent images of dizziness and slipperiness suggest a world that refuses to retain a single, clearly perceptible shape.

The first version of "Beschreibung eines Kampfes" is set out in a mock academic arrangement of sections indicated by Roman numerals, Arabic numerals, and letters of the alphabet. This makes its double story-within-story structure more readily apparent; but it also sets up a hierarchical scheme in which the primary mediator is the first narrator. In giving more prominence to this narrator, the second version shows Kafka moving toward the method of his breakthrough story, "Das Urteil," in which everything is presented through the consciousness of a single character. But he has not yet developed the limited third-person narration that was the masterstroke of "Das Urteil" and that continued to be one of Kafka's favorite narrative techniques. Despite its virtual elimination of the framework structure, the second version of "Beschreibung eines Kampfes" is still a first-person narrative.

Accounts of Kafka's subsequent literary venture, his fragmentary first novel project, *Hochzeitsvorbereitungen auf dem Lande,* of which not even a complete chapter survives, have tended not to regard it as part of the narrative apprenticeship that Kafka had embarked on in his revision of "Beschreibung eines Kampfes." *Hochzeitsvorbereitungen* has mainly been discussed in terms of its theme, a somewhat reluctant visit by a young man to his fiancée in the country, which clearly presages the development of similar themes in other texts by Kafka, as well as the ambivalence toward marriage manifested in his own life. Critics also mention the image used by the protagonist of *Hochzeitsvorbereitungen,* Raban, to capture his anxiety about the impending marriage, when he imagines he could just send his fully dressed body to the country while he himself remains lying in bed in the form of a large beetle (*NS* I 18). The opening metaphor of "Die Verwandlung" (The Metamorphosis) has already announced itself.

Hochzeitsvorbereitungen is, however, more than just thematically a key text for Kafka's subsequent development. Composed in the third person, this narrative is so constructed as to track in intricate detail the awareness of its protagonist. While it is not exactly a stream-of-consciousness narrative in the sense that we currently understand this term, it moves decisively in that direction. The reason why consciousness in this novel fragment cannot take the sorts of forms developed by James Joyce is that, unlike Joyce, Kafka did not accept the idea that consciousness might have depth. For him, as for many of his contemporaries, consciousness was essentially one-dimensional. Thus, in *Hochzeitsvorbereitungen*, the visual perceptions of the reluctant young fiancé are intermingled with occasional statements about his state of mind, his thoughts (sometimes indicated by quotation marks, but often enough unmarked), as well as passages of free indirect discourse and interior monologue.[2] *Hochzeitsvorbereitungen* is the only text of Kafka's to employ interior monologue within an essentially third-person narrative. While we can, to a certain extent, dismiss or discount some of the wilder flights of fancy in "Beschreibung eines Kampfes" by reminding ourselves that they emanate from characters who are either drunk or mentally disturbed, the oddities of *Hochzeitsvorbereitungen* cannot be so easily glossed over. The earlier story's extreme attention to gestures and body language is continued here in a more realistic vein, and frequent switches to the indefinite pronoun "man" (one) engage the reader's identification with Raban's point of view. Raban even meditates on the slippery relation of the indefinite pronoun to the pronouns "I" and "you" (*NS I* 14). Two subsequent revisions of *Hochzeitsvorbereitungen*, both from the year 1909, eliminate the mixture of narrative forms, reducing the text to a presentation of Raban's visual observation and his conversations with people he encounters. While these two versions are internally more consistent, they seem to have largely given up on the idea of presenting consciousness in all its many different forms. Kafka's urge for formal purity and logic takes over at the expense of his impulse toward narrative experiment. Like the later versions of *Hochzeitsvorbereitungen*, each of the eighteen short texts that Kafka collected in *Betrachtung* also tends, with a few exceptions, to sustain consistency of narrative perspective. Still, it was not until September 1912 that he hit upon the limited third-person point-of-view technique that he used in some of his most successful and best-known works, "Das Urteil," "Die Verwandlung," and the three unfinished novels he embarked on after abandoning *Hochzeitsvorbereitungen*.

It would be inadequate, however, to present Kafka's early narratives solely in terms of his technical development. Equally important is the way in which these texts map the multiple connections between Kafka and his contemporaries. Recent scholarship has insisted increasingly on these links, which reveal Kafka as more than a writer of abstract parables and timeless allegories. Far from being an isolated eccentric reluctant to reveal his writings to others, Kafka was an active participant in several overlapping groups of creative and intellectual friends who met not only in cafés like the Arco, but also in private literary salons or in more public forums such as the theater, cultural venues such as the Lese- und Rede-hallen, and at university lectures (Wagenbach 25–52). Alongside Max Brod, other leading figures like the professor of German literature August Sauer, founder of the journal *Deutsche Arbeit*, and Bertha Fanta, organizer of an intellectual salon, played a catalyzing role in the cultural life of young Prague at the time. Some of what now seems idiosyncratic to Kafka was in fact part of an ambience permeated by a delight in the bizarre, the grotesque, the uncanny, and the fantastic. Sexuality, mad-ness, and violence were frequent themes in literary texts of the time. While we see hints of these themes in "Beschreibung eines Kampfes," they are more strongly profiled and more effectively developed after Kafka's narrative breakthrough in 1912.

Kafka's most distinctively Prague setting is that of "Beschreibung ei-nes Kampfes." Upon leaving the party, the narrator and his new friend set out for a walk up the Laurenziberg (*NS I* 56); on the way, they walk along the quays beside the river Moldau (63), cross the Charles Bridge (66), and engage in some drunken antics near the statue of Charles IV (69). In the inset conversation between the fat man and the worshiper, other parts of Prague are mentioned by name: the Ringplatz (102) and the Wenzelsplatz (107). The fat man engages in a fantasy about Paris that is thoroughly characteristic of the relationship between the two cities at the time: while claiming that the French capital is nothing more than a kind of stage-set, he clearly expresses admiration and envy of what he regards as its more urbane culture (104–5). The servant girl, Anna, at the beginning of the story, recalls the predominance of this motif in other Prague writings of the time. *Hochzeitsvorbereitungen auf dem Lande* is less specifically tied to Prague and its environs. The market town Jung-bunzlau is the only place name mentioned. Nonetheless, the contrast between town and country that forms the backbone of this story is very much tied to Prague social history, since the turn of the century was a period when a huge influx of immigrants from the country arrived in the city in the hope of improving their economic circumstances. Against this backdrop, the fact that Raban is engaged to a young woman from the country and is on his way there to attend to his wedding preparations suggests that, socially, he is making a downward rather than an upward move. In *Betrachtung*, the opening piece, "Kinder auf der Landstraße" (Children on a Country Road), treats the country-city dichotomy through the somewhat whimsical eyes of a child, while the second text,

"Entlarvung eines Bauernfängers" (Unmasking a Confidence Trickster) depicts the common situation of a person from the country who almost falls into the trap of a city dweller who takes advantage of newcomers. Though geographic specificity tends to recede in Kafka's later works (with the exception of his amusing fantasy of America in his novel fragment of 1913), traces of Prague geography, architecture, bureaucratic structures, and so forth can be found in *Der Proceß* (The Trial) and *Das Schloß* (The Castle).

More important than these glimpses of turn-of-the-century Prague social history are the connections with its intellectual culture, which are particularly strong in "Beschreibung eines Kampfes." More than any other of Kafka's works, this early narrative is marked by the debates about philosophy and psychology that were being carried out in Berlin, Vienna, and Prague in the 1890s and the early years of the twentieth century. Although the German-language university in Prague was smaller than its Czech counterpart, it had been fortunate enough to attract leading minds during this period, especially in medicine, law, and physics. Albert Einstein and Ernst Mach both spent a period of time teaching in Prague. Ernst Mach's explorations in psychophysics and his influential book, *Analyse der Empfindungen* (Analysis of Sensations, 1886) were eagerly studied by the student groups to which Kafka belonged.[3] Students of law like Kafka were frequently also aspiring writers, and the university system gave them plenty of freedom to attend courses in areas outside their main field. Kafka himself took two courses in philosophy from adherents of the newer school of thought, indebted to an understanding of consciousness promulgated by the German philosopher Franz Brentano. He was also a member of the "Brentano Circle," a group of young intellectuals who met regularly at the Café Louvre in Prague. Brentanist theory informs Kafka's writing from his earliest stories to the very latest (Ryan 100–112). In "Beschreibung eines Kampfes," contemporary philosophy and psychology appear in an exuberantly sophomoric form, as befits the student milieu in which the narrative is set. The subtleties of the new theories are largely subordinated to a more generally Berkeleyan mode of thought, in which the external world is understood as a projection of the perceiver's subjectivity. When the framework narrator makes the landscape change according to his own desires, or the fat man urges it to go away entirely, it is perfectly possible to read these passages in terms of subjective idealism. All the same, none of Kafka's Prague contemporaries would have failed to see in these episodes of "Beschreibung eines Kampfes" allusions to Brentano's ideas about the interdependence of subject and object. By the same token, they would have read the depiction of the framework narrator, with his unsteady gait and turn-of-the-century lassitude, in terms of Mach's theory that the self was a precarious collection of attributes without internal consistency or temporal continuity.

Although Kafka and his friends had actually studied these new theories, many of their contemporaries knew them only at second hand. Hermann Bahr's essay "Das unrettbare Ich" (The Unsalvageable Self), included in his influential book, *Die Überwindung des Naturalismus* (Overcoming Naturalism, 1891), had disseminated Mach's theory of the discontinuous self well beyond the circle of specialists in turn-of-the-century philosophy or psychology. Kafka could count on his readers' familiarity with these ideas.

So, of course, could Robert Walser, one of whose earliest prose pieces (the fourth of his "Sechs kleine Geschichten" [Six Little Stories], 1901) depicts a poet who believes his fantasy is more powerful than external reality. Addressing the wall of his room, he asks it not to bother him with its continued real existence:

> Wand, ich habe dich im Kopf. Gib dir keine Mühe, mich mit deiner ruhigen, seltsamen Physiognomie zu täuschen. Fortan bist du Gefangener meiner Phantasie. Hierauf sagte er dasselbe zu den Fenstern und zu der düsteren Aussicht, welche ihm dieselben tagtäglich boten. (*Geschichten*, 10)

> [Wall, I have you in my head. Don't bother to deceive me with your quiet, strange physiognomy. From now on you're a prisoner of my fantasy. Hereupon he said the same thing to the windows and the dismal view they offered him every day.]

The fat man in "Beschreibung eines Kampfes" is another version of Walser's poet. His extravagant address to the landscape, in which he claims that it disturbs his thinking, accuses a mountain of being deceitful, and finally requests the elements of the landscape to make more space for him (*NS I* 79–81), is in essence a parody of the poet's address to the wall in Walser's little story. While Walser's poet is clearly trapped in his own narcissistic dreams of creative potency, Kafka's fat man actually does influence the landscape around him, which suddenly starts to shift and shuffle its elements around when it hears his request for more space. In another of Walser's short texts, "Das Genie" (The Genius, 1902), the writer figure is more successful than the poet of the 1901 text. Here, the genius first causes a heavy snowfall and then makes all the snow disappear again (*Geschichten*, 32). Kafka's narrator, who makes the road become stonier and steeper, conjures up a strong wind, and later makes the road become flatter, the stones disappear, and the wind become still (*NS I* 73–74), is clearly another version of Walser's playful genius figure. The larger questions raised by Walser's short prose differ, however, from those explored in Kafka's early stories. Walser's playful poet and genius figures are part of a network of reflections on the problem of narrative and narratability; Kafka's willful narrator and bizarre fat man are more concerned with epistemological issues.

Other elements of turn-of-the-century thought are woven into Kafka's "Beschreibung eines Kampfes." The language skepticism of Fritz Mauthner's *Beiträge zu einer Kritik der Sprache* (Contributions to a Critique of Language, 1901–2) and its reflection in Hugo von Hofmannsthal's influential text, "Ein Brief" (A Letter, 1902), leaves a clear imprint on Kafka's story. The fat man of the inset story recounts an episode from his childhood when, waking up from an afternoon nap, he hears his mother saying in an unremarkable tone of voice that she is taking tea in the garden (*NS I* 91). She uses an ordinary Austrian idiom ("ich jause im Grünen," meaning "I'm taking tea in the garden"), but in his sleep-dazed state, he is unable to take in its meaning. He can scarcely believe that people can use language unreflectively and in connection with everyday experiences. He meditates on the disturbingly random relationship between names and things:

> Die Pappel in den Feldern, die Ihr den "Turm von Babel" genannt habt, denn Ihr wußtet nicht oder wolltet nicht wissen, daß es eine Pappel war, schaukelt wieder namenlos und Ihr müßt sie nennen "Noah, wie er betrunken war." (*NS I* 89–90)

> [The poplar in the fields that you called the "Tower of Babel," for you didn't know or didn't want to know that it was a poplar, is shaking namelessly again and you have to call it "Noah in his cups."]

Later, he struggles to decide among several possible names for the moon: "vergessene Papierlaterne in merkwürdiger Farbe" (forgotten paper lantern in a strange color), "Mariensäule" (statue of the Virgin Mary), and "Mond, der gelbes Licht wirft" (moon casting yellow light) (*NS I* 102). His bewilderment about the nature of language in its literal and metaphorical forms is, as it were, the inverse of Hofmannsthal's fictive Lord Chandos, who desires to replace language as we know it with "eine Sprache, in welcher die stummen Dinge zu mir sprechen" (a language in which the silent things will speak to me, *Erzählungen* 472). At this early point in Kafka's development, his emphasis on gesture also has a Hofmannsthalian cast: "es liegt unendlich viel in Bewegungen: sie sind die

komplizierte und fein abgetönte Sprache des Körpers für die komplizierte und feine Gefallsucht der Seele, die eine Art Liebesbedürfnis und
eine Art Kunstbetrieb ist" (there is infinitely much in movements: they
are the complex and subtly shaded language of the body for the complex
and subtle desire of the soul to please, which is a kind of need for love
and a kind of practice of art, 36), as Hofmannsthal puts it in his story
"Das Glück am Weg" (Good Luck on the Way).[4] The depiction of body
movements in the framework narrative of "Beschreibung eines Kampfes"
is more closely related to this understanding of the "language of the
body" than is the gestural language of *Hochzeitsvorbereitungen,* where
Kafka is already moving toward a more Expressionist mode.

For Kafka's contemporaries, the dreamlike atmosphere of "Beschreibung eines Kampfes" would also have recalled the settings of some of
Arthur Schnitzler's short stories, many of which also depict party scenes
and depend heavily upon languid conversation. One might compare the
narrator's departure from the party at the beginning of Kafka's tale with
the opening of Schnitzler's "Frühlingsnacht im Seziersaal. Phantasie"
(Spring Night in the Autopsy Room. Fantasy, 1880), where the narrator
is also on his way home from a festivity in the early morning hours.
While Schnitzler's story is set at the beginning of spring, Kafka has his
narrative occur on a snowy winter's night. In both instances, however,
lassitude and exhaustion are the narrator's dominant feelings:

> Und meine Stimmung war seltsam. Freude und Lust klangen in mei-
> nem erhitzten Kopfe nach. Über den müden Blick senkten sich die Au-
> genlider und die weiche Morgenluft des erwachenden Frühlings zitterte
> um Stirn und Wangen, so weich und mild beinahe wie der warme Duft
> von herzigen Mädchenlippen, den ich heute nacht im Wirbel des Tan-
> zes übers Antlitz hauchen fühlte. (*Sterben,* 16)

> [And my mood was strange. Joy and desire resonated in my feverish
> head. My eyelids sank over my tired gaze and the soft morning air of
> awakening spring trembled about my forehead and cheeks, almost as soft
> and mild as the scent of lovely girls' lips, which I had felt breathing over
> my face tonight in the whirl of the dance.]

Despite the difference in season, the turn-of-the-century ennui is common to both stories, though it is oddly exaggerated in Kafka's. Similarly,
one might compare the discussions between the narrator and his new
friend in Kafka's story with the conversations about love in Schnitzler's
"Gespräch in der Kaffeehausecke" (Conversation in a Coffee House
Corner, 1890). Here, too, the positions are reversed in Schnitzler and
Kafka. In Kafka, the narrator's new friend is happy because he has just

enjoyed the kisses of a servant girl, while the narrator himself, alienated from social life, is choked with tears of jealousy. Schnitzler's narrator finds it hard to believe that his friend's sorrow in love is genuine. When Kafka's narrator notices that his friend has hurt his knee, he leaves him lying on the icy cobblestones, convinced that the friend can no longer be of use to him. In Schnitzler's story, the narrator's self-centeredness is explained by the inevitability of the subjective point of view, which never permits us actually to feel another's pain:

> "Wenn ich dich so reden höre, Fred, fällt es mir wieder schwer aufs Gewissen, wie subjektiv ich bin. Denn höre, ich kann dir deine Trübsal kaum glauben. Für mich gibt es in diesem Augenblick nur einen wahren Schmerz: den, den ich empfinde." (*Sterben*, 117)

> ["When I hear you speak like that, Fred, I have a bad conscience about how subjective I am. Listen, I can hardly believe your misery. For me, there is only one real pain at this moment: that which I experience."]

Kafka's "Beschreibung eines Kampfes" treats the problem of subjectivity at greater length; indeed, it is a central issue of the story, and is presented in a more overtly abstract mode that is in large measure a parody of philosophical discussions about subjectivity. Schnitzler's short stories are more tightly structured than this early text of Kafka's; even the relatively streamlined second version of "Beschreibung eines Kampfes" has a looser effect than that of Schnitzler's stories, with their more dramatic presentation of human conflicts and their more incisive narrative ironies. As a narrative, Kafka's story is rambling in structure and lacks any tight sense of psychological motivation or causality.

It may be more profitable to read "Beschreibung eines Kampfes" as a pastiche or stylistic imitation of the contemporary writers and thinkers to which it indirectly alludes. Much of its appeal depends on an intimate knowledge of the theories and stylistic peculiarities it imitates. The subtitle "Belustigungen" (Amusements) and the inebriated high jinks of the narrator suggest that the text was, among other things, a way of letting off steam about the serious intellectual debates it also represents. All the same, Kafka continued to work on this story well beyond his student years, reining in its sprawling structure and accentuating the subjective, dreamlike, and fantastic elements of the tale. We should not forget that Kafka later described his writing as a representation of his "traumhaftes innres Leben" (dreamlike inner life).

Amusing though it is, "Beschreibung eines Kampfes" does not have the black humor that later became one of Kafka's trademarks. Nor, despite its somewhat grotesque attention to detail and the unusual image of the enormous beetle beneath the bedclothes, does *Hochzeitsvorbereitungen* develop the macabre streak that runs through so many of Kafka's later stories. Only the one-paragraph text about visiting an occult sketcher ("Wir wußten nicht eigentlich," [We didn't really know], *NS I* 182) suggests something of the uncanny element that was later to appear in some of Kafka's works. From the sparse evidence of this brief text, it is hard to tell whether Kafka was here setting out to write a story in the manner of Gustav Meyrink, who was later to become famous for his novel *Der Golem* (The Golem, 1915), and who was already producing short stories about occult phenomena such as "Chimäre" (Chimera, 1904).[5] Given the spiritist craze of the turn of the century, the text may simply have emerged from an autobiographical experience, possibly his first meeting with Rudolf Steiner, whom Kafka connected with the occult (see *T* 32–35). Whatever the case may be, it reflects a somewhat skeptical view of mediums and the occult.

Kafka spent longer wrestling with "Beschreibung eines Kampfes" (from 1904 until 1911) than he did with *Hochzeitsvorbereitungen auf dem Lande* (1906–9). And it was the earlier text that ultimately provided him with several of the short pieces that he published in journals in 1908 and 1910 and finally included in his 1912 volume, *Betrachtung*. The material from his student years had remarkable staying power.

In the meantime, Kafka was clearly casting around for other writing projects. Max Brod, concerned about his friend's dissatisfaction with his writing and his inability to produce a text he felt worthy of publication, suggested two different ideas, both of them joint projects. The first, prompted perhaps by the important role played by journalism in Prague at the time, was an essay about an airplane demonstration in Northern Italy. The two friends traveled together to Brescia and produced an article that was published in fall 1909 in the Prague newspaper *Bohemia*. One of the most striking features of this essay, which distinguishes it from other pieces of contemporary journalism, is the way in which the pilots' achievements become figures for the act of creative writing. The second project was to be the novel *Richard and Samuel,* in which alternate sections would be written by Brod and Kafka, based on travel journals each had kept during trips to Switzerland, Northern Italy, and Paris. The novel did not proceed beyond the first chapter and a sketch for the introduction. The joint novel was to highlight the very different responses of the two friends to experiences they had had in common, and the chapter they completed bears out this crucial tension between the two perspectives. In particular, their different responses to women and the possibility of flirtatious adventures in the course of the trip is amusingly presented. Kafka's sketch for the introduction also emphasizes the differences in the two men's characters. The plot, as Kafka presents it in this sketch, provides for tensions between the two to increase, reaching a crisis in Stresa and finally coming to rest when they arrive in Paris. Friendship itself is presented as a struggle. Kafka's interest in the tension between dependence and independence makes itself felt in all three of his major early projects: "Beschreibung eines Kampfes," *Hochzeitsvorberei-tungen auf dem Lande,* and *Richard and Samuel.* It was an interest that was to remain with him throughout his career, surfacing again and again in his later writing.

Tracing Kafka's early development by means of his unpublished manu-scripts yields a good picture of the young writer as he must have been seen by his intimate friends. It was, after all, those friends who saved these manuscripts and thus permit us these glimpses into his initial struggle to forge a viable writing persona. A rather different impression is created if we restrict our vision to the texts Kafka himself published between March 1908 and December 1912. These were all short pieces, ranging from a few lines to a few pages long. For these early publications, then, Kafka had temporarily resolved the tension between novel- or novella-length narra-tives, on the one hand, and textual miniatures, on the other. These little pieces pointedly resist the traditional elements of the short story: develop-ment, intrigue, crisis, denouement. The two that come closest to telling a story are "Kinder auf der Landstraße" and "Unglücklichsein" (Unhappi-ness), but even in these texts, the narrative impulse is only very lightly engaged. The others range from the quasi-philosophical aperçu of "Die Bäume" (The Trees) to the prose-poem-like "Wunsch, Indianer zu wer-den" (The Wish to Be a Red Indian), the more meditative "Entschlüsse" (Resolutions), or the character sketch "Der Kaufmann" (The Tradesman). The two more narrative pieces were not among those Kafka included in the clusters of texts he published in 1908 and 1910. In other words, he had a good eye for what was suited to the magazine and newspaper format of his day. Only in 1912, when he assembled texts for *Betrachtung,* did he add the two narrative selections, using them to frame and contain the collection of shorter pieces.

Kafka was not at all happy with this first published volume. Indeed, the letter he sent to his publisher along with his manuscript gives a brilliant sketch of his writerly anxieties that could almost stand in its own right as one of the short texts in the collection. With the sharp self-critical eye he later turned to such advantage in his fiction, he presents the whole venture as the outcome of an insoluble dilemma, an intense desire to have a published book of his own, and a sense that the responsible thing would be to eliminate as imperfect more of the texts than he has done. These anxieties are equally intensely and more apologetically expressed in subsequent letters to his fiancée, Felice Bauer, who found it hard to know what to make of *Betrachtung*. It is not surprising that Kafka's next book-length publication was to be "Das Urteil," a text with all the required ingredients for a good short story, and published with a dedication to her.

Based on the texts in *Betrachtung* alone, Kafka appears primarily as a whimsical writer. If we return to our initial comparison of Kafka and Walser, however, we shall see that Kafka's short prose already diverges in important ways from that of the contemporary with whom he was at first confused. Most tellingly, the sense of gentle wonder that permeates Walser's early texts is undercut in Kafka's prose pieces by more profound anxieties. Motifs that subsequently become major themes in Kafka's work — bachelor life, the business world, family relations — put in cameo appearances, and it is already clear that these motifs are fraught with ambivalence and uncertainty. The minor epiphanies of Walser's short prose are almost entirely absent here, and where they do occur, they take place against a more equivocal and even threatening backdrop. Walser's early pieces end either with a return to fulfilled solitude or by suddenly drawing attention to the mechanics of the writing process; Kafka's often conclude with a remark even more puzzling than the text that precedes it.[6] The childlike tone of Walser's first stories is a deliberately playful posture that allows him to suggest more than he actually states; Kafka's tone is not childlike, and when children appear in his texts, they seem burdened with intimations that go beyond adult consciousness.

One of the most Walser-like texts in *Betrachtung* is "Der Nachhauseweg" (The Way Home). After an opening expression of wonder about the "Überzeugungskraft der Luft nach dem Gewitter" (persuasive power of air after a thunderstorm, *D* 25), the text proceeds to describe a walk taken by the narrator through the streets in his neighborhood. Nothing much happens in the course of this walk, and at the end the narrator simply returns to his room. Except for the old-town setting, the walk is not very different from that described in Walser's first published story, "Der Greifensee" (Lake Greifen). In this text, Walser observes that nothing more occurred during his walk than "alles das, was einem gewöhnlichen Menschen auf gewöhnlichem Wege begegnen kann" (everything that can happen to an ordinary person on an ordinary walk, *Geschichten*, 32). A page or so of ecstatic nature description culminates in an exclamation of wonder about the landscape and the little lake it contains. Suddenly the perspective shifts and the tone becomes self-mocking:

— Auf eine solche Weise spricht die Beschreibung, wahrlich: eine be-
geisterte, hingerissene Beschreibung. Und was soll ich noch sagen? Ich
müßte sprechen wie sie, wenn ich noch einmal anfangen müßte, denn
es ist ganz und gar die Beschreibung meines Herzens. (*Geschichten*, 32)

[— This is the way description speaks, in truth: an enthusiastic, ecstatic
description. And what should I say in addition? I would have to speak
like description if I were to begin over again, for it is through and
through description after my own heart.]

Walser's text ends with the speaker planning a second visit to the charming
spot while he swims out into the lake. Kafka's "Der Nachhauseweg" does
not follow this structural model. Instead, it compresses several aspects of
Walser's style into a much shorter space and handles the meta-narrative
aspects of his text with greater subtlety:

Ich marschiere und mein Tempo ist das Tempo dieser Gassenseite, dieser Gasse, dieses Viertels. Ich bin mit Recht verantwortlich für alle
Schläge gegen Türen, auf die Platten der Tische, für alle Trinksprüche,
für die Liebespaare in ihren Betten, in den Gerüsten der Neubauten, in
dunklen Gassen an die Häusermauern gepreßt, auf den Ottomanen der
Bordelle. (*D* 25)

[I walk, and my tempo is the tempo of this side of the street, this street,
this quarter. I am rightly responsible for all knocks on doors, on table-
tops, for all toasts, for all lovers in their beds, in the scaffolding of new
buildings, pressed in alleyways against walls of houses, on the ottomans
of brothels.]

Unlike the sudden recognition in Walser's story that the apparently
authentic nature description is in fact nothing other than a familiar technique of composition, the textualization of reality is taken for granted
here almost from the outset. In the sense that the narrator creates the
sights and sounds of his walk, he is "rightly responsible" for them: they
do not seem to have an existence outside the narrative itself. Unlike
Walser's text, there is no sense here of different levels of reality or of a
distinction, however playful, between reality and representation. Adapting an old literary tradition that links the walk with the act of meditation,
Kafka has the narrator of "Der Nachhauseweg" reflect upon his own
merits in the course of his stroll through the town. But although he
claims to be satisfied with himself and to find nothing really substantial
to worry about, he is somewhat out of sorts as he returns to his room:

Nur als ich in mein Zimmer trete, bin ich ein wenig nachdenklich, aber
ohne daß ich während des Treppensteigens etwas Nachdenkenswertes

gefunden hätte. Es hilft mir nicht viel, daß ich das Fenster gänzlich öffne und daß in einem Garten die Musik noch spielt. (D 25–26)

[Not until I enter my room do I feel a little concerned, but without having found anything worth being concerned about while climbing the stairs. It doesn't help me much to open wide a window and hear music still playing in a garden.]

This is a very different kind of ending from that of Walser's story about his walk out to the little lake. Walser's narrator makes plans for the future, but immerses himself — quite literally — in the present at the end of his story. There is nothing more to be said. Kafka's narrator concludes with an awareness of disjunction between his self-estimate as a writer in full control of the reality he presents and another sphere of action that seems to exist independently of him. The little text is more than just wistful, it is in fact quite disturbing.

One could do similar analyses of most of the pieces in Kafka's *Betrachtung*. Even texts from that collection that end on a more positive note, like "Der Ausflug ins Gebirge" (Excursion into the Mountains) or "Das Gassenfenster" (The Street Window), present no more than an apparent resolution to the problems posed in their opening lines. Fantasy is shown to have tremendous powers, but at the same time to come up against insurmountable limitations. The brilliant text "Wunsch, Indianer zu werden" shows fantasy in the act of deconstructing itself:

Wenn man doch ein Indianer wäre, gleich bereit, und auf dem rennenden Pferde, schief in der Luft, immer wieder kurz erzitterte über dem zitternden Boden, bis man die Sporen ließ, denn es gab keine Sporen, bis man die Zügel wegwarf, denn es gab keine Zügel, und kaum das Land vor sich als glatt gemähte Heide sah, schon ohne Pferdehals und Pferdekopf. (D 32–33)

[If only one were a Red Indian, always ready, and on the racing horse, slantwise in the air, briefly trembling again and again above the trembling ground, until one abandoned one's spurs, for there were no spurs, until one threw away the reins, for there were no reins, and scarcely saw the country ahead of one as smoothly mown heath, already without a horse's neck and a horse's head.]

This text ascribes imaginative force to the initial wish, which virtually creates the horse needed for its proper fulfillment. At the same time, it recognizes that wishes do not determine reality. As the sentence lifts off, the purely imaginative nature of the exercise becomes apparent.

Perhaps the most compelling example of this tension between fantasy and reality, words and things, is the story "Der Kaufmann." The first part of this text presents the cares of the tradesman, constantly forced to depend on risky calculations and to enter financial dealings with others whose own monies may not be secure. He longs to escape from the restrictions of his business life, but when he goes home at the end of the day, he finds no relief from this oppression. As he goes up in the elevator of his apartment building, he has what seems at first to be a paradoxical hallucination. He seems to be followed by throngs of people (at one point they appear to be birds) who will not let him alone, and in a bizarre harangue to the invisible multitude, he begs his persecutors to go away. Rising up floor by floor, he sketches one after another possible place to which the importunate throng might retreat. It is as if a series of images appears on the frosted glass walls of the elevator, or as if the banisters, which seem to glide down outside "wie stürzendes Wasser" (like falling water, *D* 23), were metamorphosing themselves into the crowd and the places he sees in his mind's eye. While at work, the tradesman seems to have longed for solitude and a chance to indulge in his own fantasies, but his isolation in the lift is so frightening that his mind involuntarily peoples this emptiness with an interfering crowd. In the tradesman's final mental image, he imagines mounted police keeping the mob in check. In the very moment when he has gained imaginative control, however, the elevator stops at his floor. The reality of home is that of a doorbell and a parlor maid who answers it; it does not appear as if the tradesman returns to a family. The narrative presents, then, three sets of constraints: oppressive life at work, solitude in the elevator, a routine arrival home. Imagination provides no respite from these oppression and isolation; instead, it summons up its own set of demons.

Given that some of the texts in *Betrachtung* had been drawn from one or another version of "Beschreibung eines Kampfes," the volume reaches far back into Kafka's first development as a writer. He notes as much, disparagingly, in a letter to Felice Bauer: "Ob Du wohl erkennst, wie sich die einzelnen Stückchen im Alter voneinander unterscheiden. Eines ist z.B. darunter, das ist gewiß 8–10 Jahre alt" (I wonder if you recognize how much the little pieces vary in age. One of them is surely 8–10 years old, *F* 175). Among the oldest texts, changed only slightly for inclusion in the new collection, was "Die Bäume," which in "Beschreibung eines Kampfes" had been attributed to the worshiper. Separated from the context of this figure's bizarre psychopathology, the brief text acquires the force of an aphorism:

Wir sind nämlich wie Baumstämme im Schnee. Scheinbar liegen sie glatt auf und man sollte sie mit kleinem Anstoß wegschieben können. Aber nein, das kann man nicht, denn sie sind fest mit dem Boden verbunden. Aber sieh, sogar das ist nur scheinbar. (*D* 33)

[For we are like tree trunks in the snow. Apparently they lie smoothly on the surface and one should be able to move them away with a slight push. But no, one can't do so, for they are firmly bound to the earth. But look, even that is only apparent.]

Characteristic of Kafka, even of the more familiar post-1912 Kafka, is the twofold reversal with which the text concludes. The complex play with an old polarity, reality and appearance, and the Berkeleyan conclusion that even reality is only appearance is evidently an aperçu Kafka does not wish to discard. Might it have been one of what he called, in a letter to Felice about *Betrachtung,* "Lichtblicke in eine unendliche Verwirrung hinein" (rays of light into an infinite confusion, *F* 218)?

The two most recent pieces in the collection were "Der plötzliche Spaziergang" (The Sudden Walk) and "Entschlüsse," written in January and February 1912 respectively. It is not surprising, therefore, that both of these texts begin to show structures characteristic of Kafka's later writing.

"Der plötzliche Spaziergang" uses the multiply extended "if-then" construction familiar to readers of Kafka's mature story "Auf der Galerie" (Up in the Gallery, written 1917). Kafka's characteristic — and very humorous — use of logic is already apparent in this text. The shift from the decision to stay home in the family living room to the wish to go out takes place almost unobtrusively in the middle of the seemingly parallel series of conditional clauses, and the conclusion drawn from these if-clauses, in the main clause of the long first sentence of the piece, is one that asserts the independence of the self from family life and its emergence as a self-assured and clearly profiled entity. The final sentence of the text undercuts this newfound independence by claiming that it is enhanced by a visit to another friend to see how he is. In terms of the polarity between solitude and life with others, however, the late-night visit to the friend merely indicates the self's inability to exist in splendid isolation.[7]

"Entschlüsse" might fruitfully be compared with a later piece like "Eine alltägliche Verwirrung" (A Common Confusion, written 1917), with its combination of broad generalization and odd particularity. It opens with what appears to be a general statement: "Aus einem elenden Zustand sich zu erheben, muß selbst mit gewollter Energie leicht sein"

(To pull oneself up out of a miserable state must be easy, even with forced energy, *D* 19). The text now turns explicitly to a first-person narrator (though at this point we recognize that the first sentence has perhaps already been spoken or thought by this narrator), who attempts to put the depression-breaking precept into practice. When his attempts to act cheerful fail to be effective, he gradually falls back into a passive slump. The text concludes with another generalization, but this time a more mystifying one: "Eine charakteristische Bewegung eines solchen Zustandes ist das Hinfahren des kleinen Fingers über die Augenbrauen" (A typical gesture of such a state is to run one's little finger over one's eyebrows, *D* 19). If we compare the first generalization with the last, we can see that something very peculiar has happened. What begins as a prescription for pulling out of a depression turns into a description of a gesture signifying bewilderment or an attempt to relieve tension. This case-study-like description of the characteristic gesture raises more questions than it resolves. Is running one's little finger over one's eyebrows a symptom of passive bewilderment? Or is this final sentence merely a desperate attempt on the part of the narrator to establish some kind of certainty, however bizarre? We are left with no indication of the truth-value — or lack thereof — of this statement. It may even be an allusion to a gesture characteristic of someone well known to Kafka and his friends.

Be that as it may, *Betrachtung* was well received by the group of writers Max Brod later called the Prague Circle. For Kafka himself, its publication served as a freeing mechanism that enabled him to move forward in a new mode. Although he continued formulating short texts in his diaries and later included a few in his volume *Ein Landarzt* (A Country Doctor, 1919), the next three works he published hew more closely to the traditional short story genre: "Das Urteil," written a scant week after he had sent off the final manuscript of *Betrachtung*, "Der Heizer" (The Stoker, 1913), and "Die Verwandlung" (1915). In part taking Kafka's lead — he had intended to collect these three stories under the title *Die Söhne* (The Sons) — these narratives have frequently been seen in terms of the Expressionist father-son theme. They also contain many elements of the peculiarly Prague culture from which Kafka's writing emerged. In a diary entry written shortly after his composition of "Das Urteil," Kafka notes that he modeled some aspects of the tale on stories by Max Brod and Franz Werfel.[8] The maze-like corridors in the bowels of the ship in "Der Heizer" are at least partly based on the labyrinthine streets of Prague and the architectural oddity of "Durchhäuser," houses that contained passageways connecting streets on either side. The protagonist's suspicion of a Slovak who shares his cabin and the ship stoker's dislike of his Rumanian supervisor reflect the tensions of a city that contained people of many different ethnic origins. The lodgers in "Die Verwandlung" represent a real aspect of contemporary Prague, where an acute housing shortage caused many people to rent out rooms to strangers. Most interestingly, we see Kafka reworking motifs from his own earlier texts in these more masterfully written stories. "Das Urteil" picks up elements from a notebook sketch he called "Die städtische Welt" (The Urban World), a brief fictional study of the effect of modern urban life on human relations. The conclusion of "Die Verwandlung" revisits the motif of a young girl about to alight from a streetcar that Kafka had first developed in "Der Fahrgast" (On the Tram, 1908), one of the texts in *Betrachtung* (*D* 27–28). Kafka's continuation of "Der Heizer" in the second chapter of *Der Verschollene* (The Missing Person, generally known as Amerika) brilliantly reworks the glass-walled lift motif of the 1908 text "Der Kaufmann."

Perhaps the most important contribution of Kafka's early writings to the works of his breakthrough period and beyond is the irony and humor of their attention to detail, their telling shifts in logic, and their experiments in registering consciousness. The short prose favored by the literary magazines of early twentieth-century Prague had created a readership that could be expected to take careful note of narrative subtleties — a group of practiced close readers, in other words. As Kafka developed the limited third-person presentation that made "Das Urteil," "Der Heizer," and "Die Verwandlung" such accomplished literary works, he could rely on this observant style of reading to suggest a more critical view of his protagonists than they themselves are able to muster. His ability to use significant detail to open up a gap between the protagonist's and the reader's perceptions had been finely honed by his early writing exercises. His pastiches and parodies of contemporary writers and thinkers provided him with a way to differentiate his own style increasingly from theirs, while remaining connected with the coffeehouse culture, which gave him intellectual and psychological support. A combination of in-house jokes with deep insights into modern culture in the broadest sense continued to inform his later work, as it did his very earliest writings. The title of his first attempt at a full-fledged narrative work, "Beschreibung eines Kampfes," remained an apt metaphor for all of his creative endeavors.

Notes

[1] On the importance of facades and surfaces in "Beschreibung eines Kampfes" and *Betrachtung,* see Mark Anderson, *Kafka's Clothes* (Oxford: Clarendon, 1992), 43.

[2] In this sense, Kafka goes beyond the use of "psychonarration" practiced by his favorite author and partial stylistic model, Flaubert. See Charles Bernheimer, "Psychopoetik: Flaubert und Kafkas *Hochzeitsvorbereitungen auf dem Lande,*" in Kurz, ed. *Der junge Kafka* (Frankfurt am Main: Suhrkamp, 1984), 154–83.

[3] For a brief account of Mach's *Analyse der Empfindungen,* see Judith Ryan, *The Vanishing Subject* (Chicago: Chicago UP, 1991), 9, 12.

[4] Jost Schillemeit notes that the scenic and visual elements of the "Belustigungen" sequence in "Beschreibung eines Kampfes" closely resemble those of Hofmannsthal's *Kleine Welttheater,* a work Kafka greatly admired. Schillemeit, "Kafkas 'Beschreibung eines Kampfes': Ein Beitrag zum Textverständnis und zur Geschichte von Kafkas Schreiben," in Kurz, ed., *Der junge Kafka,* 120–21.

[5] *Prager deutsche Erzählungen,* ed. Dieter Sudhoff and Michael M. Suchardt (Stuttgart: Reclam, 1992), 80–85.

[6] Despite the examples given by Bernhard Böschenstein (210), the ways in which the two authors conclude their texts are more often different than similar.

[7] James Rolleston speaks, in connection with such pairings of figures as the narrator and his friend in "Der plötzliche Spaziergang," of "Doppelgänger" or refractions of the self that interact in a continual process of self-confirmation and self-dissolution (*"Betrachtung:* Landschaften der Doppelgänger," in Kurz, ed. esp. 185).

[8] See my entry on "Das Urteil" in the *New History of German Literature,* ed. David Wellbery, et al. (Harvard UP, forthcoming).

Works Cited

Anderson, Mark. *Kafka's Clothes: Ornament and Aestheticism in the Habsburg Fin de Siècle.* Oxford: Clarendon, 1992.

———, ed. *Reading Kafka: Prague, Politics, and the Fin de Siècle.* New York: Schocken, 1989.

Böschenstein, Bernhard. "Nah und fern zugleich: Franz Kafka's *Betrachtung* und Robert Walsers Berliner Skizzen," in Gerhard Kurz, ed. *Der junge Kafka* (Frankfurt am Main: Suhrkamp, 1984), 200–212.

Heidsieck, Arnold. "Physiological, Phenomenological, and Linguistic Psychology in Kafka's Early Works." *German Quarterly* 62 (1989): 489–500.

Hofmannsthal, Hugo von. *Erzählungen, Erfundene Gespräche und Briefe, Reisen.* Frankfurt am Main: S. Fischer, 1979.

Kafka, Franz. *Briefe an Felice.* Ed. Erich Heller and Jürgen Born. Frankfurt am Main: S. Fischer, 1967. (*F*)

————. *Drucke zu Lebzeiten*. Ed. Wolf Kittler, Hans-Gerd Koch, and Gerhard Neumann. Frankfurt am Main: S. Fischer, 1994. (*D*)

————. *Nachgelassene Schriften und Fragmente I*. Ed. Malcolm Pasley. Frankfurt am Main: S. Fischer, 1993. (*NS I*)

————. *Tagebücher*. Ed. Hans-Gerd Koch, Michael Müller, and Malcolm Pasley. Frankfurt am Main: S. Fischer, 1990. (*T*)

Koch, Hans-Gerd. "Editorische Notiz" and "Nachbemerkung." In Franz Kafka, *Beschreibungen eines Kampfes und andere Schriften aus dem Nachlaß*, ed. Koch. Frankfurt am Main: Fischer Taschenbuch Verlag, 1994.

Kurz, Gerhard, ed. *Der junge Kafka*. Frankfurt am Main: Suhrkamp, 1984.

Musil, Robert "Literarische Chronik." *Gesammelte Werke in neun Bänden*. Ed. Adolf Frisé. Reinbek bei Hamburg: Rowohlt, 1978. Vol. 9, 1465–71. Originally published in *Die Neue Rundschau*, August 1914.

Rolleston, James. "*Betrachtung:* Landschaften der Doppelgänger." In Gerhard Kurz, ed. *Der junge Kafka*. Frankfurt am Main: Suhrkamp, 1984.

Ryan, Judith. *The Vanishing Subject: Early Psychology and Literary Modernism*. Chicago: U of Chicago P, 1991.

Schillemeit, Jost. "Kafkas 'Beschreibung eines Kampfes': Ein Beitrag zum Textverständnis und zur Geschichte von Kafkas Schreiben." In Gerhard Kurz, ed. *Der junge Kafka*. Frankfurt am Main: Suhrkamp, 1984. 120–21.

Schnitzler, Arthur. *Sterben: Erzählungen*. Frankfurt am Main: Fischer Taschenbuch Verlag, 1992.

Sudhoff, Dieter, and Michael M. Suchardt. *Prager deutsche Erzählungen*. Stuttgart: Reclam, 1992.

Wagenbach, Klaus. "Prague at the Turn of the Century," in Mark Anderson, *Reading Kafka: Prague, Politics, and the Fin de Siècle*. New York: Schocken, 1989. 25–52.

Walser, Robert. *Geschichten*. Frankfurt am Main: Suhrkamp, 1985.

Wellbery, David, et al., eds. *New History of German Literature*. Cambridge: Harvard UP, forthcoming.

Tradition and Betrayal in "Das Urteil"

Russell A. Berman

FEW WORKS AS BRIEF AND COMPACT as "Das Urteil" (The Judgment) loom so large in the landscape of literary history. This short story of deceptive simplicity but replete with unresolved questions represented a breakthrough for Kafka and became a magnet for critical readers, who were drawn to its simultaneous sparseness and intensity. Kafka himself reports how he wrote out the full text in one exhausting sitting in the night of 22–23 September 1912, marking a definitive separation between his early literary attempts and his mature accomplishments: "Die Verwandlung" (The Metamorphosis) followed in November and December, even as he made extensive progress on the novel fragment that Max Brod would later dub *Amerika* (Binder 123–25). There can be no doubt that the completion of "Das Urteil" brought Kafka's creative productivity to a new level, ushering in the series of works that has become central to modernist world literature. We know that Kafka wished to have Brod destroy much of his writing; "Das Urteil" was not on the list. On the contrary, it is one of the few texts that Kafka continued to regard with satisfaction (Stern 114). Indeed it occupies a special place as a key to Kafka's major achievement and to a much broader definition of literary sensibility in the twentieth century (Sokel 34). "Das Urteil" represents a breakthrough, redefining the literary tradition of the canon; and it is a redefinition that unfolds precisely through the logic of the text.

Why this sudden outburst of creativity and why did it take the form of "Das Urteil"? There is of course a biographical context, and much criticism has dwelled on it, endeavoring to explain the troublesome narrative with reference to data from Kafka's life. His meeting with Felice Bauer, who would become his fiancée, took place in August 1912. It is to her that he dedicated the story, she figures clearly as the model for Georg's fiancée, Frieda Brandenfeld (whose initials she shares), and in his correspondence with Felice, he refers to "Das Urteil" as her story. The prospect of marriage raised questions for Kafka regarding his own commitment to the life of a writer and the renunciation of bourgeois security, while both the conventionalism of marriage and the unconventional prospects of a literary career represented potential provocations to the troubled relationship between Kafka and his father. Hence the plausibility of referencing the prominent themes of the narrative — the father-son conflict, the relationship to the distant friend, and the imminent marriage — to Kafka's own biographical situation. Indeed critics have proposed explaining "Das Urteil," especially the altercation between Georg and his father, by mustering Kafka's letter to his father of 1919 as evidence of the strained family ties (Binder 132; Neumann 217).

Attempts to resolve the complexities of the story by drawing attention to possible literary sources are not fundamentally dissimilar to biographical connections: both attempt to explain — which is not to say, "explain away" — the phenomenon of the literary work through objective external data. In this manner, "Das Urteil" has been connected to a fairy tale from Prague, to aspects of Dostoevsky (especially *Crime and Punishment*), and to Brod's novel *Arnold Beer* (Binder 126–31). In no case is the evidence as compelling as in the estimation of the importance of Kafka's experience of Yiddish theater, which he frequently attended in the period prior to writing "Das Urteil." The family constellations, the use of unrealistic gestures, and the peripatetic reversal of fortunes all can be seen as derived from the performances that we know Kafka attended (Binder 132–34; Beck). A further, related potential source is the liturgy for the Jewish Day of Atonement, the Yom Kippur holiday, which in 1912 fell on 21–22 September, that is, the day before the night in which Kafka wrote the text. We know that he attended the synagogue that year, so the associated liturgical tropes were presumably on his mind, including most importantly the imminence of a divine judgment about to be rendered, pending atonement.

As important as these biographical and intertextual references may be in illuminating single aspects of the text, they necessarily fall short of a penetrating account of the work itself. Kafka's personal relationship to his fiancée or to his father, or for that matter, his reading habits or religious belief are ultimately private matters. Interpretations of the story that tie it too firmly to such personal information fail to account for the fascination that this text in particular has exercised on both professional critics and the larger reading public. Thus Ronald Gray comments:

> Has Kafka done more than cater for himself; is there anything here for the reader, in so far as he is a "common reader," someone who reads for pleasure and enlightenment rather than research? The quantity of biographical information needed for understanding the story suggests that it is essentially esoteric, that it has value for its position in Kafka's work, as a gateway, rather than as an accomplished achievement in itself. (72)

Treating the text as an expression of primarily private matters in effect suggests that the text has little merit as literature on its own, that Kafka's own estimation of the text was wrong, and that it should only be read symptomatically or at best merely as a study toward the mature work, beginning with "Die Verwandlung." This approach, ultimately, leaves Georg alone in the private room where the story commences: Kafka's personal vehicle, perhaps, toward a career as a writer, but not a significant imaginative accomplishment on its own terms. We should not underestimate the attraction of such a critical strategy, for it minimizes the challenge that the text poses to the reader, who must grapple with its perplexing account of human relationships: the paralogical character of the dispute between father and son, the undecided standing of the friend, the glaring discrepancy between everything we know about Georg and the severity of the verdict, and, perhaps most of all, the unquestioned obedience with which the capital sentence is carried out.

Yet we should also be very wary of adopting the underlying assumption that these apparently irresolvable tensions within "Das Urteil" undercut its literary standing. On the contrary, it is precisely this nearly impenetrable network, layer upon layer of distinct meanings, that makes up the substance of the achievement. "Das Urteil" became a breakthrough for Kafka's own career, just as it represents a crucial elaboration of his thinking on justice and guilt, the grand theme of his later writing. Moreover the very intricacy and seemingly problematic nature of the text set a new standard for the possibilities of literary writing, redefining the nature of literary achievement and therefore of literary judgment and canonicity. The topic of the text is a judgment passed on the son — and we will see how perplexing the possibility of that judgment turns out to be — but it is even more a judgment on literature, its institutionalization, and its potential. "Das Urteil" calls for a rejudgment of literary life.

The fascination of "Das Urteil" derives initially from the breathtaking discrepancy between the commencement of the story and its conclusion, a fall from complacent security to suicide, magnified by the brevity and rapid pace of the narration. All seems right in the world of Georg Bendemann, until suddenly, and without a fully compelling explanation, all seems wrong, and this reversal draws the reader into an infinite loop of rethinking, the unceasing search for the explanation of the verdict and its execution. Yet on closer examination neither the initial stability nor the concluding leap simply carries a single, fixed meaning, for the narrative is more complex than it first appears. It is of course true that the narrative commences with a seemingly familiar and conventional rhetoric of literary realism, introducing a standard figure, a young businessman, who is moreover the carrier of an unproblematic and firmly centered perspective. We find him in his own private room, seated at his desk, or more precisely, a "Schreibtisch" (writing table, *L* 39, *CS* 77) where he has just concluded a letter; meanwhile he can gaze out the window, surveying a bridge, a river, and the hills beyond. This sort of hero, and the associated epistemological integration of private and public knowledge — the personal letter and the external view — had constituted the standard requisites of poetic realism in Germany at least since 1848, with their harmonious balance of subjective and objective components (Hohendahl 376–419). Indeed long before 1912, the structures of realistic writing had been appropriated by a commercialized entertainment literature and to this day, and not only in Germany, they remain the standard fare of popular fiction. Yet Kafka flaunts the signs of realism at the outset of "Das Urteil" in a way that overstates them and thereby undermines them. The announced temporality, a Sunday morning in the height of spring, conveys a fairy tale atmosphere compounded by the "It was" with which the text begins. The generic tension between the tropes of realism and the markers of the fairy tale should set the reader on guard. Georg's smug confidence at his desk is not fully warranted, for, in broader terms, the epistemological closure promised by conventional realism, particularly in its commercial and popularized variation, is about to be called into question through a redefinition of expectations for literary authenticity.

Literary realism, strictly speaking, was about the prominence of sensuous details, the realia of life, in the literary text, and their arrangement in a presumably reasonable order. It is therefore noteworthy, as John Ellis has pointed out, that the descriptions in the first paragraph are slightly out of focus. Georg is in one of a row of houses, characterized as distinguishable only in terms of their color and height: yet surely color and height, the importance of which is casually minimized by the narrator, are precisely the most prominent sorts of qualities that realism might address. In addition, the qualification of the green of the landscape across the river as "schwach" (weak) is an odd usage in German, where an alternative adverb might have been chosen (Ellis 76–77). The very substance of the realist project of objective description seems to be breaking down, and this is corroborated by the role that Georg plays as the presumed agent of the observational perspective. He would seem to be well suited to stand in as an allegory for the writer at his desk, surveying the world before him. Yet we find him distracted and inattentive, playfully sealing the letter (as if it were of no particular importance) and surely taking little notice of the world beyond the window. There is a hint of an explanation in the professional identification of Georg as a businessman, as if the alienation from the world, his inattention, as well as the guilt that will be imputed to him in the course of the narration, were consequences of capitalist culture and the regime of private property in which he is located. At least this is a possible point of departure for a Marxist approach to "Das Urteil." Yet those class indicators are also standard markers for nineteenth-century realism, and it is that literary culture that is being prepared for scrutiny through the remarkable subtlety of the first paragraph. Realistic expectations are being raised and undermined at the same time. As J. P. Stern has noted, "In Kafka's story, the sensational is avoided because the transition from the realistic to the surrealistic or fantastic is gradual" (119). The collapse of realistic epistemology, which will be carried out in the father's judgment and Georg's death, is in effect already announced between the lines of the superficial order of the placid beginning.

In addition to this subversion of realistic description, the text, from the outset, introduces an irritation with regard to narrative perspective. From the "It was a Sunday morning" of the beginning, the reader is led to expect an omniscient narrator discussing the object of the story, Georg, his subjectivity, and his objective standing in the world. The first paragraph shifts quickly from the narrator's view of the row of houses to Georg's perspective, the landscape across the river. This perspectival disruption is continued, alternating between objectifying description and subjective point of view, when the narrator and the reader appear to be aligned with Georg's subjectivity itself, particularly through the use of indexical terms. Thus the suggestion is made that the friend in St. Petersburg move his business "here"; later, it is reported that Georg's business has "now" grown: as if the narrator and the reader were assumed to share Georg's here and now. The realistic convention of distinguishing neatly between the omniscience of the narrator and the limited subjectivity of a character has disappeared for Georg, although it is also maintained, insofar as the other figures, in particular the father, continue to be treated as objects of reportage. The father's thinking is nowhere as exposed as is Georg's, and consequently the reader is asked to accept a story about Georg, from the outside so to speak, while also participating directly in Georg's thought. The separation between the subjective interiority of the private room and the objective external view, which turns out to be unsustainable in any case, is similarly undermined through the formal structure of the narrative itself. The individual, or bourgeois, autonomy enfigured by Georg at his desk is losing its underpinnings.

The conclusion of the story is equally complex. At first, Georg's demise would appear to signify the absolute reversal of the celebration of his autonomy in the opening scene, the transition from comfortable privacy to his public execution. The complacent worldview of the outset has been demolished. Yet just as that beginning is far from one-dimensional, already signaling problems about to erupt, the conclusion cannot be read simply as the abnegation of the hero. The father is reported to collapse in the wake of the judgment, indicating a more variegated relationship to his son than the simplistic model of a stereotypical father-son conflict would permit. The encounter with the maid in the stairway, including her call to Jesus and her covering her face, is intimated to be a missed opportunity, placed in a curiously opposite relationship to Georg — "aber er war schon davon" (*L* 52; "but he was already gone," *CS* 87) — although the significance of the conjunction "but" is nowhere explicated. Even more perplexing is the role of the retarding moment, when Georg has jumped over the railing but is still holding onto the bridge. The execution has been delayed for an instant, allowing Georg to profess his love for his parents and to wait until a bus passes, presumably in order to drown out the sound of his fall and to allow for his death in a paradoxically public anonymity.

If the insistence on the security of privacy at the outset of "Das Urteil" is subverted through the unraveling of a realist epistemology, the corollary at the conclusion is that the irrevocably terminal character of Georg's plunge, the carrying out of the execution, is qualified in several different ways. It is as if the conclusion were less conclusive than the plot itself would suggest. As noted, the father collapses, and with him, the easy binary opposition of father and son, judge and criminal, is at least called into question. The two are not opposites but, on the contrary, participants in a shared regime, characterized possibly by some guilt (if such can be determined). In that case, however, it is a collective responsibility and not an individual culpability. That "Das Urteil" is not a narrative of Georg's fate alone is indicated furthermore by the complex of imagery of love: the maid's "Jesus," Georg's call to his parents, and the approach of the "Autoomnibus," a term which etymologically announces the problem of the autonomous individual in relation to the comprehensive collective (*L* 52). (To this network of signs, one should also add the references to St. Petersburg, the Russian cleric, and the father's claim to be the representative of the friend: all indications of a Christian semiotics of representation.) If the fall into the river suggests a baptismal possibility of rebirth, so too does the redemptive invocation of "unendlicher Verkehr," the last words of the story: never ceasing traffic, that is, the ongoing life of the human community, but also endless intercourse in a specifically sexual sense. Stanley Corngold writes of the "joy and sheer force of the 'Verkehr,' the erotic upsurge and infinite traffic of the concluding sentence" (40). The initial impression that the story concludes with Georg's death in the wake of the father's pronouncement turns out to be not quite right, given the father's fate, the invocations of community, and the intimation of the possibility of love and rebirth. In this light, it is especially important to note that while we read that Georg lets himself fall from the bridge, the text does not in fact report his death. On the contrary, in the place of death, we learn of the infinite traffic, with its multiple connotations, surely quite distinct from a definitive and fully terminal conclusion. Whether Georg's death is muffled beneath the passing of the bus, or the infinite traffic somehow redeems him, is left undecided by the text itself.

Thus the most basic frame of the story leads into an interpretive vortex. The reader's first approximation of the plot cannot fail to trace an arc from the protective environment of Georg's room on a Sunday morning in spring to the presumption of absolute destruction through the plunge from the bridge. The discrepancy between beginning and end necessarily elicits efforts to make sense out of the report: what could possibly justify the execution of the nice young man who had been writing a letter to his friend one fine Sunday morning? Yet the enigma of "Das Urteil" is that the beginning and end stand in a closer and less exclusive relationship than the veneer of the plot suggests. If there is an alternative path into "Das Urteil," it has to begin with the recognition that the tension between Georg at his desk and Georg on the bridge is less stringent than appears initially. In that case, the narration turns out to be not at all about a reversal of fortune, certainly not an individual's misfortune, but rather about the nature of judgment in general and its relation to fortune and the way of the world. To explore this option requires a closer look at the fabric of the story and the character of the discourse in between the opening and the end, which have turned out to be less polar in their opposition than the reader might have initially estimated.

If the beginning and the end of "Das Urteil" are linked, it is due to a stated problem, a discursive discrepancy between a normative expectation of deliberative speech and the constantly elusive, hermetic substance of individual topics. On the one hand, both Georg and the father (in different ways, to be sure) engage in processes approximating rational argument, either directly in their exchange or, in Georg's case, indirectly in his reported thought process. These deliberations invite the reader to accept rational debate as a proper standard, that is, a certain logical, nearly jurisprudential modality of argument is established as a background measure for evaluating various decisions, such as Georg's choosing to inform his friend of the engagement, or the father's verdict itself. Kafka's repeated deployment of deliberative speech frames the material and suggests that judgment is, in the end, supposed to make sense. Yet repeatedly the text demonstrates a disjunction between these deliberations and their topic. Pursuing this line of inquiry is tantamount to the recognition that what may be at stake here is a judgment not so much on Georg but on the possibility of judgment altogether.

The critique of judgment is most salient in the treatment accorded to evidence in the text. Deliberative speech presumes evidence, which is the topic of the deliberation, just as it assumes the possibility of interpreting that evidence. It insists that, in order to render judgment, reference be made to facts and to the significance that those facts are imputed to entail. These are expectations that Kafka insinuates through the justificational claims made by Georg and by his father. Yet these are hardly outlandish or unfamiliar to the reader, for they form the basis of modern understandings of legal process: proper judgment is presumed not to be arbitrary, but must instead be based on adequate evidence and its proper evaluation, according to established rules of argument.

In "Das Urteil," however, while the expectations regarding the quality of deliberation are announced, most evidence is indicated, in one way or another, to be corrupt and inconclusive, open to such a range of interpretation that it turns out to be useless for the cases at hand. Among the more salient examples of this subversion of evidentiary argumentation, one can point to the explanations for Georg's rise in the family business. The comments are part of a passage that is surely ascribed to the narrator, and therefore one might expect to find an exercise of narrative omniscience. Instead, one faces a series of three distinct accounts, each prefaced with a "perhaps," and the last of which is, in effect, no rational explanation at all, but rather an invocation of fortunate accidents (Swales 360). Thus, in the context of presumably rational deliberation on the nature of the correspondence between Georg and his friend and, more specifically, on the nature of Georg's business success, the very basis of the argument, the evidentiary underpinning, is declared to be merely conjecture. This is a crucial point, since the father will later accuse his son of conspiring against him in the business.

This disjunction between a formally rational argument and inadequate or incompatible supporting evidence occurs repeatedly. The pertinent facts are either inconclusive or inappropriate to the claims made. To prove Georg's affection for his father, the narrator references their taking lunch in the same restaurant, but the passage leaves open whether they actually eat together. Indeed the image of their evenings, each with his own newspaper, suggests more separation than comity. Similarly, it is reported that Georg's Russian friend failed to express adequate sympathy at the news of the death of Georg's mother, and this is taken to be symptomatic of the worrisome social alienation imputed to the friend alone in a distant land. Yet we also learn that the friend did in fact urge Georg to join him in Russia, an expression of affection that stands in marked contrast to Georg's own vacillation on whether to invite the friend to his wedding. Hence the very premise of Georg's judgment of his friend, the friend's social isolation, is not at all corroborated by this particular point; indeed the facts could be taken to prove the opposite, not the friend's disaffection, but Georg's.

The disjunction between argumentative claim and asserted fact even characterizes moments of seemingly uncontroversial discourse. Georg's noticing that the father has kept his window closed leads the father to indicate that this is his preference. Georg then replies that it is warm outside, "wie in Anhang zu dem Früheren" (*L* 44; "as if continuing his previous remark," *CS* 81). It is by no means clear what the innocuous comment about the weather is intended to mean: an extension of the implied criticism that the window is not open or a confirmation of the father's preference for keeping it closed. It is as if rational exchange were being simulated, but its lack of substance becomes clear at each point, even in a discussion about the weather. The text signals this slide toward a decomposition of argument, that is, the absence of a compelling logic, by indicating that the subsequent remark is only "as if continuing" what had preceded.

Finally, it should be noted that it is not only Georg but his father as well for whom deliberative pronouncements are subverted by the slipperiness of the facts. His opening attack on Georg is characterized by a series of statements that retract aspects of the implied accusations. At first he complains that Georg may not be telling him the whole truth, but then proceeds to limit his own discourse by promising to avoid matters not relevant, that is, presumably not pertinent to the discussion of the friend. Having attacked Georg for not being fully forthcoming, he is effectively announcing that he too will exclude certain topics from discussion. Yet he immediately reverses himself by invoking reportedly unfortunate events, otherwise unspecified, that have taken place since his wife's death. He emphasizes twice that "maybe" (vielleicht) the time will come for their deliberation (*CS* 82; *L* 45). Thus the accusation is suggested but nearly voided in the same instant. Similarly, he proceeds to suggest that he may be missing aspects of the business, implying that Georg could be deceiving him, while explicitly refraining from making such a claim. These several interlinear accusations become even less accessible to any potential rational defense by Georg, because the father also concedes that his own memory is fading. The consequence of the passage is therefore to suggest a wide range of misdeeds on Georg's part, within a rhetoric of rational judgment, while at the same time keeping any specific facts at arm's length and, indeed, most specific accusations as well. Any effort to explain the accusation in a manner that would allow for a properly deliberative rejoinder would be constrained by the irreducible gap between rational norm and an ultimately unreachable experience, beyond precise specification.

Deliberation in "Das Urteil" is therefore robbed of the sustenance that relatively secure factual evidence might be expected to provide. In addition, deliberation fails in a second sense with regard to summative judgments as well; that is, just as the evaluation of (elusive) particular points has been seen to be inadequate, the comprehensive verdicts turn out to be untenable. Neither Georg's judgment of the friend (the first verdict we encounter) nor the father's judgment on Georg (the second verdict) turns out, on close scrutiny, to display a compelling logic. On the contrary, argument and experience appear to be at odds in both cases, although the contradictory character of judgment functions differently in each. The text foregrounds Georg's ostentatious displays of concern for his friend. These in turn are belied however by his deep-seated reluctance to invite him to the wedding. Indeed his repeatedly professed concerns for the friend's well-being appear to be little more than excuses to keep him away. Thus Georg's judgment of the friend and his situation in Russia are a function of a complex psychological motivation, which have been explored by many critics. Hidden concerns, buried beneath the surface, force Georg to rationalize his unwillingness to issue the invitation. It is here that Kafka's interest in Freud and Nietzsche comes to the fore, the recognition of ulterior and unconscious motives. As Gerhard Kurz has written, "The archaeological impulse, the search for the 'city beneath the cities,' unites Nietzsche, Freud, and Kafka in a single configuration as modern excavators of the human psyche" (128). Georg's insistence to his father that his initial hesitation to inform his friend of the wedding was driven only by his consideration for the friend's well-being — "aus keinem anderen Grunde sonst" (*L* 45; "that was the only reason," *CS* 82) — is stated so emphatically that a critical reader must surely see through the pretextuous nature of the claim.

While Georg's judgment of his friend is patently fraudulent, the dubiousness of deliberative speech holds all the more for the father's estimation of Georg. In this second case, the tenuous nature of judgment is demonstrated emphatically by the interpolation of multiple self-contradictions into the discourse of the father. His bitter attacks on his son are undermined repeatedly by the self-negating character of his own speech. Thus he first calls into question the very existence of the friend in St. Petersburg only in order to reverse himself by insisting that he has maintained a clandestine connection to that self-same friend and indeed represents him legally in his homeland. In a second example, he appears to accuse Georg of delaying his marriage for too long and, simultaneously, to criticize his aspiration to marry at all. Georg ends in a double bind: his engagement to Frieda is both too early and too late. Finally, the father's judgment on Georg's character is equally oxymoronic. Georg stands accused of aspiring to independence and maturity too ambitiously (in the business and in the engagement), while he is also attacked for still being childish: a "Spassmacher" (joker) and his father's "Früchtchen" (offspring, literally: little fruit). Clearly the accusations hurled at Georg are mutually exclusive. It is impossible to identify a clear logic in the father's condemnation that might encompass the various and mutually incompatible elements of the tirade. In other words, judgment is certainly rendered, and quite harshly, but the judgment does not meet the standard of normativity established earlier by the deliberative discourse. In the case of Georg's evaluation of his friend, the text suggests ulterior motives that color the judgment: hence the incompatibility of argument and conclusion. In the case of the father's verdict on his son, we simply face the blatant untenability of the several assertions. In both instances, "Das Urteil" points to the structural weakness inherent in judgments, no matter how inescapable the act of judging may be.

The weakness of judgment has at least two sources. The first involves the use of language: for all of Kafka's own linguistic precision, Georg is frequently unable to control his speech. Language gets the better of him, or remains beyond his grasp, sometimes erratic, sometimes recalcitrant, but never fully under his control. Without an effective command of language, he is hardly in a position to argue his own case. Evidently, the logic of argumentative judgment cannot count on the linguistic capacity that it would require to be successful. Consequently, language can have unintended consequences, as in the correspondence with the friend: attempting to make vacuous small talk, Georg elicits a curiosity by reporting a stranger's marriage, which he had mentioned merely as a way to avoid more substantive topics. Alternatively, his several interjections during the father's outburst, all intended to ward off the attack, turn out to be pitifully inadequate. He lacks the rhetorical prowess to mount a compelling counter-argument. In addition, judgment is further destabilized by a second deficiency, the progressive decomposition of Georg's subjectivity. Facing his father, he is described as increasingly forgetful, losing the coherence of consciousness that would be necessary to mount a defense. This stands in marked contrast to the staging of a self-assured autonomy in the opening scene, although there too Georg's slide into distraction was already quite pronounced. The loss of memory in the exchange with the father can be taken to corroborate the father's implicit accusation that the son has forgotten his deceased mother. Georg's presentism entails a gradual repression of the past; if there is a judgmental moral to be drawn from his execution, it is that the loss of a past implies the loss of a future as well.

The particular genius of the work is that, demonstrating the faults that adhere to any process of judgment, it still draws the reader inexorably into an obligation to judge. Yet any judgment on "Das Urteil" is unlikely to escape the fate of judgment that the narrative itself has displayed. One possible critical response, confirmation of the verdict, must ascribe a logical coherence to the father's accusation that is absent in the text itself. Alternatively, efforts to retract the judgment and to defend Georg derive primarily from a modernist or tendentially feminist bias against the patriarchal authority of the father and would, taken consistently, argue to reverse any conviction (Neumann 220–21). Finally, to judge the text a demonstration of the impossibility of judgment altogether involves the critic in the performative contradictions of postmodern sensibility: insisting that judgment is impossible, in an imagined world of absolute indeterminacy, but nonetheless partaking willingly in the prerogatives and privileges of a judge (Corngold 40).

It is however impossible to take sides with either the accuser or the defendant, since both of their arguments are marred by major flaws. Nor can a close reader of "Das Urteil" declare the impossibility of judgment altogether — a claim obviously contradicted both by the central event of the narrative and the critic's own reading process. On the contrary, the story simultaneously demonstrates a necessity of judgment and a universal complicity in guilt. Both Georg and his father judge, and both share in a guilt (which is why the father collapses as his son runs — presumably — to his death). Moreover, in the course of his conversation with Frieda, Georg implicates his friend in the guilt, while it is after all Frieda's insistence on Georg writing the letter to the friend that precipitates the crisis. If "Das Urteil" appears on first reading to be Georg's story (an effect heightened by the interior monologues), on reflection it grows increasingly expansive. From the single, private room, it turns into a father-son conflict, which is broadened by the roles of Frieda, the friend, and the mother, and on the margins, the Russian monk and the masses, until the arrival of the "Autoomnibus" and the infinite traffic.

This widening in the course of the narrative lends extra weight to the father's accusation that Georg has only thought of himself. Guilt is inherent in the process of individuation and self-enclosure; the alternative is the embrace of the multiple relations of a community. Georg's initial self-absorption has hardly led to a genuine independence. On the contrary, the isolated autonomy of the beginning is nothing more than the beginning of the end for the weak individual, complicitous in a condition of universal alienation. Hence not only his incapacity to defend himself with argument but his obedient acceptance of the verdict. The ultimate problem of "Das Urteil" is not the dubious quality of the father's pronouncement — we know that any judgment will necessarily be tenuous — but rather Georg's acquiescence. What sort of culture produces a personality so willing to conform, even to the point of self-destruction?

It is a culture of self-absorbed isolation, a culture of narcissism, in which the individual is so self-centered that he becomes self-blind (Lasch). It is a culture in which self-interest has become congruent with betrayal: Georg's betrayal of his friend and the memory of his mother, as well as his disregard for his father. It is however above all a culture characterized by a degraded mode of writing, for the text in which Kafka achieved his own breakthrough to literary maturity is very much about writing. It is the author Georg, the type of the isolated, reflective, and distracted writer, whom we meet at the outset. We learn that he is quite satisfied to generate texts intentionally devoid of substance and that he attempts to use language strategically in order to manipulate the reader. It is a writing furthermore that appears to require no particular effort, as he closes the letter with playful slowness. Yet the most trenchant characterization of this literary world is the verb: Georg has just completed, "beendet," the text, and it is this term that recurs in an inverted variation in the conclusion, "unendlicher Verkehr," "unending" traffic (*L* 52; *CS* 88). The implicit criticism inherent in "Das Urteil" and directed against established literary life entails its complacent capacity of closure, closed forms and closed minds, associated with an isolated and therefore weakened subjectivity. Georg's text stands alone, and it is for that reason facile and mendacious, an epistolary corollary to the degraded realism of the culture industry implicitly invoked in the stereotypical images of the first sentence. "Das Urteil" presents an alternative: a literature that is open to the community, its traditions, and its past, a canonic literature that has the capacity to achieve a public and collective life. The vision of the Russian priest who has cut a cross in his hand suggests an authentic writing, presaging the corporeal script of "In der Strafkolonie" (In the Penal Colony). The liberal individual at his writing desk, for all of his professed sincerity and enlightenment, turns out to be willing to acquiesce in his own self-destruction and is incapable of an independent judgment of substance; in contrast, the religious masses can carry out a revolution. Kafka's appeal to a literature that resonates with the profundity of tradition, that is an "Angelegenheit des Volkes" (a matter of the people), as he wrote in the famous diary entry of 25 December 1911, represents one of the most severe verdicts on the culture of modernity, with its loss of memory, its atomism, and its perpetual flight from the difficult complexity inherent in any judgment.

Works Cited

Beck, Evelyn Torton. *Kafka and the Yiddish Theater: Its Impact on His Work.* Madison: U of Wisconsin P, 1971.

Binder, Hartmut. *Kafka-Kommentar zu sämtlichen Erzählungen.* Munich: Winkler Verlag, 1975.

Corngold, Stanley. "The Hermeneutic of 'The Judgment.'" In *The Problem of The Judgment: Eleven Approaches to Kafka's Story,* ed. Angel Flores. New York: Gordian Press, 1977. 39–62.

Ellis, John M. "The Bizarre Texture of 'The Judgment.'" In *The Problem of the Judgment,* ed. Angel Flores. New York: Gordian Press, 1977. 73–96.

Gray, Ronald. "Through Dream to Self-Awareness." In *The Problem of the Judgment,* ed. Angel Flores. New York: Gordian Press, 1977. 63–72.

Hohendahl, Peter Uwe. *Literarische Kultur im Zeitalter des Liberalismus: 1830–1870.* Munich: Beck, 1985.

Kafka, Franz. "The Judgment." *The Complete Stories.* Ed. Nahum N. Glatzer. New York: Schocken, 1971. 77–88. (*CS*)

———. *Ein Landarzt und andere Drucke zu Lebzeiten.* Ed. Hans-Gerd Koch. Frankfurt am Main: Fischer Taschenbuch Verlag, 1994. (*L*)

Kurz, Gerhard. "Nietzsche, Freud, and Kafka." In *Reading Kafka: Prague, Politics, and the Fin de Siècle.* Ed. Mark Anderson. New York: Schocken, 1989. 128–48.

Lasch, Christopher. *The Culture of Narcissism: American Life in an Age of Diminishing Expectations.* New York: Norton, 1979.

Neumann, Gerhard. "'The Judgment,' 'Letter to His Father,' and the Bourgeois Family." In *Reading Kafka: Prague, Politics, and the Fin de Siècle.* 215–28.

Sokel, Walter H. "Kafka and Modernism." In *Approaches to Teaching Kafka's Short Fiction.* Ed. Richard T. Gray. New York: MLA, 1995. 21–34.

Stern, J. P. "Guilt and the Feeling of Guilt." In *The Problem of the Judgment,* ed. Angel Flores. New York: Gordian Press, 1977. 114–32.

Swales, Martin. "Why Read Kafka?" *Modern Language Review* 76 (1981): 356–66.

Kafka as Anti-Christian: "Das Urteil," "Die Verwandlung," and the Aphorisms

Ritchie Robertson

THIRTY YEARS AGO, Evelyn Torton Beck broke new ground in studies of Kafka by suggesting that his contact with the Yiddish actors awakened a wide-ranging interest in Judaism that could be traced throughout his life and career. That insight has now become a commonplace. Kafka's interest in aspects of Judaism, religious and political, has been documented by Marthe Robert, Giuliano Baioni, Karl Erich Grözinger, Hans Dieter Zimmermann, Marina Cavarocchi, myself, and others; the Jewish character of his work has been sensitively studied by Robert Alter; and his personal writings have been assigned by Dieter Lamping to the "Jewish discourse" that develops within twentieth-century literature in German.

It is important, however, to remember how eclectic Kafka was in drawing on religious traditions. The story of Kafka's estrangement from the Judaism in which he had been nominally brought up, and his rediscovery at least of aspects of Judaism with the help of Max Brod, Georg Langer, and other friends, is by now familiar. But he also read Christian writers: Pascal, Augustine, Tolstoy, and of course Kierkegaard. Christian imagery enters his work more prominently than images drawn from Judaism. A crucial chapter of *Der Proceß* (The Trial) is set in a cathedral; both Kafka's other novels mention churches; yet a synagogue is mentioned only in a short fragment ("In der Thamühler Synagoge" [In the Thamühl Synagogue]). On the other hand, Jewish imagery sometimes appears more discreetly. A few months before beginning *Der Proceß*, Kafka visited Martin Buber in Berlin and asked him about the "unjust judges" in Psalm 82 (Robertson, "Von den ungerechten Richtern"). And Karl Erich Grözinger has pointed out many intriguing similarities between the imagery of the novel and that of the Kabbalah, with its judges and door-keepers, though he has not explained how Kafka knew about the Kabbalah at this stage in his life (*Kafka und die Kabbala*). It seems that Kafka borrowed images eclectically to express religious concerns that are not esoteric but find many echoes in the religious experience of humankind. He himself wrote, distancing himself both from Christians like Kierkegaard and from inheritors of Judaism like the Zionists, "Ich bin Ende oder Anfang" (*NS II* 98), "I am the end or the beginning." He drew not only on Jewish and Christian traditions but also on philosophy: a key term he frequently uses, "das Unzerstörbare" (the indestructible), comes from Schopenhauer (Zilcosky).

The purpose of this paper is to define some features of Kafka's religious outlook more sharply than before, and to continue an investigation of his contact with Christianity (begun in Robertson 1998) by examining some signs in his work of a hostile critique of Christianity. For a distinct component in Kafka's religious thought is a skepticism that was nourished by his early reading of Nietzsche. He and his friend Max Brod first met in 1902, at a meeting of a student society where Brod gave a paper on his idol Schopenhauer in which he attacked Nietzsche; Kafka, already a devoted reader of Nietzsche, sprang to the latter's defense, and they walked home in enthusiastic conversation (Brod, *Streitbares Leben* 234). In Nietzsche, Kafka found a searching critique of religion in general and Christianity in particular. Nietzsche denied that the moral and theological claims of Christianity had any divine basis. There was no single morality, but rather diverse systems of morals, whose origin could be explained historically and psychologically, and whose dominance was due not to their intrinsic excellence but to the power attained by their adherents. Christian morality represented the creative resentment felt by the physically weak against their masters, and was shot through with vengefulness and hatred. The priestly type, best realized in Judaism and Christianity, was a damaged person, lacking in vitality, maintaining power over his sick flock by psychological manipulation. Though Jesus had a valuable message, only a natural aristocracy could have understood it, whereas his disciples were mediocre individuals and St. Paul a fanatical nihilist who distorted the message to satisfy his hunger for power. Nietzsche claimed to prefer the Old Testament, with its heroic figures, to the New. And yet he acknowledged that the slave revolt in morals that produced Christianity had also made humanity more inward, more complex, more interesting, and that the asceticism exemplified by the priest was shared by the artist and the scholar in whom it was the precondition for achievement.

Kafka's religious outlook, moreover, is not a static system. It is continually developing. The problem from which Kafka starts may be defined in personal terms as follows. He wished to belong to a physical community, based on the small community of the family. He wished to found a family of his own, feeling that otherwise his life would be incomplete, indeed a failure. He quotes the Talmud: "Auch im Talmud heißt es: ein Mann ohne Weib ist kein Mensch" (*T* 266, The Talmud also says: A man without a wife is not a man).[1] But he also felt disgust for his own body, dislike of sexuality, and a desire for an ascetic form of existence. It has been argued that this aporia in Kafka's personal life reflected an aporia within Judaism (Sokel 41–42). For on the one hand, the Old Testament urges man to be fruitful and multiply, and to serve God through everyday life. But procreation means acknowledging that one is part of nature, and man is also enjoined to stand aloof from nature, to abstain from the nature-worship of the surrounding heathen, and to fix his devotion upon a God who has no physical embodiment. Hence a discomfort with sexuality can be found throughout the history of Judaism, from Old Testament times down to Zionist experiments with communal living (Biale). In Kafka's case, this conflict finds expression in the clash between two incompatible moralities. Characters like Georg Bendemann, Josef K., and the country doctor follow a worldly morality of hard work and professional devotion, expecting it to be rewarded by material and perhaps sexual success. But their lives are broken apart by the intervention of another morality — the anger of Bendemann senior, the Court, the horses that emerge from a pig-sty — in the light of which their material goals and their orderly lives are worthless, indeed reprehensible. The enigmatic, ungrammatical sentence spoken by Bendemann senior: "Ein unschuldiges Kind warst du ja eigentlich, aber noch eigentlicher warst du ein teuflischer Mensch!" (*D* 60, You were really an innocent child, but yet more really you were a devilish human being!) — contrasts the worldly, ultimately natural morality of the innocent child with the absolute morality, sharply dividing good from evil, that intervenes and annihilates the other. In the ten years that separate "Das Urteil" (The Judgment) from *Das Schloß* (The Castle), Kafka explores the implications of this dualist outlook, and in the latter text he wins through, as I have argued elsewhere, to a more tolerant morality that finds value in the mundane details of everyday life and even in bodily love, and questions the desire for contact with the transcendent as a dangerous, Faustian temptation (Robertson, *Kafka*; also Sheppard). Instead of trying to link the village with the Castle, Kafka leaves the latter in its ambiguity, and explores instead what Stephen Dowden calls an "anthropological absolute" (Dowden 125), the possibility of sublime moments that illuminate from within an otherwise frozen and painful existence.

Here I shall look briefly at two intermediate stages. One is represented by "Das Urteil" and "Die Verwandlung" (The Metamorphosis), which explore respectively questions of guilt and judgment, and the fate of humanity as an immaterial consciousness trapped in an animal body and a material world. The other is represented by the aphorisms that Kafka wrote in the winter of 1917–18 while trying to convalesce from tuberculosis in the Bohemian countryside.

Kafka's breakthrough story "Das Urteil" can obviously be read as an oedipal narrative of family conflict, but such a reading leaves many questions unanswered. Why is Georg's friendship with the man in Russia incompatible with his engagement? Why does his father charge him with violating his mother's memory (or rather, as he mysteriously puts it, "our" mother's memory ("unserer Mutter Andenken geschändet," *D* 57)? Why is Georg so helpless when faced with his angry father? And why does the father condemn his son to death? These questions seem to invite a recourse to allegory, provided we do not understand allegory as the fixed symbolic expression of eternal verities. Rather, Kafka's kind of allegory responds to our desire for meaning, teases it, and never completely satisfies it. A meaning is always just out of reach. As John Zilcosky has recently put it: "By withdrawing a traditional superstructure of meaning from above allegorical language, yet continuing to imply the negative allegory, Kafka creates texts in which more evident than their meaninglessness is their constant pointing toward a meaning" (360).

In an attempt to answer questions like those just listed, and to account for the persistence with which the story seems to point to a dimension beyond the realistic or the symbolic, Wolf-Daniel Hartwich has turned to Jewish theology. Hartwich recalls the well-known fact that Kafka wrote the story during the night following Yom Kippur, when he had failed to attend synagogue, and after a year of absorption in the full-blooded Jewish life represented by the Yiddish actors from Warsaw who were visiting Prague. Hartwich finds a contrast between Jewish assimilation, embodied by Georg with his plans to marry an apparent Gentile ("Brandenfeld" — burnt field — heath — heathen), and the friend in Russia, loyal to the home of the Eastern Jews. The father represents the authority of the Law; his back room is the Holy of Holies in the Temple; the wall visible outside is the Wailing Wall; the dead mother is both the Shekhinah (the divine wisdom, imagined in the Kabbalah as feminine) and the Virgin Mary; the father's wound recalls that of Jacob, gained by wrestling with the angel; the sick friend recalls the suffering servant in Isaiah 53, "despised and rejected of men [. . .] stricken, smitten of God, and afflicted"; Georg himself is the scapegoat, typologically represented both by Isaac and Jesus. Though Hartwich's interpretation seems often far-fetched, it does respond to the details in the story that fail to fit into a realistic or a psychoanalytic interpretation. It imputes to Kafka, however, a degree of conscious planning which is hardly compatible with the way he wrote the story or with the perplexity he himself expressed (*T* 491–92) and a thorough knowledge of Jewish theology and tradition which is not attested in any contemporary biographical documents.

Parts of Hartwich's interpretation, however, do make sense of the enigmatic overtones in the story. The "Schreckbild seines Vaters" (dreadful image of his father, *D* 56) does indeed suggest an angry Jehovah, a reminder of the authority of tradition, who punishes Georg for his apostasy into worldly pursuits. Georg and his friend, implicitly made into brothers when the father says of the friend: "Er wäre ein Sohn nach meinem Herzen" (He would have been a son after my own heart, *D* 56), faintly recall such contrasting Old Testament pairs as Jacob and Esau, or Ephraim and Manasseh (Genesis 48). More problematic is the interpretation of the Christian allusions in the story (see Kurz 171). Most directly of all, Georg and his friend suggest the Prodigal Son and his stay-at-home brother. "Petersburg," the city of Peter, recalls St. Peter and possibly Rome. We have the striking and at first sight unmotivated image of the priest in Russia who stands up before a crowd and cuts a cross into the palm of his hand. After sentence has been pronounced, the maidservant cries "Jesus!" as Georg dashes downstairs to his fate, and hides her face as though the sight of him were forbidden. Hanging from the bridge, Georg may call to mind the crucified Christ.

How are we to interpret these overtones? An obvious temptation is to discern in them a systematic key to the story, as Hartwich does when he reads the figure of the priest and the allusion to Jesus typologically: the priest's self-mutilation alludes to the alleged connection between circumcision and crucifixion; Georg, as scapegoat, represents Jesus (but also Judas, having betrayed his friend!). The trouble is that such interpretations seem over-specific, while leaving the story as open as it was before. A more perceptive, and, above all, more literary interpretation was suggested many years ago in an essay by John M. Ellis that has found too little resonance in Kafka studies. Having listed the Christian motifs, Ellis remarks that "in "Das Urteil" the values of Christianity are thrown up in the air, and come down in an unfamiliar shape" (209). He points out that the main characters keep changing their positions within the Christian scheme. Georg may resemble Jesus in his loving concern for his father, and in the manner of his death. But the friend resembles Christ in having been "denied" by Georg, as Peter did Christ ("Wenigstens zweimal habe ich ihn von dir verleugnet," *D* 54), and the father, as the representative

("Vertreter") of the friend, stands to him in the position of Christ towards his divine father.

Kafka deploys Christian imagery to question the values of Christianity, particularly through the figures of the Russian priest and Georg himself. We may notice the resemblance between the priest standing on a balcony before a crowd and the father, a little later in the story, standing on the bed and towering over Georg. Both are figures of paternal authority. Both, moreover, owe their power in part to their injury. The father bears the scar obtained during military service; the priest mutilates himself. We may get closer to the implications of Kafka's Christian imagery if we remember that as a reader of Nietzsche he would have understood Christianity, in part at least, in the skeptical light of anti-Christian texts like *The Genealogy of Morals* and *The Antichrist*. The priest who wounds his own hand is then a version of the sick priest in *The Genealogy of Morals*, who owes his power over his flock to his sharing their illness.

As for Georg, his expression of concern for his father comes late, after he and his fiancée have been planning to move away and leave the old man alone. It is formulated in suspiciously saccharine and hyperbolic language: "Tausend Freunde ersetzen mir nicht meinen Vater" (*D* 52, A thousand friends can't replace my father). Georg is clearly a determined, ambitious person with powerful material and sexual appetites. This does not correspond to the character of Christ in the Gospels. But there is something in Ellis's strongly phrased argument that "the story explores the ambiguous and dark side of the Christian ethic. Christ was crucified because his humility was felt to be arrogance, his meekness to be aggressive and his advocacy of childlike innocence to be devious and insidious" (209), and Georg really does have the duplicity that Christ was supposed to have. We may recall too that Christ rejected his own family, denying that his mother and brothers were more important to him than anyone else (Matt. 12:46–50), enjoining his followers to leave their families and follow him (Luke 14:26), and upbraiding one potential disciple for waiting till he had buried his father (Luke 9:59–60). The reader of Nietzsche would readily suspect that ostensible Christian values concealed a will to power.

Skepticism towards Christianity is also prominent in "Die Verwandlung," written two to three months after "Das Urteil." Gregor is throughout the victim of his family. A devoted, selfless son who wears himself out in supporting his family, he learns that they do not need him, since they have secretly saved some money and can in any case earn their own living. Later, when his presence in their flat risks driving away the lodgers on whom they think they depend financially, they resolve, with self-serving illogicality, that it is his duty to disappear; the self-sacrificing Gregor agrees, and on his death the family cross themselves, show some shallow grief, and then re-immerse themselves in the mundane world of work and enjoyment. Neither sacrifice was necessary. For just as the family were better off than they allowed the hard-working Gregor to realize, after his death they discover that their jobs are really quite lucrative; there is evidently no need for them to take in lodgers any more, and therefore the economic objection to Gregor's presence vanishes.

"Die Verwandlung" also depicts a consciousness trapped in matter. Gregor's transformation raises questions about the relation between consciousness and the material world. Kafka shows that one not only inhabits a body, but to a disturbing extent one is that body. Gregor's body eludes his control; he devours his disgusting food without any conscious decision to do so. Kafka is here raising another question that will bulk large, especially, in the short stories collected under the title *Ein Landarzt* (A Country Doctor, 1919). Is there any difference between human beings and animals? Is man just another animal? Kafka was well aware of Darwin (Eilittä 119), who argued that man had developed from animals by evolution. There was no discontinuity between man and the animal kingdom. Nietzsche pursued the implications of this idea, repeatedly suggesting different ways in which man differed from other animals. While other animals are healthy, man is "the sick animal"; but his inner life, which estranges him from nature, also makes him "the most interesting animal" (Nietzsche II 862, 1174). Kafka constantly elides the boundaries between man and animals. In *Der Proceß*, for example, the dog figures as an image of human degradation. Josef K. passes off the shrieks of the guard who is being whipped as the cry of a dog; he sees Block degraded into "der Hund des Advokaten" (the Advocate's dog, *P* 265); and by poetic justice, he himself dies "wie ein Hund" (like a dog, *P* 312). In the stories in *Ein Landarzt* this metaphor becomes literal. In a kind of parody of Darwinism, an ape becomes human through an accelerated process of evolution, and Bucephalus, the war-horse of Alexander the Great, adjusts to an unheroic modern age by becoming a lawyer. In both cases the transformation is uncertain: the ape Rotpeter is not accepted as a human being but as an ape who imitates human beings, and his sensual desires are satisfied at night by a half-trained female chimpanzee; while in the case of Dr. Bucephalus, his equine origins are still discernible to the practiced eye of a frequenter of race courses. Other stories contain human beings who are on the level of animals: the nomads who invade a Chinese-sounding city and sleep and eat alongside their carnivorous horses; the groom in "Ein Landarzt" who emerges from a pig-sty along with two horses whom he addresses as brother and sister. In the latter instance, animality is not simply negative. The groom, whom the doctor addresses as "Du Vieh" (you brute, *D* 254), is possessed by a brutal sexuality that makes him assault the doctor's maidservant Rosa; but the doctor, living alongside her for years, has barely noticed her, and has not treated her as an individual. Her name first occurs in the story when the groom uses it: before that, the doctor refers to her simply as "the maidservant." Here we have a split between the unbridled sensuality of the groom and the over-intellectuality of the professional man trapped in his narrow routine. The animal and intellectual sides of humanity have fallen asunder.

We might also be tempted towards a gnostic reading. Walter H. Sokel has written judiciously on the "gnostic sensibility," which produces remarkable correspondences between Kafka's writing and the doctrines, current in the early centuries of the Christian era, which are grouped under the name of Gnosticism (see Jonas). Gnostics broadly agreed in believing in two gods, a good deity who existed beyond the world, and a bad deity or demiurge who, having created the world, kept the soul a prisoner in it. The soul contained a portion of the divine essence, trapped in the world and desiring reunion with its extramundane source. Contact with the good, infinitely remote god could come only in the form of knowledge, conceived less as intellectual apprehension than as mystical union. Many Gnostics thought that such knowledge (gnosis) required a severely ascetic way of life, abstaining so far as possible from food and certainly from sex and procreation. Whether Kafka actually encountered Gnostic ideas is unknown; he owned a small book, *Die Gnosis,* published in a series of short introductions to religious topics, but probably acquired it only towards the end of his life (Wagenbach 263). Sokel is doubtless right in identifying in Kafka a gnostic sensibility, an emotional affinity to Gnostic dualism, which, however, was in severe conflict with his ideal of founding a family. In "Die Verwandlung" we can see this gnostic sensibility at work. For while Gregor's animal body does affect him, enabling him (initially at least) to enjoy food that humans would consider disgusting and to amuse himself by walking on the walls and ceiling of his room, it does not engulf his humanity. In one respect it enhances his humanity. Before his transformation, Gregor took little interest in music, but when he peeps out of his bedroom and listens to his sister playing the violin to the inattentive lodgers, Gregor appreciates music as never before, and wonders whether he can be an animal after all: "War er ein Tier, da ihn Musik so ergriff? Ihm war, als zeige sich ihm der Weg zu der ersehnten unbekannten Nahrung" (*D* 185, Was he an animal, since music moved him so? He felt as though he were being shown the way to the unknown food he longed for). If Gregor's loss of appetite expresses an unconscious wish to die to this world, his desire for something outside the world is figured as an unknown food. But what seems to offer satisfaction is music. And here another element enters the story. Although Kafka may have read Schopenhauer seriously only in 1917, he would have known a good deal about Schopenhauer from reading Nietzsche, who quotes Schopenhauer especially in *The Birth of Tragedy,* and from conversations with his friend the Schopenhauer devotee Max Brod. He would have known, therefore, about Schopenhauer's portrayal of the world as a prison from which one can only escape by renouncing the Will; it is even possible, as has recently been suggested by Michael P. Ryan, that the name Samsa was suggested by *Samsara,* the term denoting enslavement to the world, which Schopenhauer took from the Hindu Upanishads. Kafka would certainly have known also that Schopenhauer assigns a special status to music as the direct utterance of the Will, and hence as the closest we can ever come to penetrating the veil of illusion that holds us captive. As the most impalpable art form, without any material embodiment, music offers Gregor a release from his imprisonment in the body. We may say, therefore, that Kafka's imaginative affinity with Gnosticism leads him to represent the body as a prison, in which humanity is held captive by an increasing animality. His knowledge of Schopenhauer encouraged him to use music as an image for what might lie outside the corporeal prison. He is remote from any Christian acceptance of the body as the divinely created temple of the spirit. Rather, he shares the ascetic impulse that also bulks large in the history of Christianity and has been traced back in part to Gnostic influence.

Kafka's religious preoccupations crystallized in a new way in the winter of 1917–18. Having been diagnosed with tuberculosis, he went to stay in the countryside with his sister Ottla, who was working on a farm at Zürau. Deep in rural Bohemia, Kafka was officially supposed to rest and recuperate, but his real mission was to confront the prospect of death, which from being remote and ignorable had suddenly become an imminent likelihood. His task, he told Max Brod just before he left, was to get clear about the last things: "Über die letzten Dinge klar werden" (Brod, *Kafka* 147). That winter he put down his thoughts in a number of cheap school notebooks, which are now preserved, fragile and frequently blurred, in the Bodleian Library, and have been reliably edited by Jost Schillemeit for the Critical Edition of Kafka's works.

These aphorisms are first and foremost the expression of a spiritual crisis. One finds oneself in a situation that cannot be resolved, not just because the solution is impossibly difficult, but because the solution is unimaginable. "Du bist die Aufgabe. Kein Schüler weit und breit" (*NS II* 46, You are the problem. No scholar far and wide) — in an impossible act of self-reflexivity, one is required to solve a puzzle, to do a piece of homework, that is nothing other than oneself. In this situation, one feels driven to make the crisis more desperate, to reach the point of no return. "Von einem gewissen Punkt an gibt es keine Rückkehr mehr. Dieser Punkt ist zu erreichen" (*NS II* 34, From a certain point there is no longer any return. This point must be reached). When the crisis is at its most extreme, hope may emerge, as another aphorism suggests: "Vom wahren Gegner fährt grenzenloser Mut in dich" (*NS II* 46, The true antagonist fills you with boundless courage).

The situation that Kafka is writing about, in general rather than personal terms, is first of all one of self-estrangement. When writing about Kafka's thought in the past, I found it convenient to distinguish between "being" and "consciousness" (Robertson, *Kafka* 190). Consciousness is deceptive. It does not inform one about one's true being. The problem is not that one cannot know the truth; it is that one cannot know the truth and be the truth. "Es gibt nur zweierlei: Wahrheit und Lüge. Die Wahrheit ist unteilbar, kann sich also selbst nicht erkennen. Wer sie erkennen will muß Lüge sein" (*NS II* 69, There are only two things: the truth and the lie. The truth is indivisible, so cannot know itself. Anyone who seeks to know it must be [a] lie). If we wonder what it would mean to be the truth, we may be helped by a sentence from Flaubert that Kafka often repeated. Referring to a family with many children, Flaubert said gravely: "Ils sont dans le vrai" (They are in the truth, Brod, *Kafka* 89). The family, absorbed in daily tasks, seemed to inhabit the truth, compared to the writer contemplating life from outside.

For Kafka, the contemplation of life is bound to be deceptive. This is partly because the signs of the world are ambiguous. "Der Verzückte und der Ertrinkende — beide heben die Arme" (*NS II* 53, The man in ecstasy and the man drowning: both raise their arms): the same gesture can have opposite meanings. Similarly, in *Der Proceß* the all-powerful Court is incongruously located in slum tenements and neglected lumber rooms. Even photographic reproduction of reality is unreliable, as we know from *Das Schloß*, where a photograph shows a Castle messenger in a horizontal position, either lying on a board or vaulting over a rope (*S* 124–25). "Alles ist Betrug" (*NS II* 59, All is deception). But that is also because our powers of perception are inadequate. Estranged from one's true self, one perceives everything unreliably. One cannot know oneself: "Selbsterkenntnis hat nur das Böse" (*NS II* 48, Only evil has self-knowledge). One cannot know anything else, because either one is involved and hence biased, or else one is neutral and hence ignorant: "Wirklich urteilen kann nur die Partei, als Partei aber kann sie nicht urteilen. Demnach gibt es in der Welt keine Urteilsmöglichkeit, sondern nur deren Schimmer" (*NS II* 52, Only the party concerned can really judge, but as a party concerned he or she cannot judge. Hence the world contains no possibility of judgment, only its semblance).

The task of the individual, as Kafka sees it, is to resist the world. But how is one to do that if one cannot know anything for certain about the world? Worse still, since one is estranged from oneself, it may be that the self from which one is estranged is in league with the world. And that is bound to be the case insofar as estrangement divides the mind from the body. For with our bodies we are enmeshed in the world of the senses, which Kafka considers at best illusory, at worst evil. "Es gibt nichts anderes als eine geistige Welt; was wir sinnliche Welt nennen, ist das Böse in der geistigen" (*NS II* 59, There is nothing but a spiritual world; what we call the sensory world is the evil in the spiritual [world]). To fight against the sensory world is futile, because one's senses, and especially one's sexuality, are complicit with it. "Eine der wirksamsten Verführungen des Teuflischen ist die Aufforderung zum Kampf. Er ist wie der Kampf mit Frauen, die im Bett endet" (*NS II* 34–35, One of the most effective temptations practiced by the devilish [element] is the invitation to a fight. It is like the fight with women, which ends up in bed). The sensual appeal of the world is represented by the Sirens in the story, written apparently on 24 October 1917, to which Max Brod later gave the resonant title "Das Schweigen der Sirenen" (The Silence of the Sirens). Instead of singing, the Sirens give every sign of sexual desire — "die Wendungen ihrer Hälse, das Tiefatmen, die tränenvollen Augen, den halb geöffneten Mund" (*NS II* 41, the twistings of their necks, their panting, their tear-filled eyes, their half-open mouths) — but since Odysseus thinks these are the gestures that accompany singing, he does not succumb to their sexual appeal.

The struggle against the world is especially a struggle against sexuality.

Die Frau, noch schärfer ausgedrückt vielleicht die Ehe, ist der Repräsentant des Lebens mit dem Du Dich auseinandersetzen sollst. Das Verführungsmittel dieser Welt sowie das Zeichen der Bürgschaft dafür, daß diese Welt nur ein Übergang ist, ist das gleiche. Mit Recht, denn nur so könnte uns die Welt verführen und entspricht der Wahrheit. Das Schlimme ist nur daß wir nach geglückter Verführung die Bürgschaft vergessen und so eigentlich das Gute uns ins Böse, der Blick der Frau in ihr Bett uns gelockt hat. (*NS II* 95–96)

[Woman — to put it more pointedly, perhaps, marriage — is the representative of life with which you are to struggle. The means by which this world tempts you, and the sign guaranteeing that this world is only transitional, are the same. Rightly so, for it is only thus that the world could tempt us, corresponding to the truth. The bad thing is only that after the temptation has worked, we forget the guarantee, and so it is really the good that has lured us into evil, the woman's gaze has lured us into her bed.]

More generally, Kafka represents life, the physical world, in the image of a dog that has borne many puppies but is now dying and already decaying. The paragraph is headed "Ein Leben," "A Life":

Eine stinkende Hündin, reichliche Kindergebärerin, stellenweise schon faulend, die aber in meiner Kindheit mir alles war, die in Treue unaufhörlich mir folgt, die ich zu schlagen mich nicht überwinden kann und vor der ich, ihren Athem scheuend, schrittweise rückwärts weiche und die mich doch, wenn ich mich nicht anders entscheide, in den schon sichtbaren Mauerwinkel drängen wird, um dort auf mir und mit mir gänzlich zu verwesen, bis zum Ende — ehrt es mich? — das Eiter- und Wurmfleisch ihrer Zunge an meiner Hand. (*NS II* 37)

[A stinking bitch, bearer of many children, already rotting in places, but which was everything to me in my childhood, which incessantly follows me faithfully, which I cannot bring myself to strike and before which, avoiding her breath, I move back step by step, and which, if I don't make a different decision, will force me into the already visible corner, so that there she may completely decay on me and with me, to the last — does it honour me? — the pus- and worm-filled flesh of her tongue on my hand.]

This is a drastically negative portrayal of physical life, involving fertility and its counterpart, decay. The dog is an embodiment of femininity, with its many puppies, its association with the speaker's childhood, and its overpowering affection, which the speaker can hardly bear to resist, even though it seeks to drag him down into its own physical corruption. The speaker is tied to it, and thus to the world, by residual affection, by what used to be love. It is ultimately love that enslaves us to the sensual world: "Die sinnliche Liebe täuscht über die himmlische hinweg, allein könnte sie es nicht, aber da sie das Element der himmlischen Liebe unbewußt in sich hat, kann sie es" (*NS II* 68, Sensual love deceives one into ignoring heavenly love; it could not do so by itself, but as it unconsciously contains the element of heavenly love, it can). Sensual love is a version of heavenly love; it contains enough that is genuine to distract us effectively from seeking after heavenly love. For Kafka, the soul is something eternal, temporarily confined within the physical world. "Es ist mir zu eng in allem, was ich bedeute, selbst die Ewigkeit, die ich bin, ist mir zu eng"

(*NS II* 84–85, I am too confined in everything I signify; even the eternity that I am confines me too much). The soul, it seems, is conceived as disembodied, almost abstract. We recognize here Kafka's gnostic sensibility: the immaterial soul is trapped in a disgusting and decaying mortal body.

How is one to escape from this confinement? First, one must become aware of one's condition. This leads to despair. "Ein erstes Zeichen beginnender Erkenntnis ist der Wunsch zu sterben. Dieses Leben scheint unerträglich, ein anderes unerreichbar" (*NS II* 43, A first sign of the beginning of knowledge is the wish to die. This life seems unendurable, another [life] unattainable). But becoming aware of one's condition is not enough, for mere self-knowledge is a distraction from the necessary task of overcoming the world. Instead, one's motto must be: "Verkenne Dich! Zerstöre Dich!" [. . .] und nur wenn man sich sehr tief hinabbeugt, hört man auch sein Gutes, welches lautet: 'um Dich zu dem zu machen, der Du bist'" (*NS II* 42, "Fail to know yourself! Destroy yourself!" — and only when one bends very far down can one hear the good part, which runs: "in order to make yourself into that which you are"). Kafka demands active self-destruction. One must die, but not a physical death. "Unsere Rettung ist der Tod, aber nicht dieser" (*NS II* 101, Our salvation is death, but not this one). Rather, one must undergo a spiritual death, and the only development Kafka sees in human history is the development of this spiritual power: "Die Menschheitsentwicklung — ein Wachsen der Sterbenskraft" (*NS II* 101, Human development — a growth of the power to die). He represents spiritual death by the image of the burning bush in which the Lord appeared to Moses in Exodus 3:2. "Der Dornbusch ist der alte Weg-Versperrer. Er muß Feuer fangen, wenn Du weiter willst" (*NS II* 48, The thorn bush is the ancient barrier in the road. It must catch fire if you want to go any further). Spiritual progress must be through the fire, an image recalling Purgatory. Kafka, however, adopts the Jewish image of the Holy of Holies:

> Vor dem Betreten des Allerheiligsten mußt Du die Schuhe ausziehn, aber nicht nur die Schuhe, sondern alles, Reisekleid und Gepäck, und darunter die Nacktheit, und alles, was unter der Nacktheit ist, und alles, was sich unter diesem verbirgt, und dann den Kern und den Kern des Kerns, dann das Übrige und dann den Rest und dann noch den Schein des unvergänglichen Feuers. (*NS II* 77)

> [Before entering the Holy of Holies you must take off your shoes, and not only your shoes but everything, your travelling-clothes and your baggage, and beneath that your nakedness, and everything that is be-

neath your nakedness, and everything hidden beneath that, and then the core and the core of the core, then what is left and then the rest and then the light from the imperishable fire.]

Having undergone such self-destruction, such purgation, what new reality may the purified self enter? Kafka talks mysteriously of our life as being merely transitional. We need to enter the spiritual world, which is the only reality. "Es gibt nichts anderes als eine geistige Welt, was wir sinnliche Welt nennen ist das Böse in der geistigen" (*NS II* 59); when arranging a selection of aphorisms in sequence, Kafka added to this one: "und was wir böse nennen ist nur eine Notwendigkeit eines Augenblicks unserer ewigen Entwicklung" (*NS II* 124, There is nothing but a spiritual world; what we call the sensuous world is the evil in the spiritual [world], and what we call evil is only a requirement of a moment in our everlasting development). Our mission is "Aufsteigen in ein höheres Leben" (*NS II* 81, ascent into a higher life), indeed to attain eternal life. "Wirst Du nach gewonnener Erkenntnis zum ewigen Leben gelangen wollen — und Du wirst nicht anders können als es wollen, denn Erkenntnis ist dieser Wille — so wirst Du Dich, das Hindernis, zerstören müssen" (*NS II* 78, If, having gained knowledge, you want to attain eternal life — and you cannot do other than want to, for knowledge is this desire — then you will have to destroy yourself, the obstacle).

It is tempting to relate these speculations about life after death to the Kabbalistic concept of tsimtsum or rebirth (Robertson, *Kafka* 195–96); but they may also be related to the eighteenth-century concept of palingenesis (reincarnation), which some Christian theologians thought necessary so that people whose virtues were unrewarded, or vices unpunished, in this life should receive justice in another, and to conceptions of metempsychosis that the Enlightenment derived from Platonic and Pythagorean sources (see Kurth-Voigt). A preoccupation with previous and continued existence runs through Goethe's literary work from *Werther* and "Warum gabst du uns die tiefen Blicke" down to the *West-östlicher Divan* (particularly the poems "Selige Sehnsucht" and "Wiederfinden") and *Faust II*. More importantly for Kafka, who often read writers' personal documents more eagerly than their published works, these concerns often found expression in Goethe's recorded conversations. In a strange conversation recorded by Falk on the day of Wieland's funeral (25 January 1813), Goethe maintained that the simple essence of the individual, for which he borrowed the Leibnizian term "monad," must survive death, but its subsequent development would depend on its strength; powerful monads might become stars and draw weaker monads into their circle, transforming them into something appropriate. Goethe justified this idea by analogy with processes of metamorphoses in nature, which produced a flower from a seed and a caterpillar and then a butterfly from an egg. Kafka would have known this conversation from its inclusion in Biedermann's edition of Goethe's *Gespräche,* which he was reading in 1913, for he quotes another passage in a letter to Felice (*F* 347).

So far we have a sharp division between the world of the senses, which one's body inhabits, and the "geistige" world of eternity to which one is connected by one's bodiless inner or mental self. Some passages remind us strongly of Kafka's personal revulsion from sexuality, which makes him in his notebooks equate marriage with martyrdom (*NS II* 53). This revulsion underlay his curious relationships with Felice Bauer and Milena Jesenská, which were carried on largely by correspondence. The letters to Milena, especially, convey Kafka's sense of being trapped in a sexuality that is irremediably filthy: in one he compares himself to the Wandering Jew, "sinnlos wandernd durch eine sinnlos schmutzige Welt" (*M* 198, senselessly wandering through a senselessly filthy world).

There is, however, a counter-current in Kafka's thought: the idea that possibly the world of the senses can after all be made acceptable. He contemplates this possibility at first with something approaching horror:

> Was an der Vorstellung des Ewigen bedrückend ist: die uns unbegreifliche Rechtfertigung welche die Zeit in der Ewigkeit erfahren muß und die daraus folgende Rechtfertigung unserer selbst, so wie wir sind. (*NS II* 88–89)

> [What is depressing about the notion of eternity: the justification, incomprehensible to us, that time must receive in eternity, and the consequent justification of ourselves just as we are.]

Supposing our destiny were not to escape from embodied existence into a higher, non-physical reality, but to see our limited, temporal reality as part of the eternal order and having its rightful place in the eternal order? Granted that the sensory world is the evil element in the spiritual world, perhaps even it can be reclaimed. A Christian would say "redeemed"; Kafka's word is "justification," "Rechtfertigung," and as this is an important word in the notebooks the concept deserves some attention. In the Old Testament, this word expresses a relationship between human beings and God. The man who is justified is acquitted or vindicated before a judge's tribunal, as in Psalm 119:7: "I will praise thee with uprightness of heart, when I shall have learned thy righteous judgments." St. Paul transfers this concept to the effect of Christ, thanks to whom, not to any merits or actions of our own, we are justified, found righteous, before God: while Abraham was justified by his faith ("And therefore it was imputed to him for righteousness," Romans 4:22), Christians are justified both by faith in Christ and by the death of Christ for their sake: "Therefore being justified by faith, we have peace with God through our Lord Jesus Christ" (Rom. 5:1).

As Kafka develops the concept, however, justification does not come from an external source. It comes from man's own work in the world. Man does not consciously seek justification:

> daß es den Anschein hat, als arbeite er für seine Ernährung, Kleidung, u.s.w. ist nebensächlich, es wird ihm eben mit jedem sichtbaren Bissen ein unsichtbarer, mit jedem sichtbaren Kleid auch ein unsichtbares Kleid u.s.f. gereicht. Das ist jedes Menschen Rechtfertigung. (*NS II* 99)

> [That it appears as though he were working to feed and clothe himself, etc., does not matter; for with every visible mouthful he also receives an invisible one, with every visible dress he also receives an invisible dress. That is everybody's justification.]

A person who concentrates on working to support himself and his family is already justified without consciously knowing it. In such a person, being and consciousness are reconciled. Such a person, like the family Flaubert envied, is "dans le vrai." We can relate this conception to *Das Schloß*. There K. seeks a justification for his presence in the village. He wants the authorities to confirm his position as land surveyor. In his search for authorization, he becomes obsessed with the Castle and with his need to speak to an official competent to deal with his case. Early in this process, he takes up with Frieda, the girlfriend of the official Klamm, and they stumble into a relationship that both want to be lasting. K. finds work as a school janitor and maintains a grotesquely impractical household in the schoolroom. It is not the difficulties of daily life, but the lure of the Castle that ends his domestic life.

A further aphorism explores the bases of this justification. It is based on faith, not in the sense of conscious belief, but in the sense of trust, an unconscious assurance, which pervades one's whole being.

> Der Mensch kann nicht leben ohne ein dauerndes Vertrauen zu etwas Unzerstörbarem, wobei sowohl das Unzerstörbare als auch das Vertrauen ihm dauernd unbekannt bleiben können. Eine der Ausdrucks-

möglichkeiten dieses Verborgen-Bleibens ist der Glaube an einen persönlichen Gott. (*NS II* 58)

[Man cannot live without lasting trust in something indestructible, even if in lasting ignorance both of his trust and of the indestructible. One possible expression of this concealment is the belief in a personal God.]

Here Kafka affirms that life needs to be based on a relationship to something outside oneself. He is skeptical about whether that something should be conceived as a personal God. In 1913 he asked Felice about her belief in God and enlarged on what conception he thought desirable:

Fühlst Du — was die Hauptsache ist — ununterbrochene Beziehungen zwischen Dir und einer beruhigend fernen, womöglich unendlichen Höhe oder Tiefe? Wer das immer fühlt, der muß nicht wie ein verlorener Hund herumlaufen und bittend aber stumm herumschaun, der muß nicht das Verlangen haben, in das Grab zu schlüpfen, als sei es ein warmer Schlafsack und das Leben eine kalte Winternacht, der muß nicht, wenn er die Treppe in sein Bureau hinaufgeht, zu sehen glauben, daß er gleichzeitig von oben, flimmernd im unsichern Licht, sich drehend in der Eile der Bewegung, kopfschüttelnd vor Ungeduld, durch das ganze Treppenhaus hinunterfällt. (*F* 289)

[Do you feel — this is the main thing — unbroken connections between yourself and some reassuringly remote, possibly infinite, height or depth? Anyone who constantly feels that does not have to run around like a lost dog, looking around beseechingly but mutely, he need not feel the desire to slip into the grave as though it were a warm sleeping bag and life a cold winter night, and when he climbs the stairs to his office, he does not have to think he sees himself simultaneously falling from above down the entire staircase, shimmering in the uncertain light, revolving with the rapidity of his motion, shaking his head with impatience.]

This is a brilliant description of the existential insecurity that comes from lack of faith. But we have already seen how between 1913 and 1917 Kafka's insecurity had reached the point of desperation. He worked through his crisis in the Zürau notebooks. There he formulates the concept of "the indestructible," derived from Schopenhauer's famous meditation on death in Book II of *The World as Will and Representation*.

Belief in "the indestructible" is not intellectual. It is expressed in action. "Glauben heißt: das Unzerstörbare in sich befreien oder richtiger: sich befreien oder richtiger: unzerstörbar sein oder richtiger: sein" (*NS*

II 55, Belief means freeing the indestructible in oneself, or rather: freeing oneself, or rather: being indestructible, or rather: being). It bridges the gulf between consciousness and being. And it enables Kafka effortlessly to surmount a problem that worries many people who reflect on religion, namely the fact that the majority of people feel no need to reflect on religion. William James, in his *The Varieties of Religious Experience,* borrows from a Catholic writer the division of humanity into the once-born and the twice-born. The latter are the minority who feel anxiety about their relation to something beyond themselves. The former are unreflective, uncomplicated, and largely content to get on with their lives (94). For Kafka, both classes of people arrive by different routes at the same goal, that of being; the twice-born like himself have a very much longer and more arduous journey, the others can be "dans le vrai" already. Kafka also wrote: "Der Weg zum Nebenmenschen ist für mich sehr lang" (*NS II* 112, The way to my neighbor is for me very long).

Kafka's concept of "the indestructible" has further consequences. It frees the believer from isolation, for it is by definition something shared with other people. "Das Unzerstörbare ist eines, jeder einzelne Mensch ist es und gleichzeitig ist es allen gemeinsam. Daher die beispiellos untrennbare Verbindung der Menschen" (*NS II* 66, The indestructible is one; every individual is it, and simultaneously it is common to all. Hence the extraordinarily firm unity of humanity). At this point Kafka again defines his difference from Christianity:

> Alles Leiden um uns werden auch wir leiden müssen. Christus hat für die Menschheit gelitten, aber die Menschheit muß für Christus leiden. Wir alle haben nicht einen Leib aber ein Wachstum und das führt uns durch alle Schmerzen, ob in dieser oder jener Form. So wie das Kind durch alle Lebensstadien bis zum Greis und zum Tod sich entwickelt — und jedes Stadium im Grunde dem vorigen Stadium im Verlangen oder in Furcht unerreichbar scheint — ebenso entwickeln wir uns — nicht weniger tief mit der Menschheit verbunden als mit uns selbst — durch alle Leiden dieser Welt gemeinsam mit allen Mitmenschen. Für Gerechtigkeit ist in diesem Zusammenhang kein Platz, aber auch nicht für Furcht vor den Leiden oder für die Auslegung des Leidens als eines Verdienstes. (*NS II* 93–94)

> [We too shall have to suffer all the suffering around us. Christ suffered for mankind, but mankind must suffer for Christ. We all have, not one body, but one growth, and it leads us through all pains, whether in this or that form. As the child develops through all the stages of life to old age and death — and each stage basically seems unattainable to the preceding stage, whether in desire or fear — similarly we develop — no

less deeply connected with mankind than with ourselves — through all the sufferings of this world, together with all our fellow humans. In this context there is no place for justice, but nor is there one for fear of suffering, or for the interpretation of suffering as merit.]

Here Kafka relativizes the suffering of Christ. It is the task of each human being to assume Christ's role and share the suffering of the rest of humanity. And this ethical individualism, as it has been called (Heidsieck 132–39), is realized in common with the rest of humanity. Kafka implicitly denies St. Paul's claim that all are members of the one body (Rom. 12:5). Instead, a shared process of development overcomes the isolation of the individual and brings about the messianic age. But Kafka undermines the various significances assigned by Judaism and Christianity to the figure of the Messiah, showing that the Messiah thus becomes superfluous:

Der Messias wird kommen, bis der zügelloseste Individualismus des Glaubens möglich ist, niemand diese Möglichkeit vernichtet, niemand die Vernichtung duldet, also die Gräber sich öffnen. Das ist vielleicht auch die christliche Lehre, sowohl in der tatsächlichen Aufzeigung des Beispiels, als auch in der symbolischen Aufzeigung der Auferstehung des Mittlers im einzelnen Menschen. (*NS II* 55)

[The Messiah will come once the most unbridled individualism of faith is possible, nobody destroys this possibility, nobody tolerates its destruction, and thus the graves are opened. That is perhaps also the Christian doctrine, both in the actual displaying of the example and in the symbolic displaying of the resurrection of the mediator in the individual.]

There is, then, no need for a mediator like Christ to reconcile God with man. Kafka's impersonal divinity, the indestructible, is latent in every human being. To make contact with this imperishable essence is humanity's task, and when everyone does so human life will be transfigured. As a means to this goal, suffering is necessary and valuable:

Das Leiden ist das positive Element dieser Welt, ja es ist die einzige Verbindung zwischen dieser Welt und dem Positiven. Nur hier ist Leiden — Leiden. Nicht so als ob die welche hier leiden, anderswo wegen dieses Leidens erhöht werden sollen, sondern so, daß das was in dieser Welt Leiden heißt, in einer andern Welt, unverändert und nur befreit von seinem Gegensatz, Seligkeit ist. (*NS II* 83)

[Suffering is the positive element in this world, indeed it is the only link between this world and the positive. Only here is suffering suffering.

Not as though those who suffer here are elsewhere to be elevated because of this suffering; but what in this world is called suffering, in another world, unchanged and merely freed from its opposite, is bliss.]

In this hateful, prison-like world of pain, suffering connects us with higher reality. For we suffer because we are thrust down into this world. Our discomfort here reminds us that we belong to eternity. It is not the case that, as some Christians think, we shall be rewarded for our suffering here by corresponding happiness in the next world. Rather, in the next world the spiritual potential that makes us suffer here will be freed from confinement and make us happy.

Kafka is a highly individual and challenging religious thinker. His thought does not proceed within the framework of any one religion, but defines itself against a number of theologies and philosophies. That makes the historical understanding of Kafka a necessary but paradoxical exercise. For one simplifies Kafka and denies his originality and his eclecticism if one locates his thought within any religious system. Rewarding though it has been to see Kafka through lenses provided by Judaism, we need to see it only as one of the sources on which he drew for his highly personal intellectual and spiritual exploration.

Notes

[1] Translations are my own. The most reliable translations currently available of "Das Urteil," "Die Verwandlung," and other stories published during Kafka's lifetime are in: Franz Kafka, *The Transformation and Other Stories*, translated and edited by Malcolm Pasley (London: Penguin, 1992).

Works Cited

Alter, Robert. *Necessary Angels: Tradition and Modernity in Kafka, Benjamin and Scholem.* Cambridge: Harvard UP, 1991.

Baioni, Giuliano. *Kafka: letteratura ed ebraismo.* Turin: Einaudi, 1984.

Beck, Evelyn Torton. *Kafka and the Yiddish Theater.* Madison: U of Wisconsin P, 1971.

Biale, David. *Eros and the Jews: From Biblical Israel to Contemporary America.* New York: Basic Books, 1992.

Brod, Max. *Streitbares Leben: Autobiographie.* Munich: Kindler, 1960.

———. *Über Franz Kafka.* Frankfurt am Main: S. Fischer, 1966.

Cavarocchi, Marina. *La certezza che toglie la speranza: Contributi per l'approfondimento dell' aspetto ebraico in Kafka.* Florence: Giuntina, 1988.

Dowden, Stephen C. *Kafka's Castle and the Critical Imagination.* Columbia, SC: Camden House, 1995.

Eilittä, Leena. *Approaches to Personal Identity in Kafka's Short Fiction: Freud, Darwin, Kierkegaard.* Helsinki: Academia Scientiarum Fennica, 1999.

Ellis, John M. "Kafka: 'Das Urteil.'" In *Narration in the German Novelle.* Cambridge: Cambridge UP, 1974. 188–211.

Grözinger, Karl E. *Kafka und die Kabbala.* Frankfurt am Main: Eichborn, 1992.

Grözinger, Karl E., Stéphane Moses, and Hans Dieter Zimmermann, eds. *Franz Kafka und das Judentum.* Frankfurt am Main: Athenäum, 1987.

Hartwich, Wolf-Daniel. "Böser Trieb, Märtyrer und Sündenbock. Religiöse Metaphorik in Kafkas *Urteil.*" *Deutsche Vierteljahrsschrift* 67 (1993): 521–40.

Heidsieck, Arnold. *The Intellectual Contexts of Kafka's Fiction: Philosophy, Law, Religion.* Columbia, SC: Camden House, 1994.

James, William. *The Varieties of Religious Experience.* London: Collins, 1960.

Jonas, Hans. *The Gnostic Religion: The Message of the Alien God and the Beginnings of Christianity.* 2nd ed. Boston: Beacon Press, 1963.

Kafka, Franz. *Briefe an Felice und andere Korrespondenz aus der Verlobungszeit.* Ed. Erich Heller and Jürgen Born. Frankfurt am Main: S. Fischer, 1967. (*F*)

———. *Das Schloß.* Ed. Malcolm Pasley. Frankfurt am Main: S. Fischer, 1982. (*S*)

———. *Briefe an Milena.* Ed. Jürgen Born and Michael Müller. Frankfurt am Main: S. Fischer, 1983. (*M*)

———. *Der Proceß.* Ed. Malcolm Pasley. Frankfurt am Main: S. Fischer, 1990. (*P*)

———. *Tagebücher.* Ed. Hans-Gerd Koch, Michael Müller, and Malcolm Pasley. Frankfurt am Main: S. Fischer, 1990. (*T*)

———. *Nachgelassene Schriften und Fragmente II.* Ed. Jost Schillemeit. Frankfurt am Main: S. Fischer, 1992. (*NS II*)

———. *Drucke zu Lebzeiten.* Ed. Wolf Kittler, Hans-Gerd Koch, and Gerhard Neumann. Frankfurt am Main: S. Fischer, 1994. (*D*)

Kurth-Voigt, Lieselotte E. *Continued Existence, Reincarnation, and the Power of Sympathy in Classical Weimar.* Rochester, NY: Camden House, 1999.

Kurz, Gerhard. *Traum-Schrecken: Kafkas literarische Existenzanalyse.* Stuttgart: Metzler, 1980.

Lamping, Dieter. *Von Kafka bis Celan: Jüdischer Diskurs in der deutschen Literatur des 20. Jahrhunderts.* Göttingen: Vandenhoeck & Ruprecht, 1998.

Nietzsche, Friedrich. *Werke.* Ed. Karl Schlechta. 3 vols. Munich: Hanser, 1956.

Robert, Marthe. *Seul, comme Franz Kafka.* Paris: Calmann-Lévy, 1979.

Robertson, Ritchie. *Kafka: Judaism, Politics, and Literature*. Oxford: Clarendon Press, 1985.

————. "'Von den ungerechten Richtern.' Zum allegorischen Verfahren Kafkas im *Proceß*." In Hans Dieter Zimmermann, ed., *Nach erneuter Lektüre: Franz Kafkas "Der Proceß."* Würzburg: Königshausen & Neumann, 1992. 201–9.

————. "Kafka und das Christentum." *Der Deutschunterricht* 50 (1998): 60–69.

Ryan, Michael P. "Samsa and *Samsara:* Suffering, Death and Rebirth in *The Metamorphosis*." *German Quarterly* 72 (1999): 113–52.

Sheppard, Richard. *On Kafka's Castle*. London: Croom Helm, 1973.

Sokel, Walter H. "Zwischen Gnosis und Jehovah. Zur Religions-Problematik Franz Kafkas." In Wilhelm Emrich and Bernd Goldmann, eds., *Franz Kafka Symposium 1983*. Mainz: v. Hase & Koehler, 1985. 37–79.

Wagenbach, Klaus. *Franz Kafka: Eine Biographie seiner Jugend*. Berne: Francke, 1958.

Zilcosky, John. "Kafka Approaches Schopenhauer's Castle." *German Life and Letters* 44 (1990–91): 353–69.

Zimmermann, Hans Dieter. *Der babylonische Dolmetscher: Zu Franz Kafka und Robert Walser*. Frankfurt am Main: Suhrkamp, 1985.

Kafka's Aesthetics: A Primer: From the Fragments to the Novels

Henry Sussman

Introduction[1]

THE PAGES OF KAFKA'S FICTION teem with figures who, if they do not explicitly function as artists, are only a tenuous degree away from this calling. Kafka devoted so much of his fictive exposition to artists and their activities that it might be well to designate him, among other things, an aesthetician. Kafka was not, after all, gearing his writing to an academic audience. He was not under constraint to place his articulations under the rubric of some discursive subcontract,[2] whether "aesthetics" or "creative writing," that would identify his work and assure it an intellectual location and intellectual milieu. He felt as free to expend his writing on his diaries and letters as on his formal fiction.

As Kafka develops his characters, whether "people," animals, or bizarre thought-things such as Odradek,[3] he endows their artistic activities with features that, assembled in a constellation, form the parameters of a coherent aesthetics, one as distinctive as Kant's, Hegel's, or Proust's. In devising parables to serve as stage settings for his polymorphous artist-figures, he revealed himself to be a rigorous theoretician of art and its roles in "advanced" Western society and culture. While certain of Kafka's ideas about art clearly derived from the encounter with Western metaphysics and systematic philosophy conducted, among others, by the German Romanticists, Kant, Hegel, Kierkegaard, and Nietzsche, under the illumination of his fictive exposition his aesthetic postulates took on a singular character and cast. Kafka's aesthetics is infused with the rich and non-reproducible imprint of his specific writerly, formal, stylistic, and tonal experiments. The display of such "art-games"[4] may well constitute one of the pivotal features of fiction, at least where a distinctive vision has been allowed to coalesce: serving as a theater in which the elements of reference, possibly related to "experience," are distilled into aesthetic design-parameters and moods.

The mood of an aesthetics, perhaps the artist's most distinctive trace, is the palette of tonalities under which a gradation of design-parameters assembles. The singular imprint enabling us to discern the lineaments of an aesthetics within the production of a particular artist is a function of the cohesion of a fictive world combined with aesthetic maturity. If a production is not so extensive as to contain a set of well-articulated aesthetic parameters, it had better reflect the full range of the artist's maneuvers. I am not sure that we could credit Charles Dickens, on the evidence of *Oliver Twist* alone, or even on the basis of the "full body" of his novels, with a distinctive aesthetic theory, but the claim might be well worth pressing in relation to Robert Musil's *Der Mann ohne Eigenschaften*.

The Trapeze Artist of "Erstes Leid" (First Sorrow), the Hunger Artist, and Titorelli of *Der Proceß* literally function as artists with aesthetic practices and even styles. Yet a full range of near-artists or quasi-artists amply populates the pages of Kafka's fiction. As untoward as his metamorphosis may be, Gregor Samsa as "ungeheueres Ungeziefer" (monstrous vermin) hangs from the ceiling, in symbiosis with the later Trapeze Artist's performance through suspension and resisting the law of gravity. The bizarre kitten/lamb of "Eine Kreuzung" (A Crossbreed [A Sport]), is not merely an inherited house pet and occasion for endless mirth and contemplation. It is a possession marking the narrator who owns it as a social pariah and as a writer. In the case of "Eine Kreuzung," the dramatic stage property of an amalgamation of species distinct from the narrator nonetheless marks the text as a parable of aesthetic activity.

We may credit the same Romantic engagement with the expansionist and systematic aspirations of Enlightenment ideology evident in Benjamin's earliest understanding of the critical vocation with setting the agenda for certain of Kafka's bounded fiction games. Kafka's experiments with the fragment and with narrative irony, for example, arise very much in this context. But Kafka's aesthetics cannot be reduced to these subcontractual negotiations of Romanticism. Out of the very particular formal, tonal, and modal interventions that Kafka was willing to make arise the lineaments of a singular, that is, iterable[5] but not reproducible, aesthetics. To whatever extent the participation of philosophy and critical theory are indispensable to naming and articulating the arenas of cultural activity and the transactions taking place within their bounds, the mutations arising from literary composition are singular and irreplaceable, and cannot be reduced to these formats.

Literariness, then — the intangibles of formal iteration and distortion, style, literary naming, diction, syntax, meter, and other features — is as quintessential a feature of Kafka's aesthetics as generalizable observations regarding his theories and approaches to art. Kafka's aesthetics is the amalgam or hybridity between literarity and critical theory in the same sense in which Gregor Samsa is at the same time a man and a "monstrous vermin" and in which the subject, if not protagonist of "Eine Kreuzung" is a kitten/lamb.

Every aesthetics fuses a specific literary or scriptural practice with a set of generalizable formulations, even in the hands of a philosopher, who is among other things a philosophical writer. The literary dimension of an aesthetics may comprise an indelible imprint, as in the case of Kierkegaard or Kafka, or it may function as a secret sharer, and need to be *read out* of Kant, Fichte, or Hegel. It is on the vitality and strength of this fusion and interpenetration that any comparative literary or cultural "discipline" rises and falls.

The Aesthetics of Fragmentation

This is a proper as well as strategic place to start, for at least two compelling reasons: first, because from the moment it begins to precipitate out of his "private" writing, Kafka's fictive discourse is explicitly engaged in experiments of narrative scale and framing or contextualization; and second, because in a literal sense, the fragment comprised Romantic theory's most visible trace of its opposition to a priori systematic orders and the ideological conditions under which they thrive. Kafka's explorations of the writerly phenomenon of fragmentation are many. In "Beim Bau der chinesischen Mauer" (The Great Wall of China, 1917) it appears as an indispensable feature of artistic and cultural production, particularly in projects of larger scale. The meditation on the fragment in this pivotal tale belongs to the culture-critique that may be extrapolated from the pages of Kafka's novels as well as his tales. Yet fragmentation is also at the crux of a Kafkan enterprise that we could call a deconstructive experimentation with and undermining of conventional fiction as one manifestation of an entire metaphysics of representation. To play on the fragment as a fictive or narrative device, as Kafka does, is to test the scale, duration, perspectivism, and marginal delineation of fictive discourse.

The gravitation toward considerations of scale, a fundamental questioning of writing's dimensionality, links Kafka's fictional project to the critical systems of Kant. Kafka is never closer to Kant than when the narrative of "Beim Bau der chinesischen Mauer" registers the wonder of the Wall's construction and the socio-communicative vastness, tending toward chaos, that it bespeaks.[6] Or when *Das Schloß* surveys the gaps and misprisions in the bureaucratic approaches linking the power-nexus to the village below it. Sublimity, the terrain that Kant, in a long tradition of thinkers, devised as a field for the interpenetration of the measured and everyday by the awesome, an interstitial space logically and culturally necessitated by his system, is the fullest backdrop on which Kafka's fictive plays of fragmentation register. Kafka's plays on fragmentation are twentieth-century literature's response to awe, magnificence, and cultural grandiosity generated systematically.[7] In its grandiose scale and design, the Great Wall is inseparable from the High Command that conceives and executes it:

> Wir — ich rede hier wohl im Namen vieler — haben eigentlich erst im Nachbuchstabieren der Anordungen der obersten Führerschaft uns selbst kennengelernt und gefunden, daß ohne die Führerschaft weder unsere Schulweisheit noch unser Menschenverstand für das kleine Amt, das wir innerhalb des großen Ganzen hatten, ausgereicht hätte. In der Stube der Führerschaft — wo sie war und wer dort saß, weiß und wußte niemand, den ich fragte — in dieser Stube kreisten wohl alle menschlichen Gedanken und Wünsche und in Gegenkreisen alle menschlichen Ziele und Erfüllungen . . . Bleibt also nur die Folgerung, daß die Führerschaft den Teilbau beabsichtigte. Aber der Teilbau war nur ein Notbehelf und unzweckmäßig. Bleibt die Folgerung, daß die Führerschaft etwas Unzweckmäßiges wollte. — Sonderbare Folgerung! (*SE* 292–93)

> [We — and I here speak in the name of many people — did not really know ourselves until we had carefully scrutinized the decrees of the high command, when we discovered that without the high command neither our book learning nor our human understanding would have sufficed for the humble tasks which were performed in the great whole. In the office of the high command — where it was and who sat there no one whom I have asked knew then or knows now — in that office one may be certain that all human thoughts and desires revolved in a circle and all human aims and fulfillments in a countercircle. . . . There remains, therefore, nothing but the conclusion that the command deliberately chose the system of piecemeal construction. But the piecemeal construction was only a makeshift and therefore inexpedient. Remains the conclusion that the command had willed something inexpedient. Strange conclusion! (*CS* 239–40)]

Kafka's narrator wonders in bemusement how a project so grand and magnificent could have emerged from a procedure so piecemeal and expedient. Piecemeal construction (*Teilbau*) is a blueprint for literary as well as architectural construction. Through the elaboration of this *modus scribendi* in this tale, Kafka betrays the plan underlying many distinctive literary phenomena in his work: a truncated and discontinuous architecture that follows through into the installations of Court and Castle; the Benjaminian "cloudy spots"[8] that intervene toward the end of *Der Proceß* (The Trial) and *Das Schloß* (The Castle); enunciation of a "fragment's eye-view" in literary production, whether in the breathless laughter of Odradek, or in the ruminations of the Burrow Creature, or in Josephine's piping.

In "Beim Bau der chinesischen Mauer," the High Command is as remote and inscrutable as the Wall is extensive. Kafka makes sure to place the Wall and the High Command in a reciprocal genealogy and culpability. It is precisely in the domain of the Law, with its preordained, a priori (in a Kantian sense) absolutism and closure that the expedients of fragmentation and other plays of writing find their origin.

From his delving into the fragment and its anomalous potentials, Kafka mines new potentials for the sublime, above all as a resource for twentieth-century literature. Speaking again of "Beim Bau der chinesischen Mauer," it is but a stone's throw from the dissolution of the clarity of the High Command's strictures into a runaway river (*CS* 240), or, later in the tale, from the torrent of inconsistencies released by a messenger's mission to the hinterlands (244) to a collection of parallel oddities by like-minded twentieth-century authors. I think of the sublime literary spaces in "The Library of Babel," "Death and the Compass," and related Borgesian *ficciones;* or the incessant parabolas, made by guided missiles, sexual desire and arousal, and schemes of colonial domination, crisscrossing Pynchon's *Gravity's Rainbow.*[9] Kafka's literary space is even more sublime in the confusions to which it gives rise, as in "Eine alltägliche Verwirrung" (A Common Confusion), than in its endless reaches. Following above all the Poe of "Eureka" in this respect, Kafka bequeathed this distinctive literary space to kindred twentieth-century writers.

Kafka's plays on fragmentation are systematically structured by the Kantian system. The architects and masons of Qin China are left to fulfill a plan preordained at a transcendental (that is, synthetic a priori) remove. In Kafka's fiction, as well as in Kant's philosophy, only paradoxes (or Kantian antinomies) can reside at the interstice where the perspectives of the transcendental and the empirical fix each other in a mutual gaze. "Beim Bau der chinesischen Mauer" may be read as Kafka's most extensive transcript of the paradoxes emerging where the preordained exigencies of the High Command give way to the transgressions of writing. The exotic setting of ancient China underlines only too dramatically for Kafka's Western readers the Kantian antinomies[10] surfacing at the interface between civilized repression and scriptural disruptions of order.

The Aesthetics of Inversion

Besonders oben auf der Decke hing er gern; es war ganz anders, als das Liegen auf dem Fußboden; man atmete freier; ein leichtes Schwingen ging durch den Körper; und in der fast glücklichen Zerstreutheit, in der sich Gregor dort oben befand, konnte es geschehen, daß er zu seiner eigenen Überraschung sich losließ und auf den Boden klatschte. (*SE* 78–79)

[He especially enjoyed hanging suspended from the ceiling; it was quite different from lying on the floor; one could breathe more freely; one's body swung and rocked lightly; and in the almost blissful absorption induced by this suspension it could happen to his own surprise that he let go and fell plump on the floor. (*CS* 115, translation modified)]

The image of Gregor hanging suspended from the ceiling of his bedroom looms over the extent of Kafka's aesthetics in several senses. The power of this snapshot derives not only from a bizarre projection of the human state, but from the multiple transpositions of images elsewhere in the body of Kafka's fiction that make it possible. Gregor's position is inverted, but the stance claims nothing of the fanciful or magical with which the topsy-turvy worlds of Shakespeare, Goethe, and Joyce are laced. A compelling aesthetic sense or non-logic has precipitated Gregor's upside-downness with respect to his familiar world, his family environment.

In the citation at the head of this section, the narrative, in lauding the benefits of Gregor's inverse posture, abandons its putative neutrality, as it does in "Erstes Leid," rationalizing the compulsion to minimize the Trapeze Artist's contact with the pedestrian world below. Gregor's new stance "was quite different from lying on the floor" (*CS* 115). "Besides," argues the narrative voice of "Erstes Leid," "it was quite healthful up there. . . . True, [the Trapeze Artist's] social life was somewhat limited. . . . Otherwise nothing disturbed his seclusion" (*CS* 446–47; "Doch war es oben auch sonst gesund. . . . Freilich, sein menschlicher Verkehr war eingeschränkt . . . Sonst blieb es um ihn still," *SE* 155). In "Erstes Leid," an antipodal stance to the world, striving to be suspended above in contrast to the entire world below, implements an aesthetic of resistance to the fundamental, ultimately most ineluctable force of all, gravity. This aesthetics of resistance also marks the Hunger Artist, body and soul. The Hunger Artist's triumph is a successful, sustained resistance to the most basic instinct of all, for self-preservation through nourishment.

Er war sehr gerne bereit, mit solchen Wächtern die Nacht gänzlich ohne Schlaf zu verbringen; er war bereit, mit ihnen zu scherzen, ihnen Geschichten aus seinem Wanderleben zu erzählen, dann wieder ihre Erzählungen anzuhören, alles nur um sie wachzuhalten, um ihnen immer wieder zeigen zu können, daß er nichts Eßbares im Käfig hatte . . . Am glücklichsten aber war er, wenn dann der Morgen kam, und ihnen auf seine Rechnung ein überreiches Frühstück gebracht wurde, auf das sie sich warfen mit dem Appetit gesunder Männer nach einer mühevoll durchwachten Nacht. (*SE* 164–65)

[He was quite happy at the prospect of spending a sleepless night with such watchers; he was ready to exchange jokes with them, to tell them stories out of his nomadic life, anything at all to keep them awake and demonstrate to them that he had no eatables in the cage. . . . But his happiest moment was when the morning came and an enormous breakfast was brought out, at his expense, on which they flung themselves with the keen appetite of healthy men after a weary night of wakefulness. (*CS* 269)]

Everything about the Hunger Artist's position in relation to the world of "healthy men" is inverse: his thriving on self-denial in place of their unproblematic consumption; his *jouissance* in their satisfaction at the literal expense of his corporeal misery as well as his pocketbook; his residence on the far side of a barrier of ocular and spatial Otherness. Art, for Kafka, as personified by the Hunger Artist, is a multifaceted inversion of the values regulating bourgeois culture and economics. Like the optical aberrations that Kant attributes to the Transcendental's appearances in the domain of mutability, art regards the pedestrian world with the inverse gaze of radical Otherness: "This is an *illusion* which can no more be prevented than we can prevent the sea appearing higher at the horizon than at the shore, since we see it through higher light rays; or to cite still a better example, than the astronomer can prevent the moon from appearing larger at its rising, although he is not deceived by this illusion" (*Critique of Pure Reason* 299–300). In Kafka's novel *Der Verschollene* (often known as it was titled by Max Brod: *Amerika*) this inversion defines the location of the balcony where Karl Rossmann, incarcerated by Delamarche, Robinson, and Brunelda, encounters the student, another subject in a state of aggravated becoming, before the "cloudy spot" trailing off toward the work's utopian coda.

Kafka's aesthetics of inversion skirts the margin of speculative dialectics, on the in- and the outside. In the opposition it stages to the imperative, whether of human survival, bureaucratic process, or physics, it pertains to the economy of dialectical assertion and resistance. In this instance, the self-demolition of the machine of execution in the Penal Colony is an instance of the reversal of authoritarian machines. Even fragments as brief as "Bäume" (Trees) and "Prometheus" stage the progressive negation and denial of any sense of stability that may be grounded in their formulations. This destabilization was the basis for Benjamin's characterization of Kafka's fictions as "fairy-tales for dialecticians" (*Selected Writings* 2: 799). Yet the multifaceted inversion staged by Kafka's fictive world also transgresses beyond the parameters of dialectical oversight. Gregor, Odradek, the assistants of *Das Schloß*, the migratory bullies of *Amerika* all relate to the prescriptive ideologies and orders of modern life in an inverse way. With vertiginous uncanniness, their realms penetrate, question, and disable normative actuality as it evolved in Western society in the early twentieth century. The pivotal parable "Vor dem Gesetz" (Before the Law) may be apprehended in precisely this fashion: as the inscription and instrument of an inversion so complex and polymorphous as to break free of dialectical constraints. The aesthetics of inversion is the hinge or pivot opening Kafka's fiction to sustained marginality, to big Otherness, to doubling on the cosmic scale of an alternate universe reporting to the human domain on its status via the allegory of sustained writerliness and textuality.

The Aesthetics of Doubling

It was Kafka's innovation to metamorphose the Romantic tradition of literary doubling — and he was as aware as any European writer of the narrative, perspectival, and thematic potentials exploited by, among others, Poe, Hoffmann, and Dostoyevsky — into an extended allegory of writing.[11] The life of letters and its exactions is the ultimate secret sharer that spies and preys upon, invades, and subverts the existence of Kafka's protagonists. Indeed, it is the inverse life and domain of writing that is the only recompense that the Court, however grudgingly, even punitively, furnishes to Joseph K. in *Der Proceß*, having isolated him from family, friends, and neighbors, made his employment impossible, and, in the end, cost him his life.

The aesthetics of doubling marks Kafka's work as indelibly as it has tinged the writing of any major author of fiction. But the doubles are not perfect look-alikes; instead their contrary activities and attitudes, whether nearby or at great distance, ultimately bracket and question the protagonist's articles of faith. There is no better example of a double in Kafka's fiction than the kitten/lamb of "Eine Kreuzung," an unwanted "remarkable legacy" ("eigentümliches Tier . . . Erbstück aus meines Vaters Besitz") from the narrator's father, which, despite an anomalous status that the brief tale investigates in every logical nuance and existential implication, bears an uncanny affinity to the narrator. "It sometimes gazes at me with a look of understanding, challenging me to do the thing of which both of us are thinking" (*CS* 427; "mich wie aus verständigen Menschenaugen ansieht, die zu verständigem Tun auffordern," *SE* 303). The kitten/lamb is precisely the narrator's double in anomaly, Otherness, and a perverse posture toward the protocols of everyday communal existence. In brief, the kitten/lamb and narrator share in the obverse and invariably marginal and supplemental economy of writing, which is a universe and worldview as well as a vocation.

The broader doubling that Kafka explores and exploits is nothing less than the writer's predicament and irreducible credo. It pervades Kafka's fiction to the same degree that it usurps control over the "lives" of his protagonists. Manifestations of the Kafkan double run a full range of elaboration from the sister in "Der Schlag ans Hoftor" (The Knock at the Manor Gate, 1917), whose minimal action, intimated in the tale's title, may not qualify as an action at all, yet becomes the pretext for the looming, bloodthirsty, medieval execution of the brother/narrator; to the Court of *Der Proceß*, which may be described as a "full-service" counter-world to the interests of social conformity, stability, and advancement.

The Kafkan protagonist is torn, in a non-dialectical way, between the worldviews and economies of communal participation and writing. The troubled no-person's land, or seismic fault, between the linguistic and the sociological runs the course of Kafka's fictive creation. These counter-modalities of being intersect and interpenetrate in the subject, whose normative existence is already over. As Maurice Blanchot noted before anyone else, the Kafkan protagonist is the survivor of a death that has already taken place.[12] Doubling, in Kafka's writing, is the ultimately insurmountable tension between the exigencies and triumphs of writing, and the husks of existence it leaves in its wake. Kafka's animals are subject-units that have succumbed to hard-core writing conditions. Gregor Samsa, the Burrow Creature, the kitten/lamb, and Josephine have devolved into the non-human in the wake of their writerly apprehensions. When the Burrow Creature imagines for itself a double, probably boring "its great snout into the earth with a mighty push and tear[ing] out a great lump" (*CS* 354), a doubling already constitutive of the Creature's very being doubles itself. The fantasmatic creature that the burrow's major-domo encounters is a read-out of its own writerly status, a feedback loop of its own transposition from fairy-tale animal icon into text.

It's easy to overlook, by the same token, the shrewdness of Gregor Samsa's metamorphosis into his writerly double, the giant vermin. At the mere cost of some damage to his mandibles, Gregor excuses himself from an alienating and demeaning job and communicates his disgust at his family's exploitation of his goodwill and good offices (*CS* 110–11), allowing himself to enjoy the antipodal Kafkan life of artistry. Gregor becomes Kafka's most indelible talisman for an existence doubled between socio-existential *Sorge* and writerly resistance.

We should by no means underestimate the rigor and inventiveness with which Kafka surveyed the frontier marked by this — dare we call it systematic? — doubling. Kafka's most striking legacy may have assumed the form of literary fragments, stories, and novels, but he assayed the features, activities, and environmental impacts of writing with the persistence of a philosopher. For this reason I have no difficulty in numbering him among the twentieth-century philosophers of writing,[13] among them Wittgenstein, Heidegger, Benjamin, Adorno, Blanchot, de Man, and Derrida, who have endowed this period of intellectual production with so much of its distinctive flavor. Kafka's pervasive aesthetics of doubling is one rubric marking this decisive turn toward an ethos and bearing of inscription.

The Aesthetics of Confusion

So ominously did Kafka's fiction lay out the coordinates of authoritarian control and death-centeredness in the twentieth century that it is easy to forget that he reduced his friends to convulsive laughter during his informal readings of "Die Verwandlung" (The Metamorphosis) and other works. There is a pervasive strain of humor in Kafka's fiction, and it is more often than not occasioned by the confusions, misprisions, and misdirections endemic to systems of language and communication. Kafka looms large in Deleuze and Guattari's cultural sights because he maintains an acutely schizo sense of the wider flows of energy, violence, and repression in "advanced" society through a sharp attentiveness to conditions in the microeconomies of language and the media through which it is disseminated.[14] Deleuze and Guattari understand that a humorous confusion within a confined sector of the civil order, say the co-presence of Castle bureaucrats named "Sordini" and "Sortini," could on a systematic level cause dire human problems.

Kafka pushes to the limit a range of dimensions intrinsic to the communicative and referential premises of language: time, space, acceleration, density, complexity. These are to the domain of Kafka's writing what time, space, and intuition are to Kant's speculations: a priori givens. It is within the parameters of these dimensions that Kafka revels at the confusions that language — and its interpersonal media — is capable of engendering. Thus, as the village mayor explains in chapter 5 of *Das Schloß*, K.'s very calling by the Castle hierarchy, and its belated reconsideration after his arrival, is the result of the misplacement of crucial correspondence between departments A. and B. It can be no accident in a novel in which Castle officials and village residents systematically misrecognize one another that K.'s assistants, Arthur and Jeremias, are constantly taken for each other. Indeed, they barely claim the discreteness conventionally accorded to "identities." The blueprint for the Great Wall of China, the telephone systems in *Das Schloß* and in the Hotel Occidental in *Amerika,* and, in the latter novel, the elevators in the same hotel as well as the traffic patterns on the way to Ramses are all material configurations of a language system whose primary byproducts may well be confusion. It is no accident, given this propensity for linguistic misplacement, misprision, and misrecognition that "Es gibt nur Kontrollbehörden" (*S* 82; "There are only control authorities," *Castle* 84) in the Castle, according to the village mayor. The proliferation of bureaucrats, court officials, and military officers in Kafka's fiction is a sign that in the social sphere, the play of language and its pervasive confusions are greeted with suspicion and repression. In the domain of Deleuze and Guattari's *Capitalism and Schizophrenia* diptych,[15] such figures appear as Keystone Cops in the belated effort to monitor and repress the inevitability of flow. In certain key sites, Kafka's fiction rises to the paradoxical endeavor of formulating a science of confusion. The set-up to "Eine alltägliche Verwirrung" runs as follows:

> A hat mit B aus H ein wichtiges Geschäft abzuschließen. Er geht zur Vorbesprechung nach H, legt den Hin- und Herweg in je zehn Minuten zurück und rühmt sich zu Hause dieser besonderen Schnelligkeit. Am nächsten Tag geht er wieder nach H, diesmal zum endgültigen Geschäftsabschluß. Da dieser voraussichtlich mehrere Stunden erfordern wird, geht A sehr früh morgens fort. (*SE* 303)

> [A. has to transact important business with B. in H. He goes to H. for a preliminary interview, accomplishes the journey there in ten minutes, and the journey back in the same time, and on returning boasts to his family of this unusual speediness. Next day he goes again to H., this time to settle his business finally. As that by all appearances will require several hours, A. leaves very early in the morning. (*CS* 429, translation modified)]

This discourse of scientific parody, which is not devoid of its own good scientific sense, becomes a significant legacy to, among others, Beckett, Calvino, Borges, and Pynchon. In the brief tale cited directly above, Kafka undermines the textbook presentation of time and acceleration by juxtaposing it to an experience of temporality of a far more speculative and hypothetical character. Needless to say, in its day this concern amounted to serious business indeed. The writings of Bergson and the calculations of Einstein represent the merest tip of the iceberg.[16] The Kafkan speculation in this field results in a parable in which the same local space takes a hypothetical character, who is not named except with an initial, ten hours, ten minutes, and "practically . . . an instant" to traverse (CS 429–30), depending, it would seem, on the universe's need to frustrate its inhabitants. At the tale's conclusion, the characters, who have very rationally arranged to meet, literally stumble over each other, bringing Kafka's aesthetics of confusion to its logical and not-so-logical culminations.

In terms of narratology, the correlative to this thematic and logical confusion is a narrative voice whose loyalties, points of view, and functions are often obscure. Kafka silently dismantles the conventions enabling disinterest and objectivity to be imputed to the narrative voice. There are unmarked carryovers from the patent misogyny of the manager in "Ein Hungerkünstler" (A Hunger Artist) and of the Officer in "In der Strafkolonie" (In the Penal Colony) to the narrator. These characters berate women for their role in belittling and devaluing the feats and tensions of performance, whether of art or justice. It is the narrator who assumes the Hunger Artist's irritation at giving up his fast at a ceremony presided over, in part, by women: "[Er] sollte sich nun hoch und lang aufrichten und zu dem Essen gehn, das ihm schon allein in der Vorstellung Übelkeiten verursachte, deren Äußerung er nur mit Rücksicht auf die Damen mühselig unterdrückte" (SE 166; "And now he was supposed to lift himself up to his full height and go down to a meal the very thought of which gave him a nausea that only the presence of the ladies kept him from betraying," CS 271). The narrator's allegiance in, among other texts, "Erstes Leid," "Das Urteil" (The Judgment), and "Die Verwandlung" is surely as questionable as the ladies' support for the social values that they purportedly revere. This leads to a systematic confusion in Kafka's fiction. As one example of linearity, the progression of narrative is by definition continuous. Yet the narrative line becomes a Möbius strip if its values and sympathies, unannounced, loop back and around. A minefield of confusions will have been planted.

Kafka excelled in this experiment. This is precisely what happened in "Das Urteil," his September 1912 breakthrough, the inauguration of his fully realized fictive discourse, with plots, surrogates, and differences of perspective. Onto Georg Bendemann's best-case scenario of his role in his family, his forthcoming marriage, his business success, and his empathy for his friend, Kafka seamlessly splices, within the continuity of narrative, his father's very different account of the events and arenas in Georg's "life." The "hinge," or graft[17] between the counter-narratives, is a fulcrum for a confusion existing at least *in potentia* for the duration of Kafka's fiction. Kafka's contemporaries and followers, by means of various experiments, have exploited this potential for duplicity embedded in all narration, the inscription of an uncanny Otherness pervading, precisely, the most intimate human ties and allegiances. Beckett divides Molloy between two narrators, each with his own existential as well as narrative baggage. The narrative of Woolf's *The Waves* assumes the form of unidentified shards of utterance, multiplying, exponentially, their potential attributions, meanings, and implications. Confusion, as fundamental feature of language systems, thus spans a gamut of epiphenomena in Kafka's fiction, ranging from the comical to the deeply disturbing and uncanny.

The Aesthetics of Proliferation

Nowhere is Kafka's literary imagination more striking than in his configuration of complexity-generators that may be regarded as either signifying machines or self-composing texts. The instrument of execution in the Penal Colony and the telephone systems in the Castle and the Hotel Occidental are obvious instances of this recurrent figure, on which Kafka left an unmistakable imprint; but as I argued many years ago and still maintain, the culminating parable of *Der Proceß*, although arrayed in the intimacy of a folktale, is also, at its core, a signifying machine, a core matrix whose product is as much a succession of variants or interpretations as any master narrative.[18] The novel devotes more material to the ambiguities in "Vor dem Gesetz," as they are hashed over by Joseph K. and the priest, than to the parable itself. The priest sets the stage for the parable's unsettling open-endedness, its refusal to serve as the answer to the Court's multiple enigmas, when he insists: "Die Erklärer sagen hiezu: Richtiges Auffassen einer Sache und Mißverstehn der gleichen Sache schließen einander nicht vollständig aus" (*P* 297; "The commentators note in this connection: 'The right perception of a matter and a misunderstanding of the same matter do not wholly exclude each other'" [*The Trial*, trans. Willa and Edwin Muir [New York, Schocken Books, 1974], 216]). This exegetical ethos becomes the basis for a Talmudic deliberation on "Vor dem Gesetz" that postulates even the doorkeeper's victimization as somehow central to the impasse forever excluding the man from the country from the Law's splendor.

As it is for Jorge Luis Borges, literature is very much an expansive medium for Kafka.[19] The expansion may be figured as the immensity of China and the project of walling it in, but more often Kafka sets his text-generators to the task of multiplication, or chronicling the matrix of alternatives that literature opens. We see this on a microscopic scale in "Prometheus" where, in a proto-structuralist performance, three variants on the traditional myth progressively weaken and retract its meaning and place in culture. And in *Der Proceß*, the multiplication of the potential meanings of "Vor dem Gesetz" could not be on a grander scale, questioning the very validity of canonical texts as messengers of clear signification.

Not only do the structural variables that Kafka's fiction often takes pains to explore implant a gravitation toward expansiveness within the literary medium; they cancel each other out, undermining the truth-value of the states of affairs that the narrative seems bent on establishing. We have observed this tendency with respect to the parable "Vor dem Gesetz." The Kafkan text, in its specific entertainment of so many possibilities, accelerates the implosion of any clear world-picture or sense of reality that can be gleaned from its language. The sense of a bounded set of conditions and choices that the protagonist faces is even further undermined by the alternatives that the narrative takes up, whether the mayor's explanation of K.'s initial appointment as village land surveyor in *Das Schloß*, or Titorelli's review of the collective but congenitally flawed possibilities for acquittal in the face of a Court prosecution.

The aesthetics of proliferation, then, implicates expansiveness as the most pervasive form of literary negation in Kafka's fiction. Within this domain, dialectic proceeds not by precipitating a new thesis out of controversy, but by undermining the very possibility of resolution, leaving an array of half-baked alternatives in its wake. If psychological terms applied to a situation of this nature, we could say that Kafka devised a passive-aggressive dialectic for his fictive universe. In a fashion that was truly momentous to such writers as Borges, Cortázar, Calvino, and Eco, his fiction opens a breathtaking array of alternatives. But in contrast to speculative fiction or magical realism, Kafka sabotages any sense of exhilaration that might accrue from their realization or tangibility. Kafka leaves us with a universe of narrative possibilities produced under conditions of rigor, but subdued into the indifference on whose plain Samuel Beckett will take up his own endless tale.[20] The aesthetics of proliferation never strays far from the ethos of a very distinctive negation that Kafka borrowed from philosophy and reprogrammed for twentieth-century Western literature with excruciating subtlety and congenital frailty.

The Aesthetics of Suspension

It is no accident, then, that at the ends of things, when matters might be wrapping themselves up, whether in Kafka's novels or toward the end of his corpus as a whole, conditions reach a dead end, a stalemate, an impasse, whose fullest expression is a never-ending sentence, one at which Kafka eventuated, by chance, in the company of Proust, Joyce, Stein, and Beckett. Yet none of Kafka's partners in this venture were as explicit or multifaceted in their demonstration that a crucial measure of writing's freedom, autonomy, and contrariety consists in its capacity to sustain, that is, suspend itself.

A goodly share of Kafka's most memorable images, whether of the Trapeze Artist's travail, the Great Wall's vast compass, the Burrow Creature's self-enclosing labyrinth, or of Gregor, in tribute to the Trapeze Artist, hanging in an inverted posture from the ceiling, circle around literature's capacity to sustain itself in a full range of inhospitable environments. Gregor's and the Trapeze Artist's resistance to gravity and the Hunger Artist's putting off of his nourishment become positional correlatives to a writing practice one of whose prominent characteristics is its inability, or refusal, to end. A significant body of telling twentieth-century literary artifacts shares, or commiserates, in this virtual impossibility of reaching a decisive termination.

The run-on, endlessly self-sustaining and qualifying sentence that Kafka and cohorts bequeath to twentieth-century literature becomes a hallmark of postmodern indifference. By what steps has this artifice of absorption, as Charles Bernstein has termed it,[21] emerged, more often than not, in an enclosed, self-contained setting of sensory deprivation? This is a question, for one, of formal convention and the materiality of language.

The discursive mega-experiment common to "Der Bau" (The Burrow), *Finnegans Wake,* Beckett's *Trilogy,* and Bernhard's *Correction* eludes the *ficciones* of Borges. Why so? I would argue that Borges, at all times, invests so heavily in pastiche, miniaturization, and parody that his fictive discourse is never free to overrun the boundaries set by these forms. "The Library of Babel" may take the liberty to postulate a literary space as vast and sublime as that prevailing in Poe's "Eureka," or in "Beim Bau der Chinesischen Mauer," but it never abandons the parameters of a sci-fi tale. Amid the ebb and flow of their specifically endless elaboration, it is often unclear to what generic conventions "Der Bau" or Beckett's *Trilogy* adhere. "The Garden of Forking Paths," by the same token, is a spy-thriller, condensed to the smallest possible fictive scale. "Death and the Compass" is a work of detective fiction. Borges's demolition of such generic conventions through a strict adherence to their formal specifications belongs to the contractual arrangements of the "structural fabulation"[22] so pivotal to literary modernism.

Kafka, in his gravitation toward the aesthetics of suspension, absorbed his fictive discourse in the materiality of language to a degree beyond the possibilities afforded by the disfiguration and play of structures. "Der Bau" not only synthesizes a relatively new *Stoff* or material for fictive discourse, one distinguished both by density and prolixity; it transpires literally in the ground (or Heideggerian Earth) of language.[23] The location signals a new explicitness in fictive language regarding the material features and accidents that it encompasses. We may thus characterize Kafka's "Der Bau" as a "scene of materiality," to which other distinctive twentieth-century literary productions, as diverse as Beckett's "The Lost Ones,"[24] Bernhard's *Correction,* and Pynchon's *Gravity's Rainbow,* compulsively revert.

Displaced to a setting of subterranean self-enclosure, as in "Der Bau," or to one of antipodal alienation and marginality, as in "Die Verwandlung," the metaphoric substrate to literary figuration achieves an acrobatic extension and prolongation. Indeed, through his exploration of this aesthetics, Kafka contributes to a radical redefinition of literary performance, scale, value, and expectation extending well beyond his works and his days.

The Aesthetics of Transformation

Kafkan metamorphosis, then, in its widest sense, pursues the transmogrification of circumstance, life, existence, futurity, and necessity in and out of writing. It matters not a jot whether Gregor is a dung-beetle, centipede, millipede, praying mantis, or "giant vermin." The true gist and force of his *Verwandlung* is that he becomes a creature of writing. The significance of his predilections, tastes, and desires on the "other side of the looking-glass" of his transformation — really the far side of the picture frame in his bedroom, with its generic "Venus in Furs" photo — is entirely mediated by the obverse worldview of writing. His tastes for bad cheese and good music receive their glimmer of illumination from the travails and contingencies of literary composition. The Burrow Creature's subterranean refuge, fortress, and repository makes sense only as a written space, a writing environment.

The Creature surveys and edits its passages (*CS* 331, 340, 342); it calculates how many carcasses of its prey to allocate from one chamber to the next (329); the compartmental walls are the product of literal head-labor, banging its head against the wall (328). Gregor is a monster who lives out writerly conditions, while the Burrow Creature's lifetime production would be most succinctly characterized as a text.

If Nietzsche subjected the matrix of Western core attitudes to a transvaluation of all values, Kafka effected a comprehensive translation of this broad deconstructive campaign into the materials and resources of literature. (This is in no way to undervalue the literary quality of such works as *Also sprach Zarathustra* or *Der Wille zur Macht*. But Nietzsche, with the gravity that he deplores above all in *Zarathustra*, is nonetheless repeatedly drawn back into ideological confrontations,[25] while Kafka, in the utter marginality ascribed to literature, is free to wander far afield: to China, coal-cellars, and subterranean animal lairs.) Kafka freely exercises his license to extend a wide-ranging ideological transvaluation of values to considerations of sentence-length and fictive dimensionality, narrative perspective and reliability, human and non-human characterization. Indeed, the transition from the radical Nietzschean transvaluation of values to Kafka's abysmal theater of writing may well be indicative of the discursive parameters under which philosophical notation and literary performance both intersect and diverge.

Kafka's extension of a philosophical transvaluation of all values assures that literature, in his wake, will be particularly attentive and susceptible to *becoming*, a becoming-animal, thing, or machine en route to *becoming-text*.[26] Many of the uncanny and sublime features of "Die Verwandlung," "Eine Kreuzung," "Die Sorge des Hausvaters" (The Cares of a Family Man), "Forschungen eines Hundes" (Investigations of a Dog), and "Der Bau" derive simply from the positing of this becoming. Yet as all these tales make clear, there is a destination or horizon to this flux. They eventuate at the intimate, disconcerting, and alien simulation of a textual double: translation into a medium utterly responsive to human faculties, drives, and predilections, but inimical to them, irreducibly, disturbingly. Gregor's transformation transpires in a theater of becoming. Yet more discomfiting than the disfigurations that overcome him is the utter lack of a path back to normality. The reader is an unindicted co-conspirator in this transformative license. For the reader as well, having borne witness to the Kafkan protagonist's doubling and transmogrification into an inhuman simulacrum, the path back to the existential status quo is definitively barred. Gregor's bizarre adventure, like Joseph K.'s trial, initiates the reader into the antipodal sensibility of the philosophy of writing. The reader becomes yet another character implicated and swept beyond recognition by the aesthetics of transformation.

The Aesthetics of Inscription

The prevalent drift of the foregoing is to suggest that for Kafka, art and aesthetics were inseparable from the systematicity and self-propulsion of writing. Inscription — its composition, "read-out," interpretation, sensibility, and effects upon its readers — is the nexus at which Kafka's works originate and where they deposit us in their wake. Kafka's fiction surely draws on the events and features of domains beyond the writer's desk for its settings and their atmosphere, just as it furnishes a critique of extratextual phenomena. Yet such developments as the deterritorialization of Josephine,[27] her fellow mice, and the Burrow Creature, the blatant colonialism and racism prevalent in the Penal Colony, the ambivalent status of the female onlookers in "Ein Hungerkünstler" and "In der Strafkolonie," and even the twentieth-century machines of execution in the latter tale and, of course, at the end of *Der Proceß*, are all explicitly negotiated within a writing process and sensibility set in relief within Kafka's works. At its worst, writing is the terrain that sociopolitical trends, to which Kafka was uncannily acute, had to invade in order to benefit from a distinctly Kafkan poetic transvaluation. In its broadest sense, script encompasses the full range of linguistic devices and textual shapings into which sociopsychological observation must project itself.[28]

Brutal social engineering, the deterritorialization of minorities, and the totalitarian sensibility have all been inscribed in Kafka's work in a telling, because unpredictable, fashion. Kafka's writing makes perfect material for Deleuze and Guattari's joint endeavor, in the *Capitalism and Schizophrenia* diptych as well as in their Kafka study, to fuse a liberationist social critique with a rich appreciation for the complexity of communications systems, the most general of which is language itself. In their terms, Kafka is an aesthetically superior instance of a schizo mentality that bristles at the underlying violence of twentieth-century ideological assemblages and other formations. Yet Deleuze and Guattari themselves demonstrate an exquisite sensibility to the complexities of language, which do not escape the schizo. In view of the foregoing, Deleuze and Guattari should not be taken as a pretext for an essentialistic treatment of identity, gender, class, or race in Kafka. All these factors in social existence register themselves upon the writer. They cannot be processed, however, as somehow discrete or separate from the counter-economy of writing. To impose essentialism on Kafka or any writer ethically engaged in the sorting out and reprogramming of cultural codes is to deprive their implicit critiques of their most trenchant fire. I would argue that the judges, attorneys, and minor officials of the Court in *Der Proceß* survive as one of culture's all-time indictments against authoritarian corruption and excess, not because they comment upon any particular case, injustice, or tangible state of affairs, but because they succeed so thoroughly as creatures of a text in which Kafka addresses such issues with full writerly contrariety. It is because their features and "actions" are so exquisitely formulated that characters such as the examining magistrate, Huld, and Titorelli are infused with the equivocation and the deferral of justice that they embody. To impose essentialisms upon complex cultural artifacts is to short-circuit the critique that they render by way of their writerly and poetic dynamism. At the same time, one can hardly overestimate the healthy skepticism toward and resistance against corrupt sociopolitical systems, evident in the political as well as the artistic domain, that Kafka, as a property of twentieth-century public culture in the West, has inspired. Writing, in the hands of such a practitioner as Kafka, may systematically produce enigmas and complexities; it is never an instrument of repression.

The politics of writing maintains a critical distance from any prevalent state of affairs at the same time that it refuses appreciation by any particular political position, however laudable or deplorable. Kafka had little to regret politically over the course of his too-brief adult life. In "real life," he championed his father's Czech employees, maintained an active interest in the *Ostjuden* who were a cut below the aspirations of assimilated Jews in German-speaking lands, and worked to improve working conditions and workman's compensation at Central European industrial installations. Pound and Borges, whose values and positions were far more suspect, nonetheless achieved in their writings a polyvalence that superseded their political identities. Their senses of social justice surely did not equal Kafka's. The latter, by crystallizing so many of the writerly terrains that were to become the distinctive landscape of twentieth-century literature, facilitated an ongoing critique of that century's unprecedented military aggression, genocide, and disregard for the value of life, a skeptical urgency that extended well beyond his day.

Conclusion

In the above pages, I have attempted to outline and characterize the elements of a highly distinctive aesthetics that may be extrapolated from the pages of Kafka's fiction. I hope to have alighted upon at least a significant number of its interlocking elements. I am certain that other readers can isolate more. I was tempted to posit, for example, "The Aesthetics of Distortion," surely a significant player in the Kafkan modality of representation. But I balked at formulating an overarching model that could account for epiphenomena as singular as Odradek's vocal rattle, the bucket rider's lightness of being, and Leni's webbed digits.

Kafka's prevalent experiments, or art-games, are interrelated, but in no simple way. Their sequence in this essay may be no accident, but I have not discovered any "unified field theory" making each one a specific stage in a plotted game-plan. Surely much of Kafka's fictive "working through," like Benjamin's critical sensibility, extends from the Romantic fascination with the claims and drawbacks of systematicity. Friedrich Schlegel, Kierkegaard, and Nietzsche partially read-out and partially invented the complex interplay of fragmentation, perspectivism, and irony at the margins of the Kantian and Hegelian systems. With uncanny acuity, they zeroed in on the dimensions of systematic aspiration that would be generative of poetic invention. Although in a fictive sphere, Kafka took these writers at their word. From the outset of his fictive production, he was engaged in a literary translation of philosophical objections raised against systematic composition and the ideology accompanying it. There are thus many historical as well as aesthetic pretexts for the placement of the section titled "The Aesthetics of Fragmentation" at the head of the present essay. Yet the other prevalent arenas of Kafka's artwork follow according to no master plot. Instead, there are local neighborhoods of interrelation. It is not difficult to see, for example, how the aesthetics of proliferation and the aesthetics of suspension both follow from the expansive dimension in Kafka's approach to literature, possibly as a shadow system. Or how the aesthetics of inversion and the aesthetics of transformation both emerge from a pervasive Kafkan sense that art should illuminate an antipodal stance toward prevailing norms, values, social structures, and even paradigms of being and existence. All the elements of Kafka's artwork that I have singled out are ultimately interwoven on a common map, which becomes the fingerprint or signature of Kafka's practice of art and writing.

In certain instances, I have indicated which of Kafka's aesthetic experiments and stances were held in common with other, more-or-less contemporary writers. Kafka's singularity does not inhere in the nature of the art-games he played. These belong, in turn, to the universality and impersonality of language, conjured with such power in "Tlön, Uqbar, Orbis Tertius" and other Borgesian *ficciones*. Kafka's singular imprint derives, rather, from the particular combination of the language- and art-games he played, from the relative emphases and values they achieved in his novels and tales, and the very specific linkages between them.

We are drawn again, in closing, to the question why, so obviously and quintessentially, Kafka's productions convey an aesthetics of their own, when other writers, some several times more prolific, do not elicit this sense of system. When this question confronts us, we are implicitly dealing with the issue of whether the weight of an artist's innovation rests upon the generic aesthetic contracts to which her or his contributions subscribe or upon singular revisions to those prevailing conventions.

Not every writer engages in art-games experimental enough and in a distinctive enough combination to merit an aesthetics attributed to him or her. In determining which authors evolved a practice of art and inscription so idiosyncratic that a discrete aesthetics may be ascribed to them, and which, rather, subsumed their productions within pre-existing aesthetic contracts, fine distinctions, no doubt controversy-laden, need to be drawn. Were we hesitant to attribute an autonomous aesthetics to the novels of Honoré de Balzac, Charles Dickens, and George Eliot, this is less owing to any lack of creativity on their part than to the powerful traditions that had accrued to the European post-Romantic novel. It might, on the other hand, prove worthwhile to tease out the values, emphases, and "mix" in a kind of aesthetics initiated by Lawrence Sterne, as Bakhtin and others have done.[29] Kafka and his contemporaries, some of whom have been noted in passing above, ushered in a highly transgressive moment of literary production. I would consider it eminently worthwhile to crystallize the aesthetics of Bruno Schulz and Witold Gombrowicz, even though their work is an outgrowth of a World, in the Heideggerian sense, already familiar to Kafka. Fine work has already been devoted to the particular aesthetic conventions that were appropriated, violated, and retrofitted by the likes of Proust, Joyce, Stein, Beckett, and Borges. The phrase, "a distinctive aesthetics," in this sense, can even be applied to a philosopher or a critic, if of substantial enough cultural vision: to Plato, Wittgenstein, Benjamin, Heidegger, Blanchot, or Derrida, among many others.

I am arguing here that a writer verges on the crystallization of his or her own aesthetics when he or she participates in a substantial transvaluation of prevailing aesthetic contracts. But when an artist's production is easily valorized and legitimated by the conventions in place, when there is a dearth of the tension between new productions and established canons, when there has been no vertigo of uncertainty regarding a production's place in culture, possibly extending to its very comprehensibility, then little new aesthetic groundwork has been laid. Kafka's fiction continues to amuse, disturb, and inspire us in large measure because its parameters at once bound a highly distinctive universe of invention and a singular aesthetic practice that, for all its imitations, appropriations, and other spin-offs, can only be Kafka's.

Notes

[1] I am deeply indebted to James Rolleston for the care and helpfulness of his numerous suggestions.

[2] The present essay may be regarded as an attempt on my part to extend the contractual notion of aesthetics I developed in *The Aesthetic Contract: Statutes of Art and Intellectual Work in Modernity* (Stanford: Stanford UP, 1997) to my lifelong obsession with the writings of Franz Kafka. The central notion of my book is that since the outset of the broader modernity, the ideology of artistic production has been couched in terms of unique and brilliant creativity, a transcendental attribute, inhering to the individuated artist. This ideology has been undermined by the disposition and canonization of artworks according to (collective) contractual understandings of what "works," that is, what answers fundamental epistemological and ontological questions under particular socio-cultural formations. I argue as well that the contractual dynamic so evident, say, in the histories of art and literature, also applies to the market in academic paradigms and models.

[3] An odd creature, part organic, part inorganic, on which the narrator meditates in "Die Sorge des Hausvaters" (The Cares of a Family Man, *CS* 427).

[4] The Wittgensteinian notion of "language games" accords well with my contractual understanding of artistic production as a socio-linguistic phenomenon. In this sense, artists under any particular historico-cultural formation engage in, and stylize, the particular art-games they require in the quest for the epistemological and ontological solutions they seek. The present essay is a by no means comprehensive compendium or primer of the art-games that Kafka, in his fiction and other texts, perfected. It may well be that the distinctive aesthetics of a particular cultural programmer or producer amounts to a survey of the art-games he or she plays and his or her particular delivery with respect to these games. For the pivotal notion of language games, see Ludwig Wittgenstein, *The Blue and the Brown Books* (Oxford: Basil Blackwell, 1964), 17, 81, 92, 116, 125, 138; *Philosophical Investigations* (Oxford: Basil Blackwell, 1984), 179–80, 184, 190, 197, 200, 217, 224–25.

[5] Iterability is a philosophical term found in the work of John Austin and John Searle that regards possibilities of repetition and contextualization in language. Jacques Derrida, in his engagement with these philosophers, enlarges the meaning of this term, taking issue with Austin and Searle's limited deployment of it. See the following articles by John R. Searle: *Speech Acts: An Essay in the Philosophy of Language* 55, 74; "Austin on Locutionary and Illocutionary Acts," *Philosophical Review* (1968); "A Taxonomy of Illocutionary Acts," *Minnesota Studies in the Philosophy of Science 6* (1975); "The Logical Status of Fictional Discourse," *New Literary History* 5 (1975); "Reiterating the Differences: A Reply to Derrida," in *Glyph 1*, ed. Samuel Weber and

Henry Sussman, 198–208. Also see Jacques Derrida, "Signature, Event, Context," in *Glyph 1* 172–97; "Limited Inc," in *Glyph 2,* 162–254.

[6] I think above all of the systematic architecture of *The Critique of Pure Reason,* also known as the First Critique, surely Kant's most comprehensive attempt to synchronize human faculties and tendencies with the limited superhuman infrastructure, the Kantian Transcendental, embedded in the universe. None of Kant's other works convey this degree of systematic aspiration. It sets the standard to which, among others, Hegel, Kierkegaard, Nietzsche, and Kafka react.

[7] "The Analytic of the Sublime," of course, forms part of Kant's *Critique of Judgment,* otherwise known as his Third Critique. I have elsewhere commented on the Kantian sublime and its implications for psychology and aesthetics. See my *Psyche and Text: The Sublime and the Grandiose in Literature, Psychopathology, and Culture* (Albany: SUNY Press, 1993), 27–43; *The Aesthetic Contract,* 134–62.

[8] This is a term that Walter Benjamin, in his 1934 Kafka study, devised to characterize the fragmentariness of the novels and the parables. Walter Benjamin, "Franz Kafka," in *Selected Writings* (Cambridge: Harvard UP, 1999), 2: 802.

[9] Thomas Pynchon, *Gravity's Rainbow* (New York: Penguin, 1987), 48, 90, 192, 237, 241, 251, 262.

[10] Immanuel Kant, *Critique of Pure Reason,* trans. Norman Kemp Smith (New York: St. Martin's, 1933), 384–484.

[11] Kant 299–300.

[12] One thinks, among many other possible texts, of Poe's "William Wilson," E. T. A. Hoffmann's "Die Doppeltgänger," Joseph Conrad's "The Secret Sharer" and Fyodor Dostoyevsky's "The Double" and *Notes from the Underground.*

[13] Maurice Blanchot, *The Space of Literature* (Lincoln: U of Nebraska P, 1989), 21–22, 31, 58–59, 61–62, 75, 77, 87–96; *The Gaze of Literature* (Barrytown, NY: Station Hill, 1981), 51, 56–62, 81–89.

[14] See my *The Aesthetic Contract* 202–4, 246, 258–59.

[15] Gilles Deleuze and Félix Guattari, *Anti-Oedipus* (Minneapolis: U of Minnesota P, 1983), 2–4, 33–37, 86–87, 132–33, 232–33, 243–46.

[16] The two "wings" of the diptych are *Anti-Oedipus* and *A Thousand Plateaus* (Minneapolis: U of Minnesota P, 1983, 1987).

[17] I am thinking, of course, of Einsteinian relativity and Bergsonian duration. See Henri Bergson, *Matter and Memory* (New York: Zone, 1991), 34–41, 70–74, 138, 186–91, 221.

[18] The first of these terms is developed by Jacques Derrida relatively early in his writings to figure a possible relationship between the mainstream of systematic philosophy to its margins or "outside"; the second is also a long-standing Derridean term for textual appropriation in all its admiration and violence. See Jacques Derrida, *Of Grammatology,* trans. Gayatri Chakravorty Spivak (Baltimore: Johns Hopkins UP, 1976), 65–73, 265; "The Double Session," in *Dissemination,* trans. Barbara Johnson (Chicago: U of Chicago P, 1981), 202.

[19] Readers of a certain morbid disposition may wish to track down this very old case, "The Court as Text: Inversion, Supplanting, and Derangement in Kafka's *Der Pro-*

zeß," *PMLA* 92: 41–55, reprinted in my *Franz Kafka: Geometrician of Metaphor* (Madison, WI: Coda, 1978), 83–112.

[20] I think of the "boundless odor of the eucalypti" awaiting the Borgesian detective Lönnrot at the villa in "Death and the Compass," where he both solves a series of murders and meets his fate. See Jorge Luis Borges, *Ficciones* (New York: Grove, 1962), 122.

[21] For a discussion of postmodern indifference and its operation in Beckett's fiction, see my *Afterimages of Modernity* 175–84.

[22] See Charles Bernstein, "Artifice of Absorption," in *A Poetics* (Cambridge: Harvard UP, 1992), 9–89.

[23] This is a wonderful term devised by Robert Scholes. See his *Structural Fabulation: An Essay on Fiction of the Future* (Notre Dame: U of Notre Dame P, 1975).

[24] For a discussion of how a distinctive fabric or material becomes a major aim of twentieth-century American poetry and poetics, see my *High Resolution: Critical Theory and the Problem of Literacy* (New York: Oxford UP, 1989), 128–31. According to the historiography that Martin Heidegger embeds in his pivotal essay, "The Origin of the Work of Art," the artwork resides at the interstice between Earth and World, that is, between ongoing features of culture and subjectivity and time-specific considerations, whatever their modality (e.g., nationality, historical epoch). The Heideggerian distinction here bears striking similarities to the Saussurian division of labor between, respectively, the synchronic and the diachronic. See Martin Heidegger, "The Origin of the Work of Art," in his *Poetry, Language, Thought* (New York: Harper and Row, 1971), 34, 42, 44–46, 48–49, 53. For Saussure's distinction between the synchronic and the diachronic, see Ferdinand de Saussure, *Course in General Linguistics* (New York: McGraw-Hill, 1959), 81–89, 98–102.

[24] Samuel Beckett, "The Lost Ones," in *The Complete Short Prose: 1929–1989* (New York: Grove, 1995), 202–23.

[25] The camel, in the animal symbolism of *Also sprach Zarathustra,* is the beast of gravity. See *Thus Spoke Zarathustra,* trans. Walter Kaufmann (New York: Penguin, 1966), 25–26, 41, 107, 187, 191–95, 197, 310.

[26] Becoming-text is, of course, a variant on explorations of the concept of becoming, such as becoming-animal and becoming-death, that Deleuze and Guattari explore, above all in the *Capitalism and Schizophrenia* diptych. I am also much indebted to the possibilities of becoming that my colleague Elizabeth Grosz has elaborated, above all in relation to Bergson and Darwin, in recent writings and in several lectures coinciding with her arrival on the University at Buffalo campus.

[27] The notion of deterritorialization is a construct worked out by Deleuze and Guattari with particular force in their Kafka study. See Gilles Deleuze and Félix Guattari, *Kafka: Pour une littérature mineure* (Paris: Minuit, 1975), 27–30, 34–38, 142. Also see their *A Thousand Plateaus* 32–33, 40, 54, 61, 65, 70, 87–88, 91, 99, 109, 112, 117, 129, 133–35, 180.

[28] The fullest current exploration of inscription, in relation to ideology, culture, and academic debate, has been made by Tom Cohen. I strongly recommend his *Ideology and Inscription* (New York: Cambridge UP, 1998).

[29] See Mikhail Bakhtin, *The Dialogic Imagination* (Austin: U of Texas P, 1981), 164–66, 235–37, 275, 301–10, 362.

Works Cited

Bakhtin, Mikhail. *The Dialogic Imagination.* Trans. C. Emerson and M. Holquist. Austin: U of Texas P, 1981.

Beckett, Samuel. *The Complete Short Prose: 1929–1989.* New York: Grove, 1995.

Benjamin, Walter. *Selected Writings.* Cambridge: Harvard UP, 1999.

Bergson, Henri. *Matter and Memory.* Trans. N. M. Paul and W. S. Palmer. New York: Zone, 1991.

Bernstein, Charles. *A Poetics.* Cambridge: Harvard UP, 1992.

Blanchot, Maurice. *The Gaze of Literature.* Trans. Lydia Davis. Barrytown, NY: Station Hill, 1981.

———. *The Space of Literature.* Trans. Ann Smock. Lincoln: U of Nebraska P, 1989.

Borges, Jorge Luis. *Ficciones.* New York: Grove, 1962.

Cohen, Tom. *Ideology and Inscription.* New York: Cambridge UP, 1998.

Deleuze, Gilles, and Felix Guattari. *Kafka: Pour une littérature mineure.* Paris: Minuit, 1975.

———. *Anti-Oedipus.* Trans. R. Hurley, M. Seem, and H. R. Lane. Minneapolis: U of Minnesota P, 1983.

———. *A Thousand Plateaus.* Trans. Brian Massumi. Minneapolis: U of Minnesota P, 1987.

Derrida, Jacques. *Of Grammatology.* Trans. Gayatri Chakravorty Spivak. Baltimore: The Johns Hopkins UP, 1976.

———. "Limited Inc." *Glyph 2* (1977): 162–254.

———. "Signature, Event, Context." *Glyph 1* (1977): 198–208.

———. *Dissemination.* Trans. Barbara Johnson. Chicago: U of Chicago P, 1981.

Heidegger, Martin. *Poetry, Language, Thought.* Trans. Albert Hofstadter. New York: Harper and Row, 1971.

Kafka, Franz. *Sämtliche Erzählungen.* Ed. Paul Raabe. Frankfurt am Main: S. Fischer, 1967. (*SE*)

———. *The Castle.* Trans. Willa and Edwin Muir. New York: Schocken, 1974. (*Castle*)

———. *The Trial.* Trans. Willa and Edwin Muir. New York: Schocken, 1974.

―――. *The Complete Stories*. Ed. Nahum N. Glatzer. New York: Schocken, 1976. (*CS*)

―――. *Das Schloss*. Ed. Malcolm Pasley. Frankfurt am Main: S. Fischer, 1982, 1994. (*S*)

―――. *Der Process*. Ed. Malcolm Pasley. Frankfurt am Main: S. Fischer, 1990. (*P*).

Kant, Immanuel. *Critique of Pure Reason*. Trans. Norman Kemp Smith. New York: St. Martin's, 1933.

Nietzsche, Friedrich. *Thus Spoke Zarathustra*. Trans. Walter Kaufmann. New York: Penguin, 1966.

Pynchon, Thomas. *Gravity's Rainbow*. New York: Penguin, 1987.

Saussure, Ferdinand de. *Course in General Linguistics*. Trans. Wade Baskin. New York: McGraw-Hill, 1959.

Searle, John R. "Austin on Locutionary and Illocutionary Acts." *Philosophical Review* (1968).

―――. *Speech Acts: An Essay in the Philosophy of Language*. London: Cambridge UP, 1970.

―――. "The Logical Status of Fictional Discourse." *New Literary History* 5 (1975).

―――. "A Taxonomy of Illocutionary Acts." *Minnesota Studies in the Philosophy of Science* 6 (1975).

―――. "Reiterating the Differences: A Reply to Derrida." *Glyph 1* (1977).

Scholes, Robert. *Structural Fabulation: An Essay on Fiction of the Future*. Notre Dame: U of Notre Dame P, 1975.

Sussman, Henry. *Franz Kafka: Geometrician of Metaphor*. Madison: Coda Press, 1978.

―――. *High Resolution: Critical Theory and the Problem of Literacy*. New York: Oxford UP, 1989.

―――. *Afterimages of Modernity*. Baltimore: The Johns Hopkins UP, 1990.

―――. *Psyche and Text: The Sublime and the Grandiose in Literature, Psychopathology and Culture*. Albany: SUNY Press, 1993.

―――. *The Aesthetic Contract: Statutes of Art and Intellectual Work in Modernity*. Stanford: Stanford UP, 1997.

Wittgenstein, Ludwig. *The Blue and the Brown Books*. Oxford: Basil Blackwell, 1964.

―――. *Philosophical Investigations*. Oxford: Basil Blackwell, 1984.

Medial Allusions at the Outset of *Der Proceß*; or, *res in media*

Stanley Corngold

"Schuldig ist die Organisation"

FROM THE OUTSET, the narrative of *Der Proceß* (The Trial) displays medial variations of more than one kind. The basic medial intrusion is theater.[1] This theatrical performance includes ("intermediates"), however, a second and a third medial instance: first, popular literature, especially travel literature; and second, the consciousness of the archive, of the very manuscript from which the diegesis, the world of the novel, emerges. Kafka's seemingly inexhaustible ability to enact and dramatize modes of presentation (*Vorstellung*) and of reading includes even the kinds of critical attention paid to his work by readers having a fully saturated consciousness of media. "Types of Kafka interpretation can be identified and their validity measured by a scrutiny of the work, which unfolds as the adventurous combat of principles authorizing interpretations" (Corngold, *The Commentators' Despair* v). This sentence was written in 1973. Some thirty years later — after guerilla theater; after the emergent claim that modernism in literature is defined by its absorption of popular culture; above all, after the expansion of the electronic archive — this point about Kafka's wide consciousness of the formal, medial constraints on interpretation still seems correct.

In *Der Proceß*, the scenic element of theater ("die Schaustellung" [the "show"]; "die Komödie" [the "farce"]: *P* 12; *Tr* 7)[2] is penetrated throughout by a scriptive element ("das in Schrift Gestellte" [that which is put in writing], "das Buch" [the book]: *P* 9; "das Schriftstück," "die Papiere" [the papers]: *P* 12). Here the problematic imbrication of the visible Court and the (in principle) readable Law is enacted by the crossing of the media — the visible and the readable — *res in media*. The outcome of this scriptive medial intrusion will be — not the "clarification" ("Klarstellung": *P* 22, *Tr* 14) that K. requires — but, rather, his being stabbed to death.

Consider how these medial interferences play out. From the very first page, *Der Proceß* is a play within a narrative. On awakening, Josef K. is "put out" ("befremdet": *P* 7, *Tr* 3) not to have been brought his breakfast: it is past eight o'clock and Anna the cook, a holdover from "Die Verwandlung" (The Metamorphosis), usually brings him his breakfast before eight o'clock.[3] Upon noting this absence of cook and breakfast, K. does immediately notice the presence of something. This is a scene made instructive by Jean-Jacques Rousseau's *Second Walk,* in which Rousseau, having fallen unconscious as a result of a collision with a Great Dane ("un gros chien danois"), awakens — and bit by bit perceives — and hence constitutes, as if for the first time, the human world as a pastoral: "the sky, some stars, and a little greenery" ("le ciel, quelques étoiles, et un peu de verdure," *Oeuvres* 1:1004–1005). "This first sensation was a delicious moment. I still had no feeling of myself except as being 'over there' (*par là*). I was born into life at that instant, and it seemed to me that I filled all the objects I perceived with my frail existence. . . . A rapturous calm pervaded my whole being. . . ." (*Reveries* 15–16, translation modified, SC).

Otherwise with Josef K., who on awakening sees — what? Another's stare: "die alte Frau die ihm gegenüber wohnte und die ihn mit einer an ihr ganz ungewöhnlichen Neugierde beobachtete" (*P* 7; "the old woman who lived across the way, who was peering at him with a curiosity quite unusual for her," *Tr* 3). K. constitutes his world as the event of being stared at by another, so that anything he thereafter sees and does falls under the sway of the Other's stare. His moment of awakening out of his bewilderment is to see himself figure as the element in another's seen world. His attempt to constitute a world performs the Other's world, meaning that he is no longer a subject — which is to say: the protected spectator of his own actions — but the exposed object of another's spectatorship — he is an "actor." And now it is as if every judgment he makes on his own experience must be referred to a complex of powers or forces stemming from the Other, must be seen as capable of vexing or, then again, as appeasing the judgment implicit in the Other's stare — and henceforth his judgments can be made only in spite of the Other or in accord with the Other. It all must figure as something of a clamp, as if to be "verhaftet" (arrested) were principally to be trapped in the niche of the prisoner of the panopticon.

On next ringing for his breakfast (and with this ringing of the bell: Let the play begin!), Josef K. is disarmed by the appearance in his bedroom of a man he has never seen before. The man is wearing a jacket suggestive of a tourist's, "mit verschiedenen Falten, Taschen, Schnallen, Knöpfen und einem Gürtel . . . [das,] ohne daß man sich darüber klar wurde, wozu es dienen sollte, besonders praktisch erschien" (*P 7*; "with a variety of pleats, pockets, buckles, buttons and a belt — [one that looks] eminently practical [although] its purpose remained obscure," *Tr 3*).

The fit of this event with the event of being seen is perfect: the effect of being seen (and hence judged in the act of seeing) by a remote pair of eyes — hence, quite possibly always thus being seen — must provoke the second question: On the inevitable appearance of another (real) human counterpart, how shall one figure the stare of this particular Other? Does it belong together with the stare of the abstract Other, as constituted by the old woman in her loge? The question on the face of it is undecidable — and as worrisome as it is undecidable. The only relief might be in the super-identification of the particular Other, his minute specification. Scrutinized with great precision, do the colors he wears suggest his allegiance to the party of the Other or his independence of it: is he friend or foe?

One could recall, for corroboration of this gesture, the moment in "Erste Untersuchung," when K., at his most paranoid, studies

> . . . [die] Gesichter rings um ihn! Kleine schwarze Äuglein huschten hin und her, die Wangen hiengen herab, wie bei Versoffenen, die langen Bärte waren steif und schütter und griff man in sie, so war es als bilde man bloß Krallen, nicht als griffe man in Bärte. Unter den Bärten aber — und das war die eigentliche Entdeckung, die K. machte — schimmerten am Rockkragen Abzeichen in verschiedener Größe und Farbe. Alle hatten diese Abzeichen, soweit man sehen konnte. Alle gehörten zu einander, die scheinbaren Parteien rechts und links, und als er sich plötzlich umdrehte, sah er die gleichen Abzeichen am Kragen des Untersuchungsrichters . . . (*P 71*)

> [The faces that surrounded him! *Tiny black eyes darted about,* cheeks drooped like those of drunken men, the long beards were stiff and scraggly, and when they pulled on them, it seemed as if they were merely forming claws, not pulling beards. Beneath the beards, however — and this was the true discovery K. made — badges of various sizes and colors shimmered on the collars of their jackets. They all had badges, so far as he could see. They were all one group, the parties on the left and right, and as he suddenly turned, he saw the same badges on the collar of the examining magistrate. . . . *Tr 51–52*, emphasis added, SC)]

His paranoia is accomplished.

Now, at the opening scene of his process, K. studies the rich specificity of the tourist-figure before him, the abundance of pleats, pockets, buckles, buttons, and belts sewed into this fetish-bearer whose name will be: Franz — K.'s, Kafka's, monstrous and seductive bisexual Other within — but here outed and exposed in the service of an adversarial world, a structure of relations unsurprising in an author who wrote, "Im Kampf zwischen Dir und der Welt sekundiere der Welt" (*BB* 236; In the struggle between you and the world, back the world). This "Franz" is now a killing agent of the Court.

But beyond perceiving the purposiveness of his costume or mask, K. cannot tell what its purpose is and hence cannot tell the purpose of the figure. This abundance, this surplus of signs without meaning, points to a certain remoteness in relation to the scene: and indeed this Franz is a traveler, though we cannot say whether it is because he is now prepared to travel away from Josef K.'s bedroom, with Josef K. in tow (his black jacket might anticipate the deadly black "Gehröcke" [*P* 305; "frock coats," *Tr* 225] worn by K.'s executioners in the final chapter); or, perhaps, more tellingly, whether he is a traveler whose long journey has now come to an end with his arrival at K.'s; and the pleats, belts, buckles are to serve a purpose that K. will experience at first hand, at home. Says the warden: "You'll feel it eventually" (*Tr* 9) or — more potently, more menacingly in the German — "Sie werden es zu fühlen bekommen" (*P* 15; You'll find out first-hand).

This, now — after the theater or indeed inside the theater — is the second medial allusion, an allusion to Kafka's ongoing preoccupation with travel literature and especially, as one can learn from a book in preparation by John Zilcosky, an allusion to "Kafka's beloved imperial adventure novels, *Schaffsteins Grüne Bändchen* (Little Green Books) (1910ff)" (ms 26). Zilcosky's work suggests that Kafka dreamt of traveling to a newfound land — on the model of his Uncle Alfred, who did indeed become director general of the Spanish Railways in Madrid (Pawel 10). Kafka then abandoned the dream; and the punishment for the abandonment of the dream is to stay at home and become the destination of another's travels, the second self who went away.

The presence of a second self will be marked, as I've said, with the name "Franz"; and I am proposing "paranoia" as the perverse of Kafka's Green-book-colored travel-lust, which invariably has a fin-de-siècle sexual and exploitative character. The charm of foreign lands is that they offer a pool of available "subjects" of erotic and sadistic exploitation. What would it mean to guiltily abandon — not renounce — but abandon through anxiety and lassitude one's erotic and sadistic desires, if not to court the punishment that is its mirror obverse: one will become oneself the impending subject of erotic and sadistic exploitation by the traveler who does travel, who does set off on the long journey that will bring him into the bedroom of Josef K.

Mark Anderson suggests that K. has been raped; Zilcosky develops the argument:

> This [black tourist's] suit is one of Kafka's trademark symbols of "Verkehr," a conceptual node that, through the word's double meaning, connects "traffic" with "(sexual) intercourse" throughout Kafka's work [Cf. Anderson].[4] The warder's suit, as a marker for "Verkehr," indeed points to what Anderson refers to as the "rape" of K. (161). K., we remember, claims to have been "molested" [belästigt] (*P* 88) in his bed, dressed, like a Kleistian rape victim, only in a blouse-like "nightshirt" [Nachthemd] (*Tr* 5, *P* 10). As we discover later, the man in the "traveling" suit leaves K.'s room with his usual sexual trophies (K.'s underwear). . . . (ms 131–32)

The rape is K.'s undercurrent projection.[5] The wider name for his predicament is paranoia; the more anodyne term, "performance" — a play: K. will perform a play to escape his paranoid arrest or seizure, by clarifying it. With this gesture (the play), the more drastic workings of his paranoia will be delayed, just as the violence of his sexual imagination will be pushed into the background until it too springs out.

The analogy of K.'s opening moves with the opening of a play is explicit. K. says to Franz: "Ich will weder hierbleiben noch von Ihnen angesprochen werden, solange Sie sich mir nicht vorstellen" (*P* 8; "I have no wish to stay here, nor to be addressed by you, until you've introduced yourself," *Tr* 4). The act of "Sichvorstellen" (introducing himself) is not forthcoming in the bedroom and hence dictates that if there is to be such a *Vorstellung* or theatrical presentation of sorts, it will have to be provoked by K. and take place in another room. With perfect consistency, "der Fremde" (the stranger) — "Franz" — "öffnete nun freiwillig die Tür" (*P* 8; "opened the door of his own accord," *Tr* 4). This way K. can escape the oppression of his bedroom, the world of "Fr-," exchanging it for the adjacent room, Frau G.'s sitting room [thus, by connotation, also exchanging Frieda (Felice Bauer's cover name) for Grete Bloch/Grubach],[6] a room that appears unchanged except for seeming less cluttered, more open: the impression is of the deck having been cleared, of a room that has been turned into a stage, now in the service of a play, in which K. will attempt to affirm his public authority.

More than once, it is K. who forces the metaphor of the play onto his effort to escape his situation of being seen. He thinks: "War es eine Komödie, so wollte er mitspielen" (*P* 12; "If this was a farce, he was going to play along," *Tr* 7). This prepares the language of his protest to the inspector: "Sie wollen einen Sinn [dafür, daß ich dem Staatsanwalt telephonieren will] und führen das Sinnloseste auf was es gibt?" (*P* 23; "You ask what sense it makes [to telephone the public prosecutor], while you stage the most senseless performance imaginable?" *Tr* 15). Even of his killers, at the close, he says, to diminish their power, "Alte untergeordnete Schauspieler schickt man um mich . . ." and to them: "An welchem Teater spielen Sie [?]" (*P* 306; "They've sent old supporting actors for me . . ."; "Which theater are you playing at?" *Tr* 226).

Now, in Frau Grubach's sitting room, the second warder, not Franz, is the first to speak, in effect ordering K. to return to his bedroom, whereupon K. replies, "Ja, was wollen Sie denn?" (*P* 9; "What is it you want, then?" *Tr* 5) and with this "wollen" appears to constitute the Other as "Einer, der was will" (someone who wants something), "einer, dessen Willen eine Absicht zugeschrieben wird" (someone, to whose will an object is attributed), "einem Willen" — or, put simply: Will*em*. That is the name the guard is given, in this scene of name-giving; and later we have a corroborative formulation, for, on replying to K. he is identified as "der Wächter, der Willem genannt worden war" (*P* 15; the guard who had been named Willem) and not as Breon Mitchell has it, in his otherwise admirable translation, "the guard called Willem" (*Tr* 9). To this extent, not only a situation, with charges and countercharges, but even named persons are constituted performatively.

Consistently, in this scene of naming, the main import of what Willem says is to refer K. to the second warder, who is now formally introduced as "Franz," a gesture that produces K.'s — Kafka's? — wondering stare — Franz? — as one might expect. (It is not surprising, with touches like these, that Kafka and his listeners, when Kafka read this chapter aloud to them, could not go on for sheer hilarity.) So what we've chiefly had, then, in this scene, is an exchange of glances between K. and a man reading a book by an open window and then a glance back to Franz before K. must experience with a renewed impact his situation as a player of a play. The window, even as an open window, is not an opening out and away to a freer zone but a space filled entirely by the perception of being perceived, for "Durch das offene Fenster erblickte man wieder die alte Frau, die mit wahrhaft greisenhafter Neugierde zu dem jetzt gegenüberliegenden Fenster getreten war, um auch weiterhin alles zu sehen" (*P* 9; "through the open window the old woman was visible again, having moved with truly senile curiosity to the window directly opposite, so she could keep an eye on everything," *Tr* 5). Moments later, too, "er [K.] sah die alte Frau, die einen noch viel ältern Greis zum Fenster gezerrt hatte, den sie umschlungen hielt" (*P* 15; "He [K.] saw the old woman, who had pulled an ancient man far older than herself to the window and had her arms wrapped about him," *Tr* 9); and that's not all:

> "Im gegenüberliegenden Fenster lagen wieder die zwei Alten, doch hatte sich ihre Gesellschaft vergrößert, denn hinter ihnen sie weit überragend stand ein Mann mit einem auf der Brust offenen Hemd, der seinen rötlichen Spitzbart mit den Fingern drückte und drehte." (*P* 20)

> [Across the way, the old couple were again at the opposite window, but their party had increased in number, for towering behind them stood a man with his shirt open at the chest, pinching and twisting his reddish goatee. (*Tr* 12–13)]

They are members of the audience to join the gaping cast already on stage. Even K. identifies the figures in the window as such: "Dort sind auch solche Zuschauer" (*P* 24; "There's more of the audience over there," *Tr* 15). A persecutory audience on all sides seals the theatrical space: *fenêtres closes*.

Whereupon K., depriving Willem in advance of an answer to the question of what he wants, answers the question for him: "Ich will doch Frau Grubach —" (*P* 9; "I'd still like Frau Grubach —" *Tr* 5). Just as in the first instance of his perceiving himself being perceived, Josef K.'s remedial move was to ring for a woman — Anna, Frau Grubach's maid; now, again perceiving himself being perceived, he demands Frau Grubach: The woman will rescue him from this space of windows opening onto yet other windows to reveal the stare of the Other reflecting himself. Woman as beneficent reality, woman as the anti-paranoid: K. will say later on, "Nur Ihr Urteil [der Frau Grubach], das Urteil einer vernünftigen Frau wollte ich hören und bin sehr froh, daß wir darin übereinstimmen" (*P* 34; "I just wanted to hear your judgment on the matter [Frau Grubach], the judgment of a sensible woman, and I'm glad we agree about it," *Tr* 23–24). Is this not a figure in small for the construction of interpersonality throughout the entire work? The chaplain, moreover, will reprove K. for this expedient; one recalls: "Du suchst zuviel fremde Hilfe . . . und besonders bei Frauen" (*P* 289; "You seek too much outside help, . . . particularly from women," *Tr* 213).

The Archive

What has been happening at the order of scenic event and gesture is now mirrored in remarkable fashion at the order of verbal exchange: the third — and most surprising — medial intrusion.

In response to K.'s *Willensäußerung,* to the expression of his will, Willem throws down his book. In response to K.'s "I'd still like Frau Grubach," Willem produces his key reply: "Nein . . . Sie dürfen nicht weggehen, Sie sind ja gefangen" (*P* 9; "No, . . . you may not go, you're being held," *Tr* 5), with the word "ja" connoting "as things are" or "as anyone can see" or "right?" It is evident from Reuß's manuscript edition[7] that Kafka indeed wrote the word "gefangen" (held, caught) (Reuß ed., "Jemand," 9). Yet in the older, until recently standard German edition — that of Max Brod — the sentence reads: "Sie sind ja verhaftet" (11); and, hence, in the older, until recently standard English translation of Willa and Edwin Muir, as revised by E. M. Butler, the sentence reads: "You are arrested" (5–6). It is as if Willem has found his (correct) lines in the script/manuscript that he was reading and can now toss "the book" aside and speak his line — a line that, with its little word "ja," is very productive and very apt at the outset of a drama. Why?

Consider that the opening spoken lines of a drama are drastically more limited in their power to stage a scene than the principally long and reflective lines of a novel. The opening lines of a drama require the greater suspension of the claim on intelligibility by an audience or by a performer who does not possess the script in advance, because neither we nor he knows the world to which the words refer. Every successive line is in principle clearer, since it has more evidence, within the stage world, to refer back to; the first lines have nothing. What is eye-catching and fitting is the little word "ja" with which Willem announces K.'s being "held" or "caught," since its thrust is to move the drama back to a virtual moment when an understanding had already been reached, as if the communicative situation among the players had been pre-established. The "ja" seeks to quench the thirst for intelligible reference of the referentially-deprived opening lines of the drama.

Now, the play within *Der Proceß* is, to be sure, a play within a frame narrative. Hence a certain kind of precedence does go to the frame in which it is embedded, though that precedent narrative is decidedly brief, consisting entirely of the sentence: "Jemand mußte Josef K. verleumdet [Reuß: "verläumdet"] haben, denn ohne daß er etwas Böses getan hätte, wurde [Reuß: "war" crossed out] er eines Morgens verhaftet [Reuß: "gefangen" crossed out]" (*P* 7 [variants from Reuß ed., "Jemand," 2]; "Someone must have slandered Josef K., for one morning, without having done anything truly wrong, he was arrested," *Tr* 3). This is a rhetorical moment of great importance. In the manuscript, the German word "gefangen" (held, caught) has been crossed out by Kafka and replaced by "verhaftet" (arrested). We must keep this frame sentence in mind, since it will establish the crux that we now intend to resolve.

Let us return to Willem's odd remark, "Sie sind ja gefangen" (*P* 9; "You're being held," *Tr* 5). Clayton Koelb was the first to elaborate the speech-act implications of the little word "ja," to point out the performative character of this utterance owing to this little word, since the intelligibility of the utterance is not based on anything that precedes it in the diegesis (Koelb 43–50); its intelligibility must be constituted for the first time by the person to whom it is addressed and who is free (1) to consent to a prior understanding, which the sentence assumes — or (2) deny it — or (3) evade it — or (4) simulate any of the foregoing. Furthermore: Willem's statement must provoke an acknowledgement of (or a refusal to acknowledge) the communicative situation as such, since this "ja," meaning, "Well, isn't it so?" refers to a communicative state of affairs allegedly already established between the speakers. Finally — the bottom line — with either a yes or no answer, K. is agreeing to perform the speech act scripted by the Other and to accede to his own captivity. So with typical, but in this instance quite understandable indecision, K. replies: "Es sieht so aus" (*P* 9; "So it appears," *Tr* 5), which is just enough to keep the communicative situation unsettled but not destroyed and *Der Proceß* in motion.

What follows is indeed a crazy speech, a discussion about K.'s bribing his warders with silk underwear. It is talk of the rhetorical ilk that Kafka calls "family language," of the kind memorably illustrated in the following 1912 passage from his *Tagebücher:*

Im Nebenzimmer . . . sprechen sie über Ungeziefer und Hühneraugen . . . Man sieht leicht an, daß durch solche Gespräche kein eigentlicher Fortschritt eintritt. Es sind Mitteilungen, die von beiden wieder vergessen werden und die schon jetzt ohne Verantwortungsgefühl in Selbstvergessenheit vor sich gehn. Eben deshalb aber weil solche Gespräche ohne Entrückung nicht denkbar sind, zeigen sie leere Räume, die wenn man dabei bleiben will, nur mit Nachdenken oder besser Träumen ausgefüllt werden können. (*T* 412–13)

[In the next room . . . they are talking about vermin and corns. . . . It is easy to see that there is no real progress made in conversations of this sort. It is information that will be forgotten again by both and that even now proceeds along in self-forgetfulness without any sense of responsibility. But for the very reason that such conversations are unthinkable without absent-mindedness, they reveal empty spaces which, if one insists, can be filled only by thinking, or, better yet, by dreams. (*Diaries* 258)]

This act of critical augmentation, in the absence of dreams, is exactly what we are attempting.

Finally, we need to look at one more short exchange; for I plan to resolve an aporia — the crux concerning the terms "gefangen" and "verhaftet" — by means of a medial segue to the manuscripts.

A few pages later, then, after K. has asked why Frau Grubach wasn't permitted to enter, Willem says: "Sie darf nicht. . . . Sie sind doch verhaftet" (*P* 13; "She's not allowed to. . . . After all, you're under arrest," *Tr* 8). Thus the manuscript sequence has read, starting with the frame narrative: Josef K. was "gefangen," which was crossed out and replaced by "verhaftet" (*P* 7); next: "Sie sind ja gefangen" (*P* 9; "You're being held" *Tr* 5); thereafter, "Sie sind doch verhaftet" (*P* 13; "After all, you're under arrest," *Tr* 8).

In a previous paper on this question, I argued for emending the word "gefangen" in the second case, à la Max Brod, to "verhaftet," on the putative grounds that "Kafka nodded," in order to bring this moment into the hermeneutically rich force field established by the two other instances of "verhaftet," the one preceding it and the one following it. I concluded: "What effect on Koelb's discussion [of the interesting manner in which the authority of the Court is constituted recursively, SC] have Pasley's and Reuß's 'purification' of Brod's version of the second of the three instances from '*verhaftet*' (arrested, under arrest) to '*gefangen*' (held)? For, in the present situation, the third exchange no longer returns to the second (since the third is about being '*verhaftet*' [arrested] but the second is about being '*gefangen*' [held]); and, hence, the entire argument about how the authority of the Court is constituted by an endless recursiveness of the performative utterance (from '*doch*' [after all] back to '*ja*' [implying 'Well, isn't it so?'] and the pseudo-agreement of 'so it appears') is jeopardized. Or does the purification, in the second instance, of '*verhaftet*' to the original '*gefangen*' only make matters more complexly interesting?"

That is what I hope to show in the remainder of this essay. Let us attribute to Kafka himself, the author of *Der Proceß*, a complete knowledge of the process of composition. Then he is fully aware of a history of events occurring not only at the level of the diegesis but at the level, too, of scription — the making of the manuscript. Now, Malcolm Pasley has already discussed a number of explicit intersections of these worlds as part of what he calls "the parallel process run through by fictional events and the acts of writing that produced them." These intersections produce effects of wit, as the forcible yoking together of dissimilars. "The two processes — the two 'trials,'" Pasley continues, "reciprocally determine one another and at certain places even appear to fuse — in an amazing way" (22).

One such prize example occurs in "Ende," the chapter Kafka wrote as he was writing the first chapter, called by Pasley in his edition "Verhaftung" (Arrest). K. is on the way to his execution and urges himself "den ruhig einteilenden Verstand [zu] behalten" ("to keep my mind calm and analytical to the last"), adding: "Soll ich nun zeigen, daß nicht einmal der einjährige Process mich belehren konnte? . . . Soll man mir nachsagen dürfen, daß ich am Anfang des Processes ihn beenden und jetzt an seinem Ende ihn wieder beginnen will" (*P* 308; "Do I want to show now that even a yearlong trial could teach me nothing? . . . Shall they say of me that at the beginning of my trial I wanted to end it, and now, at its end, I want to begin it again?" *Tr* 228). This play of beginnings and ends is amazing when one reflects that of course Kafka did want to end his writing of *Der Proceß* at the very beginning (of his writing it, with K.'s execution); and now, at its end, that he did want to begin it again, with chapter 2. What K. in no way wants to be said on his account, Kafka wants, above all, to be said on his account. These semi-private games are, Pasley continues, using a phrase of Goethe's, "quite serious jests" (24). They are effects too striking to suppose that Kafka did not cultivate them.

The second of Pasley's demonstrations is even more amazing, if this is thinkable. Around the beginning of October 1914, Kafka asked for leave from the office in order to get on with *Der Proceß*. Meanwhile, in a passage that Pasley holds must have been written at this time, Josef K. plays with the idea of asking for leave from the bank so that he can devote himself uninterruptedly to composing the "Eingabe" (petition) that he means to submit to the Court. The text of *Der Proceß* reads:

> Wenn er im Bureau keine Zeit für sie fand, was sehr wahrscheinlich war, dann mußte er sie zuhause in den Nächten machen. Würden auch die Nächte nicht genügen, dann mußte er einen Urlaub nehmen. Nur nicht auf halbem Wege stehn bleiben, das war nicht nur in Geschäften sondern immer und überall das Unsinnigste. (*P* 170)

> [If he couldn't find time for it at the office, which was quite likely, he would have to do it nights at home. And if the nights weren't sufficient, he would have to take a leave of absence. Anything but stop halfway, that was the most senseless course of all. (*Tr* 126–27)]

And thereafter:

> Was für Tage standen ihm bevor! Würde er den Weg finden, der durch alles hindurch zum guten Ende führte? Bedeutete nicht eine sorgfältige

Verteidigung . . . gleichzeitig die Notwendigkeit sich von allem andern möglichst abzuschließen? Würde er das glücklich überstehn? Und wie sollte ihm die Durchführung dessen in der Bank gelingen? Es handelte sich ja nicht nur um die Eingabe, für die ein Urlaub vielleicht genügt hätte, . . . es handelte [in the MS "handelt"] sich doch um einen ganzen Proceß, dessen Dauer unabsehbar war. (*P* 177)

[The days that lay ahead! Would he find the path that led through it all to a favorable end? Didn't a painstaking defense . . . simultaneously imply the necessity of cutting himself off as far as possible from everything else? Would he successfully survive that? And how was he supposed to do that here at the bank? It wasn't just a matter of the petition, for which a leave might perhaps suffice . . .; it was a matter of an entire trial, the length of which was unforeseeable. (*Tr* 132)]

This "petition" is a manuscript that will cover up, so to speak — "zudek-ken"[8] — the script, the papers, the book of the Law.

Pasley notes that, presumably without meaning to, Kafka composed this sentence in the present tense: "es *handelt* sich um einen ganzen Proceß" ("it *is* a matter of an entire trial,"emphasis added, SC). This gives the allegory away. And furthermore, before writing the word "Dauer" (length, duration), Kafka initially wrote "Länge," which also means "length" or "duration" but with connotations both of "long-lastingness" and even of "body length," for which reasons Pasley presumably considers the first word to better fit Kafka's own lifelong "process" than the trial of Josef K. (24).

Thus methodologically instructed, we can return to the specific matter at hand: of "gefangen" versus "verhaftet." And given our knowledge of the manuscript, we are now able to understand Willem's declaration to K: "Sie sind ja gefangen!" ("You're being held"). The puzzled response that might spring up in the mind of an uninstructed reader of the novel at this point would be: "How so? Josef K. isn't just 'being held'; he's been 'arrested.' You have only to recall the opening of the text, you have only to read the book of his 'Process'" — the book in which Willem was reading and has now emphatically tossed aside. But, in light of the manuscript, this response is no longer permitted because, here, Willem is reciting to K. from the manuscript *before* Kafka emended the first line of it. *At this moment Kafka has not yet made the change from "gefangen" to "verhaftet"* in the first sentence of the novel. This is my thesis, and I know no other, short of the punitively deficient one that Kafka blundered and required the editorial ministrations of Max Brod to set him right. The "gefangen" that both text and book offer in this instant is the same word that concludes the first sentence, K.'s special sentence, in its *original* conception: "K. wurde gefangen." What else can K. — who can be held to be conscious of the first sentence — say now to what actually stands in the text except, "Es sieht so aus" ("So it appears"). But, through the uncertainty of K.'s utterance, the author may well be registering at this point his uncertainty about this word and category choice. On the one hand, there is the word "gefangen," with its at once exaltedly metaphysical and primitively naturalistic connotations — since in addition to meaning "being held," it can mean both "captured," as in the gravitational field of mortality, and also "caught," as in the child's game "Gefangen," quite in the way that the word "Böses" (truly wrong, evil), which figures centrally in the opening sentence of the novel, as Breon Mitchell points out, can mean both preternaturally "evil" and also merely "naughty."[9] (The two terms — "Böses" and "gefangen" — support one another in this way.) On the other hand, Kafka will finally opt for the category "verhaftet," with the definitive connotations of a civil-juridical technical term of law.

It is only some pages later, with the repetition of this conversation between Willem and K., that — I propose — the news of the emendation has arrived from the archive (news of which Willem, unlike K., might be said to have been subcutaneously informed), announcing that the conclusion to the opening sentence of the manuscript has now been changed from "gefangen" to "verhaftet." Ergo, says Willem, "Sie sind *doch verhaftet*" ("After all, you're under arrest"), for, as an agent of the Court, he is entitled to a better insight (or to allege such insight) into the law and its now no longer alterable "letter" (Schrift).

To state this plainly: Willem, as authorial agent, has registered the change in the first sentence from "gefangen" to "verhaftet." Kafka's serious jest is to have him be *au courant* with the script or manuscript of K.'s process and to inform K. of the truth of his arrest. But K. is now to be denied access to the text of his trial: he has been alienated from the author; he knows only the first "sentence" of his "Process" — his likely reaction in advance to the fact of being held — but he is not allowed to see any of the further protocols. As he is afterwards told by his lawyer, "die Schriften des Gerichtes, vor allem die Anklageschrift [sind] dem Angeklagten . . . unzugänglich" (*P* 152; "The court records, and above all the writ of indictment are not available to the accused," *Tr* 113); and all the attempts of K. and his lawyer to read them are only expressions of the commentators' despair. Having heard from Willem previously that he had been "gefangen," how can he react now, on hearing that he is "after all, . . . under arrest," except to cry out, "Wie kann ich denn *ver-*

haftet sein?" (*P* 13; "How can I be under arrest?" *Tr* 8). It is then entirely apropos that the conversation immediately following should turn on the legitimacy of various sorts of "Schriftstücke" (papers). "Hier sind meine Legitimationspapiere," says K., "zeigen Sie mir jetzt die Ihrigen" (*P* 13; "Here are my papers, now show me yours," *Tr* 8). K. offers up a puny text, but we may now imagine what papers the Court has access to.

This is my summing up: Kafka can have introduced into the world of the novel a manuscript "figure" — the (irregularly) crossed-out word-choice. He can have incorporated into the sequence of plot-events the event of emendation. Certainly this conceit gains support not only from Pasley's reflections, as above, but also from Roland Reuß's way of requiring that moments of uncertainty in Kafka's manuscript — Kafka, as it were, between emendations — be left uncertain and active.[10] All these voices together make uncertainty, especially this uncertainty, a forcible poetic event.

Interesting, noteworthy, and corroborative, too, is the way in which the inspector subsequently mentions the fact of K.'s being under arrest. "Sie sind verhaftet, *das ist richtig*" (*P* 22; "You've been arrested, *that's true*," *Tr* 14, emphasis added, SC). Why this otherwise inexplicable emphasis, uncalled for in context, if Kafka weren't here working out the conclusion of his uncertainty?

All these contributions of various critics appear to hold together: I am in the same cathedral as Pasley and Reuß, but then again I am in a different pew, because I want to emphasize a hermeneutically important difference. In the examples that Pasley gives, there is after all his rather striking failure to introduce a key differentiation between them: In the first instance of an imbrication of manuscript and diegesis at the ostensible close of the novel, "Ende," K. is ignorant of the irony that is being played out around him or through him or over his head. The ironist is Kafka; the fall guy, Josef K. But that is not at all the case in the second example: here Kafka the author and K., the potential author of a petition, fuse. And yet Pasley presents both textual parallels as instances of the same sort of thing.

In my own example, where the news of the emendation of "gefangen" to "verhaftet" at the opening of *Der Proceß* is only subsequently introduced into the diegesis, K. is again the fall guy; the jest is on the side of the author, who here sides with Willem and the inspector. The Court knows the score — or script — as K. does not. But it is quite revealing that the first example of such medial interference that Pasley gives — at the end of the novel, concerning K.'s reluctance to begin his trial all over again — and my example — of the delayed introduction into the novel of the news of the emendation — were both written at around the same time (11 August 1914) and are quite consistent in marking Kafka's distance from K. — his more than formal authorial distance. The mode is distantiation and the goal is murder, with Kafka functioning as loyal officer, friend of the Court, and executioner. With some indignation, Brod retitled Günther Anders's incisive polemic against the fatalistic, demoralized character of Kafka's heroes "Die Ermordung einer Puppe" (The assassination of a puppet):[11] an accurate description of things at the outset of the scription of *Der Proceß* (after the chapters "Verhaftung" and "Ende") but not as the diegesis began to unravel and Kafka evidently became less and less capable of imagining his superiority to K. and functioning as officer of the Old Law. One knows that he wrote "In der Strafkolonie" (In the Penal Colony) midway through the writing of *Der Proceß*, in which it is the machine, and not the initial culprit, who shatters: "Schuldig ist die Organisation" (*P* 112; "It's the organization that's guilty," *Tr* 83), just as K. had maintained; and no identification on Kafka's part with this murderous Law is any longer defensible.

What is at stake in my reading of the "gefangen"/"verhaftet" crux is Kafka's reflection on how K.'s entire process is to be figured. I repeat the question: is K.'s plight to be "Gefangensein" (being captured), with its at once natural and metaphysical openings (corresponding to the at once brutally natural — infantile — and also metaphysically open sense of "Böses"), or is it to be a civic-legal "Verhaftetsein" (being under arrest), corresponding to a category in Austrian civic law? What self has been fixated: the animal/metaphysical, the "natural" self, or the civic-legal public identity?

The author Kafka's final shift from "gefangen" to "verhaftet" makes it obligatory for K. to figure the trial as a civic-legal affair, but the minute he does so he is doomed: he cannot be "saved" by playing the role of the person accused in a civic-legal sense, since his protestations of innocence in the absence of a charge have no role to play in a court of law; his is a fundamentally different sort of case. K. is doomed by this message broadcast into his world, through Willem, from the archive, the world of the manuscript. More than "gefangen," he has been "verhaftet" — "das ist richtig" (that's true): he is condemned to think his case through the prism of such an arrest, and for this blunder he shall surely die.

But with this decisive change of descriptor from "gefangen" to "verhaftet," Kafka not only sentences K. to death but implicitly sentences his authorial personality to death as K.'s guilty executioner. "Death," here — the death of the author — means precisely: Kafka's failure as author to survive K., the impossibility of his bringing *Der Proceß*, after all, to a close on a note of mastery. In "In der Strafkolonie" it is asked of the culprit,

"Er kennt sein eigenes Urteil nicht?" (*L* 1, 167; "He doesn't know the sentence that has been passed on him?" *CS* 144–45), which may well be an allusion to the author who does not know the mastery he once possessed as author of "Das Urteil."[12] That means that in 1914 Kafka was unable to reproduce the authorial-manuscriptive-diegetic structure of 1912, in which he could literally survive the death of his puppet as "an unending stream of traffic" that "was just going over the bridge" (*CS* 88). To be sure, he was otherwise diverted.

Postscript

Two more examples of intersections "from the archive" seem especially interesting to note here — one occurring early in the manuscript, and one at the very end, though written, as I have mentioned, at approximately the same time as the beginning, around 11 August 1914. On returning home the evening of his arrest, K. encounters at the house landing the porter's son, who says to K., after K. has shown some signs of impatience,

> "Wünscht der gnädige Herr etwas? Soll ich den Vater holen?" "Nein, nein," sagte K., in seiner Stimme lag etwas Verzeihendes, als habe der Bursche etwas *Böses* ausgeführt, er aber verzeihe ihm. "Es ist gut," sagte er dann und gieng weiter, *aber ehe er die Treppe hinaufstieg, drehte er sich noch einmal um.* (*P* 31; emphasis added, SC)

> ["Is there anything I can do for you, sir? Shall I get my father?" "No, no," said K. with a note of forgiveness, as if the fellow had done something *truly wrong*, but he was willing to forgive him. "That's all right," he said, and passed on; *but before he went up the stairs, he turned around once more*" (*Tr* 21; emphasis added, SC)].

Now what on earth can have prompted K. to whirl about except the recurrence of the key word "Böses," not in the immediate context of his world but in the immediate context of the script, the narration of his world? It is as if K. had just remembered the first sentence of his life-text and grasped the coincidence of the word that has just occurred to him with the sinister marker "*Böses*" that had been introduced at the outset but then dismissed as a likely explanation of K.'s capture or arrest.

That first "*Böses*" to which this "*Böses*" returns, I stress, is not part of the consciousness that belongs to the Court but part of the text ("spoken" in thought by K. or by a narrator who at this stage of the game maintains his sly advantage of attitude over him) — a piece of language or thought that rhetorically precedes the first event in K.'s world at which the Court is present, the event of his awakening to his capture or arrest.

A second remarkable moment of scriptive interference has been pointed out by May Mergenthaler, who has studied the last line in the manuscript of the concluding chapter "Ende." Here, after Josef K. has been brutally stabbed, Kafka's narrator observes, "es war, als sollte die Scham ihn überleben" (*P* 312; "it seemed as though the shame was to outlive him," *Tr* 231). A look at the manuscript shows that Kafka formulated three versions of this concluding piece of a sentence ("Ende" 25). After writing the phrase "'Wie ein Hund!' sagte er" ("'Like a dog!' he said"), he wrote a first, then a second, rejected sentence that reads "bis ins letzte Sterben blieb ihm die Scham nicht erspart" ("up until his last dying moment, shame was not to be spared him"). At this point, a line in the manuscript is drawn through each one of the words *except* the concluding word, which in the German is "Scham" (shame). The word "shame" survives the crossing out.

The *word* shame outlives Josef K. If one needed additional confirmation of the haughty distance that Kafka was able to manifest toward his hero/victim at the outset of the process of scription (though not as the scription of *Der Proceß* advanced), one could scarcely find stronger evidence. Kafka the author is in control of the scription as K. is not; Kafka generates K.'s world through scription when it is the illusion of the diegesis that K.'s world is at least co-constituted by his perception of it. Not true, not true even of his gravest moment, of his dying instant. Dorrit Cohn has written that "No instant of life (if one can call it that) highlights more dramatically" the distinction of fiction. For fiction is able "to represent an experience that cannot be conveyed by 'natural' discourse in *any* manner or form. This may well be why novelists — great realists no less than great antirealists — perennially give us the mimesis of a dying consciousness" (22). But here it appears to be less a mimesis of a consciousness than, finally, a "logomimesis" that Kafka has given us.[13] A shame so great that it survives K., a consciousness of shame that might be attributed to the dying hero and so might be reckoned his achievement, is in fact an accident of the scription: not K.'s shame but Kafka's word "shame" survives him for not having been crossed out. This haughty distance will close.

Given the evident heuristic fruitfulness of this principle of "scriptive interference," with the onset of electronic and electronically generated reproductions of Kafka's manuscripts, "a vast and profitable entertainment" ("eine große und nützliche Unterhaltung" *BB* 6, 167) now awaits the reader of Kafka in the electronic age.

Notes

[1] The question of Kafka's theatricality was originally posed by Walter Benjamin in 1934: "Kafka's world is a world theater. For him, man is on the stage from the very beginning" ("Franz Kafka: On the Tenth Anniversary of his Death," in *Illuminations,* trans. Harry Zohn, ed. Hannah Arendt [New York: Harcourt, Brace and World, 1960], 124). In an exchange of letters with Benjamin, Theodor Adorno found much to criticize in this idea: "The form of Kafka's art . . . is the most extreme antithesis to the theatrical," perceiving in Benjamin's remark the (for him) pernicious presence of Brecht's idea of epic theater (Schweppenhäuser, ed. *Benjamin über Benjamin* [Frankfurt am Main: Suhrkamp Taschenbuch, 1981], 105). Since then, there have been many rich discussions of the theatrical character of Kafka's literary imagination, especially Rolleston (1974). The theatrical character of the opening of *Der Proceß* is an often acknowledged fact. The American translator of *Der Proceß* — Breon Mitchell — terms it "farce": "*The Trial* begins as farce and ends as tragedy" (Mitchell, trans., *The Trial* [New York: Schocken, 1998], xxi). Theodore Ziolkowski considers the whole of *Der Proceß* a "burlesque" of Austrian legal procedure (*The Mirror of Justice: Literary Reflections of Legal Crises* [Princeton, NJ: Princeton UP, 1997], 226). Still, a great many details of the theatrical opening of *Der Proceß* call for additional exploration.

[2] The German word "Schaustellung" is from *Der Proceß,* ed. Malcolm Pasley (Frankfurt am Main: Fischer, 1990), 15. The English word "show" is from Mitchell's translation of *The Trial,* 9. Henceforth, citations from Pasley's edition of *Der Proceß* will be indicated by *P* plus page number; citations from Mitchell's translation of *The Trial* will be indicated by *Tr* plus page number.

[3] Anna, it will be recalled, was last seen fleeing the Samsa household after having gone in search of a locksmith and/or doctor; now she has evidently taken up lodging at Frau Grubach's. There is the trace here of an unwritten Prague epic of the demimonde: *Anna Mutzenbacher* — but this is an only virtual medial intrusion.

[4] To these senses of the word "Verkehr," one should add "the flow and exchange of commodities." This idea was first identified by Gayatri Chakravorty Spivak, who wrote: "In Kafka's code the word translated as 'traffic' (*Verkehr*) is also the word for 'commerce,' and it is the word that is used everywhere in all the literature of political economy (including, most significantly, Marx) in German" (Spivak, "Discussion," in *Literature and Anthropology,* ed. Jonathan Hall and Ackbar Abbas [Hong Kong: Hong Kong UP, 1986], 192).

[5] The rape is a suggestion but more than a "mere" suggestion: it is the powerful apparition of a cathexis and fully part of the atmosphere throughout *Der Proceß* of a more than free-floating sexual violence. Compare such moments as K.'s assault of Fräulein Bürstner in the scene following, the scene of the whippers, the prurient behavior of the girls who pursue K. in Titorelli's chambers. Perhaps it is such an atmosphere of waxing sexual violence that now fixates the bystanders in their window. They seem worried, ashamed of their curiosity. Consider such telling details as that the curiosity of the old woman in the window is "quite unusual for her" (*Tr* 3); subsequent scenes of their gaping always include acts of nervous or physical agitation.

[6] Especially in the months before the composition of *Der Proceß,* Kafka was engaged in an intricate correspondence with Grete Bloch, the friend of his fiancée Felice Bauer, bearing on reasons for and against his marrying Felice. In Ernst Pawel's subtle account of their relations, Grete was "his most solid human contact" (*The Nightmare of Reason: A Life of Franz Kafka* [New York: Farrar, Straus, Giroux, 1984], 309).

[7] Franz Kafka, *Der Process: Faksimile-Edition,* ed. Roland Reuß (Stroemfeld Verlag: Frankfurt am Main, 1997). This is the first volume of Stroemfeld Verlag's planned Frankfurter Kafka Ausgabe (FKA), in which Kafka's handwritten manuscript pages are printed in facsimile form alongside a transcription in type on the facing pages. The fragmentary pieces of the manuscript are each provided in a separately bound folio, in keeping with the editor Roland Reuß's contention that there is no sound editorial principle for ordering them. The fragments referred to here are listed separately in the works cited list in addition to the volume as a whole, and are abbreviated as "Reuß, ed." plus short title of fragment and page number.

[8] "Zudecken" is a key word in the murderous discourse held between father and son in Kafka's "breakthrough" story, "Das Urteil" (*GW* 1, 48; *CS* 84). The word has the connotation of "covering up" a dangerous, adversarial truth.

[9] Theodore Ziolkowski has shown that the word/concept "*Böses*" (evil, deep wrong), if it alludes to the phrase "böser Vorsatz" (malicious intent), is, in Austro-Hungarian jurisprudence, also a technical term of law: the malicious intention indispensable to a punitive judgment (236).

[10] For instance, Kafka appeared to waver in deciding whether to write, in the so-called "Türhüter-Legende" (Legend of the Doorkeeper) — a portion of the chapter "Im Dom" (In the Cathedral) — "der Türhüter . . . fragt ihn [den "Mann vom Lande"] "nach seiner Heimat aus" or "über seine Heimat aus," both expressions meaning: "the doorkeeper inquired about his home" (*Tr* 216). The manuscript passage can be read in facsimile in the fascicle titled "Im Dom" (Reuß, *Der Process,* 45). Pasley, in his edition, settles the matter by simply choosing "über seine Heimat aus" (*P* 293). The manuscript, however, does not support one decision over the other. Roland Reuß observes that once an edition, like Pasley's, is governed by the idea of producing a reader's text, it is going to have to make univocal decisions, whether or not they do justice to cases like these where Kafka evidently wavered. At this point supplementary apparatuses do not provide a solution (*"Zur kritischen Edition von Der Process," Franz Kafka-Hefte* 1[1997]: 23).

[11] Günther Anders, "Franz Kafka — pro und contra," *Die neue Rundschau* 58 (1947): 119–57. Incorporated in Anders, *Kafka, pro und contra* (Munich: Beck, 1951). English version (not a literal translation) in Anders, *Franz Kafka,* trans. A. Steer and A. K. Thorlby (London: Bowes and Bowes, 1960). See Brod's hostile reply ("Ermordung einer Puppe namens Franz Kafka," *Neue Schweizer Rundschau* 19 [1952]: 613–25) and Anders's response ("Franz Kafka: pro und contra," *Neue Schweizer Rundschau* 20 [1952]: 43–50).

[12] The English translation misses the fact that in writing the phrase "sein Urteil" (his judgment), Kafka was quite probably alluding to his breakthrough story "Das Urteil." See the illuminating commentary by Anderson in "Kafka in America: Notes on a Travelling Narrative," in his *Kafka's Clothes* (Oxford: Clarendon Press, 1992), 185–86.

[13] This is Clayton Koelb's term of art (Koelb, *Kafka's Rhetoric* [Ithaca: Cornell UP, 1989], 41–42).

Works Cited

Anders, Günther. "Franz Kafka — pro und contra." *Die neue Rundschau* 58 (1947): 119–57.

———. *Kafka, pro und contra*. Munich: Beck, 1951.

———. "Franz Kafka: pro und contra," *Neue Schweizer Rundschau*, 20 (1952): 43–50.

———. *Franz Kafka*. Trans. A. Steer and A.K. Thorlby. London: Bowes and Bowes, 1960.

Anderson, Mark. "Kafka in America: Notes on a Travelling Narrative." *Kafka's Clothes: Ornament and Aestheticism in the Habsburg Fin de Siècle*. Oxford: Clarendon Press, 1992. 98–122.

Benjamin, Walter. "Franz Kafka: On the Tenth Anniversary of his Death." *Illuminations*. Trans. Harry Zohn. Ed. Hannah Arendt. New York: Harcourt, Brace, and World, 1960.

Brod, Max. "Ermordung einer Puppe namens Franz Kafka," *Neue Schweizer Rundschau* 19 (1952): 613–25.

Cohn, Dorrit. *The Distinction of Fiction*. Baltimore: The Johns Hopkins UP, 1999.

Corngold, Stanley. The Commentators' Despair. *The Interpretation of Kafka's "Metamorphosis."* National University Publications. Port Washington, NY: Kennikat Press, 1973.

———. "Pre-Reading *The Trial*." An unpublished paper given at Annual Meeting of MLA, San Francisco, 1998.

Kafka, Franz. *The Diaries of Franz Kafka 1910–1913*. Trans. Joseph Kresh. Ed. Max Brod. New York: Schocken, 1948.

———. *Dearest Father: Stories and Other Writings*. Trans. Ernst Kaiser and Eithne Wilkins. New York: Schocken, 1954.

———. *The Trial*. Trans. Willa and Edwin Muir and E. M. Butler. New York: The Modern Library, 1956.

———. *Der Prozess, Roman*. Ed. Max Brod. Frankfurt am Main: S. Fischer, 1965.

———. *The Complete Stories*. Ed. Nahum Glatzer. New York: Schocken, 1971.. (*CS*)

———. *Der Proceß, Roman, in der Fassung der Handschrift*. Ed. Malcolm Pasley. Frankfurt am Main: S. Fischer, 1990. (*P*)

————. *Tagebücher.* Ed. Hans-Gerd Koch, Michael Müller, and Malcolm Pasley Frankfurt am Main: S. Fischer. 1990. (*T*)

————. *Beim Bau der chinesischen Mauer.* Ed. Hans-Gerd Koch. Frankfurt am Main: S. Fischer, 1994. (*BB*)

————. *Ein Landarzt und andere Drucke zu Lebzeiten.* Ed. Hans-Gerd Koch. Frankfurt am Main: S. Fischer, 1994. (*L*)

————. *Der Process: Faksimile-Edition.* Ed. Roland Reuß. Frankfurter Kafka Ausgabe. Stroemfeld Verlag: Frankfurt am Main, 1997.

————. "Ende." *Der Process,* ed. Reuß. ("Ende")

————. "Im Dom." *Der Process,* ed. Reuß.

————. "Jemand musste Josef K. verläumdet haben." *Der Process,* ed. Reuß. ("Jemand")

————. *The Trial.* Trans. Breon Mitchell. New York: Schocken, 1998. (*Tr*)

Koelb, Clayton. *Kafka's Rhetoric: The Passion of Reading.* Ithaca: Cornell UP, 1989.

Mergenthaler, May. "Arguing with a Friend: Writing and Reading Kafka's *Process* in a New Edition." An unpublished paper given at the Colloquium "Authorship and Work in the Age of New Media," Princeton University, February 19, 2000.

Pasley, Malcolm. *Franz Kafka, Der Proceß: Die Handschrift redet.* Marbacher Magazin 52 (1990). Marbach: Deutsche Schillergesellschaft.

Pawel, Ernst. *The Nightmare of Reason: A Life of Franz Kafka.* New York: Farrar, Straus, Giroux, 1984.

Reuß, Roland. "Zur kritischen Edition von *Der Process* im Rahmen der Historischen-Kritischen Franz Kafka-Ausgabe." *Franz Kafka-Hefte 1.* Frankfurt am Main: Stroemfeld, 1997.

Reuß, Roland, ed. in cooperation with Peter Staengle. *Der Process, Historisch-Kritische Ausgabe sämtlicher Handschriften, Drucke und Typoskripte.* Basel/Frankfurt am Main: Stroemfeld/ Roter Stern, 1998.

Rolleston, James. *Kafka's Narrative Theater.* University Park, PA: Penn State UP, 1974.

Rousseau, Jean-Jacques. *Oeuvres Complètes.* Bibliothèque de la Pléiade. 3 vols. Paris: Gallimard, 1959.

————. *The Reveries of the Solitary Walker.* Trans. Charles E. Butterworth. New York: New York UP, 1979.

Schweppenhäuser, Hermann, ed. *Benjamin über Benjamin.* Frankfurt am Main: Suhrkamp Taschenbuch, 1981.

Spivak, Gayatri Chakravorty. "Discussion." *Literature and Anthropology.* Ed. Jonathan Hall and Ackbar Abbas. Hong Kong: Hong Kong UP, 1986. 189–96.

Zilcosky, John. *Kafka's Travels: Exoticism, Imperialism, Modernism.* New York: St. Martins Press, forthcoming.

Ziolkowski, Theodore. *The Mirror of Justice: Literary Reflections of Legal Crises.* Princeton: Princeton UP, 1997.

Kafka's Circus Turns:
"Auf der Galerie" and "Erstes Leid"

Bianca Theisen

A M I A CIRCUS RIDER ON 2 HORSES?" Kafka concludes a letter to
Felice Bauer on 7 October 1916, and adds with regret: "Alas, I am
no rider, but lie prostrate on the ground." ("Bin ich ein Cirkusreiter auf
2 Pferden? Leider bin ich kein Reiter, sondern liege am Boden." [*F*
720]). The circus seems to defy even the basic rules of balance, while
Kafka, trying to establish a precarious equilibrium between his everyday
life and his writing, time and again loses his footing.

Kafka regularly patronized the Prague varietés and cabarets (Wagenbach 155) and was an avid reader of two journals on circus culture,
*Artist: Central-Organ des Circus, der Varietébühnen, reisenden Kapellen
und Ensembles,* and its Austrian counterpart *Proscenium* (Bauer-Wabnegg
1986, 10). Well-informed references to the popular art form of the circus
and its various types of performances pervade his literary writings, notes,
and letters. In the diaries and the *Oktavhefte,* he mentions aquatic pantomime — which had been introduced by Ernst Renz in 1891 and had
also been a great success for the Busch circus — and notes his admiration
for the great juggler "K" and for the acrobatic skill of a contortionist. In
"Ein Hungerkünstler" (A Hunger Artist) and *Der Verschollene,* he emphasizes the inclusive aspect of the circus institution, which welcomes all
kinds of different artistic skills: "Ein großer Zirkus mit seiner Unzahl von
einander immer wieder ausgleichenden und ergänzenden Menschen und
Tieren und Apparaten kann jeden und zu jeder Zeit gebrauchen" (*L*
269; "A large circus with its enormous traffic in replacing and recruiting
men, animals, and apparatus can always find a use for people at any
time," *CollS* 228). Kafka's Hunger Artist is modeled on the human
skeletons exhibited in sideshows (Bauer-Wabnegg 1990, 374). The
anthropomorphized ape Rotpeter in "Bericht für eine Akademie" (Report to an Academy) recalls the enfreaked bodies and people exhibited
before the Berlin Anthropological Society in the late nineteenth and early
twentieth centuries; the case of Krao, a putative ape-girl who was pur-

ported to be the missing evolutionary link between nature and culture, was discussed in the popular journal *Die Gartenlaube* in 1888 and put on show at the Frankfurt Zoological Gardens in 1884 and 1894 (Rothfels).

With his acute interest in the circus, it has been argued, Kafka partakes in a modernist aesthetics fascinated with the lowly, the miserable, the alienated, the anonymous, and the existentially threatening (Kurz 73). Kafka's circus figures — the pitiful Hunger Artist, the sad cabaret success Rotpeter, the distressed equestrienne, the tormented aerialist — have been read as nihilistic allegories of the modern artist (Ritter 1974). Such an immediate equation between entertainment and art seems to overlook the "great divide" (Huyssen) between mass culture and high art still operative at Kafka's time. Of course we could, if we wanted to follow such a line of argument, supplement it with Theodor W. Adorno's emphatic analysis of art. Adorno believes that "in its very existence," each art work "conjures up" the circus and is nevertheless "doomed as soon as it tries to imitate the circus." With the ghost of the circus, as it were, the sensual, physical elements repressed by the increasing spiritualization of art returns. Corporeal skill, Adorno suggests, is not only the "complement" of art but, as long as it is skill without aim or intention, art's "model," and even its well-kept "secret" (Adorno 126, 180). But the recurrence of the body — of the contorted and often freakish body — and the emphasis on gesture and pantomime is so ubiquitous in Kafka, and, it seems to me, derives so much more from his equally keen interest in another mass medium of his time, the cinema, that it cannot be seen as specific to his fascination with the circus. Certainly the story "Ein Hungerkünstler" could be understood as a puzzling self-reflection of art on art, in which the Hunger Artist paradoxically affirms his art in his last moments by denying that his staged starvation was art at all, that he only fasted because there was not a single food he craved, and that he could never obtain the fare he desired. But this self-consumption of art relies on a double transformation: the spectacle of fasting, exhibiting a precarious balance between life and death, always rests on an oscillation between artistic skill and illusion (Neumann 1984); in Kafka's narrative, the suspension of binarisms and the transformation of cultural codes characteristic of circus performances (such as life and death, skill and illusion) are reorganized in turn, so that illusion can finally appear as the ultimate, perfect artistic skill, because it no longer is one. Kafka twists and further transforms the semiotic transformations underlying circus acts in order to explore the cultural matrix from within which he was writing, to address the constantly threatened and re-established equilibrium of his writing, and to test whether writing — the literary medium — could be set on a par with the media of popular culture.

"Auf der Galerie" (Up in the Gallery)

Kafka's two-sentence narrative "Auf der Galerie," written in 1917 and published in the collection of stories *Ein Landarzt* (A Country Doctor, 1919) has elicited much critical attention. It has mostly been read as if it were an epistemological or ontological parable (Beicken) on the enigmatic status of reality or on the relationship between reality and illusion (Foulkes; Reschke; Jones). Starting with a subjunctive "If," the first sentence already frames the circus situation it describes as hypothetical: "Wenn irgendeine hinfällige, lungensüchtige Kunstreiterin in der Manege auf schwankendem Pferd vor einem unermüdlichen Publikum vom peitschenschwingenden erbarmungslosen Chef monatelang ohne Unterbrechung im Kreise rundum getrieben würde" (*L* 207; "If some frail, consumptive equestrienne in the circus were to be urged around and around on an undulating horse for months on end without respite by a ruthless, whip-flourishing ringmaster, before an insatiable public," *CollS* 170). The sentence then extends this hypothetical situation into an indeterminate future: "und wenn dieses Spiel [. . .] in die immerfort weiter sich öffnende graue Zukunft sich fortsetzte" ("if this performance were likely to continue in the infinite perspective of a drab future"). A visitor from the gallery may then "perhaps" run down to bring this shabby spectacle of exploitation to a halt. Kafka underscores the conditional aspect of the sentence with the repeated subjunctive, highlights its mere potentiality with "vielleicht" (perhaps), and reinforces its hypothetical status again with the stark contrast presented by the second sentence: "Da es aber nicht so ist" ("But since that is not so"). Now, since a lovely lady in lavish costume flies into the arena to exhibit astounding artistic skill ("Kunstfertigkeit") to a devoted and protective ringmaster and to an admiring public raving with applause, the potential reality of exploitation described by the first sentence seems to be negated.

Kafka's text establishes strict incongruity between the two paragraphs, which offer different versions of what appears to be the same circus act. Whereas equestrienne, ringmaster, and audience are referred to with indefinite articles in the first sentence, the entire situation is made more specific with the use of definite articles in the second sentence. Whereas the relationship between performer and ringmaster is determined by labor, exploitation, and abusive power (the performer is "rundum getrieben" ["urged around"] by a "peitschenschwingenden erbarmungslosen Chef" ["ruthless, whip-flourishing ringmaster"]) in the first paragraph, it is described in terms of familial love and protectiveness in the second (the ringmaster lifts her up "als wäre sie seine über alles geliebte Enkelin" ["as if she were his own most precious granddaughter"]). Whereas the equestrienne is first characterized as frail and consumptive, giving at best a mediocre, endlessly repeated performance "auf dem Pferde schwirrend" ("whizzing along on her horse"; "schwirrend" implies non-direction and imprecision in this context), she is then depicted as "eine schöne Dame, weiß und rot" ("a lovely lady, pink and white") who triumphs in her artistic skill. Whereas the orchestra accompanying the drab show in paragraph one is likened to mechanical noise ("dem nichtaussetzenden Brausen des Orchesters und der Ventilatoren" [the "unceasing roar of the orchestra and hum of the ventilators"]), the orchestra in paragraph two is implored by the ringmaster to be silent just before the highlight of the performance. Whereas in paragraph one the audience's applause is mechanized by being equated with — and not just compared to — steamhammers: "Beifallsklatschen der Hände, die eigentlich Dampfhämmer sind" ("bursts of applause [from hands] which are really steam-hammers"), in paragraph two all the audience's ovations cannot suffice to show their appreciation for the performer's mastery. Whereas the individual spectator from the gallery reacts to the conditional reality of the first paragraph with his imperative "Halt!" ("Stop!") his reaction to the indicative reality of the second paragraph is merely affective: he weeps "ohne es zu wissen" ("without knowing it").

This highly ambivalent gesture, an involuntary, if not necessarily unconscious, physical expression, at first seems to problematize the overt incongruity between the two scenes. What is the significance of these tears? Is the spectator, faced with a perfected illusion shared by everyone except him, unable to act, to stop the exploitative, dehumanized circus act now glossed over by the deceptive illusion of an auratic performance? Is he the only "human being" in a dehumanized audience, the only person who understands the automated nature of the performance as a "universal puppet show" (Politzer 92–94)? Does the spectator find himself trapped by an incapacity to act? Even though he wishes to act, even though he wants to come to the equestrienne's rescue, taking such action would conflict with and upset the (illusionary) reality constructed by the circus act and perceived by the rest of the audience (Reschke 50). Is he therefore caught between wish and frustrated wish fulfillment (Margetts 82)? Is the spectator an outsider who "observes, but does not participate" and who confronts the reader with the "tragic existence" of a powerless "life on the sidelines" (Spahr 214)? Or are the spectator's tears an expression of an

impotent pity, and does Kafka's short text thereby pose the epistemological problem that being part of a situation prevents its understanding even
though it is its precondition (Binder 1976, 193, 489)? Can power, exploitation, and inhuman discipline — expressed in images of circus training — be masked so completely that their perception fades into one dim,
inarticulate expression of sorrow within the communal feeling of "bliss,"
into an expression that ultimately marks nothing but a textual void (Vogl
109)? The assumption that the spectator's tears are tears of sorrow, and
thus an affective reaction to the hypothetical reality described in paragraph one, relies on an interpretation that takes as reality what Kafka
presents in the subjunctive, and takes as lie or illusion what Kafka offers
in the indicative. Weeping is not univocal; tears can also indicate joy, for
instance. The ambivalence of the text's final gesture offers no clear exege-
sis to the incongruities and contrasts set up by the two paragraphs and
reproduces the circular relationship between negation and affirmation that
organizes and reorganizes a miserable reality as mere fiction and an illusionary mirage as reality (Heller 87). The position of the reader is clearly
modeled on the role of the circus spectator (Nemec 46). Moreover, the
text's play on rules of congruity and compatibility mimes the semiotic
structure of a circus act.

According to Paul Bouissac, circus performances solicit ambivalent
reactions of both fascination and contempt because they present metacultural codes that implicitly refer to, but at the same time depragmatize,
the governing cultural codes. The circus, Bouissac says, is "at the same
time both 'within' and 'outside' culture" (1976, 7). Suspending, transforming, and manipulating the dominant communicative and behavioral
codes, circus performances virtualize the semantics with which we actu-
alize and organize our world as meaningful. What seems to be incompatible is made compatible when an ape displays human table manners,
or when a predator shows off artistic tricks in unison with an animal that
would otherwise be his prey. The cultural meaning of objects becomes
ambivalent in the circus, when a clown fights with a chair as if this object
were an ill-willed subject, or when an equilibrist integrates a chair as an
additional perturbation into his trapeze act. The semantic function of
each element staged in a circus act changes with the context of its performance, while its common, everyday use is kept virtual: a chair is no
longer a seating device but is anthropomorphized by a clown, functions
as an instance of perturbation for an equilibrist, or serves as a possible
weapon for a wild animal trainer. Differences in costume can vary the
semantic effect of what is technically the same acrobatic skill: if the artist
is dressed as a clown, the accomplishment of his acrobatic feat will be

read as mere chance and evoke laughter; if he wears a bright leotard, his accomplishment will be perceived as superhuman skill and arouse anxiety and admiration (19). The circus thus develops a "multimedia language" in which sequentialized audio-visual events, played on a dense net of metacultural codes and subcodes, anticipated and integrated the spectators' reactions in feedback loops. For Bouissac the metacultural semiotics of the circus is transgressive — a fact that may explain its ill repute and the oscillation between fascination and repression it calls forth: "The circus freely manipulates a cultural system to such an extent that it leaves the audience contemplating a demonstration of humanity freed from the constraints of the culture within which the performance takes place. Circus tradition, contrary to what many assume, is not an invariable repetition of the same tricks but a set of rules for cultural transformations, displayed in a ritualistic manner that tempers this transgressive aspect" (8). Such potentially transgressive cultural transformations require a neutralized spatial and temporal realm dissociated from but also related to the surrounding cultural systems; this realm is constituted by the circle or ring, with which the circus creates a "parenthesis," as Bouissac says, a semantic void or a neutral ground without "intrinsic structuration." This circular differentiation of the surrounding culture from itself, which allows for the self-description and transformation of cultural codes, is replicated in the space reserved for the audience, the surrounding crown. The peripheral position of the spectators is thereby made part of the circular recoding of the circus message, which is not unidirectional and does not present "face to face interaction," but resides in "the totality of the patterned behavior performed." The circus message, inasmuch as it "focuses on the general biological aspects of the situations which are displayed," includes the patterned behavior of the audience (Bouissac 1977, 146). Circus programs typically encompass metadiscursive acts that transgress the border between performers and spectators: an individual spectator may keep clapping his hands after the applause from the audience has stopped, and, in the ensuing dialogue with a performer in the ring, this troublemaker will then turn out to be a clown (150).

If such meta-discursive involvement indeed has to be seen as constitutive of circus performances, the spectator in Kafka's "Auf der Galerie" by no means presents us with the completely unreal situation Jones has seen in it: that a spectator who "had to rush into the ring to rescue a performer in distress" would be an "impossibility in the world on view at the circus"; consequently, Kafka's text does not draw on the circus theme "as an embodiment" of the "severe separation between audience and performer" that also troubles the modern writer (Jones 105, 97). Within the transformative logic of a circus act, the seemingly insignificant, trouble-making spectator who comes to the rescue of an equestrienne whipped around the ring could well, after he has halted the shabby spectacle, emerge as the best bare-back rider of the circus, who then performs his artistic skills together with the equestrienne, now also auratically transformed, and earn raving applause. Bouissac has described the narrative syntax of a circus act in terms of Greimas's actantial narrative as the relationship between an addresser (the circus director), an addressee (the audience), and the hero (the artist) who performs a feat, and has specified this performance as the survival of a test or the control of a disturbance in which, similar to the basic plot of folktales, the hero typically defeats an opponent with the aid of a helper — a prop, another performer, sheer luck (Bouissac 1976:25). According to this narrative syntax, the equestrienne (the hero) in Kafka's first paragraph would conquer an opponent (the circus director and the audience) with the aid of a helper (the young spectator who stops the performance), and survive a test (being urged around on an undulating horse) or control a perturbation (the roar of the orchestra, the hum of the ventilators, the steam-hammer bursts of applause) with the help of a disturbance (the trouble-making spectator). In the logic of the circus act, this disturbance would be transformed into control, the troublemaker would emerge as artist, and what appears to be a perturbation would thus point to the very transformational operations circus performances show. Kafka models his narrative on this transformational syntax, but the transformation from paragraph one to paragraph two remains unaccounted for: the spectator does not emerge as a performer, disturbance is not turned into the control provided by artistic skill. The incongruity typically made congruent in the transformational structure of circus acts — realized in Kafka's text with the opposition between alienated, depressing work and effortless, triumphant skill — is never quite resolved. Even though the survival of a test or the control of a disturbance can be seen as the micro-narrative that structures this as well as other Kafka texts (most notably, "Bericht für eine Akademie" and "Der Bau" [The Burrow]), Kafka's stories consume the basic narrative structure they are modeled on by offering disturbances that *can no longer be controlled,* but paradoxically re-establish a precarious balance in and through their proliferation.

The affective reaction of the weeping spectator in paragraph two can be understood as just such a disturbance. Weeping (as well as laughing) expresses not this or that, be it pity (even self-pity), empathy, or joy; it indicates only loss of control: Kafka's spectator weeps "im Schlußmarsch wie in einem schweren Traum versinkend" ("sinking into the closing march as into a heavy dream," *CollS* 171). Helmuth Plessner has analyzed weeping as the expression of a disturbed relationship to our own body: we fall into and lose ourselves in an involuntary physical process that compels us and remains obscure; with our inner balance perturbed or even undone, however, we at the same time relinquish and re-establish the relationship to our body. Weeping shows that it is impossible to find an adequate response to an overpowering situation, but this very impossibility of responding constitutes the only apposite response (Plessner 274) — weeping balances and reorganizes lost control. Even the intimate, affective reaction of the spectator in paragraph two, then, takes up the transformational syntax of disturbance and control constitutive of circus acts, but, like the public, assertive reaction of the spectator in paragraph one, also disturbs this syntax. Within the narrative logic of a circus act, the accomplishment of a feat, the exhibition of effortless and successful artistic skill (as re-establishment of control) would solicit the public acclaim Kafka's text mentions, only to again replace this expected response in turn with one that strikes us as inapt and puzzling, because it takes the transformation of disturbance into control onto yet another level. The feat is never accomplished, the text never ends. With highly artistic skill, the text simultaneously invites public acclaim and refutes it — controls it by disturbing it. In "Auf der Galerie" the circus does not allegorize art as "torture" in the tradition of the saltimbanques who have come to stand for the social degrading and the powerlessness of the artist in modern literature and art, as Kurz suggests (59); and it does not, as metaphor for a futile art that destroys itself, stand in for the "transcendent nihilism of modern art," as Ritter maintains (1981, 69). The circus provides the micro-structure of a transformational logic that Kafka transforms again to account, in the last instance, for his own writing process. When Kafka notes in his diary: "Nun stehen vor mir vier oder fünf Geschichten aufgerichtet, wie die Pferde vor dem Zirkusdirektor Schumann" (Now four or five stories stand up for me like the horses for circus director Schumann, *T* 718), he transfers the metacommunicative displacements at stake in circus training — the usual cultural codification of the horse (its primarily zoological classification) is corroded and transformed, the circus horse is still a "horse" but also a multivalent element whose significance can span from a moving platform in bareback riding to an anthropomorphized, even superhuman status in training acts (Bouissac 1976, 22) — onto his writing process. Kafka's circus turns doubly transgress the reality of cultural codes already transformed in the circus, a mass medium still very popular in Kafka's time. With such double transformation, the circus comes to function as a medium from which Kafka generates new literary form.

"Erstes Leid" (First Sorrow)

Lamenting his inability to write, in an early diary fragment from 1910, Kafka compares himself to Japanese acrobats: the creative ideas he can come up with, he cannot grasp at their root but only imagine and show somewhere in their median state — as if he tried to hold on to a blade of grass that, without roots, only grows from the middle of its stem. Only Japanese acrobats were able to accomplish such an impossible feat, climbing a ladder that does not stably rest on the floor but on the lifted soles of a reclining artist, or one that does not lean against a wall but is suspended in mid-air. Kafka believes he is incapable of performing such precarious balancing acts, in particular since he does not even have someone else's soles to employ as a platform, however unsteady (T 14). Kafka's writing process indeed strikes an uncertain equilibrium between the private and the public, between the narrative sediments and fragments in his notebooks — a flow of writing constantly modifying and transforming itself — and a desire to publish a "work" (Neumann 1982a; 1982b; 1988). "Erstes Leid," a narrative about a perfectionist acrobat who has come to live on his trapeze night and day, was published separately in 1922 in *Genius: Zeitschrift für werdende und alte Kunst* and was also included in the collection of stories *Ein Hungerkünstler,* published in 1924. Kafka was editing it just before his death; but even though it seems to fall on one side of the scale between fragmented manuscript and authorized publication (Kafka had also immediately regretted that he had published the piece in *Genius*), the narrative's peculiar genesis allows it to be read as an artistic performance with which Kafka regained mastery of an interrupted writing process. "Erstes Leid" was scribbled on a blank page torn from the notebook in which Kafka was writing *Das Schloß* (The Castle), apparently at a point where his writing process had come to a standstill (Kittler and Neumann 68; for a different account, see Binder 1977, 252). Kafka used the two sides of this one blank page to note down the short text, cramming his writing more and more and writing even around the margins to the point of illegibility. Wolf Kittler and Gerhard Neumann interpret the peculiarity of the manuscript as a meta-poetological statement on Kafka's own writing process: the empty page, symptom of his interrupted productivity, then served as an acrobatic digression, a one-trapeze act on a single page, as it were, that allowed for leaping back into the more complex acrobatics of novel writing (Kittler/Neumann 68–69). The micro-structure of the circus act — a balancing of disruption and control — is here employed on a meta-level to transform arrested productivity, to regain mastery over the writing process.

The micro-structure of the circus act can be seen as the basic plot of the narrative. Kafka's trapeze artist has found what seems a perfect, if odd, balance between work and life: he never comes down from his trapeze, and all his modest needs are catered to while he lives high up in the vaulted dome of the variété. As if following the sequencing of a circus act, Kafka's narrator identifies his hero as "non-autochthon" (Bouissac 1976, 25) — superior to man, as if he were not of human origin — when he introduces his art as "eine der schwierigsten unter allen, Menschen erreichbaren" (*L* 249; "one of the most difficult humanity can achieve," *CollS* 211). The trapeze artist is characterized as superhuman in the almost absurd perfection of his skill, living high up on his trapeze, and also as subhuman, in the unhappy limitation of his social life: perfecting his skill to such a degree as to turn it into a "Gewohnheit" (custom), he excludes himself from the company of others. With its theme of artistic perfection and social exclusion, the narrative at first seems to call for one of the autobiographical readings Kafka criticism is often tempted to give: writing, Kafka often complained, locked him into loneliness, excluded him from the expected normalcy of the family and forced him into the life of a bachelor, who, lacking any safety net, had even less foothold than a trapeze artist (*T* 118). It is possible to read the short narrative as a message about social standing — be it as autobiographic reflection or as allegory of the socially alienated artist destroyed by his striving for "more and more perfection" (Politzer 303), caught up in self-deceit (Beicken 303), or narcissistically doubling himself (through his desire for a second trapeze) in a helpless attempt to break out of his self-enclosure (Kurz 75). However, doing so short-circuits the underlying transformational logic of disturbance and control with which Kafka here, as in "Auf der Galerie," aligns artistry and distress. The narrative transformations evolve around the German word "Störung" (disturbance): the trapeze artist's continuous presence in the dome is perceived as "störend" (disrupting), because he occasionally draws stray glances from the audience during other performances. But in the set ways of his odd life high up on the trapeze, the artist himself nevertheless could have lived "ungestört" (undisturbed), had it not been for being on tour, traveling from one city to the next. In fact, the moves from city to city are said to become more and more "zerstörend" (ruinous) for the artist's nerves, even though the circus manager does his utmost to speed up these necessary interruptions of the artist's life on the trapeze by using

the fastest means of transportation. During one of these train trips between cities — on which the artist stays up in the luggage rack as a poor
substitute for his usual lifestyle — he suddenly asks for a second trapeze.
Although the manager immediately agrees to accommodate this wish,
the artist bursts into tears when the manager mentions that the addition
of a second bar would also bring more variety to the performance. Urged
by the empathy of his manager, the artist eventually confesses "Nur diese
eine Stange in den Händen — wie kann ich denn leben!" (*L* 251; "Only
the one bar in my hands — how can I go on living!" *CollS* 213). As in
"Auf der Galerie," weeping here again comes into play as the inarticulate
utterance of a disturbed relationship to the body. For an aerialist, any
loss of balance could of course prove fatal. Even though the manager is
able to reassure the artist by promising to telegraph and arrange for a
second trapeze right away, he himself is worried by concerns about the
artist's inner equilibrium. If an acrobat entertains such thoughts, the
manager believes, they could be "existenzbedrohend" (*L* 252; they could
"threaten his very existence," *CollS* 213); and the first wrinkles he suddenly perceives on the artist's childlike forehead seem apt proof for what
critics, following the manager's reasoning, have also seen as a loss of the
innocence and grace of unreflected self-assurance (Kurz 75) or as the
artist's potential self-destruction by an increasing desire for artistic perfection (Politzer 303).

The micro-narrative underlying "Erstes Leid," however, is at the
same time more simple and more complex than the far-reaching meditations on existence or art it has solicited. Kafka's trapeze artist has established an equilibrium between his art form and his life. Bothered only by
the necessary and unavoidable interruptions of this lifestyle, he re-
establishes control and regains balance by demanding a second trapeze
as a counter-irritant, which, however, in turn damages his communication with and perception by others. Just as objects or animals alter their
cultural meaning in the dually patterned language of circus acts and can
be used as means of control or as means of perturbation (Bouissac 1976,
23), the meaning of the trapeze in Kafka's story also changes. Taken out
of, but still referring to, the circus context (reducing it to a statement on
the transgression of the basic rules of balance), the trapeze becomes a
polyvalent element operative on different levels of the narrative's reflection on art and communication. For Kafka's artist, the trapeze as the
medium of his art has become an "extension" of himself, as we could say
with Marshall McLuhan. For McLuhan, technological innovations are
"all extensions of ourselves" — whether they are means of increased
acceleration like the railway or means of distance communication like the

telegraph. Both figure prominently in Kafka's story: train travel as a hardship of the artist's lifestyle and the telegraph as a means of re-establishing balance by speeding the desired installment of a second trapeze; comforting the artist, the manager "versprach, gleich aus der nächsten Station an den nächsten Gastspielort zu telegraphieren" (*L* 251; "promised to wire from the very next station for a second trapeze to be installed in the first town on their circuit," (*CollS* 213). McLuhan characterizes technological innovations as "attempts to maintain equilibrium." New media are stressors or irritants to which we can adequately react only with a counter-irritant: the acceleration of exchange brought about by the introduction of money and writing, McLuhan suggests, prompted the invention of speedier modes of transportation that increasingly replaced or, in McLuhan's terms, "amputated" body functions such as walking (McLuhan 42). Accelerated transportation, introduced as a new medium to counter the irritation of modified forms of exchange, then in turn sets another equilibrium off kilter: it alters the perception of space and introduces new possibilities of long-distance communication. At the basis of media technology and its impact on social change, McLuhan detects what we can call a cybernetic dynamic between disturbance and re-established equilibrium, a dynamic that ultimately leads one to the precept his media theory is perhaps best known for: "the medium is the message" — meaning that "the 'content' of any medium is always another medium" (McLuhan 52).

In Kafka, the "content" of writing is not so much speech, as McLuhan has it, but the body with its mute gestures, its contrived performances, its "extensions." But this is not to say that the telegraph becomes "the actual hero" of "Erstes Leid" because it can span distances, an accomplishment the trapeze artist desires but does not achieve; Kafka also does not simply posit acrobatics — as an aimless art with its end only in itself — against the media of transport and information (Bauer-Wabnegg 1986, 163). The telegraph here rather seems to indicate the narrative reduction ubiquitous in Kafka's work; for McLuhan, the increasing reduction of literary form to headlines and catchwords in its modernist fragmentation was contemporaneous with the emergence of the telegraph and indicated a general shift from the typographical to the visual and the graphical (McLuhan 190). Reduction leaves its mark on all communication within Kafka's story — workmen repairing the roof exchange only "einige Worte" (a few words) with the artist; a fireman inspecting the emergency lighting calls out something respectful that can, however, hardly be heard; the artist does not respond to the manager; and even when he finally replies, he does so sobbingly and with a condensed, enigmatic statement.

When Kafka's stories draw on the reduced narrative syntax of disturbance and control also operative in circus performances, they do not simply mirror the crisis circus acrobatics faced through the emergence of competing mass media such as the cinema or the gramophone. Within the semiotics of the circus, the acrobat's body does not signify an authenticity or immediacy that could be posited against technological mediation. And Kafka's circus stories are more than critical narrative reflections on technological certainties (Bauer-Wabnegg 1990, 340). What Kafka's stories do reflect on when they assimilate structural elements of the circus is their own mediality, the reality of the literary medium at a time of increasing media saturation and of the rising hybridity of the media such saturation called forth. Kafka's writings abound with references to the parlograph, the photograph, the gramophone (Kittler), and the cinema (Zischler). Especially the multi-media language of the circus, with its audio-visual events and its formation of a semantically blank space that allowed for a transgression and transformation of cultural codes, creating a cultural "reality" of its own for the duration of the performance, served as a structural model, as a medium for Kafka's experiments with new literary form, such as the reduction of his narrative syntax to a dynamic of disturbance and control. Kafka no longer tells stories, Gerhard Neuman has suggested, rather his "narratives," particularly in the volume *Ein Landarzt*, are all concerned with the transfer of messages and with the interruption of that transfer (Neumann 1988, 79–80). The precarious balance between interruption and equilibrium, thematized in his circus stories, is also employed as the basic structure underlying many of his narratives; moreover, at the heart of his writing process, such unstable equilibria corrode a pre-modernist poetics of the work, based on concepts of authorial agency or expressive creativity, and replace it with a circular process, a flow of writing, a network of notes, with circuits of information creating neutralized semantic spaces.

Works Cited

Adorno, Theodor W. *Ästhetische Theorie*. Frankfurt am Main: Suhrkamp, 1973.

Bauer-Wabnegg, Walter. *Zirkus und Artisten in Franz Kafkas Werk: Ein Beitrag über Körper und Literatur im Zeitalter der Technik*. Erlangen: Verlag Palm & Enke, 1986.

———. "Monster und Maschinen, Artisten und Technik in Franz Kafkas Werk." *Franz Kafka: Schriftverkehr*. Ed. Wolf Kittler and Gerhard Neumann. Freiburg: Rombach, 1990. 316–82.

Beicken, Peter U. *Franz Kafka: Eine kritische Einführung in die Forschung*. Frankfurt am Main: Athenäum Fischer Taschenbuch Verlag, 1974.

Binder, Hartmut. *Kafka in neuer Sicht: Mimik, Gestik, and Personengefüge als Darstellungsformen des Autobiographischen*. Stuttgart: Metzler, 1976.

———. *Kafka Kommentar zu sämtlichen Erzählungen*. Munich: Winkler, 1977.

Bouissac, Paul. *Circus and Culture: A Semiotic Approach*. Bloomington: Indiana UP, 1976.

———. "Semiotics and Spectacles: The Circus Institution and Representations." In *A Perfusion of Signs*. Ed. Thomas A. Sebeok. Bloomington: Indiana UP, 1977. 143–52.

Foulkes, A. P. "'Auf der Galerie': Some Remarks Concerning Kafka's Concept and Portrayal of Reality." *Seminar* 2 (1966): 34–42.

Heller, Peter. "'Up in the Gallery': Incongruity and Alienation." In *Franz Kafka*. Ed. Harold Bloom. New York: Chelsea House Publishers, 1986. 77–94.

Huyssen, Andreas. *After the Great Divide: Modernism, Mass Culture, Postmodernism*. Bloomington: Indiana UP, 1986.

Jones, Robert A. *Art and Entertainment: German Literature and the Circus 1890–1933*. Heidelberg: Carl Winter Universitätsverlag, 1985.

Kafka, Franz. *Briefe an Felice*. Ed. Erich Heller and Jürgen Born. Frankfurt am Main: S. Fischer, 1967. (*F*)

———. *Letters to Felice*. Trans. James Stern and Elisabeth Duckworth. Ed. Erich Heller and Jürgen Born. New York: Schocken Books, 1973. (*LF*)

———. *Erzählungen. Taschenbuchausgabe in sieben Bänden*. Ed. Max Brod. Frankfurt am Main: S. Fischer, 1983.

———. *Tagebücher*. Ed. Hans-Gerd Koch, Michael Müller, Malcolm Pasley. Frankfurt am Main: S. Fischer, 1990. (*T*)

———. *Collected Stories*. Ed. and introduced by Gabriel Josipovici. New York: Knopf/Everyman's Library, 1993. (*CollS*)

———. *Ein Landarzt und andere Drucke zu Lebzeiten*. Ed. Hans-Gerd Koch. Frankfurt am Main: S. Fischer, 1994. (*L*)

Kittler, Wolf. "Schreibmaschinen, Sprechmaschinen. Effekte technischer Medien im Werk Franz Kafkas." In *Franz Kafka: Schriftverkehr*. Ed. Wolf Kittler and Gerhard Neumann. Freiburg: Rombach, 1990. 75–163.

Kittler, Wolf and Gerhard Neumann. "Kafkas 'Drucke zu Lebzeiten' — Editorische Technik und hermeneutische Entscheidung." *Freiburger Universitätsblätter* 78 (1982): 45–84.

Kurz, Gerhard. *Traum-Schrecken: Kafkas literarische Existenzanalyse*. Stuttgart: Metzler, 1980.

Margetts, John. "Satzsyntaktisches Spiel mit der Sprache. Zu Franz Kafkas 'Auf der Galerie.'" *Colloquia Germanica* 6 (1970): 76–82.

McLuhan, Marshall. *Understanding Media: The Extensions of Man*. Cambridge: MIT Press, 1995.

Nemec, Friedrich. *Kafka-Kritik: Die Kunst der Ausweglosigkeit*. Munich: Fink, 1981.

Neumann, Gerhard. "Schrift und Druck." *Zeitschrift für deutsche Philologie* 101 Sonderheft (1982a): 115–39.

———. "Der Verschleppte Prozess. Literarisches Schaffen zwischen Schreibstrom und Werkidol." *Poetica* 14 (1982b): 92–112.

———. "Hungerkünstler und Menschenfresser. Zum Verhältnis von Kunst und kulturellem Ritual im Werk Franz Kafkas." *Archiv für Kulturgeschichte* 66, 2 (1984): 347–88.

———. "Script, Work and Published Form: Franz Kafka's Incomplete Text." *Studies in Bibliography* 41 (1988): 77–99.

Plessner, Helmuth. "Lachen und Weinen. Eine Untersuchung der Grenzen menschlichen Verhaltens." Plessner, *Gesammelte Schriften*. Ed. Günter Dux, Odo Marquard, Elisabeth Ströker, vol. VII. Frankfurt am Main: Suhrkamp, 1982. 201–388.

Politzer, Heinz. *Franz Kafka: Parable and Paradox*. Ithaca: Cornell UP, 1962.

Reschke, Claus. "The Problem of Reality in Kafka's 'Auf der Galerie.'" *Germanic Review* 51 (1976): 41–51.

Ritter, Naomi. "On the Circus-Motif in Modern German Literature." *German Life and Letters* 27 (1974): 273–85.

———. "Art as Spectacle: Kafka and the Circus." *OCLC* 2 (1981): 65–69.

Rothfels, Nigel. "Aztecs, Aborigines, and Ape-People: Science and Freaks in Germany, 1850–1900." *Freakery: Cultural Spectacles of the Extraordinary Body*. Ed. Rosemarie Garland Thomson. New York: New York UP, 1996. 158–72.

Spahr, Blake Lee. "Kafka's 'Auf der Galerie': A Stylistic Analysis." *German Quarterly* 23 (1960): 211–15.

Vogl, Joseph. *Ort der Gewalt: Kafkas literarische Ethik*. Munich: Fink, 1990.

Wagenbach, Klaus. *Franz Kafka*. Bern: Francke 1958.

Zischler, Hanns. *Kafka geht ins Kino*. Reinbek: Rowohlt, 1996.

Kafka and Postcolonial Critique: *Der Verschollene,* "In der Strafkolonie," "Beim Bau der chinesischen Mauer"

Rolf J. Goebel

I

THE TOPIC OF KAFKA AND POSTCOLONIALITY emerges from the productive supplementation of the hermeneutic and philological traditions of *Germanistik* with cultural studies paradigms. This disciplinary self-revision has lead to a new awareness of the multiple ways in which the signifying practices of politics, history, and social processes interact with literary texts. One of the most fertile of cultural studies approaches, postcolonial theory interrogates the historical ramifications and discursive articulations of the interaction between metropolitan centers and colonial peripheries, focusing on imperialism, resistance, decolonialization, as well as cultural or political forms of neo-colonialism. Topics commonly discussed include the subversion of Western discourse by the uncanny inscription of the signs of the foreign in processes of crosscultural hybridization; the problematic of the silenced, suppressed, or manipulated "native" voice; the authenticity of indigenous cultures; and the signifying body of the colonized subject.

There, are, however, significant problems of cross-disciplinary mediation. Russell A. Berman cautions against the uncritical application to German colonialism of postcolonial theories about hybridity and transculturalism as developed by critics such as Homi K. Bhabha and Mary Louise Pratt. The "underlying assumption" of these theories "appears to be that British imperialism is the normative imperial structure," Berman says, going on to argue that the British situation was very different from German colonialism, its particular position in European Enlightenment, and Germany's supposedly more flexible notions of cultural Otherness (15). Berman is certainly right to oppose the disciplinary hegemony of theories derived from British and, one might add, French imperialisms. Unfortunately, though, there are as yet no postcolonial theories in German studies that have the conceptual breadth and analytic effectiveness of the models proposed by Bhabha, Edward W. Said, Rey Chow, and other critics who are working in U.S. cultural studies and do not primarily focus on German cultural material.[1] Nonetheless, these figures have made significant theoretical contributions to the very issues of hybridity and crosscultural communication that Berman is concerned with in his study of German colonialism. Therefore, it seems to me, one should bring together Anglo-French colonial theories and German texts in a conceptual field of mutual illumination and critique, allowing for an eclectic borrowing and translating of current theoretical terms within the indigenous field of German colonial literature. In such a quasi-dialogic situation, postcolonial theory is not treated as a monolithic system foreign to the particularities of German literary production. Rather, it serves as a heuristic tool that, despite cultural differences, is employed to elucidate textual details that could not necessarily be understood in their fullest implications from within the German context alone. On the other hand, the specifics of the individual text — its narrative rhetoric, aesthetic value, and cultural specificity — function as factors of resistance against homogenizing or totalizing tendencies in postcolonial theory.

As Bhabha's influential work shows, concepts of postcoloniality can be productively employed to understand postmodernity as a world in spatial-temporal flux. Its dominant features — cultural displacement, migration, minority issues, etc. require theoretical reflection on culture's hybridized, "transnational" character and its "translational" forms of signification across the boundaries of the "natural(ized), unifying discourse of 'nation,' 'peoples,' or authentic 'folk' tradition" (171–72). In the context of Kafka's colonial writings, Karen Piper has given a useful definition of the issue of transnationality. She argues that Austro-Hungary's "pre-nationalist nostalgia for empire" and "multinational rhetoric," even if that ideology was increasingly seen as anachronistic, is reflected in Kafka's tendency to erase clear markers of ethnicity in stories like "In der Strafkolonie" (In the Penal Colony). Instead, Kafka projects "international" characters largely abstracted from geographically or culturally recognizable locales. Thus this and other texts of his express homelessness, deterritorialization, and the "dislocated nature of the human condition" (48–49).[2]

As a result of these conditions, the issue of crosscultural translation is central to Kafka's work. Not only does he repeatedly depict protagonists who leave their geographic origins behind and must come to terms — personally, socially, and politically — with radically new cultural terrains. But most important, these narratives of dislocation, migration, and estrangement are really allegories of transcultural hermeneutics. Their protagonists are called upon to "read" the puzzling signs of the foreign culture across established geopolitical boundaries in terms of their own national, ethnic, or ideological preconceptions. But while the hermeneutic paradigm, either in Hans-Georg Gadamer's philosophy of the temporality of understanding or in ethnographic theories such as those of Clifford Geertz and James Clifford, generally expects cross-cultural understanding to be effective and successful, this is not at all the case in Kafka's writings. For here, the stark and often unbridgeable difference between cultures — often as a result of political hegemony and colonial power — is a factor that tends to lead to far-reaching misunderstanding and, ultimately, to a breakdown of the attempt to decipher the disturbing signs of the Other. In the texts discussed here, this incommensurability of cultures, even if they relate and interact with one another in the sense of postcolonial hybridity, frequently results in madness, physical disappearance, brutal rejection of and by the foreign, and a narrative lapse into silence.

In short, transnationality and crosscultural translation as inescapable impasses are the unifying tropes of Kafka's imaginative exploration of non-European and colonial spaces. A passage from his "Oktavheft G" (18 October 1917–late January 1918) gives these terms a special, highly ironic twist:

> Der Neger, der von der Weltausstellung nachhause gebracht wird und, irrsinnig geworden von Heimweh, mitten in seinem Dorf unter dem Wehklagen des Stammes mit ernstestem Gesicht als Überlieferung und Pflicht die Späße aufführt, welche das europäische Publikum als Sitten und Gebräuche Afrikas entzückten. (*NS II* 64)

> [The Negro who is brought home from the world exhibition and, gone crazy with homesickness, performs, in the midst of his village and under the lament of his tribe, his face dead-serious, those entertainments as tradition and duty that delighted the European audience as the life and customs of Africa.][3]

In Kafka's ironic evocation and subversion of the tropes of colonial discourse, the "Negro" figures against his will as a "translator" who performs African customs for the Europeans and reflects the European image of the colonial scene back to its origins, the "native" culture. Moving across the boundaries between metropolis and colonial periphery, he resembles the "hybrid" subject of multiple significations celebrated by postcolonial theory, but only in a debased, effectively desubjectified manner. As the victim of the insidious European interplay between longing for the exotic and the capitalist exploitation of human capital, the African must play the role of the indigenous, "authentic" representative of his own culture in the midst of the metropolis. However, the world exhibition's spectacular glamor and purported internationalism cannot conceal his violent dislocation, the displacement and display of his enslaved body, a condition that articulates itself bluntly in the terrifying madness of the actor. This psychological disfigurement outlasts the "Negro's" temporary physical bondage; once taken back to Africa, he can no longer distinguish between performance and seriousness. Due to the inescapable role forced upon him by the European exhibitors, he shows symptoms of a compulsive exhibitionism that makes him replay for his helpless peers the very stereotypes the Europeans had projected onto his body. Authentic African customs, after being displayed as an exotic spectacle in the metropolis, reappear in the "periphery" as split theatricality. For the "Negro," the showing of African traditions and duties appears as a "serious" resumption of genuine native life, whereas the other tribe members recognize it as the horrendous image of colonial victimization. What they see in his performance is only the ruin of an authentic mode of self-presentation that this native has irretrievably lost in his back-and-forth passage between the "First" and the "Third" Worlds.

Three of Kafka's larger texts, *Der Verschollene* (The Missing Person), "In der Strafkolonie," and "Beim Bau der chinesischen Mauer" (The Great Wall of China) reflect such typical colonial issues in a more intricate way. To link these works under the rubric of postcoloniality may seem strange at first, set as they are in vastly dissimilar geographic and ideological spaces — capitalist America, a colonial island in the tropics, and imperial China. Critics have argued that the term "postcolonial" may lose its clearly defined meaning if it is used to refer not only to the "historical fact" of European colonialism and its many effects, but also to a wider range of more general "cultural, economic, and political practices" (Ashcroft, et al. 2). While I am sympathetic to these concerns, it seems to me that postcolonial theory gains its very strength as an instrument of cultural critique by virtue of its conceptual translatability from its original context — the interaction between Empire and resistance, metropolis and periphery — into different geographical terrains, time-spaces, and ideological frameworks. This is not to argue for an ahistorical or abstract use of the term postcolonial, but to draw attention to the fact that theories, like human subjects, can travel across vastly different disciplinary and territorial boundaries. In the process, they redefine their own meanings, purposes, and effectiveness without losing contact with the specificity of their original fields and definitions. Although, as Edward W. Said has shown, such transplantation into new contexts of "representation and institutionalization different from those at the point of origin" may have to overcome considerable obstacles and resistances, it is an immensely productive form of crosscultural intellectual activity (1983, 226–27).

Allowing postcolonial theory to travel across the range of Kafka's texts, one notices, without giving too much weight to chronological development, an interesting progression in these works from First World centrality to non-Western difference. In *Der Verschollene*, which was written between 1911 and 1914, Karl Rossmann must negotiate between the European immigrant perspective and the foreign world of American capitalism, urban alienation, and dehumanizing technology — the exorbitant signs of Western hypermodernity. Significant references to *non*-Western cultures appear in "In der Strafkolonie" (1914), which focuses on the encounter of a European traveler with the colonial regime — although less so with the "natives" — on a tropical island. The representation of the fictionalized perspective of the non-Western subject itself has to wait until "Beim Bau der chinesischen Mauer" (1917), which features a Chinese scholar attempting to reconstruct his own imperial history. Thus Kafka's work performs a gradual decentering of the European perspective. This process involves an increasing subversion of Western ethnocentrism through the exploration of cultural displacements and encounters with alternative worlds, similar to the complex negotiations among different forms of identity and signification across geotemporal borders that Bhabha calls cultural translation.

The comparability of these three texts, then, is found not so much on the level of content or plot, but rather on the structural level of crosscultural negotiation between the dislocated protagonists and a foreign culture or estranged tradition that they simultaneously desire to understand and yet are bound to miscomprehend. The protagonists' crosscultural encounters share the internal splitting and ambiguities that Bhabha finds typical of colonial discourse. For him, the colonialist construction of reality is a hybridized discourse whose authority and hegemony are continually deconstructed by self-contradiction and the inscription of foreign, denied, or suppressed forms of knowledge (33–39; 102–22). As Kafka's texts show, these features are not restricted to colonial discourse formations. Rather, in various ways, they are characteristic of any process of intercultural translation or historiographic reconstruction, where multiple signs of the Other must be appropriated, reinterpreted, and integrated into new horizons or regimes of writing across — and against the resistance of — geopolitical borders, ideological divides, or temporal distances.

II

Condemned for involuntary sexual transgression — his seduction by his parents' servant girl — Karl Rossmann in *Der Verschollene* finds himself embarking on another type of transgression — across the Atlantic Ocean — that he has not initiated himself. He enters America with a mixture of fear and desire similar to the colonial experience of non-Western terrain. The boy encounters an alien — and alienated — space of crosscultural hybridity in which the promising yet mostly hostile signs of the New World — from ruthless economic competition and technological dehumanization to the sufferings of the disenfranchised and the moral depravity of people living on the fringes of society — inscribe themselves subversively into the fabric of his cultural preconceptions: nationalistic essentialism, political innocence, and desperate dreams of success. Kafka's disfiguration of the Statue of Liberty exemplifies this hybridity of self and Other. Karl perceives the statue as the Goddess of Freedom; surrounded by intense sunlight and open air, she holds in her hand a threatening sword instead of the customary torch. On a personal level, this contradictory image reflects the boy's mixed feelings of sexual guilt and desire for atonement or self-improvement. But on a more general level, it represents the inscription of entrepreneurial freedom and fearsome capitalist power politics into the psyche of the hopeful immigrant. The statue's new meaning mirrors Karl's own sense of dislocation and his urgent need for crosscultural "translation," for mechanisms of mediation between the foreign reality and his fears and expectations, values and principles.

Ironically, though, it is cultural *un*translatability that becomes the determining feature of Karl's displacement.[4] Its first manifestation is the boy's well-meant but pitifully inept and self-servingly moralistic defense of the German stoker against the exploitations of the Romanian Schubal, the "foreign" head machinist of the German steamer that takes Karl to New York. A poor immigrant without a homeland (54), Karl is temporarily rescued by his uncle, the Senator Jacob, a frightening caricature of a German immigrant turned American self-made capitalist, who, unlike his nephew, has deliberately severed all his ties to his European relatives (38). Profiting from rapid economic expansion and shady hiring practices, his monumental enterprise distributes goods, not between producers and customers or retailers, but between big factory cartels. For this purpose it is dependent on a huge telephone and telegraph network (66). The uncle's business, then, thrives on endless economic mediation and human alienation by technological media, a principle that Karl admires but one that also allegorically reflects the problematics of cultural translation that the boy cannot resolve in his own life.

The Senator asks his nephew to examine everything closely without being captured by American reality. The first days of a European in America are comparable to a birth, the uncle points out, advising him that despite the relatively rapid progress of cultural assimilation, the immigrant needs to be mindful of initial pre-judgments that could easily throw all later opinions about the new country into disarray. On the other hand, the passive enjoyment of a typical busy day in the streets of New York may be the prerogative of a superficial tourist, but will be fatal for an immigrant intent on staying (56). Here Kafka draws attention to the quasi-ethnographic problem of distinguishing between critical observation and imaginative projection, and of mediating between dispassionate contemplation and active involvement in foreign society. His uncle's advice, though, is of little help to him. Neither a tourist/guest nor a fully assimilated immigrant like the powerful Senator, Karl finds himself perpetually lost in the interstices between his displaced European cultural memory and the indifference or hostility of American society. Naïve and nostalgic, he hopes to influence the American conditions by playing old soldier's songs from his home country on the piano. Outside the open window, however, the street noise and the incalculable circulation of public life go on totally unaffected (60). Karl tries hard to learn English and to adopt the new country's customs; thus he can even employ a manner of speaking colored by a typical New York accent and idiomatic usage — to the delight of his uncle and his shady business associates, Mr. Green and Mr. Pollunder (69). It is clear, though, that here and elsewhere, Karl *imitates* American life without genuinely adopting its customs, values, and traditions. He performs a kind of mimicry by trying to emulate the entrepreneurial spirit and ambitious work ethic of the capitalist system. But unlike colonial mimicry, where the "native" mocks the self-representations of the foreign master,[5] the boy's efforts are more a sign of assimilationist ideology — however, unsuccessful — than an expression of political opposition. The sad failure of Karl's exercises in crosscultural imitation only confirms the seemingly invincible strength of the American power hierarchy that promises but ultimately denies integration.

The immigrant experience reveals itself as a typically liminal encounter, a way of life that seeks to transcend boundaries and leaves origins behind without ever really arriving or being at home again. Having been kicked out by his stern and unforgiving uncle for failing to return from Mr. Pollunder's country estate on time, Karl finds himself on the road in the company of two tramps, Delamarche and Robinson. Contemplating the fields, factories, and tenement houses alongside the highway, the boy is reminded of his distant homeland. He wonders if he should really leave New York and give up on the possibility of returning to Europe. Yet, as he tells himself, it would be better to venture into the country's interior, where there is less prospect of returning home but a greater chance of finding employment (143). The only terrain, then, that Karl can "inhabit" is — to adapt a term from Bhabha — a "Third Space" (36–39) of unsettling in-betweenness and ambiguity — geographically, ideologically, and psychologically. This space is marked neither by the Old World nor by the New World alone; nor is it delineated either by the boy's past — parental scorn, exile, moral guilt feelings — or by his expectations for the future — the stereotypes of life, liberty, and the pursuit of happiness. Rather, Karl's space is outlined as a perpetual fluctuation between these seemingly binary poles; it is a radically unstable realm constituted through a continual alternation of moments of memory and desire, deceptive acceptance and disillusioning experiences of rejection. The boy's intercultural instability is mirrored in a string of geographical experiences: expulsion, automobile excursions, homelessness, road trips, the final train journey, etc. These tropes turn the novel into a radically pessimistic and inconclusive "travel narrative," which, as Mark M. Anderson has noted, works to "deterritorialize and disfigure America's identifying signs" while destabilizing Karl's perception of the world (105).

Although — or perhaps because — Karl clearly senses that he is trapped in this profoundly unsettling space between cultures, he takes refuge in the treacherous world of nationalistic essentialisms. When first meeting Robinson and Delamarche while sharing a room at an inn with them, he proposes that they tell each other their names and nationalities. He learns that Robinson is Irish and Delamarche is French, but the two tramps seem to prefer sleep to the tedious discussion of cultural identity. Karl, not quite logically, thinks that danger has temporarily been averted. Nonetheless, he remains bothered by the presence of the Irishman simply because at home he had read that in America one should be wary of the Irish. The boy regrets that he did not examine this issue more deeply while staying with his uncle; now though, he actually finds the peacefully sleeping Robinson's appearance more tolerable than the Frenchman's (132–34). Here the boy's perception of cultural Otherness resembles the structure of colonial stereotype, which Bhabha, in analogy to Freud's understanding of the fetish, defines as an ambivalent vacillation between acknowledgment and disavowal of racial, cultural, or historical differences. Bhabha departs from common notions about the stereotype as a distortion or "false representation of a given reality." For him, the stereotype is rather an "arrested, fixated form of representation that, in denying the play of difference . . . constitutes a problem for the *representation* of the subject in significations of psychic and social relations" (74–75). Karl uses imported national stereotypes in a similar way, as a strategy that, rather than simply fixating and discriminating the Other, expresses a deeply ambiguous and self-contradictory mixture of preconceived ethnic generalization and the perception of actual individual difference. In other words, the boy vacillates uneasily between the trust in the written authority of ethnic prejudice — the book he has read about minorities in America — and the empirical evidence of the visual — the tramps peacefully sleeping in their beds. He senses that the image of the Irish immigrants is a generalized and homogenizing projection that may not be substantiated by real people and lived experience. Nonetheless, Karl's relation with Delamarche and Robinson remains defined by suspicion and fear, by a fixed and fixating image of the Other that develops long before the roguish behavior of the two actually confirms his preconceptions.

While his companions call him a false and uncouth German because he claims they have plundered his suitcase, Karl leaves the tramps because they fail to apologize and because they have insulted him and his entire people ("mein Volk," 163). In this scene, the indiscriminate and essentialist identification of individuals with their ethnic community proves to be a ridiculously inadequate strategy for figuring out the intentions and motivations of strangers in extremely unpredictable situations on the fringes of society. Later, however, national essentialism seems to have the opposite effect, establishing solidarity between persons who share little more than their displacement and immigrant status. The head cook at the Hotel Occidental offers Karl her personal help and a job as a liftboy simply because the boy introduces himself as a German from Prague in Bohemia. She in turn identifies herself as a native of Vienna who worked for half a year in Karl's hometown (171–72). It is interesting that she calls this coincidental encounter between two very different individuals from the multicultural and multiethnic Austro-Hungarian Empire a meeting of "Landsleute" (compatriots). This term, with its connotations of regionalism and cultural homogeneity, suggests the extent to which Kafka ridicules the imported assertion of ethnic commonalities as a basis for recognition and survival in a country like America, which takes pride in its principles of cultural diversity and individual worth regardless of ethnic origins.

After spending time as a virtual captive in the former singer Brunelda's decadent milieu of human exploitation and sexual perversity, Karl enters the "Teater von Oklahoma" [*sic*], a strange scenario of demagogic fakery, eschatological promise, and egalitarian social policy. Not until then is the boy willing and able to undergo that total erasure of personal identity, cultural origins, and national affiliation that seems to lead to social redemption and individual success. Karl is at first classified as "Negro, ein europäischer Mittelschüler" (Negro, a European middle-school pupil, 405), a deeply emblematic signifier for his hybrid position between cultures, perhaps suggesting the boy's uneasy position between European petit-bourgeois values and discriminated minority status in the New World. He gets himself accepted as an actor only to be demoted to technical worker; this happens because in Europe he had wanted to be an engineer. He must learn, however, that his original career plans are as much a part of his irretrievable past as are the shores of distant Europe themselves (407–8). Renamed "Negro, technischer Arbeiter" (Negro, technical worker, 409), Karl comes to shed the pretenses of theatrical artistry for the stereotypical affiliation of minority status with menial labor. Not until this transformation is he allowed to embark on the train journey into the interior that may either liberate him from his troubles or — as the novel's title suggests — lead to his untraceable disappearance. Concluding the fragmentary narrative, this entirely unpredictable, open-ended travel experience functions as a final allegory of the dialectic of exploration and confusion, hope and despair that has characterized Karl's adventures in crosscultural translation all along.

III

"In der Strafkolonie" transfers this theme from the immigrant's journey through First World capitalism to the ethnological construction of the colonial "periphery" by European metropolitan consciousness. Together with the geopolitical terrain, the protagonist's perspective changes from naïveté to sophistication, from attempted integration to indifference. As a result, the terms of hybridity — the crossing of cultural boundaries, the mediation between different ideological positions, and the inscription of the disturbing signs of the Other into the protagonist's consciousness — are transformed dramatically. Whereas Karl seeks to assimilate to American society, the Explorer-Traveler has not come to learn but to observe and to criticize, even though his attitude shifts from initial indifference to gradual interest (208). If the boy's journey necessitates forgetting his European origins and giving up his national identity, the Explorer's voyage to the penal island only strengthens — and is strengthened by — his ethnocentric belief in the superiority of his European enlightened rationality and morals. Correspondingly, the promise of freedom offered by the mechanism of American capitalist hypermodernity turns into the terrifying finality of the torture machine etching the legal sentence onto the naked body of the Prisoner.

Here, the failure of crosscultural translation between colonial periphery and European metropolitan rationality far surpasses Karl's unsuccessful mediation between his European consciousness and American society. This predicament is ironically reflected in the paradox that the Explorer and the Officer constantly talk to each other without engaging in a genuine dialogue that could lead to a gradual closing of personal differences and ideological gaps.[6] On the contrary, the elaborate lectures about the method of execution only confirm the Traveler's dispassionate and disinterested attitude. As he tells himself, although the execution method is clearly in violation of his enlightened ethics, a penal colony requires special rules and military discipline (214). It is always questionable to interfere with foreign realities, he reasons, especially since he is a foreigner, neither an inhabitant of the island nor a citizen of the state that administers the colony (222). But soon the Traveler realizes that, no matter how eagerly he seeks to detach himself, he will inevitably be drawn into the controversy between the New Commandant and the Officer about the validity of the execution ritual (227–35). Thus Kafka suggests that the colonial situation allows for no neutral position, no ideological or — in the case of the Prisoner — physical escape. Faced with this problem, the Explorer announces that he will inform the Commandant of his opposition to the cruel procedure, though not in public, but during a private conversation (236). Yet such privacy — the intimate exchange of opinions and judgments among like-minded individuals outside the realm of social power relations — is something that colonialism, dependent on the public performativity of its political power, cannot tolerate. It is the Officer, the most brutal and uncompromising of all the players in this drama, who demonstrates this characteristically public self-legitimation of the colonial regime with fatal logic. Giving up his hope to defend the outdated system, he frees the condemned and, to the horror of the Explorer and delight of the Prisoner, submits himself to the gruesome ritual of the execution. The machine, the symbol of colonial power but also of the regime's internal contradictions and vulnerability, disintegrates dramatically after killing its last heroic defender.

The Officer remains convinced of the absolute righteousness of the execution ideology even though he realizes its anachronistic nature. By contrast, the Explorer, as Berman has pointed out, is the "prototype of the effete liberal" who is trapped in his "anticolonialist presumption of the absolute incompatibility of primitive life in the colony with the ideals and aspirations of enlightened Europe." It is because of this binary thinking, without the possibility for productive crosscultural understanding, that the Traveler is unable to offer practical aid to the colonial victim, refusing to allow the Prisoner and his guard to join him on the boat that takes him away from the island (Berman 232–33).[7] If the Officer represents colonial dogmatism at its most horrific, the Traveler turns out to be a typical representative of radical ethnographic relativism, believing as he does in the mere coexistence of different and incommensurable — if morally unequal — cultures. There seems to be no "Third Space," no mediating perspective of productive hybridity available to him. Rather, the Explorer seeks to guard himself against the charge of Eurocentrism by situating himself outside the binary opposition of metropolis and colony while pursuing an unattainable subject position beyond ideology. But the execution process, no longer effective as a method to punish prisoners, becomes a catalyst that brings about the self-deconstruction of the Traveler's ideology of detached scientific reason and liberal-bourgeois tolerance. By refusing the Prisoner help to leave the island, the Explorer must, against his will and lofty intention, become complicit with the very mechanism of colonial domination and discrimination that he set out to denounce. So strong is the hegemonic influence of colonialism, then, that it draws even the most critical voices of opposition into its orbit. Ironically, colonial power shows itself at its most irresistible precisely when the Traveler is about to extricate himself physically from its territory to return to his own metropolitan sphere.

It is interesting that Kafka concentrates primarily on the conflict between the enlightened traveler and the colonial administration, rather than on the exploitation of the oppressed or silent "native" by hegemonic colonialism. As Berman argues, the "real 'primitives,' to use the term in its most provocatively derogatory sense, are not the 'natives' or 'noble savages' but the colonial riffraff" (232). This focus is typical of Kafka's doubts about the authentic representability of other cultures, and his preference for deconstructing the very regimes of exoticism or colonial power projected by his own explorations of cultural Otherness. Nonetheless, the figure of the native is by no means absent from the penal colony. He is represented by the many prisoners executed by the torture machine; their body and voice, the physical sites signifying their cultural authenticity, are both indelibly marked and obliterated by the writing expressing colonial authority. As Piper argues, the native, "refusing or unable to speak the language of the colonizers," has the ruling language inscribed upon his silent body. This suggests that "the only crime in this penal colony" may be the "failure of the natives to assimilate or adapt to the colonizing culture or to become European" (47). The execution machine's writing of the sentence on the naked, immobilized body of the condemned is indeed emblematic of the imperialist denunciation of cultural difference. But the colonial system must in the end realize its own limitations, its inability to obliterate the potential resistance found in even the most oppressed native voices, customs, and subject positions. This self-recognition is built into colonialism's own theatricality, its need to perform its power publicly as a ritualistic spectacle. While for the Officer this theatrical self-representation is an entirely unironic medium for demonstrating the regime's seemingly indubitable truth and unshakable dogma, it encounters surprising subversion when viewed from the perspective of the least likely participant, the abused and apparently helpless victim.

For what makes the fate of the present and, as it turns out, last Prisoner different is that he situates himself ambiguously between acceptance and disturbance. First, he tries to assert his human rights against the arbitrary system when he refuses to follow the meaningless and mean-spirited order to salute his superior's door once every hour during the night. Since his sentencing, however, he appears as a dumb, apathetic man who seems to accept his fate like a dog (203–4). But still, the Prisoner manages to insert an irrepressible element of mockery into the inhumane legal process by exercising what Bhabha has called colonial mimicry. This term denotes a particular strategy in colonial representation, where the "native" is described as someone who partially imitates the colonial master's manners, morals, or intellect. Without concealing any presence or identity, this form of parodic imitation, by reflecting an incomplete, strangely distorted image of the colonizer, constitutes a menace that subverts the authority of his discourse (Bhabha 85–92). Similarly, Kafka's Prisoner imitates the traveler at the very moment when the European visitor begins to show signs of interest in the execution (209). The condemned man strains to hear the Officer's explanations, although the silent movements of his thick lips indicate that he does not understand anything (211). To the horror of the Traveler, the Prisoner again mimics him by following the Officer's invitation to look at the machine from close up, pulling the sleepy soldier with him by his chain. The Traveler sees how the Prisoner searches "mit unsicheren Augen" (with uncertain eyes) what the Officer and the guest have just observed, even though his inquiry, for want of an explanation, remains unsuccessful (216). This partial mimicry, imitating the masters' actions but lacking their motivations, rationales, and forms of communication, has an unsettling effect on the authority of the colonial scene. The Prisoner's transgression results in a comic interlude that disrupts the high seriousness of the impending execution. Upset about the Prisoner's insolence, the Officer throws a piece of dirt at the guard, who tries to pull the Prisoner back. The man stumbles to the ground, writhing in his chains, and the Officer himself, clearly unnerved, has a hard time helping the Soldier put the condemned man back on his feet (216–17).

Even after the Prisoner has been installed in the machine, he succeeds in disturbing the demonstration. He seems to treat his guard as a friend, gesturing and whispering something in the Soldier's ear (236). Once pronounced free, he shows for the first time signs of "real life" in his face, tearing at the straps that hold him to the machine. Taken off the device, he "lachte ohne Worte leise vor sich hin" (laughed wordlessly to himself), ominously gazing at the Officer, the Soldier, and even the Traveler (237). While the Officer prepares the machine for his own execution, the man performs a silly dance of sorts as if to entertain the loudly laughing Soldier (239). Finally, the ex-Prisoner refuses to leave the execution site. Noticing the loose straps that are to hold the Officer on the machine, he asks the guard to help him adjust them properly and begs desperately to be allowed to watch his former oppressor's self-execution (242–43). In this farcical reversal of roles, colonial mimicry amounts to taking the position of the colonial master's controlling gaze. Viewing the carefully staged execution ritual from the perspective of the disenfranchised "native," mimicry forces the dominant point of view — represented by the deeply perturbed Traveler and the dying Officer — to recognize the ideological limitations of the colonial regime.

But while the Prisoner's mimicry questions the Traveler's complacent practice of ethnographic inquiry as well as the self-justification of the Officer's legal doctrine, it does not entail the articulation of genuine political consciousness. The thoughts and emotions, aspirations and concerns of the "native" remain hidden behind the surface signifiers of his indecipherable antics, his facial grimaces and contorted gestures. A "breites, lautloses Lachen" (broad, silent laughter) appears in the Prisoner's face when he discovers that the Officer himself will suffer the fate that had been meted out for him earlier — possibly an act of revenge instigated by the Explorer. But what here seems to be an account of the Prisoner's point of view is actually little more than "ethnological" guesswork on the part of the Traveler. Trying to read the Prisoner's psychological motivation from his body language, the Explorer seeks to explain what the "native" does not or cannot explicitly articulate himself (241). While the Officer and the Traveler engage in extensive rhetorical combat, carefully presenting their own ideological positions through elaborate, if inconclusive dialogue, the Prisoner's voice is literally reduced to a whisper audible only to his guard. There is, then, no space — political, social, or even discursive — outside the dominant regime of colonial and ethnographic language in which the Prisoner could represent himself. It is not even clear, after all, if the Prisoner really *is* a native in the literal sense of the word — an indigenous inhabitant of the island whose subject position was formed before the arrival of the French-speaking colonialists. In other words, unlike all the other actors in this cruel farce, the Prisoner has no clear identity, history, or personal agenda, only his social role as the oppressed, silenced "subaltern." In this way, Kafka's text questions the possibility of reconstructing the voice of cultural authenticity — the essence or the subjective self-understanding — of the colonial "native" from within his own literary representation of the colonial regime. The enunciatory hegemony of the Traveler and the Officer — the fact that all events are narrated from their points of view and in their ideological language — precludes the active self-articulation of the victim of colonial power and ethnographic indifference.

This narrative technique can be read as Kafka's anticipation of an interesting debate in postcolonial studies. For Benita Parry, a politically effective opposition to the representational regime of imperialism needs to move from Bhabha's notion of the native's subversive appropriation of the foreign discourse to a more clearly combative articulation of "another knowledge" — the emergence of national consciousness — resulting in a "rejection of imperialism's signifying system." Only when recognizing the importance of such a type of indigenous self-presentation, she believes, can postcolonial theory develop a "conception of the native as historical subject and agent of an oppositional discourse" (43–44). By contrast, Rey Chow argues against the very attempt to restore a native subjectivity or authentic voice behind or beneath the "defiled image" as constructed by imperialism. Such a project, she contends, is problematic because it "tries to combat the politics of the image, a politics that is conducted on surfaces, by a politics of depth, hidden truths, and inner voices." Instead, the critic ought to focus on the image's "power precisely as image and nothing else" (29). To reconstruct the self-articulation of the "native" or "subaltern" behind the colonialist image must fail, "not because there are [no] activities in which we can locate a subaltern mode of life/culture/ subjectivity," but because "speaking itself belongs to an already well-defined structure and history of domination." She cites Gayatri Spivak as saying, "If the subaltern can speak then, thank God, the subaltern is not a subaltern any more" (Chow 35–36). Chow rejects both the notion of the native's presence in the split or hybrid structure of dominant discourse *and* the call for restoring the native to an "authentic" context. Since that context has been irremediably destroyed by colonial hegemony, one should instead argue that "it is the native's silence which is the most important clue to her displacement. That silence is at once the *evidence* of imperialist oppression (the naked body, the defiled image) and what, in the absence of the original witness to that oppression, must act in its place by *performing* or *feigning* as the pre-imperialist gaze" (38; Chow's emphases).[8]

Although Chow does not refer to Kafka's story, her argument helps to understand why "In der Strafkolonie" foregrounds the Prisoner's "naked body" and his "defiled image" as well as the unreadable spectacle of the silent man's farcical mimicry, instead of explicating his "authentic" thoughts and emotions. It is as if the text's refusal to go behind the surfaces of these images and to give the Prisoner a voice is the most appropriate way of expressing what the "native" simply *cannot* express himself: his irreversible degradation by the political power and oppressive discursive hegemony exerted by the colonial Officer and the Traveler. The Prisoner's virtual silence and contorted facial features are the only signs of what cannot be reconstructed: his pre-imperialist original voice and hidden subjectivity. To paraphrase Spivak: if the Prisoner (whose political confinement on the island continues even after he has physically been released from the torture machine) could speak, he would no longer be a prisoner. Or more precisely: only if the Prisoner could actually follow the Explorer and leave the penal colony for Europe, would he be free to speak, albeit in the language of the colonial masters. Only then could he acquire a subject position from which to articulate his own consciousness and agency in the subversive contest of the imperialist system of signification and control.

IV

The "pre-imperialist gaze" Chow speaks of has further implications for Kafka's work beyond "In der Strafkolonie." Somewhat freely adapting her phrase, I suggest that this gaze can be found, in fictionalized — or feigned — form, in "Beim Bau der chinesischen Mauer." Concentrating on the national project of building a protective wall against the Northern nomads and on the politically ignorant people's worship of the decadent and ineffective emperor, the story telescopes Chinese history from the Ch'in period (221–206 B.C..) to the Ming Dynasty (1368–1644) (Nicolai 20). Moreover, the text borrows heavily from classical European tropes about pre-modern China during the Ch'ing era (1644–1912) — the country's immense size; the alienation between imperial institutions and the politically immature people; endless cycles of revolutions and new dynasties without true historical change in the Hegelian sense. Kafka's ironic and parodic images of dynastic China's ahistoricality can be seen as a subversion of what, following Chow, one may call the "imperialist gaze" and its identification of historical change in the colonies with Western-style modernization. For example, the travel writer Julius Dittmar, whose work Kafka probably knew, asserted that progress after the demise of the corrupt and exhausted Ch'ing dynasty would be possible only when the Chinese people shed their political passivity and followed the model of the technologically and economically superior Western powers (Dittmar 78–79; Goebel 1997, 65–90). Now, it is highly significant that Kafka's story does *not* expressly mention any of these political and rhetorical affiliations between China and the West, even though it was composed several years after the collapse of the Ch'ing regime and the onset of Western political presence in the Asian country. In other words, while Kafka quite obviously parodies classical Western stereotypes about pre-modern China, he deliberately suppresses the contemporary imperialist context of his story.

What this means, I suggest, is that Kafka seeks to project a kind of "pre-imperialist gaze" — the self-representation of the "native" point of view. The narrator here is not a European traveler or a colonial administrator, but a nameless Chinese historian. In other words, he is a "native" who seeks to reconstruct his own past — the building of the wall, the people's veneration for the emperor, the endless cycles of dynasties — before China's contact with Western-style modernity. Nonetheless, it is important to note that the narrator's voice, while not yet affected directly by Western imperialism, speaks in those classical orientalist images that Kafka employs to construct his version of dynastic China. What we have here, then, is neither simply a Western misrepresentation of China nor the uncontaminated voice of authentic Chinese self-understanding. Instead, to appropriate Bhabha's terminology of the "Third Space" again, Kafka's text constitutes something in-between, an intercultural terrain, in which the Chinese scholar represents the "native" who must adopt Western stereotypes in order to narrate his own indigenous past. In the very process of this self-orientalization, the Chinese historian's voice confounds the traditional binarism of European orientalism vs. Chinese "authenticity."

The scholar's reconstruction of his own past is not simply identical with the revival of some essentialist or nativist ideal of a "pure" Chinese self-understanding outside the influence of foreign discursive regimes. Instead, his historiographic pursuits are generated by the hybrid interplay between Chinese self-construction and Western imagery.

This is of great importance for the content as well as the form of the scholar's discourse because his use of Western orientalist stereotypes of China's ahistoricality, emperor worship, and political immaturity undermines the possibility of historical knowledge and political agency. The Great Wall remains forever incomplete, the symbol of fragile national unity among doubtful workers who have been displaced from their home provinces and who rely on the continual encouragement they gain from witnessing the successful completion of small parts of the wall. But the people are not just alienated from their national construction project and its questionable origins in an unmotivated injunction from the "obersten Führerschaft" (supreme leadership, 344). They are also estranged from their quasi-divine, but in fact utterly human and decadent emperor. In Kafka's China, history collapses into absurd cycles of dynasties that rise and decay endlessly. Behaving like belated arrivals and strangers in their own capital, the scholar notes, the ordinary folks stand in crowded side streets stupidly munching their snacks while their ruler is being executed on the market square (350–51). Thus, the people, deprived of political consciousness, agency, and voice by centuries of authoritarian rule and social suppression, transform the realities of imperial change into a theatricalized scenario that may be aesthetically spectacular but has little or no actual import for their daily lives in the provinces.

Even worse, the people confuse past and present rulers and battles because the news about political affairs brought to the distant provinces by ill-informed priests, over-excited neighbors, and seemingly untrustworthy tax inspectors fails to retain any sense of actuality and accuracy (352–54). No wonder, then, that even the Chinese historian himself, much like Karl Rossmann and the Traveler in the penal colony, is precluded from complete understanding of these events, in which he does not participate directly. If the Traveler insists on the autonomy and dispassionate objectivity of his ethnographic observation, the Chinese scholar emphasizes the considerable temporal distance between his preoccupation with comparative ethnology and the events he studies. Walter Benjamin has famously described materialist historiography as the forging of a flash-like constellation between the present moment and the citation of fragments from the past that are deliberately torn out of their original contexts in order to be incorporated into the historian's interpretive horizon. Benjamin calls the image or constellation resulting from this procedure a "dialectic at a standstill" (576–78; 594–95).[9] Kafka's narrator employs a metaphoric language reminiscent of Benjamin, but in a strangely reversed way, comparing the estranged past to "längst verflogenen Gewitterwolken" (long-vanished thunderclouds) from which "kein Blitz mehr [zuckt]" (346; no lightning flashes any longer). Like Benjamin's historian, the Chinese scholar realizes that historiography deals less with continuous traditions and a complete, totalizing vision of the past than with discontinuities and fragmentary objects of cognition. But his inquiry, entirely unlike Benjamin's, amounts only to a disinterested speculation about bygone events that are as dispersed and lost in time as the Chinese workers are dislocated across vast geographical expanses.

Kafka's intriguing passage has further, more directly colonial implications. In *The Wretched of the Earth*, Frantz Fanon writes of intellectuals who combat the overwhelming colonialist power by "renew[ing] contact once more with the oldest and most pre-colonial springs of life of their people" (209–10). But, as he argues, this recapturing of national culture cannot simply be the expression of folkloristic nostalgia or the abstract discovery of the "people's true nature." The anti-colonial revival of indigenous history and tradition can only be effective if it recognizes that culture "is not made up of the inert dregs of gratuitous actions, that is to say actions which are less and less attached to the ever-present reality of the people." Rather, national culture must be reinterpreted as the signifying body of actions through which "that people has created itself and keeps itself in existence" (233). Therefore, instead of retelling "inert episodes" from a remote past, native storytellers need to bring narratives of national struggle up to date, thus relating them directly to present issues of anti-colonial resistance (240). Although, as I have suggested, the narrative of Kafka's Chinese historian can be read as a recapitulation of indigenous national strife before the onset of Western colonial presence, it lacks the connection between past and present political concerns that Fanon emphasizes. All that is left to Kafka's intellectual is to reflect on the impasses of his historical speculation, whose sheer infinitude exceeds any individual's hermeneutic horizon and analytic capabilities and no longer has any significance for the historian's own time. Since the scholar is unable to forge the fragments of past endeavors — the building of the wall, battles, dynastic changes, court intrigues — into a coherent narrative that defines a unified vision of the present and future, he can only seek recourse to those elements of "comedy and farce" that, according to Fanon, dominate if the storyteller is *not* able to revive the past in a meaningful way (241). Or, more precisely, these elements are the ironic author's tropes to critique a defeatist attitude of his "native intellectual": an attitude that the Chinese scholar can barely recognize in himself.

V

What I have argued so far is that "Beim Bau der chinesischen Mauer" explores the possibility of opening up a discursive space in which the "pre-imperialist gaze" can narrate its own indigenous, pre-modern history. Yet the pervasive presence of orientalist images about dynastic China's political immaturity and historical stagnation precludes any assertion of authentic culture and any self-representation of political agency. Instead, in a move that is as self-reflexive textually as it is impotent politically, the historian can only record his own failure to understand his people's history of social powerlessness and alienation. When evaluating the ideological implications of the narrator's position, one needs to keep in mind that Kafka's text, while being something of an ethnographic "thought experiment," is *not* an example of that plurivocal type of ethnography that incorporates into its own narrative the real testimonies of indigenous speakers as supplements or alternatives to the Western perspective.[10] It is, rather, a piece of modernist fiction self-ironically exploring issues of crosscultural translation, by projecting a European image of Chinese reality through the eyes and writing strategies of a fictional *native* speaker. What is necessarily left out of an account like this is the actual voice of the Other, the documentary evidence of Chinese self-articulation.

However, the indigenous Chinese perspective that Kafka's text is unable to accommodate can be brought into the discussion through what Edward W. Said has called a "contrapuntal reading." He defines it as a strategy that examines the "great canonical texts, and perhaps also the entire archive of modern and pre-modern European and American culture, with an effort to draw out, extend, give emphasis and voice to what is silent or marginally present or ideologically represented in such works" (1993, 66). For an example of such a possible counterpoint to Kafka's European representation of the Other, I want to look at the policy of self-strengthening advanced in China since the 1860s. This program was meant as a strategic response to the increasing political, economic, and military presence of the West in Ch'ing Dynasty China. One of its earlier proponents was Feng Kuei-Fen (1809–74), a Confucian scholar and influential advisor to statesmen. Feng advocated strategies of modernization — the adoption of Western mechanical skills and scientific knowl-

edge, the foundation of a school of Western languages and sciences —
to revitalize the intellectual resources of the Chinese and define a new
sense of national identity in an age of inevitable Western contact (see de
Bary, Chan, Watson 707; Schirokauer 398–99, 448–49). No uncritical
proponent of wholesale Westernization, Feng notes in 1861 that "We
have only one thing to learn from the barbarians, and that is strong ships
and effective guns." Responding to initiatives taken by the government,
"people of extraordinary intelligence" ought to develop "new ideas and
improve on Western methods. At first they may take the foreigners as
their teachers and models; then they may come to the same level and be
their equals; finally they may move ahead and surpass them" (708–9).

At that time, threats to China's sovereignty were numerous, such as
indemnities, import tariffs, the opening of the British trade base in Hong
Kong, and legal extraterritoriality enforced as a result of the Opium War
of 1843 (Schirokauer 387–89). Although the establishment in 1854 of
the Foreign Inspectorate of Customs in Shanghai was to become a
source of support for the ailing Ch'ing dynasty, hostilities between the
Europeans and China continued. In 1860, the Western allies entered the
capital, and the British, most infamously, burned down the Peking summer palace (Schirokauer 390). Although none of these events turned
China into a full-fledged colony, Feng's writing displays tropes of mimicry and hybridity resembling those that Bhabha finds typical of colonial
discourse. Referring to Bhabha's theory, Gareth Griffiths has argued that
it is a "powerful need" of indigenous peoples — here seen as an analogy
to colonized subjects — "to re-assert their pre-colonized cultures and to
struggle for the recuperation of their cultural difference and its resilience
in and through the local and specific." However, similar to Rey Chow,
he warns against the mythologizing of such assertions of anti-imperialist
authenticity. It tends to disregard the "powerful weapons" — displacement, disruption, ambivalence, mimicry — that can be found in the
multiple transformations of subaltern subject positions within hybridized
encounters between the colonized and the colonizers. By contrast, the
self-enclosed assertion of a "pure authentic sign" of indigenous tradition
precludes the awareness of such transformations (75–76).

In light of this comment, Feng's position takes on a virtually postcolonial significance, for instead of opposing Western power and nativist
tradition, he seeks to open up a "Third Space" between them. Feng
envisions a dialectic whereby the imitation of Western military and technological skills acknowledges the present weakness of the Chinese political situation while asserting the dormant but ineradicable cultural
ingenuity of his country, and thus its superiority over the Western bar-

barians. Combining the advocacy of pragmatically motivated Westernization with a revival of the "Middle Kingdom's" indigenous cultural resources, Feng inscribes an indigenous — one could even say, ethnocentrist — core of resistance into the politics of internationalism. This procedure, he speculates, will ultimately enable the Chinese to surpass the authoritative model of the foreigners; the Chinese should employ the "instruments of the barbarians" — without adopting their culture — in order to "repel them" ultimately (709).

A comparable, but more radical position was later taken by Sun Yat-Sen (1866–1925), the leader of the Nationalist Revolution that in 1911 overthrew the decadent and corrupt Manchu Dynasty in order to establish a Chinese republic based on Western democratic principles and economic theory (Schirokauer 473–74). By 1924 Sun's pro-Western stance had changed into a critique of foreign economic imperialism, Western materialism, and cosmopolitanism (Schirokauer 768). Since the 1911 revolution, Sun argues, the overthrowing of the oppressive dynasty of the foreign (non-Han) Manchu has strengthened the people's spirit of resistance against Western control by political force. In response to this resistance, the West has turned to economic pressure to keep China down; this however is a form of oppression to which the Chinese are hardly sensitive. "As a consequence," Sun contends, "China is being transformed everywhere into a colony of the foreign powers." The country is not just a "semi-colony" as many argue; rather, its situation is worse than that of a full-fledged colony. China is, in fact, "the colony of every nation with which it has concluded treaties; each of them is China's master," rendering the country effectively what Sun calls a "hypo-colony," that is, a colony of the lowest order (769–70). Considering this national crisis and foreign exploitation, Sun continues, the idea of cosmopolitanism, as embraced by England, Germany, and Russia as well as by many young Chinese, needs to be re-examined. Echoing China's self-conception as world empire, cosmopolitanism is theoretically sound, but in concrete political terms, "it is because formerly the Chinese intellectual class had cosmopolitan ideas that, when the Manchus crossed China's frontier, the whole country was lost to them" (770).

Like Feng, Sun seeks inspiration for his cause of nationalist resistance to foreign hegemony in traditional Chinese morality — "loyalty and filial piety, then humanity and love, faithfulness and duty, harmony and peace" (771). The question is, of course, whether these are not precisely the values that contributed to the attitude of political subservience and emperor-worship criticized by Western observers like Kafka. In this sense it is ironic that Sun strategically revives these traditional sentiments in order to forge a new "national spirit" and a new sense of social solidarity supposed to extricate China from its present position as the "poorest and weakest nation in the world" (769). Nonetheless, what is interesting in terms of postcolonial hybridity is that Sun's discourse defines national resistance through a critical revaluation of the very terms — Western economic power, cosmopolitanism, colonialism — that contributed to the self-formation of modern China.

In Feng's and Sun's texts, we encounter a sophisticated re-assertion of Chinese intellectual self-understanding and political agency that is very different from Kafka's projection of national dispersion, passive emperor-worship, and historiographic confusion. Yet it would be unproductive simply to play off the discursive authenticity of these real Chinese voices against Kafka's fictive orientalism. Rather, the immense value of "Beim Bau der chinesischen Mauer" as a cultural statement — supplementing its undeniably great aesthetic merits — lies in its propensity for rhetorical and ideological self-transgression. The text's ironic deconstruction of its own orientalist stereotypes — the fact that Kafka himself is thoroughly critical about the tropes of political inertia recorded by his own narrator — points to its own "beyond," to what it leaves out of its discursive projection of Chinese reality — agency, resistance, self-articulation. Although "Beim Bau der chinesischen Mauer" undeniably originates from within the ideological horizon of colonialism and orientalist discourse, its potential meaning is not at all confined to this horizon. Rather, because of the very one-sidedness of the Chinese narrator's point of view, the story almost necessarily calls for a critical juxtaposition of its account of Chinese history with that of alternative voices such as Feng's and Sun's. While they are not postcolonial in the chronological sense of the term, they do open up a historical dimension, a geopolitical terrain, and an ideological horizon that simultaneously supplement, critique, and transcend the European vision of the non-Western Other. In exploring figures of displacement and hybridity, and by suggesting the need for contrapuntal readings, Kafka's texts thus point beyond their own times to our contemporary world. Its dominant trope, according to Bhabha, is "to locate the question of culture in the realm of the *beyond*" and in a "moment of transit where space and time cross to produce complex figures of difference and identity, past and present, inside and outside, inclusion and exclusion" (1). It is for these profoundly temporal reasons, and not, ultimately, because of their seemingly ahistorical universality, that Kafka's explorations of cultural translation continue to speak to our postcolonial situation.

Notes

[1] Chow's work, though, while concerned with Chinese cultural studies, has drawn on Walter Benjamin for theoretical issues of cross-cultural negation. See my "Postkoloniale Kritik und kulturelle Authentizität: Zur Rezeption Walter Benjamins in der amerikanischen Kulturtheorie," *Weimarer Beiträge* 45 (1999): 532–46. It should also be noted that Anglo-American theories are increasingly being appropriated, critiqued, and expanded in German Studies. For the reception of anthropological and post-colonial approaches in Germany, see the excellent volumes *Kultur als Text* (Frankfurt am Main: S. Fischer, 1996), edited by Bachmann-Medick, and *Figuren der/des Dritten* (Amsterdam: Rodopi, 1998), edited by Breger and Döring.

[2] This does not mean, of course, that Kafka's texts are themselves ahistorical. Müller-Seidel's study is the most extensive discussion of "In der Strafkolonie" in a colonial context, covering the story's origins in literary modernism and the First World War as well as the background of legal history, deportations, sociology, and ethnographic travel. See Piper for further aspects of the Hapsburg Empire as a context for "In der Strafkolonie." Discussing Kafka's rewriting of stereotypical representations of the Jewish body defined by race, illness, and gender, Gilman offers a detailed reading of "In der Strafkolonie" as fictional reworking of the imprisonment of Alfred Dreyfus, the French officer accused of high treason, on Devil's Island (68–88). See also Müller-Seidel 29–30 and *passim*. Piper doubts that any character of "In der Strafkolonie" refers specifically to the Dreyfus affair (44).

[3] All citations of Kafka's works are from the Fischer/Schocken Critical Edition. All translations are my own.

[4] For remarks on "culture's untranslatability" and the "assimilationist's dream," see Bhabha, *The Location of Culture* (London: Routledge, 1994), 224.

[5] I discuss Kafka's employment of this figure (see Bhabha 85–92) in greater detail in my comments on "In der Strafkolonie."

[6] See also Müller-Seidel, *Die Deportation des Menschen: Kafka's Erzählung "In der Strafkolonie" im europäischen Kontext* (Stuttgart: Metzler, 1986) on the story's connection between mastery and discourse (122–26).

[7] Müller-Seidel comments extensively on the traveler's views on the legal system and human rights (130–41).

[8] See also Gareth Griffiths' point that even "when the subaltern appears to 'speak' there is a real concern as to whether what we are listening to is really a subaltern voice, or whether the subaltern[s are] being spoken by the subject position they occupy within the larger discursive economy" ("The Myth of Authenticity," in *De-Scribing Empire,* ed. Tiffin and Lawson [London: Routledge, 1994], 75).

[9] Bhabha refers several times to Benjamin's famous phrase (4, 8, 18, 233). For reflections on the importance of Benjamin's notion of translation for cultural theory, see Bhabha 224 and 227.

[10] See Clifford, "On Ethnographic Authority," in *The Predicament of Culture* (Cambridge: Harvard UP, 1988), 46–54 for the theory and examples of this type of ethnographic inquiry.

Works Cited

Anderson, Mark M. *Kafka's Clothes: Ornament and Aestheticism in the Habsburg Fin de Siècle.* Oxford: Clarendon P, 1992.

Ashcroft, Bill, Gareth Griffiths, and Helen Tiffin, eds. *The Post-Colonial Studies Reader.* London: Routledge, 1995.

Bachmann-Medick, Doris, ed. *Kultur als Text: Die anthropologische Wende in der Literaturwissenschaft.* Frankfurt am Main: Fischer, 1996.

Benjamin, Walter. *Das Passagen-Werk.* Ed. Rolf Tiedemann. Frankfurt am Main: Suhrkamp, 1982.

Berman, Russell A. *Enlightenment or Empire: Colonial Discourse in German Culture.* Lincoln: U of Nebraska P, 1998.

Bhabha, Homi K. *The Location of Culture.* London: Routledge, 1994.

Breger, Claudia and Tobias Döring. *Figuren der/des Dritten: Erkundungen kultureller Zwischenräume.* Amsterdam: Rodopi, 1998.

Chow, Rey. "Where Have all the Natives Gone?" *Writing Diaspora: Tactics of Intervention in Contemporary Cultural Studies.* Bloomington: Indiana UP, 1993. 27–54.

Clifford, James. "On Ethnographic Authority." *The Predicament of Culture: Twentieth-Century Ethnography, Literature, and Art.* Cambridge: Harvard UP, 1988. 21–54.

de Bary, William Theodore, Wing-tsit Chan, and Burton Watson, eds. *Sources of Chinese Tradition.* New York: Columbia UP, 1960.

Dittmar, Julius. *Im neuen China: Reiseeindrücke von J. Dittmar.* Cologne: Schaffstein, 1912.

Feng Kuei-Fen. "On the Manufacture of Foreign Weapons." De Bary, Chan, and Watson 707–10.

Gilman, Sander L. *Franz Kafka: The Jewish Patient.* New York: Routledge, 1995.

Goebel, Rolf J. *Constructing China: Kafka's Orientalist Discourse.* Columbia, SC: Camden House, 1997.

———. "Postkoloniale Kritik und kulturelle Authentizität: Zur Rezeption Walter Benjamins in der amerikanischen Kulturtheorie." *Weimarer Beiträge* 45 (1999): 532–46.

Griffiths, Gareth. "The Myth of Authenticity: Representation, Discourse and Social Practice." *De-Scribing Empire: Post-Colonialism and Textuality.* Ed. Chris Tiffin and Alan Lawson. London: Routledge, 1994. 70–85.

Fanon, Frantz. *The Wretched of the Earth.* Preface Jean-Paul Sartre. Trans. Constance Farrington. New York: Grove P, 1968.

Kafka, Franz. "Beim Bau der chinesischen Mauer." *Nachgelassene Schriften und Fragmente I*. Ed. Malcolm Pasley. Frankfurt am Main: S. Fischer; New York: Schocken, 1993. 337–57.

———. *Der Verschollene*. Ed. Jost Schillemeit. Frankfurt am Main: S. Fischer; New York: Schocken, 1983.

———. "In der Strafkolonie." *Drucke zu Lebzeiten*. Ed. Hans-Gerd Koch, Wolf Kittler, and Gerhard Neumann. Frankfurt am Main: S. Fischer; New York: Schocken, 1994. 201–48.

———. *Nachgelassene Schriften und Fragmente II*. Ed. Jost Schillemeit. Frankfurt am Main: S. Fischer; New York: Schocken, 1992. (*NS II*)

Müller-Seidel, Walter. *Die Deportation des Menschen: Kafkas Erzählung "In der Strafkolonie" im europäischen Kontext*. Stuttgart: Metzler, 1986.

Nicolai, Ralf R. *Kafkas "Beim Bau der chinesischen Mauer" im Lichte themenverwandter Texte*. Würzburg: Königshausen und Neumann, 1991.

Parry, Benita. "Problems in Current Theories of Colonial Discourse." Ashcroft, Griffiths, and Tiffin 36–44.

Piper, Karen. "The Language of the Machine: A Post-Colonial Reading of Kafka." *Journal of the Kafka Society of America* 20 (1996): 42–54.

Said, Edward W. *Culture and Imperialism*. New York: Knopf, 1993.

———. "Traveling Theory." *The World, the Text, and the Critic*. Cambridge, MA: Harvard UP, 1983. 226–47.

Schirokauer, Conrad. *A Brief History of Chinese and Japanese Civilizations*. San Diego: Harcourt Brace Jovanovich, 1978.

Sun Yat-Sen. "The Three People's Principles." De Bary, Chan, and Watson 767–71.

Disjunctive Signs: Semiotics, Aesthetics, and Failed Mediation in "In der Strafkolonie"

Richard T. Gray

IN DER STRAFKOLONIE" (In the Penal Colony) is a text that has often been accorded a special place in Kafka's oeuvre. In his authoritative early study *Tragik und Ironie,* first published in 1964, Walter Sokel seeks to establish the transitional status of this text in two principal respects: with regard to its narrative structure, Sokel identifies in "Strafkolonie" a shift from the perspectival, "expressionistic" narratives of Kafka's earlier period to the "parabolic" writing of his later years (103); and in terms of tone and thematic approach, Sokel views this text as a first step away from the "tragic" dramatization of Kafka's father conflict in the early texts to the ironic presentation of this problematic in the later works (129–31). If Sokel views the uniqueness of this text as deriving precisely from the complexities and polyvalence constituted by its transitional, quasi-experimental nature, other critics have insisted, on the contrary, that what makes "Strafkolonie" anomalous in the context of Kafka's other works is its closure and univocality. For Heinz Politzer, for example, it is "outwardly the most conclusive" of all of Kafka's short stories (98). Similarly Ingeborg Henel, in an influential 1973 essay on the form of this work and its relative place in Kafka's overall literary production, claims that this story's peculiarity resides in the absence of the mysterious, opaque, and riddle-like quality characteristic of Kafka's other works (500).

The thesis that "Strafkolonie" is the most straightforward and transparent of Kafka's longer narratives seems to be belied by the critical reception of this text, which has produced a plethora of diverse interpretations rivaled only by the critical response to the novels *Der Proceß* (The Trial) and *Das Schloß* (The Castle) and such seminal stories as "Das Urteil" (The Judgment) and "Die Verwandlung" (The Metamorphosis). Indeed, one might justifiably claim that the spectrum of hermeneutic engagements with "In der Strafkolonie" is broader than that evoked by most of Kafka's other works. This is due, I believe, to two powerful countertendencies manifest in this text. One of these is the almost nebulous, highly abstract quality of the plot and central images of the story. For Roy Pascal, for example, this greater abstraction, in particular the distance Kafka places between himself and the biographical connection to his father, so clearly mirrored in the breakthrough stories "Das Urteil" and "Die Verwandlung," marks "a distinct maturing of Kafka's art" and defines the centrality of this text in Kafka's development (143). The other tendency, which is highly unusual for Kafka's fiction, is the clear allusion to specific realities of Kafka's day, namely to the institution of the penal colony and to the problematic of deportation as a legal-forensic remedy made possible by the conditions of colonialism. This dimension of the story leads Walter Müller-Seidel to read it as a "document of humanity" that voices a scathing critique of the death penalty, the modern institutions of penal justice, and state-sponsored terror in general (160; see also 87, 111).[1]

Axel Hecker has recently noted that interpreters of "In der Strafkolonie" fall into two general categories, "officers" and "explorers," who neatly reflect the attitudes of the two central figures in Kafka's tale. For Hecker the hermeneutical "officers" are those who, like the Officer in the story, muster all the rhetoric at their disposal to identify and defend a specific, often narrow meaning for the story, whereas the "explorers," like Kafka's "Forschungsreisender" (D 203),[2] are less definitive, refuse to take a clear side, and seek judiciously to weigh the evidence of the text (Hecker 115–17). But one could also describe this critical divide as one between predominantly figurative interpreters, on the one hand, and critics who, on the other hand, focus more on the literal, textual level of the story. For critics such as Henel it is precisely the obviously allegorical nature of this text that sets it apart from Kafka's other longer narratives (482). Significantly, Henel's hypothesis that the allegorical character of "Strafkolonie" is what constitutes its uniqueness among Kafka's stories has received veritable critical enshrinement since being adopted in Hartmut Binder's *Kafka-Handbuch* as the final word on this text. In the section of the *Handbuch* authored by Henel and dedicated to the periodization and historical development of Kafka's art, this thesis is given its strongest formulation. Here we can read that "Strafkolonie" "is the only allegory Kafka ever wrote, and as such it represents the extreme pole of his proclivity for abstraction" (2: 229). To be sure, Henel's statement receives some confirmation from the interpretive history of this text: allegorical readings of widely divergent sorts clearly constitute one of the most prominent directions in the critical reception of "Strafkolonie." Such allegorical approaches tend to fall into two main groups: those that interpret the text along various Judeo-Christian lines (see, for example, the essays by Fickert, Steinberg, and Thomas); and those ontological approaches that view the text as the demonstration of an existential guilt that inheres in the very substance of human life (for example, Beckmann 1989, 1994; Davey; Emrich, 221–26, and even Henel, 483).[3] To the extent that these allegorical interpreters of "Strafkolonie" almost invariably take sides with the Officer as the representative of the Old Commandant and the system he created, there is additional justification for identifying them with Hecker's hermeneutical "officers." To be sure, this valorization of the Officer and the brutal, unenlightened, irrational penal system he defends contains an inherent and wry paradox. This irony is most clearly in evidence in a recent interpretation by David Pan that follows the general pattern of earlier allegorical approaches but offers a new set of referents, "primitivism" and "universalist culture," as the abstract entities represented by the old and new systems in Kafka's text (see esp. 4–5 and 39–40). Pan glorifies the Officer as the avatar of primitivism and condemns the Explorer as the representative of a tyrannical universalist culture that seeks mastery and dominance, and in doing so repeats the black-and-white portraiture of previous allegorical readings and fails to resolve the contradiction that the system represented by the Officer, and allegedly defended by Kafka, is all too obviously characterized by that very brutality, dominance, and tyranny over others that Kafka is supposed to be criticizing in the hegemony of "universalist" culture. If Kafka had wanted to justify the Officer and his brand of penal justice, wouldn't he have played down the obvious fanaticism of this character and the unmitigated violence of the machine he serves and services?

The faction of literalist interpreters, led above all by Walter Müller-Seidel, insists that Kafka's text is grounded primarily in "contemporary history," not in "metaphysics, a theology of redemption, or other such themes" (87). For Müller-Seidel, Kafka's text alludes above all to the specific historico-empirical facts of justice under the conditions of deportation made possible by the modern penal colony, and the obvious distortions the text enforces upon these empirical facts reflect Kafka's strategy of employing exaggeration for the purpose of more prominent demonstration (111). Müller-Seidel seeks corroboration of this perspective largely in an examination of Kafka's possible sources and his acquaintance, as a trained lawyer, with relevant debates in the discipline of jurisprudence about deportation as a viable punitive measure. But the most prominent tack of recent literalist readers is to understand the torture machine of "Strafkolonie" as a writing and/or reading machine, and from here to interpret the story in terms of Kafka's reflections on his own writing practice or his vision of reading at the time the story was composed in 1914. Clayton Koelb's essay "Kafka and the Scene of Reading" initiates this series of analyses. Koelb discerns in the penal writing machine defended by the Officer the literalization of a process of reading, enacted as the twelve-hour torture the Prisoner undergoes as he deciphers the message engraved into his flesh. Mark Anderson provides a valuable variation on this theme by reading the metaphors of writing performed in this text in the context of aesthetic discussions, especially that of the theory and practice of decadence that were current during Kafka's day. Axel Hecker sees the apparatus as a "deconstruction machine" whose malfunctioning in the narrative of the story anticipates and mimics the malfunctioning of Kafka's text itself, its inability to achieve resolution. Wolf Kittler interprets the writing machine at the center of "Strafkolonie" as a reflection of technological innovations in mechanical language reproduction, such as the typewriter and the Dictaphone, focusing especially on the secondary impact these inventions had on legal institutions and procedures during Kafka's lifetime. Klaus Mladek, finally, sees the destruction of the penal machine as Kafka's ironization of his own imperfect act of writing. A set of related interpretations, most notable those by Norris and Horn, follow the critical model established by Gilles Deleuze and Felix Guattari, interpreting "Strafkolonie" as a subversive performance of sadistic rituals that serves ultimately to undermine the very foundation of enlightened reason.

This brief and schematic summary should suffice as an indication that, contrary to the assertions of Politzer and Henel, "In der Strafkolonie" is anything but a conclusive, univocal, or non-enigmatic text. On the contrary, of all the texts published by Kafka during his lifetime, it is perhaps the most fractured, disjunctive, and inconclusive. It is well known, of course, that Kafka himself was extremely dissatisfied with the conclusion of this story, calling it "Machwerk" (botched, *B* 159), and that it was this dissatisfaction that motivated the five-year hiatus between its composition in 1914 and its first publication in 1919. Moreover, when Kafka returned to the story in August 1917 at the prompting of his publisher Kurt Wolff, he invested his energies almost exclusively in revisions of the ending (see *Tagebücher* 822–27), all of which he ultimately discarded, retaining with a small deletion the initial, objectionable conclusion. My approach to "Strafkolonie" will cast me in the role of one of the interpretive "explorers" of this text; for my aim is not to take sides and present a presumptively conclusive reading of this story, but instead to reflect on the reasons why this text resists any neat and simple interpretive reduction. My hypothesis is that the very prominence of disparities and disjunctive structures suggests that what this story thematizes is nothing other than disjunction itself. If critics noted early on that Kafka's Explorer is one of the most peculiar characters in all his fiction (Politzer 112; Sokel 118), none has adequately reflected on the mediating role this character is called upon to play — and, moreover, the miserable way in which he fails to perform any mediating function whatsoever.[4] From this position, which stakes out the territory of failed mediation in this text, I believe one can discover a perspective that allows a reading of the story as a self-reflection on Kafka's art and artistry, but one that focuses not so much on acts of writing and reading, as previous interpreters have stressed, but rather on the act of *narration* as a fundamentally mediative event. Here it is important to recall that Kafka's text centers on an act of narration performed by the Officer as he attempts to "mediate" an understanding of the penal machine and the system of the Old Commandant to the Explorer, an outsider who has neither any knowledge of, nor any sympathy for this system. Indeed, a large portion of Kafka's text is made up of the Officer's act of narration; and when we as readers exit the fictional world of the past invoked by the Officer — which includes the presumed wiles of the New Commandant intended to subvert this system, as well as the Officer's counter-machinations against this ostensible plot — and enter the real time of the Explorer's experiences in the penal colony, the events that transpire, in particular the operation of the penal machine, run absolutely counter to the fictions invoked in the Officer's narrative. In other words, the fictional world of the story and that of the Officer's narrated story within the story are almost entirely discontinuous.

Walter Benjamin was one of the first to point out the dialectical nature of Kafka's literature, claiming as early as 1934 in his essay "Franz Kafka: Zur zehnten Wiederkehr seines Todestages," that Kafka composed "fairy tales for dialecticians" (15). But of all Kafka's stories and novels, "In der Strafkolonie" is unquestionably the most dialectical. Indeed, dialectic, in the venerable form of dialogic exchange enshrined in the works of Plato, is inscribed into the very structure of this text and concretized most manifestly in the opposition between its two primary characters, the Officer and the Explorer. This is the only text by Kafka in which we find two potential protagonists (see Henel 482; Politzer 105; Thieberger 304), and interpretations of the story depend fundamentally, as previous critics have indicated (Hecker 115; Beckmann 1989, 391), on whose side the individual interpreter is inclined to take. But unlike the classically dialectical debaters Naphta and Settembrini in Thomas Mann's novel *Der Zauberberg*, who engage critically, following the Platonic pattern, in each other's ideas and arguments, the dialogic positions of Kafka's Officer and Explorer seem to run on parallel tracks in a Euclidean world, so that they tend to speak or even think past one another.[5] The dialectic in Kafka's text is, in other words, a fractured dialectic, one that from the outset allows no possibility for resolution and Hegelian sublation, for a happy — or, for that matter, even an unhappy — synthesis of the opposing positions.

The impossibility of reconciliation between the standpoints of the Officer and the Explorer is brought out clearly in one of the rare instances of narrative intervention in this text. This occurs at the crucial juncture in which the Officer, explaining the public solidarity and sense of communion that, according to his narrative of the past, used to emerge in response to the Prisoner's transfiguration during his punishment by the machine, physically embraces the Explorer.

> Der Reisende wollte sein Gesicht dem Offizier entziehen und blickte ziellos herum. Der Offizier glaubte, er betrachte die Öde des Tales; er ergriff deshalb seine Hände, drehte sich um ihn, um seine Blicke zu fassen, und fragte: "Merken Sie die Schande?"
>
> Aber der Reisende schwieg. Der Offizier ließ für ein Weilchen von ihm ab [. . .] (D 227)

> [The Explorer wanted to withdraw his face from the Officer and looked around aimlessly. The Officer thought he was observing the desolation of the valley; therefore he grasped his hands, circled around him in order to catch his gaze, and asked: "Do you recognize the infamy?"
>
> But the Explorer remained silent. The Officer left him alone for a little while [. . .]]

Kafka turns necessarily to the authority of the narrator here in order to illuminate the opposing intentions of each character and the way in which his own desires shape his interpretation of the other's gestures and actions. The Officer, in fact, seeks to exploit what he sees as the Explorer's distracted observation of the surrounding desolation to try to win him over to his point of view. It is no coincidence that he once again uses physical contact, the grasping of the Explorer's hands, in an attempt to evoke an air of intimacy and shared community. The "grasping" of the Explorer's hands explicitly parallels the "fassen" (catching) of his gaze. But instead of receiving the desired signs of agreement and solidarity, the Officer is confronted by the Explorer's silence and evasive glances.

When semiotic mediation occurs between these two figures, no transformation takes place in the horizon of understanding that informs the interlocutors' positions, as would be the ideal case in hermeneutic interaction. Instead, each interpreter simply ascribes a meaning to the signs of the other such that these willfully confirm the significance the interpreter wants them to have. For example, when the Officer asks the Explorer whether the New Commandant has already explained the penal apparatus to him, the Explorer responds merely with "eine ungewisse Handbewegung" (an uncertain movement of his hand, D 205), which the Officer arbitrarily interprets in accordance with his own wishes, taking it as his cue to supply the detailed explanation he is bent on providing: "der Offizier verlangte nichts Besseres, denn nun konnte er selbst den Apparat erklären" (D 205; the Officer desired nothing better, for now he could explain the apparatus himself). When the Officer later attributes just such interpretive tyranny to the New Commandant in his interactions with the Explorer, he is both projecting onto the Commandant his own herme-neutical strategy and simultaneously describing the universal semiotic disjunction operative in this text. Explaining how the New Commandant is bound to understand the statements of the Explorer in a way that will confirm his, the Commandant's, own opinions, the Officer asserts: "Ein flüchtiges, ein bloß unvorsichtiges Wort genügt. Es muß gar nicht Ihrer Überzeugung entsprechen, wenn es nur scheinbar seinem Wunsche ent-gegenkommt" (D 228; A fleeting, a merely incautious word will suffice. It doesn't even have to correspond with your conviction, as long as it apparently conforms with his wish). What people seek from interpersonal contact in the world of Kafka's "Strafkolonie" is nothing but *apparent* confirmation of their own desires.

The only counterpoint to this fractured dialectic in Kafka's story is the interaction between the Prisoner and the Soldier. Using the doubling technique Kafka employs so frequently in his stories and novels, this relationship doubles but also distorts the basic dialectic between the two primary characters. If the Officer and Explorer find no common ground, then the Prisoner and Soldier discover almost nothing but intimate, immediate solidarity, exaggerated and perverted into nearly Chap-linesque slapstick. This occurs, moreover, despite the hierarchically con-structed opposition between the transgressor and defender of the law that defines their basic relationship. The object around which this soli-darity emerges is the rice purée placed in a container on the machine for the nourishment of the Prisoner during the twelve-hour process of his execution. As they witness the interaction between the Officer and the Explorer, centered around the explanation of the machine and its opera-tion, the Prisoner and the Soldier share a kind of communal meal (D 227, 235). The solidarity that unexpectedly arises between these two secondary figures ironically mirrors, of course, exactly that solidarity the Officer would like to achieve with the Explorer, his wish of winning him over to support the machine and the system of the Old Commandant against the opposition of the New Commandant. When, carried away by his own rhetoric and by the soporific emotionality inherent in his portrayal of the glory days of the Old Commandant and his machine, the Officer hugs the Explorer and calls him "comrade," he is attempting to construct a kind of subliminal solidarity between himself and his dialogic partner that is similar to the relationship that emerges between the Prisoner and the Soldier.

> "Wie nahmen wir alle den Ausdruck der Verklärung von dem gemarterten Gesicht, wie hielten wir unsere Wangen in den Schein dieser endlich erreichten und schon vergehenden Gerechtigkeit! Was für Zeiten, mein Kamerad!" Der Offizier hatte offenbar vergessen, wer vor ihm stand; er hatte den Reisenden umarmt und den Kopf auf seine Schulter gelegt. Der Reisende war in großer Verlegenheit [. . .] (*D* 226)

> ["How we all took the expression of transfiguration from the martyred face, how we held our cheeks in the glow of this justice that was finally achieved and already fading! What great times those were, my comrade!" The Officer had apparently forgotten who was standing before him; he had embraced the Explorer and placed his head on his shoulder. The Explorer was greatly embarrassed.]

Although the pseudo-narrator intervenes here, suggesting that the Officer commits this act in a moment of self-forgetfulness, there is good reason to believe that he is actually pursuing a calculated strategy, deploying touch and other signs of social intimacy to overcome the Explorer's resistance. It is no coincidence, of course, that the Officer enacts this gesture of cordial camaraderie with the Explorer at precisely that point in his narrative in which he describes the moment of communion that, in his account of the past, formed the culminating event of public executions. Here again Kafka's text constructs an ironic contrast between the fictional world invoked in the Officer's narrative and the real-time experience of the fictional characters themselves, marked in this instance by the Explorer's embarrassed response to the Officer's verbal and physical entreaties. But as we have seen, no semiotic mediation, no meeting of the minds, ever takes place between the Officer and the Explorer.

By contrast, the Soldier and the Prisoner not only experience successful semiotic exchange, but even come together in an apparent friendship.

Der Soldat und der Verurteilte schienen sich miteinander befreundet zu haben; der Verurteilte machte, so schwierig dies bei der festen Ein-schnallung durchzuführen war, dem Soldaten Zeichen; der Soldat beugte sich zu ihm; der Verurteilte flüsterte ihm etwas zu, und der Sol-dat nickte. (*D* 236)

[The Soldier and the Prisoner seemed to have formed a friendship; as difficult as this was, given how tightly he was bound, the Prisoner made signs to the Soldier; the Soldier bent down to him; the Prisoner whis-pered something to him and the Soldier nodded.]

Even in spite of his limited mobility, the Prisoner succeeds in communi-cating via gestural signs with the Soldier; and when he expresses himself through verbal signs, he receives the affirmation of his interlocutor. Their relationship, then, can be seen as a kind of parodistic exaggeration of the ideal of spontaneous communicative understanding described by the Officer in his explanation of the glory days of the penal machine.[6] The interaction between the Officer and Explorer, however, belies any such communicative mediation, and when the Explorer banishes the Soldier and Prisoner from his boat at the end of the story, perhaps what he is signaling is precisely a rejection of the apparent solidarity they have realized, or at least the Explorer's recognition that he cannot participate in such mindless communitarianism.[7]

The complex interactions between these two sets of characters have not yet been completely illuminated; the structures of parallelism and ironic contrast extend into yet further dimensions of this relationship. In an important sense, the Soldier and the Prisoner have assumed the posi-tion in the real-time events of the story that the spectators at the execu-tion — in particular the two children the Officer holds in his left and right arm (*D* 226) — take up in the Officer's narrative about the past. Like the standpoint of this audience vis-à-vis the execution, the perspec-tive of the Soldier and the Prisoner is one based on pure spectatorship, since they do not comprehend a single word of the verbal exchange that passes between the Officer and the Explorer, which is conducted in French, a language they do not understand (*D* 207). This is an impor-tant detail, of course, since it highlights once more the issue of problem-atized mediation in this text. Shut out from the verbal interaction that transpires between the Officer and the Explorer, the Prisoner is reduced to struggling to comprehend the machine and the procedure to which he will be subjected by following the movements and the reactions of the Explorer (*D* 209): he is already, in effect, forced into that situation of complex hermeneutic decipherment on the basis of limited sensual stimuli that forms the essence of the punishment and eventual "illumination" he is supposed to experience on the penal machine.

Kafka brilliantly choreographs this parallelism in the scene in which the Officer explains to the Explorer the operation of the harrow, that part of the machine responsible for carving the condemned man's sentence into his flesh. During this episode the Explorer notices with dismay that the Prisoner is trying to follow this explanation, even mimicking the position and pose the Explorer assumes vis-à-vis the machine.

> Da sah er [der Reisende] zu seinem Schrecken, daß auch der Verurteilte gleich ihm der Einladung des Offiziers, sich die Einrichtung der Egge aus der Nähe anzusehen, gefolgt war. [. . .] Man sah, wie er [der Verurteilte] mit unsicheren Augen auch das suchte, was die zwei Herren eben beobachtet hatten, wie es ihm aber, da ihm die Erklärung fehlte, nicht gelingen wollte. Er beugte sich hierhin und dorthin. Immer wieder lief er mit den Augen das Glas ab. (*D* 216)

> [Then he [the Explorer] saw to his dismay that, like him, the Prisoner had accepted the Officer's invitation to view the structure of the harrow from close up. [. . .] One saw how he [the Prisoner] sought with uncertain eyes what the two other men had just observed, but how he was not successful at this, since he was deprived of an explanation. He bent down this way and that way. He repeatedly ran his eyes up and down the glass.]

As an enactment of a rebuffed search for transparency, this scene is emblematic of the problems at the heart of Kafka's story. Lacking any verbal clues that might give him some stable points of orientation, the Prisoner is reduced to imitating the pose of objective, comprehending observation assumed by the Explorer. The glass he thoroughly, if futilely, examines with his "uncertain eyes" is the glass out of which the harrow itself is constructed. But instead of peering *through* this glass, using it as a transparent medium that will reveal to him the secrets he seeks, the Prisoner stares *at* it. The medium itself, not what it potentially mediates, has become the object of his attention. But it is not a case — to allude to Marshall McLuhan's claim — of the medium being the message. On the contrary, it is the medium, or rather the very lack of an adequate, "transparent" medium, that banishes any hope of communicating any message whatsoever. The Explorer is jockeyed into the structural position of a Hermes, as the potential mediator of information between the Officer and the Prisoner. Himself excluded from acquiring definitive information about the machine and the penal procedure, the Prisoner trains his gaze on the Explorer; "er schien zu fragen, ob er den geschilderten Vorgang billigen könne" (*D* 211; he seemed to be asking whether the Explorer was inclined to sanction the depicted procedure). The Explorer unwittingly — and unwillingly — takes on the role of a hermeneutical intermediary, without, however, ever being able to satisfy the demands for meaning and clarification addressed to him by the Prisoner.

The fictional world of "In der Strafkolonie" is one in which translation of any sort seems utterly impossible: it is a world without a divine Hermes capable of transmitting messages from one sphere to another. Only those like the Soldier and the Prisoner, who from the outset share a common ground, have any hope of shared understanding. To comprehend this we need only consider the alienation and total incomprehension with which the Explorer responds to the messages encoded on the manuscript pages written by the Old Commandant and used for programming the operations of the penal machine.

> Er [der Offizier] zeigte das erste Blatt. Der Reisende hätte gerne etwas Anerkennendes gesagt, aber er sah nur labyrinthartige, einander vielfach kreuzende Linien, die so dicht das Papier bedeckten, daß man nur mit Mühe die weißen Zwischenräume erkannte. "Lesen Sie," sagte der Offizier. "Ich kann nicht," sagte der Reisende. "Es ist doch deutlich," sagte der Offizier. "Es ist sehr kunstvoll," sagte der Reisende ausweichend, "aber ich kann es nicht entziffern." (*D* 217)

> [He [the Officer] showed the first page. The Explorer would have liked to say something appreciative, but all he saw were labyrinth-like lines that constantly intersected and covered the paper so completely that one could only discern with difficulty the white interstices. "Read it," the Officer said. "I can't," the Explorer replied. "But it's perfectly clear," the Officer said. "It's very ornate," the Explorer replied evasively, "but I can't decipher it."]

Although the manuscript page is intended to help bridge the chasm that separates the Officer from the Explorer, instead it merely reinforces the incommensurability of their respective positions. What is perfectly clear and self-evident ("deutlich") to the Officer appears to the Explorer as nothing but a chaos of intersecting lines without any significance. Indeed, the signs on the page — if they are, in fact, signs at all — barely fulfill the minimum criterion necessary for the constitution of writing: the differential contrast between the written marks themselves and the background from which they must be isolated is practically non-existent. Hence the Explorer can scarcely discern the white interstices of the manuscript page against which the writing should be set off. The "evasiveness" with which he responds to the disjunction between the Officer's position and his own — what the Officer interprets as "clear," the Explorer describes politely as "ornate" — anticipates that final act of evasion he will undertake at the conclusion of the story: his headlong flight from the island and his refusal to embrace the Soldier and the Prisoner, who seek refuge with him on his ship. This refusal, signaled by the implied violence with which the Explorer wields the knotted line of the boat (*D* 248), marks his ultimate refusal to accept any mediating function, to play the role of Hermes.

If we turn now to a detailed examination of the penal apparatus itself, we can observe how it simultaneously represents an ideal of perfect mediation and subverts this very ideal by highlighting moments of disjunction. The first thing the Officer emphasizes about the apparatus is its tripartite structure, made up of the "bed," onto which the condemned man is strapped, the "designer," which functions something like the electronic and mechanical brain, or software, for the entire mechanism, and the "harrow," which, moving between the bed and the designer, has the task of inscribing the actual sentence onto the condemned man's body (*D* 206–8). Critics have often assigned symbolic or allegorical significance to the three-part structure of the machine. Those interpreters who approach the text from a Judeo-Christian perspective discover in this structure allusions to the trinity or other religious motifs or paraphernalia structured around the mystical number three (see, for example, Thomas 15); those who pursue a Freudian approach view this structure as a reference to Freud's tripartite division of the psyche into id, ego, and superego (e.g. Dodd 129). But there is no compelling reason to seek the significance of the apparatus's structure beyond a purely literal reading of the machine itself, the described interrelation of its parts, and the role played by the apparatus in the fictional world of the story itself.

According to the Officer's description, the bed and the designer operate wholly independently of one another: each has its own electrical battery, the bed to power its own movement, the designer to enable it to control the movement of the harrow, which is attached to it and which hovers between the designer and the bed (*D* 209). The perfect operation of the apparatus depends on the precise coordination of the otherwise independent movements of the harrow and the bed: only when they interact, as it were, in perfect collaboration, can the machine perform with precision and perfection.

> Sowohl das Bett, als auch der Zeichner haben ihre eigene elektrische Batterie; das Bett braucht sie für sich selbst, der Zeichner für die Egge. Sobald der Mann festgeschnallt ist, wird das Bett in Bewegung gesetzt. Es zittert in winzigen, sehr schnellen Zuckungen gleichzeitig seitlich, wie auch auf und ab. [. . .] [N]ur sind bei unserem Bett alle Bewegun-

gen genau berechnet; sie müssen nämlich peinlich auf die Bewegungen der Egge abgestimmt sein. (*D* 209)

[Both the bed and the designer have their own electric battery; the bed needs it for itself, the designer for the harrow. As soon as the man is strapped down, the bed is set in motion. It vibrates in tiny, very fast convulsive movements, both sideways as well as up and down. [. . .] [B]ut in the case of our bed all the movements are precisely calculated; for they must be painstakingly coordinated with the movements of the harrow.]

Now the kind of collaboration the Officer attributes here to the machine also describes exactly what he expects from the "comradeship" he hopes to establish with the Explorer. Only if the Explorer willingly accepts and executes the detailed plans — the "design" — the Officer has concocted for outmaneuvering the New Commandant, his lackeys, and his ladies, can the counterrevolution the Officer envisions ever be realized. Requisite for this successful joint action, in other words, is a perfectly mediated understanding that will turn the coordinated actions of the Explorer and the Officer into the rigorous operation of a well-programmed, well-maintained machine.

Viewed literally, the machine can be interpreted as a semiotic instrument of mediation insofar as its structure replicates the threefold character of the modern sign. The designer, into which the plans of the Old Commandant are programmed, manifests the conceptual signified, the "transcendental" meaning that must be communicated. The harrow, as the concrete writing instrument, represents the medium, the signifier, by means of which this signified content will be transmitted. The bed is nothing but a placeholder for the interpretant, the intelligent being who will receive the message and decode its significance. The fact that the harrow inscribes its message directly into the flesh of the interpretant alludes to an immediacy of understanding — the signifier and the interpretant become, as it were, one and the same entity — that essentially belies the mediacy of the process itself. In other words, what Clayton Koelb felicitously calls the "scene of reading" enacted by the machine can be described somewhat more precisely as a scene of perfectly transparent semiotic functioning: when the bed (the interpretant) is perfectly coordinated with the inscription of the harrow (the signifier) and this latter is under the careful control of the designer (the signified), perfect, for all intents and purposes *immediate* semiotic transmission of the signified will occur.[8] This is the ideology represented by the Officer and the system of the Old Commandant: the dream of perfect communicative transparency. We should recall in this context that the harrow is explicitly made of glass, a transparent medium, so that the spectators can observe or "read," if they so desire, the sign being branded into the Prisoner's flesh. The glass harrow thereby concretizes the drive for transparency associated with the machine as semiotic apparatus.

This totalizing ideology of transparency explains, among other things, why the Officer can take pride in combining the roles of judge, jury, and executioner in one figure; for only when one and the same person represents all these roles is there no necessity for mediation between distinct agencies or functions, and the final judgment is never clouded by imperfect translation as it passes to successive agents. The Officer implies as much when he explains to the Explorer why it is superfluous to interrogate the Prisoner:

> Hätte ich den Mann zuerst vorgerufen und ausgefragt, so wäre nur Verwirrung entstanden. Er hätte gelogen, hätte, wenn es mir gelungen wäre, die Lügen zu widerlegen, diese durch neue Lügen ersetzt und so fort. Jetzt aber halte ich ihn und lasse ihn nicht mehr. (*D* 213)

> [If I had first made the man appear before me and interrogated him, the result would have been nothing but confusion. He would have lied, would have replaced these lies, if I succeeded in exposing them, with other lies, and so on. But now I have him in my grasp and will no longer let him go.]

Entering the dialogic situation, especially when one can assume opposing views from the outset, is not merely futile, but actually — according to the Officer — counterproductive. What this interaction produces is disjunction, lies, and diversions; in such situations, successful mediation can never take place. It is no coincidence, of course, that, viewed in these terms, the process of interrogation as described by the Officer reflects precisely the situation in which he finds himself in his dealings with the Explorer. He is, after all, well aware of the Explorer's putative opposition to the system he himself glorifies; indeed, he even anticipates the basis of the Explorer's objections: he acknowledges the "European outlooks" that are likely to influence the Explorer's judgment about the machine and its operation, even suggesting that the Explorer might be a committed opponent of the death penalty (*D* 228). The Officer must be able to anticipate as well, then, that, as in the case of interrogating a prisoner, his dialogue with the Explorer will be constructed out of lies, evasions, counter-strategies, and rhetorical tactics. And in fact, this is largely how the dialogue between these two central characters develops.

It would be incorrect, however, to assume that the semiotic transparency so fanatically advocated by the Officer is deserving of our admiration. Indeed, by contextualizing this semiotic-hermeneutic problematic in the sphere of legal justice and concretizing it in the symbol of this violent penal machine, Kafka alludes precisely to the tyranny, brutality, and mastery over others that such an ideology necessarily entails. The text itself calls attention to the ideological blindness of the Officer by ironically exposing the gulf between his idealized theoretical adumbration and the pitifully banal practical reality of the apparatus's operation. Thus, when the Officer finally puts the machine into motion his exposition is irreverently interrupted by a squeaking cog.

> "Können Sie jetzt die Arbeit der Egge und des ganzen Apparates würdigen? — Sehen Sie doch!" Er sprang auf die Leiter, drehte ein Rad, rief hinunter: "Achtung, treten Sie zur Seite!," und alles kam in Gang. Hätte das Rad nicht gekreischt, es wäre herrlich gewesen. (*D* 218)

> ["Are you now able to appreciate the work of the harrow and of the entire apparatus? — Just look!" He jumped onto the ladder, turned a knob, called down "Careful, move to one side!," and everything went into motion. If the cog had not squeaked, it would have been magnificent.]

This is an inherently humorous scene: for at precisely that moment when the Officer expects the Explorer to be able to appreciate the sophistication of the apparatus, the squeaking cog deflates the illusion of grandeur he has sought so painstakingly to conjure up. Moreover, it is significant that the final comment, "Hätte das Rad nicht gekreischt, es wäre herrlich gewesen," is impossible to attribute conclusively to either of the two characters. Who actually makes this remark? Its content, affirming the majesty of the machine and bemoaning this simple flaw, seems to suggest that this is the Officer's thought, presented in narrated monologue. But throughout this text Kafka is careful to give the Officer's ideas strictly in direct speech rather than narrated monologue (Lange-Kirchheim 213). If this passage is in fact narrated monologue, then the pattern established by the text would lead one to attribute this thought to the Explorer. But it is hard to accept the idea that at this stage in the Officer's diatribe the Explorer could be so won over by his rhetoric and the machine. That leaves one final possibility: namely, that this comment is made by the narrator (Hecker 108). But such a gnomic commentary on the fictional action is out of keeping with the stance of the narrator, who otherwise tends more or less scrupulously to hide behind one or another of the characters. Ultimately, then, attribution of this statement to a specific perspective proves impossible, and this opens up a crucial "wolkige Stelle" (cloudy passage) — the term is Benjamin's (20) — an area of significant indeterminacy in the text.

One is left to wonder, then, why Kafka included this strangely gnomic, unattributable utterance in the final version of the story. The answer to this question, I believe, is a relatively simple one: the statement functions primarily to unmask the Officer's description of the machine as a purely fabricated, ideologically biased, perhaps even mendacious portrayal. In other words, this statement reveals the disjunction between the discursive-ideological construction of the machine in the Officer's narrative and the reality of the machine in the Explorer's experience. The Officer's portrayal of the apparatus, in short, is divulged to be nothing but an act of *narration:* a mediative bridge between the mythology he seeks to defend and the rationalist stance of the Explorer. In this sense the discrepancy between the Officer's idealized portrait of the machine's perfect functioning and the squeaking cog anticipates what will become the major disjunction of this text: the gulf that separates the Officer's idealized theoretical exposition of the apparatus and the brutal reality of its actual operation when the Officer himself becomes its victim.

The radicality of this discrepancy is foregrounded in the text itself. For at the end of his exposition, when he admits that the glory days of the Old Commandant cannot be fathomed from the perspective of the present, the Officer appeals to the continued efficacy of the machine as evidence for the living proof of this past.

> Im übrigen arbeitet die Maschine noch und wirkt für sich. Sie wirkt für sich, auch wenn sie allein in diesem Tale steht. Und die Leiche fällt zum Schluß noch immer in dem unbegreiflich sanften Flug in die Grube, auch wenn nicht, wie damals, Hunderte wie Fliegen um die Grube sich versammeln. (*D* 227)

> [Furthermore, the machine still functions and it operates autonomously. It operates autonomously even if it stands alone in this valley. And at the end the corpse still falls in the same incomprehensibly gentle arc into the pit, even if, as in former times, hundreds of people do not gather like flies around the pit.]

The Officer insists that the machine and its operation have remained intact, and as proof he points to the beautiful arc with which, at the end of the process, the corpse falls into the pit. The only difference between the grandiose past and the banal present, he maintains, is the lack of public support under which the penal procedure suffers. But the Officer's death belies even this statement: for one of the important malfunctions of the machine in this instance is precisely its failure to release the corpse and drop it into the pit:

> Und nun versagte noch das letzte, der Körper löste sich von den langen Nadeln nicht, strömte sein Blut aus, hing aber über der Grube ohne zu fallen. (D 245)

> [And now the ultimate breakdown occurred, the body did not free itself from the long needles, its blood gushed out, but it hung over the pit without falling.]

With this the Officer's crowning example for the perfection of the penal process, the gentle arc with which the corpse falls into the ditch, has been explicitly undermined: narrative is revealed to be mere discourse that finds no confirmation in experiential reality. But the violent impaling of the Officer only appears as a malfunction if one accepts as accurate the Officer's own previous description of the transfiguring and redemptive nature of the penal process. The Explorer clearly does, at least partially, buy into this ideological stance (see Schmidt 62), since he examines the face of the Officer's corpse and notes that "kein Zeichen der versprochenen Erlösung war zu entdecken" (no sign of the promised redemption could be discovered, D 245). This is one of the most compelling signals that the Explorer is actually in danger of being influenced or swayed by the Officer's discourse and arguments. But as opposed to the Explorer, we as readers of Kafka's text must have become aware at this point that the reality of the machine contradicts point for point the Officer's portrayal of its magnificence, revealing his narrative as nothing but ideologically motivated salesmanship. His tale about the past, which makes pretense to being a transparent account of real events, is exposed as illusion, deception, perhaps even lie.[9]

If we return once more to the Officer's narrative about the halcyon days of penal justice under the regime of the Old Commandant, we can identify a further area, beyond the mere structure and functioning of the apparatus itself, that invokes the mythology of im-mediate, perfectly transparent semiotic transference. Here the Prisoner no longer plays the role of the interpretant who deciphers, through the signifiers carved into his body, the transcendental signified of the Old Commandant's manuscript; rather, the Prisoner now is himself transformed into a sign or semiotic mediator for others: namely, for the spectators who congregate en masse to witness his execution (see Koelb 513).

Wie war die Exekution anders in früherer Zeit! Schon einen Tag vor der Hinrichtung war das ganze Tal von Menschen überfüllt; alle kamen nur um zu sehen. [. . .] Vor hundert Augen — alle Zuschauer standen auf den Fußspitzen bis dort zu den Anhöhen — wurde der Verurteilte vom Kommandanten selbst unter die Egge gelegt. [. . .] Kein Mißton störte die Arbeit der Maschine. Manche sahen nun gar nicht mehr zu, sondern lagen mit geschlossenen Augen im Sand; alle wußten: Jetzt geschieht Gerechtigkeit. [. . .] Nun, und dann kam die sechste Stunde! [. . .] Wie nahmen wir alle den Ausdruck der Verklärung von dem gemarterten Gesicht, wie hielten wir unsere Wangen in den Schein dieser endlich erreichten und schon vergehenden Gerechtigkeit! (*D* 225–26)

[How different the execution was in former days! Already the day before the execution the entire valley was overrun with people; everyone came just to see. [. . .] In front of hundreds of eyes — all the spectators stood on their tiptoes all the way up to the hillocks — the Prisoner was placed under the harrow by the Commandant himself. [. . .] No discordant sound disrupted the operation of the machine. Some people didn't even bother to watch, but instead lay with closed eyes in the sand; everyone knew: Now justice is being done. [. . .] Well, then the sixth hour arrived! [. . .] How we all took the expression of transfiguration from the martyred face, how we held our cheeks in the glow/ semblance of this justice that was finally achieved and already fading!]

We recall that the harrow is made of glass and contains an extra set of needles, whose sole purpose is to wash away the Prisoner's blood so the script on his back will remain legible throughout the twelve-hour procedure (*D* 215). These measures are clearly taken not for the benefit of the Prisoner's comprehension, but rather for that of the audience. But if the spectators truly had to rely on this mediated process of reading, the effect of the machine and what it demonstrates would be severely compromised. Hence the Officer's description of audience participation at previous executions makes no mention of such an imperfect, mediated mode of reception. While his portrayal does emphasize the importance of spectatorship, stressing the significance of vision and of the eyes as the organs of understanding, he also indicates that many spectators close their eyes, content in the absolute foreknowledge that justice is being done. Here again the ideological premise of the Officer's narrative makes itself evident; for the efficacy of the spectacle itself seems to rely not so much on the actual witnessing of the events as in the simple *belief* that justice is occurring. In this sense, there is actually no new knowledge that needs to be transmitted; the process simply confirms and affirms a manner of thought and a worldview that the audience already shares with the Officer and the ideological system he represents.

In direct contrast to this, however, the Officer presents the process of transmission from the Prisoner to the audience in terms of an exchange of knowledge, the insight of the Prisoner being communicated almost by means of mystical osmosis to the spectators. They simply "*take* [nehmen] the expression of transfiguration from [the Prisoner's] martyred face," a formulation that suggests an immediate transfer of the Prisoner's expression to the faces of the audience participants themselves. This idea of immediate transference is further highlighted when the spectators expose their cheeks to the glow ("Schein") that emanates from the Prisoner's dying face. The Officer's point seems to be that the edification experienced by the Prisoner immediately on his own body is somehow transmitted, in the act of spectatorial reception, vicariously but nonetheless with the very same immediacy, to the members of the audience as well. The Prisoner has in effect been transformed into a communicative medium (see Kittler 116), but a medium that, like the apparatus itself, operates with such transparency that the act of mediation appears as though it were nonmediated. The transparency of the Prisoner's illumination is communicated with the very same immediacy to the audience. In the Officer's narrative, the community that gathers around and finds its ritualized ideological center in the penal apparatus is one predicated upon the unquestioned immediacy of this shared "illumination": it is, in short, held together by nothing other than its faith in a common ideology. In this instance, however, the Officer's own language threatens to betray his portrayal as an ideological fiction; for the *Schein* of justice in which the audience basks their cheeks can be translated not only as "glow," but also as "semblance." Double entendre is a technique Kafka, in this sense a disciple of Freud's, often uses to expose the thoughts of his characters hidden behind their verbal utterances; in this instance the double meaning undercuts the Officer's portrayal by casting what he depicts as the reality of a magnificent past as nothing but the deceptive semblance of narrative fiction.

It is important to note that the Prisoner subjected to the machine is not the only human agent in this story who is transmuted into a transparent communicative mediator. In fact, the Officer himself assumes exactly this kind of intermediary role with relation to the Old Commandant, whose system he is trying to preserve, and the Explorer, whom he hopes to enlist as a further emissary of this system. Thus, when the dénouement of the story is reached and the Officer decides to make himself into a martyr for the machine and the Old Commandant, he intently stares at the Explorer "with bright eyes" that seem to contain a silent message.

"Dann ist es also Zeit," sagte er [der Offizier] schließlich und blickte plötzlich mit hellen Augen, die irgendeine Aufforderung, irgendeinen Aufruf zur Beteiligung entheilten, den Reisenden an. (*D* 236)

["Then the time has come," he [the Officer] finally said and suddenly looked at the Explorer with bright eyes that contained some kind of demand, some kind of summons to participation.]

If the illumination of the Prisoner tortured by the machine begins at the eyes ("um die Augen beginnt," *D* 218), the "bright eyes" of the Officer are a symptom of his own illumination at the moment when he has committed himself to dying for the machine. The "demand" or "summons to participation" expressed in the Officer's eyes is the very same call to participation, related in the Officer's narrative about past executions, manifest in the transfigured eyes of the Prisoner and immediately communicated to and shared by the audience. The Officer clearly hopes to re-enact this transferral of illumination in his interaction with the Explorer; this is the final trump card he can play in his game of rhetorical persuasion designed to trigger the Explorer's solidarity and thereby enlist him as the Officer's ally. His hopes that his own illumination will infect the Explorer are in vain, of course, and to the Officer's assertion that "Dann ist es also Zeit" (the time has come), the Explorer naïvely replies "unruhig" (with a note of agitation), "Wozu ist es Zeit?" (Time for what?, *D* 236–37). The Explorer's agitation indicates that he has comprehended the summons to participation expressed in the Officer's eyes; but he resists this summons, as he has consistently resisted the Officer's importunings, asking instead an affectedly naïve and hence evasive question.

If we understand the Officer's self-immolation as an attempt to re-create the ideological bond between victim and audience that he projects in his idealized narrative of earlier times, then it also becomes possible to explain why the Explorer fails to detect any illumination or transfiguration in the face of the Officer's corpse. On the one hand, if the Officer already radiated the expression of this illumination in life, in particular after his decision to subject himself to the machine, then it is not surprising if his face appears in death "wie es im Leben gewesen war" (as it had in life, *D* 245). Unlike the condemned prisoners, the Officer does not need to acquire conviction and transfiguration in death; he possesses them already in life. On the other hand, however, it is important that it is none other than the Explorer who fails to discover this illumination in the face of the Officer, either in life or in death; for this underscores precisely his absolute lack of receptivity for the Officer's "message." The Explorer does not fit the mold of the Officer's idealized audience that immediately comprehends and shares the expression it "takes" from the victim's martyred face. Once again the Officer's attempt to translate his theoretical vision of perfect, transparent communication into concrete practice is dashed by the very real resistance of the Explorer.

The conflict that structures "In der Strafkolonie" is not so much one between the Old Commandant and the New, between political dema-goguery and democracy, between faith and enlightened rationality; rather, it is a conflict between a myth of immediacy and transparency, predicated on ideological identity, and the reality that in a world defined by ideological difference, mediation is either imperfect or impossible and semiotic disjunction is the norm. The relevance of this problematic for Kafka's own experience, especially in the fall of 1914 when this story was first composed, seems self-evident. It is well known that in response to Kurt Wolff's objections to the "distressing aspect" of this story, Kafka sought self-justification by appealing to all that was "distressing" in the contemporary age in general and in his own experience in particular. In a letter to Wolff dated 11 October 1916 Kafka asserted:

> Ihr Aussetzen des Peinlichen [in "In der Strafkolonie"] trifft ganz mit meiner Meinung zusammen. [. . .] Zur Erklärung dieser letzten Er-zählung füge ich nur hinzu, daß nicht nur sie peinlich ist, daß vielmehr unsere allgemeine und meine besondere Zeit gleichfalls sehr peinlich war und ist. (*B* 150).

> [Your complaint about the distressing aspect [of "In The Penal Col-ony"] conforms completely with my own opinion. [. . .] By way of ex-plaining this last story let me simply add that it is not alone in being distressing, but rather that our general time and especially my particular time was and is very distressing.]

Written in October 1914, shortly after the outbreak of the First World War, it is clear that Kafka was referring to this cataclysmic event as the distressing aspect of the age in general. Perhaps we should remind our-selves, however, that the onset of war — and the onset of this war in particular — results from a hardening of ideological positions and the ultimate failure of attempts to find ways to mediate between these ideo-logical extremes. The violence of war, we might then maintain, results from the impossibility of mediation or compromise. It is commonly assumed, moreover, that what Kafka was alluding to as the distressing aspect of his personal life at the time of writing this story, and through to the time of his letter to Wolff in 1916 and beyond, was the crisis surrounding his relationship with Felice Bauer. Shortly before "Strafko-lonie" was composed, Kafka was subjected to Felice's recriminations in the Hotel Askanischer Hof in Berlin, which resulted in the dissolution of their first engagement. The on-again, off-again relationship with Felice lasted through December 1917, and hence spanned the period both of the original composition and the subsequent revisions of "In der Strafkolonie." From Kafka's perspective, of course, what caused the frictions and ultimately doomed the relationship between him and Felice was the absolute difference in their lifestyles and their ways of thinking — something Kafka saw as ultimately detrimental to his ambitions as a writer.[10] In this relationship as well, then, Kafka recognized that the principal problem was one of mediation between two incommensurable positions. Indeed, one of the things he likely learned during the confrontation at the Hotel Askanischer Hof was that Felice was less compromising than he had hitherto hoped or expected. Of his own inability — or was it unwillingness? — to make compromises in lifestyle he was always painfully aware. Thus the "distress" that forms the common thread connecting the war as Kafka's general historical experience, the crisis with Felice as his immediate personal experience, and the content of "In der Strafkolonie" is the problematic of mediation between two absolutely opposed and incommensurable positions.

A close look at the opening lines of this story reveals that the interaction between the Officer and the Explorer is marked from the outset by opposition with little promise of mutual understanding or compromise.

> "Es ist ein eigentümlicher Apparat," sagte der Offizier zu dem Forschungsreisenden und überblickte mit einem gewissermaßen bewundernden Blick den ihm doch wohlbekannten Apparat. Der Reisende schien nur aus Höflichkeit der Einladung des Kommandanten gefolgt zu sein, der ihn aufgefordert hatte, der Exekution eines Soldaten beizuwohnen, der wegen Ungehorsam und Beleidigung des Vorgesetzten verurteilt worden war. (*D* 203)

> ["It is a peculiar apparatus," the Officer said to the Explorer and observed with a more or less admiring gaze the apparatus with which he was, after all, certainly quite familiar. The Explorer appeared only to have accepted out of politeness the invitation of the Commandant to witness the execution of a soldier who had been sentenced for insubordination and insulting a superior officer.]

Although critics who have analyzed the complex narrative structure and stance of this text have generally assumed that these lines exhibit the presence of an objective narrator (see Pascal 126; Jayne 124), I tend to agree with Klaus Mladek (132) that Kafka's text provides little evidence of such a narrative metaperspective. The voice of the Officer is presented predominantly, as in the opening sentence of the text, as direct speech. The voice of the Explorer, by contrast, is given almost exclusively by means of narrated monologue. This is consistent with their respective attitudes and positions vis-à-vis their interaction: the Officer trying to persuade by means of rhetorical speech acts, the Explorer evading these implied imperatives and deliberating silently about the Officer's motivations and how he, the Explorer, should respond. I would like to suggest that the first sentence of the story already adumbrates these two distinct narrative stances in a way that highlights the incommensurability of the two characters and their positions. For the commentary that describes the "more or less admiring gaze" of the Officer at the machine with which he is "after all, certainly quite familiar" seems to be grounded in the perspective of the Explorer himself, not in that of an omniscient narrator. An objective narrator would not have to qualify the Officer's stare as "more or less" admiring, but could simply state this admiration as a fact. Nor would an omniscient narrator need to question this admiration by contrasting it with the fact that the Officer is "after all, certainly quite familiar" with the apparatus. This suggests that the perspective from which we hear the voice of the Officer is actually that of the Explorer. This would seem to confirm Sokel's and Pascal's hypothesis that throughout the text we as readers hear through the ears and see through the eyes of the Explorer (Sokel 1964, 123; Pascal 129). But already the second sentence of the text provides us with a counterexample. The comment about the Explorer's apparent motivations (or lack thereof) for attending the execution clearly cannot be interpreted as his own narrated monologue: the introductory verb *schien* already indicates that this observation is being made from a perspective outside the Explorer himself. But this cannot be the perspective of an omniscient narrator, for once again he (or she) would not have to qualify this comment by saying that it "appeared" to be so; it could simply be stated as fact to which the "omniscient" narrator is privy. Indeed, what we are presented with here is nothing other than the perspective of the Officer as he reflects on the Explorer: *the Officer* is the one to whom the Explorer appears only to have accepted the invitation out of politeness. Thus the first two sentences of the narrative are constructed as a careful and complex dialectic between the two main characters.[11] In the first sentence the Officer speaks, and we are given the Explorer's reactions to his comment; in the second sentence the Explorer is the subject, but only insofar as we are presented with the Officer's interpretation of unspecified non-verbal signs regarding his thoughts. These first two sentences set the pattern for the rest of the text up to the point of the Officer's death, a narrative structured around a wandering point of view that is split between the perspectives of the Explorer and the Officer and moves back and forth between them in subtle and unpredictable ways.[12] These erratic shifts in perspective from one character to the other account for the profound confusion and interpretive instability of this story. It also is the primary factor that makes this the most dialectical of all of Kafka's longer texts.[13] But more to the point in the present context is that this fluctuation in perspective enacts on the level of narrative structure, and as a consequence in the sphere of reader-response as well, the problematic of successful mediation that lies at the heart of this story. The reader is constantly placed in the position of having to negotiate between the positions of the two characters: *we* ultimately play roles similar to that of the Explorer in the story, called upon to mediate between stances that offer no obvious ground for successful mediation. In other words, in the split between the two predominant characters and the shift between their respective narrative perspectives, Kafka's text choreographs the very problematic of mediation that this story thematizes, ultimately forcing the reader to perform and experience this mediative function.

Given the prominence of this split perspective and the grounding of the theme of mediation in the constant fluctuations between the two main characters, it should come as no surprise that Kafka was unhappy with the story's conclusion. After the death of the Officer the dialectical structure of the text breaks down. This is not the only time Kafka had notorious difficulties in finding a solution for a story once he had killed off his central character. We need only think here of the conclusion to "Die Verwandlung" after Gregor Samsa's death, with which Kafka was likewise dissatisfied (*F* 163). In the case of "In der Strafkolonie" it seems as though it would have been easier for Kafka to find a felicitous resolution, since one of the story's two main figures remains alive. But this is not the case, simply because the entire dialectic around which the story is structured has collapsed. If we examine the alternative endings Kafka drafted for this story in August 1917, we can discern how he sought in various ways to recover the dialectical structure of the text and reintroduce the central problematic of mediation.

Without exception these drafts for revised endings pick up with the death of the Officer and eliminate the initial conclusion containing the scene at the teahouse, the discovery of the Old Commandant's grave, and the flight of the Explorer. This episode seems to be what Kafka was referring to as "Machwerk" (botched) in his letter to Kurt Wolff, written just a month later, on 4 September 1917 (*B* 159). The last draft Kafka attempted, found in a diary entry dated 9 August 1917 (*T* 825–27), represents his longest, most sustained attempt to find a resolution for this story. This version begins with the Explorer reporting his feeling that with the death of the Officer "eine vollkommene Ordnung geschaffen sei" (complete order has been reached in this case, *T* 825). Thus the passage begins by introducing a sense of closure. The Explorer goes on to observe that the Officer's gruesome death provides a "maschinen-mäßige Widerlegung" (mechanical refutation) of his opinion, and that following his death the Explorer has lost all connection with the Prisoner and the Soldier. But at this point the fragment abruptly changes modes, shifting from realistic portrayal to the Explorer's imagined fantasy. He pictures his ship motoring up through the sand to fetch him, reflects on how he will reveal at home the horror of the execution process he witnessed here, and expresses a reproach against the Officer for the "grau-sam[e] Hinrichtung des Verurteilten" (gruesome execution of the Prisoner, *T* 826), an event, of course, that in the story never actually occurred. At this point, the ghost of the Officer returns to the scene:

"Hingerichtet?" hätte daraufhin der Offizier mit Recht gefragt. "Hier ist er doch" hätte er gesagt und auf des Reisenden Kofferträger gezeigt. Und tatsächlich war dies der Verurteilte, wie sich der R.[eisende] durch scharfes Hinschauen und genaues Prüfen der Gesichtszüge überzeugte. "Meine Anerkennung" mußte der R.[eisende] sagen und sagte es gern. "Ein Taschenspielerkunststück?" fragte er noch. "Nein" sagte der O.[ffizier] "ein Irrtum ihrerseits ich bin hingerichtet, wie Sie es befahlen." Noch aufmerksamer horchten jetzt Kapitän und Matrosen. Und sahen sämtlich wie jetzt der O.[ffizier] über seine Stirn hinstrich und einen krumm aus der geborstenen Stirn vorragenden Stachel enthüllte. (*T* 826–27).

["Executed?" the Officer would have then justifiably asked. "But here he is," he would have said and pointed at the Explorer's luggage porter. And indeed this was the Prisoner, a fact of which the Explorer persuaded himself by keen observation and careful inspection of the man's face. "My compliments," the Explorer was forced to say, and he said it gladly. Then he asked, "a conjurer's trick?" "No," the Officer replied, "an error on your part, I was executed just as you commanded." The captain and the sailors now listened more attentively. And everyone then saw how the Officer brushed his hand across his forehead to reveal a crooked spike protruding from his shattered forehead.]

We should note, first of all, that although this passage is initially marked, through the use of the subjunctive, as a wish-fulfillment fantasy on the part of the Explorer, eventually the subjunctive is dropped and the fantasy enters the real-time dimension of the fictional world. We are familiar with this transitional tactic from other texts by Kafka; but in "Strafkolonie," which contains so many allusions to the historical reality of Kafka's time and which otherwise refuses to breach the pseudo-empiricism of its fictional world, such a flight into imaginative fantasy is out of place. Kafka surely knew this, which may explain why he rejected this version as a potential conclusion. But the fantasy is necessary for the simple reason that it allows Kafka to resurrect the Officer and re-establish the dialectical interchange between him and the Explorer that constitutes the structural underpinning of the text. If anything, the incommensurability of the positions assumed by the Officer and the Explorer is even more extreme in this fragment than in the published conclusion of the story. The Explorer displays no uncertainty, he doesn't flee, and he is even made responsible for the Officer's death. Here there is clearly no possibility of mediation. But at the same time, the scales have been tipped in favor of the Explorer, who appears to come away as victor in the engagement with the Officer. That may also explain why Kafka ultimately rejected this alternative conclusion.

Other fragments propose completely different alternatives. In one (*T* 825) the Explorer enters into an open solidarity with the Prisoner and the Soldier, culminating in the remark that "alle drei gehörten jetzt zusammen" (now all three belonged together). This version obviously runs wholly counter to the conclusion in the published text, in which the Explorer fends off the Soldier and the Prisoner by threatening violence. Another fragment shows the Explorer asserting he would be a "Hundsfott" (dirty dog) if he refused to condemn the Old Commandant's penal procedure, but then, as if to retract this statement, he takes his own metaphor literally and begins to act like a dog. Here the dialectic between Officer and Explorer has been concentrated into the ambivalent and contradictory thoughts and actions of the Explorer himself.

The most interesting — and to my mind the most telling — fragment is a very brief one in which the Explorer appeals in his thoughts for help in sorting out the chaos of the situation that follows the Officer's death.

> "Wie?" sagte der Reisende plötzlich. War etwas vergessen? Ein entscheidendes Wort? Ein Griff? Eine Handreichung? Wer kann in das Wirrsal eindringen? Verdammte böse tropische Luft, was machst Du aus mir? Ich weiß nicht was geschieht. Meine Urteilskraft ist zuhause im Norden geblieben. (*T* 823)[14]

> ["What?," the Explorer suddenly said. Had something been forgotten? A decisive word? A firm grip? An extended hand? Who can penetrate

this chaos? Damned, evil tropical air, what are you doing to me? I don't know what is happening. I left my power of judgment at home in the Northland.]

In essence the Explorer bemoans the laming of his own power of judgment and expresses his desire for a mediator who might intervene and dispel the confusion. However, this reference to the Explorer's power of judgment, his *Urteilskraft* that has been left at home in the Northland, contains a not very subtle allusion to Immanuel Kant's *Kritik der Urteilskraft* (Critique of Judgment, 1790), one of the founding documents of modern German aesthetic theory. What function, we might properly ask, can an allusion to Kant possibly have in this context? The answer is actually quite simple: in Kant's theory, aesthetic judgment plays the crucial role of mediating between pure reason, representing the sphere of nature and the laws of causality, and practical reason, subsuming the domain of human freedom and morality. Indeed, the introduction to the *Kritik der Urteilskraft* contains an entire section with the title "Von der Urteilskraft, als einem Verbindungsmittel der zwei Teile der Philosophie zu einem Ganzen" (On the Critique of Judgment as a Medium for Connecting the Two Parts of Philosophy into a Whole, Kant 84–87). The two parts of critical philosophy to which Kant is referring are his *Kritik der reinen Vernunft* (Critique of Pure Reason, 1781) and his *Kritik der praktischen Vernunft* (Critique of Practical Reason, 1788); and the role he ascribes to aesthetic judgment is none other than the central function of mediating between these two separate epistemological domains and fusing them into an organic whole. "Allein in der Familie der oberen Erkenntnisvermögen," Kant maintains, "gibt es doch ein Mittelglied zwischen dem Verstande und der Vernunft. Dieses ist die *Urteilskraft*" (However, in the family of the superior intellectual faculties, there is a mediating formation between the faculty of pure reason and the faculty of practical reason. This is the power of judgment, 85).

If, as Axel Hecker has maintained, "In der Strafkolonie" represents a kind of abbreviated intellectual history (97), then its focus would seem to be a critical history of German aesthetics and aesthetic theory. Several themes suggest themselves immediately. The machine itself, in the Officer's idealized narrative, manifests that harmonious organicism that was the watchword of bourgeois aesthetic theory; to be sure, its self-destruction in the real time of the Explorer's experience unmasks this organicism as mere ideological hype (see Mladek 133). Indeed, Kafka's very choice of a mechanical apparatus as a symbol for the organic aesthetic entity already indicates his ironical, critical perspective: one might even go so far as to read the machine as a parody of the aesthetic totality, one that reveals it to be always already mechanical rather than organic. Even the Officer's own admission that the machine, especially under the regime of the New Commandant, is "zusammengesetzt" (pieced together, *D* 221) seems to undercut his own assertions of its harmonious totality. Moreover, the Officer's assertion that the apparatus "wirkt für sich" (operates autonomously, *D* 227) alludes to another fundamental doctrine of bourgeois aesthetics: the principle of aesthetic autonomy (see Anderson 185). Once again this theory appears to be radically perverted when the machine enters this mode of autonomous operation and becomes a symbiotic extension of the Officer's will only in order to effect the latter's brutal execution (*D* 242). One might also interpret the tripartite structure of the machine as an allusion to the threefold character of Kant's epistemology, with the harrow assuming the mediating role of aesthetics in Kant's system. This reading, too — which borders, to my way of thinking, almost too much on the allegorical — would ultimately produce a critique of aesthetics as a mechanism that strategically inscribes the ruling ideology into the very body of its aesthetic "subjects," thereby insuring their subjugation to this ideology. This critical hypothesis can piggyback in some respects on Mark Anderson's thesis that in "Strafkolonie" Kafka sought to express a critique of the aesthetics of decadence so prominent in Central Europe at the turn of the last century. The advantage (if it indeed is one) of the reading I am proposing is that it sublates Anderson's more local aesthetic critique into a wider ranging criticism of aesthetics as one of the principal areas in which modern German thought attempted to define that domain where the principles of its own epistemology could find mediation and dialectical resolution. One need not think only of the Kantian model. The theory Friedrich von Schiller propounded in his classical treatise *Über die ästhetische Erziehung des Menschen* also positioned aesthetic "Spiel" (play) as the mediating agency between the rational drive for form and the demands of physical materiality. One might also pursue a reading of "In der Strafkolonie" that aligns the three functions of Schiller's treatise, form, matter, and play, with the characters of Kafka's story, the Officer, the Prisoner (and perhaps the Soldier as well), and the Explorer, respectively, whereby the Explorer would be assigned — and would fail at — the task of mediating between the hyperrationalism of the Officer and the animalistic materiality of the Prisoner.

To follow up on these suggestions here would go well beyond the confines of the present essay. My sole intention has been to indicate that "In der Strafkolonie" can be productively read as a critical meditation on the problematic of mediation, and that the dialectical structure of this story, which makes it unique among Kafka's longer narrative texts, reflects on the level of form the thematic problem with which Kafka was attempting to grapple.

The opposition between the Officer and the Explorer, or, if you will, between the Old Commandant and the New, appears here as the conflict between an ideology of immediacy, semiotic transparency, and harmonious aesthetic mediation, on the one hand, and an insistence on the imperfection, indeed, the impossibility of adequate mediation, on the other. Extended to the self-reflective dimension of the text, this critique of transparent mediation calls into question not only the very act of narration the Officer employs as a strategy for mediating between his own position and the antithetical standpoint of the Explorer, but also Kafka's own characteristic flights into narrative — one might think not only of his literary writing, but also of his epistolary relationship with Felice Bauer — as a manner of seeking mediation between the (writing) self and the Other. Read in the manner I have proposed here, "In der Strafkolonie" presents a scathing critique not only of the idealistic fantasies of semiotic immediacy and aesthetic mediation, but also of the acts of narrative mediation concretized in Kafka's own fiction. If we as interpreters of this text ultimately find ourselves in the position of the Explorer in Kafka's alternative conclusion who asks "Wer kann in das Wirrsal eindringen?" (Who can penetrate this confusion?, *T* 823), then this is because this story stages precisely the omnipresence of disjunction without hope of interpretive mediation.

Notes

[1] Throughout this essay translations from the German are my own.

[2] Citations from "In der Strafkolonie" follow the text in the volume *Drucke zu Lebzeiten* (*D*) of the Critical Edition.

[3] Dietrich Krusche in his *Kafka und Kafka Deutung: Die problematisierte Interaktion* (Munich: Fink, 1974), 130–31, subsumes the allegorical readings of Kafka in general under what he calls "speculative approaches," and his first two categories, the religious and the ontological, describe precisely the two primary early critical views of "Strafkolonie." Krusche's third "speculative" approach, sociological interpretation, differs radically from the first two insofar as it does not rely on allegorical reduction.

[4] Sokel was one of the first to maintain that the Explorer is the figure through whose eyes and ears the reader experiences the events of the story (*Tragik und Ironie* [Munich: Langen/Müller, 1964], 109, 123), but he fails to question or problematize the Explorer's function as mediator between the fictional events and the reader. Pascal likewise sees the Explorer as the transparent mediator of the fictional events ("Kafka's 'In der Strafkolonie': Narrative Structure and Interpretation," *Oxford German Studies* 11 [1980]: 135). However, it is precisely such mediative transparency that this text constantly calls into question.

[5] Kramer has correctly observed that the Officer and the Explorer are alike insofar as they both represent absolutist, non-compromising personalities. ("The Aesthetics of Theme: Kafka's 'In the Penal Colony,'" *Studies in Short Fiction* 5 [1969]: 363–64).

[6] In the early sketch "Beschreibung eines Kampfes" one of Kafka's characters nostalgically expresses his amazement at, and envy of, those who can communicate with such spontaneity. Here people speak "ohne Nachdenken und nicht allzu deutlich, als müßte [das Gesagte] jeder erwartet haben" (*NS I* 91–92; without reflection and not very clearly, as if everyone would have anticipated [what was said]). Walter Sokel has called this the "naturalist pole" of Kafka's existence ("Language and Truth in the Two Worlds of Franz Kafka," *German Quarterly* 52 [1979]: 374). This "naturalist" approach to communication defines the interaction between the Soldier and the Prisoner in "Strafkolonie."

[7] Kafka seems to have at least considered the possibility of having the story conclude with an affirmation of solidarity among the Prisoner, the Soldier, and the Explorer. See the alternate conclusion he drafted in his diary on 9 August 1917 (*Tagebücher* 825). Kafka certainly recognized that the addition of such a harmonious conclusion to a text that has continuously highlighted disharmony threatened to give the story an inauthentic, even parodistic ring.

[8] Koelb also stresses — in my view, correctly — that the machine passes on, and hence mediates, the message of the Old Commandant to the prisoner ("'In der Strafkolonie': Kafka and the Scene of Reading," *German Quarterly* 55 (1982): 513). On the machine's function as that of mediation, see also Weinstein ("Kafka's Writing Machine: Metamorphosis in 'The Penal Colony,'" *Studies in Twentieth-Century Literature* 7 [1982]: 26).

[9] Mladek likewise points out that the Officer's claims to truth are infected by deceptions and ultimately constituted purely as linguistic phenomena ("'Ein eigentümlicher Apparat': Franz Kafkas 'In der Strafkolonie,'" *Text und Kritik: Sonderband Franz Kafka,* ed. Heinz Ludwig Arnold [Munich: Text und Kritik, 1994], 122). Further evidence of the deceptive and rhetorical nature of the Officer's discourse can be found in the self-contradictions into which he unwittingly falls, for example when he accuses the New Commandant's ladies of feeding candy to the Prisoner on the day before the execution when the Prisoner has in fact only been arraigned one hour ago (*D* 223), or when he indicates that the Explorer was invited to attend the execution "yesterday" (*D* 227) even though at that time the Prisoner's act of insubordination had not yet even been reported.

[10] See in this regard Kafka's long letter to Felice dated end of October, early November 1914 (*Briefe an Felice* 615–22).

[11] Krusche gives a similar analysis of these opening lines, but he draws a quite different conclusion, claiming that the text ultimately finds resolution as the perspective increasingly drifts away from the Officer and is concentrated in the figure of the Explorer (*Kafka und Kafka-Deutung,* 25–26).

[12] I thus am inclined to agree with Thieberger ("The Botched Ending of 'In the Penal Colony,'" in *The Kafka Debate: New Perspectives for Our Time,* ed. Angel Flores [New York: Gordian, 1977], 304) that this text is principally built around a split, dualistic perspective. There are, admittedly, a few notable, if necessary, excep-

tions to this limitation to the views of the Officer and the Explorer. There are some cases in the story, as we have already seen, when the presence of an objective narrator can be detected. These generally occur as expositions of the thoughts, emotions, and motivations of the Officer, who, limited to the more restricted expression of direct speech, sometimes requires a narrator to reveal sentiments he could not otherwise display (see, for example, *D* 204, 208, 210, 212, 214). Narrated monologue is generally reserved exclusively for the Explorer, but in at least two instances this privilege is passed on to the Prisoner (see *D* 237, 242). In the first case, the internal perspective of the Prisoner is relativized by the inclusion of an addendum stating that this is what he appeared to be thinking; in the second instance no such qualifier is added, and it hence provides an example of pure narrated monologue that transcends the perspective of the Explorer. Indeed, it marks one of those few instances when the narrative perspective is not that of either the Officer or the Explorer.

[13] I am purposely excluding here the short parables of Kafka's later creative period, which are often quite conscientiously dialectical in nature. One need only consider, for example, Kafka's famous metaparable "Von den Gleichnissen."

[14] The importance of this sketch for a new conclusion is underscored by the fact that the fragment immediately following it in Kafka's diary offers a revised version of this same idea.

Works Cited

Anderson, Mark. "The Ornaments of Writing: 'In the Penal Colony.'" *Kafka's Clothes: Ornament and Aestheticism in the Habsburg Fin de Siècle*. Oxford: Clarendon, 1992. 173–93.

Beckmann, Martin. "Franz Kafkas Erzählung 'In der Strafkolonie': Ein Deutungsversuch." *Wirkendes Wort* 39 (1989): 375–92.

———. "Zeitverfallenheit und Existenzerfahrung: Franz Kafkas Erzählung 'In der Strafkolonie.'" *Seminar* 30 (1994): 286–302.

Benjamin, Walter. *Benjamin über Kafka: Texte, Briefzeugnisse, Aufzeichnungen*. Ed. Hermann Schweppenhäuser. Frankfurt am Main: Suhrkamp, 1981.

Binder, Hartmut, ed. *Kafka-Handbuch*. 2 vols. Stuttgart: Kröner, 1979.

Davey, E. R. "The Broken Engine: A Study of Franz Kafka's "In der Strafkolonie.'" *Journal of European Studies* 14 (1984): 271–83.

Deleuze, Gilles, and Felix Guattari. *Kafka: Toward a Minor Literature*. Trans. Dana Polan. Minneapolis: U of Minnesota P, 1986.

Dodd, William J. "Kafka and Freud: A Note on 'In der Strafkolonie.'" *Monatshefte* 70 (1978): 129–37.

Emrich, Wilhelm. *Franz Kafka*. 5th ed. Frankfurt am Main: Athenäum, 1965.

Fickert, Kurt J. "A Literal Interpretation of 'In the Penal Colony.'" *Modern Fiction Studies* 17 (1971): 31–36.

Hecker, Axel. "Die Dekonstruktionsmaschine — 'In der Strafkolonie.'" *An den Rändern des Lesbaren: Dekonstruktive Lektüren zu Franz Kafka.* Vienna: Passagen, 1998. 79–119.

Henel, Ingeborg. "Kafkas 'In der Strafkolonie': Form, Sinn und Stellung der Erzählung im Gesamtwerk." *Untersuchungen zur Literatur als Geschichte: Festschrift für Benno von Wiese.* Ed. Vincent J. Günther, Hellmut Koopmann, and Joachim E. Krause. Berlin: Erich Schmidt, 1973. 480–504.

Horn, Peter. "'Ein eigentümlicher Apparat' im Blick eines Forschungsreisenden: Zur anthropologischen Methode Kafkas in 'In der Strafkolonie.'" *Acta Germanica* 19 (1988): 49–78.

Jayne, Richard. "Kafka's 'In der Strafkolonie' and the Aporias of Textual Interpretation." *Deutsche Vierteljahrsschrift für Literaturwissenschaft und Geistesgeschichte* 66 (1992): 94–128.

Kafka, Franz. *Briefe 1902–1924.* Ed. Max Brod. Frankfurt am Main: S. Fischer, 1958. (*B*)

———. *Briefe an Felice und andere Korrespondenz aus der Verlobungszeit.* Ed. Erich Heller and Jürgen Born. Frankfurt am Main: S. Fischer, 1967. (*F*)

———. *Drucke zu Lebzeiten: Kritische Ausgabe.* Ed. Wolf Kittler, Hans-Gerd Koch, and Gerhard Neumann. Frankfurt am Main: S. Fischer, 1994. (*D*)

———. *Nachgelassene Schriften und Fragmente: Kritische Ausgabe.* Ed. Jürgen Born, Gerhard Neumann, Malcolm Pasley, and Jost Schillemeit. 2 vols. Frankfurt am Main: S. Fischer, 1992–93.

———. *Tagebücher in der Fassung der Handschrift: Kritische Ausgabe.* Ed. Hans-Gerd Koch, Michael Müller, and Malcolm Pasley. Frankfurt am Main: S. Fischer, 1990. (*T*)

Kant, Immanuel. *Kritik der Urteilskraft.* Vol. 10 of Immanuel Kant *Werkausgabe.* Ed. Wilhelm Weischedel. Frankfurt am Main: Suhrkamp, 1974.

Kittler, Wolf. "Schreibmaschinen, Sprechmaschinen: Effekte technischer Medien im Werk Franz Kafkas." *Franz Kafka: Schriftverkehr.* Ed. Wolf Kittler and Gerhard Neumann. Freiburg im Breisgau: Rombach, 1990. 75–163.

Koelb, Clayton. "'In der Strafkolonie': Kafka and the Scene of Reading." *German Quarterly* 55 (1982): 511–25.

Kramer, Dale. "The Aesthetics of Theme: Kafka's 'In the Penal Colony.'" *Studies in Short Fiction* 5 (1969): 362–67.

Krusche, Dietrich. *Kafka und Kafka-Deutung: Die problematisierte Interaktion.* Munich: Fink, 1974.

Lange-Kirchheim, Astrid. "Franz Kafka, 'In der Strafkolonie' und Alfred Weber, 'Der Beamte.'" *Germanisch-Romanische Monatsschrift* 27 (1977): 202–21.

Mladek, Klaus. "'Ein eigentümlicher Apparat': Franz Kafkas 'In der Strafkolonie.'" *Text und Kritik: Sonderband Franz Kafka*. Ed. Heinz Ludwig Arnold. Munich: Text und Kritik, 1994. 115–42.

Müller-Seidel, Walter. *Die Deportation des Menschen: Kafkas "In der Strafkolonie" im europäischen Kontext*. Stuttgart: Metzler, 1986.

Norris, Margot. "Sadism and Masochism in 'In the Penal Colony' and 'A Hunger Artist.'" *Reading Kafka: Prague, Politics, and the Fin de Siècle*. Ed. Mark Anderson. New York: Schocken, 1989. 170–86.

Pan, David. "Kafka as a Populist: Re-Reading 'In the Penal Colony.'" *Telos* 101 (Fall 1994): 3–40.

Pascal, Roy. "Kafka's 'In der Strafkolonie': Narrative Structure and Interpretation." *Oxford German Studies* 11 (1980): 123–45.

Politzer, Heinz. *Franz Kafka: Parable and Paradox*. Revised ed. Ithaca, NY: Cornell UP, 1966.

Schmidt, Ulrich. "'Tat-Beobachtung': Kafkas Erzählung 'In der Strafkolonie' im literarisch-historischen Kontext." *Franz Kafka und die Prager deutsche Literatur: Deutungen und Wirkungen*. Ed. Hartmut Binder. Bonn: Kulturstiftung der Deutschen Vertriebenen, 1988. 55–69.

Sokel, Walter. *Franz Kafka: Tragik und Ironie*. Munich: Langen/Müller, 1964.

———. "Language and Truth in the Two Worlds of Franz Kafka." *German Quarterly* 52 (1979): 364–84.

Steinberg, Erwin R. "Die zwei Kommandanten in Kafkas 'In der Strafkolonie.'" *Franz Kafka: Eine Aufsatzsammlung*. Ed. Maria Luise Caputo-Mayr. Berlin: Agora, 1978. 144–53.

Thieberger, Richard. "The Botched Ending of 'In the Penal Colony.'" *The Kafka Debate: New Perspectives for Our Time*. Ed. Angel Flores. New York: Gordian, 1977. 304–10.

Thomas, J. D. "The Dark at the End of the Tunnel: Kafka's 'In the Penal Colony.'" *Studies in Short Fiction* 4 (1966): 12–18.

Weinstein, Arnold. "Kafka's Writing Machine: Metamorphosis in 'The Penal Colony.'" *Studies in Twentieth-Century Literature* 7 (1982): 21–33.

Hunting Kafka Out of Season:
Enigmatics in the Short Fictions

Ruth V. Gross

IN THE PREFACE TO THE 1995 English edition of his 1990 philosophical work *Enigmas: The Egyptian Moment in Society and Art,* Mario Perniola asks the following questions about our own state at the end of the twentieth century:

> What is the fear that is taking hold of our feelings in this end of the millennium? What troubles and confounds our experience and reason? What is it that threatens, intimidates and terrifies us? Is it something dreadful coming back from the past, something that we wrongly believed had been completely subdued, but that now reemerges to drag us back to the insecurity and danger we thought we had escaped forever? Or is it something totally new that shakes and dissolves all our certainties, throwing open before us unpredictable, unthinkable horizons where the very notions of humankind and nature appear to crumble? What do we fear most? Repetition or difference? The return of a barbarism that is remote and prehistoric or the advent of a barbarism that is technological and post-human? (vii)

Perniola goes on to explain that the questions themselves are not an enigma — they simply express a fear; enigma emerges when the two poles of these questions, the world of the past and the world of the future, pass into one another without border — when they are "collapsed into an ambiguous, supremely problematic present" (vii).

This sense of an extremely problematic present is the basis of much of the anxiety that we sense when reading the works of Franz Kafka. Whether read as modern, postmodern, existential, surreal, or what you will, Kafka's works have been interpreted to explain ways of looking at the present moment, whenever that present moment occurred, be it 1925, 1965, or 2000. Because Kafka indicated no precise dates in his stories, and because his stories are not set in any definite time, their characters tend to be interpreted by readers as actors in an always present. The working conditions portrayed in "Die Verwandlung" (The

Metamorphosis) or *Der Proceß* (The Trial), though seemingly antiquated by modern computerized office standards, do not locate the works historically. If anything, they take Kafka's works out of time rather than place them into a known age. This Kafkan time-zone, in which very unpredictable, often unthinkable events occur, is rife with anxiety for the characters who inhabit it, and it is equally anxiety producing for Kafka's readers. To quote Perniola once more, it "shakes and dissolves all our certainties." It is not new, of course, to consider Kafka's works "enigmatic" in the sense of being puzzling and inexplicable; however, if we take the sense of enigma further and define it as that moment when fear of the past and fear of the future collide in the present, that is, Perniola's sense of enigma — perhaps new insights into some of Kafka's stories may be gleaned.

With the figure of the Hunter Gracchus, in Kafka's short fictional texts of the same name, "Der Jäger Gracchus," written in 1917, Kafka created one of his most enigmatic situations. Both the story and fragments remained unpublished during Kafka's life. After Kafka's death, Max Brod titled the story and published it and a longer fragment; Nahum Glatzer also published not only the story, but also the fragment in his collection of Kafka's complete stories in translation.[1] Each of these two versions is a dialogue between the wandering body, not to say corpse, of Gracchus and a visitor, be it the Mayor of Riva, as in the more complete text, or an unnamed interlocutor, as in "Fragment zum 'Jäger Gracchus'" (The Hunter Gracchus: A Fragment). There is no action, only a conversation, and the conversation ultimately reveals little more than who the hunter is, the hunter's origins, how he died, and his lack of understanding of his situation. Each of the versions introduces a death ship sailing into a harbor. In the longer version, the hunter's arrival goes unnoticed by the populace, but is heralded by a flock of doves; and the Mayor says that a dove "gross wie ein Hahn" ("as big as a cock") decreed that he should be received "im Namen der Stadt" (*SE* 330; "in the name of the city," *CS* 228). In the fragment, the interlocutor has happened on the scene by chance because of his business (*BK* 333; *CS* 233).

Perhaps because the essence of reality is enigmatic, Kafka began his tale with one of the most "real" settings in all of his fictional works. Remarkable is the description of the scene leading up to the conversation between the hunter and the Mayor of Riva in the more complete "story." Kafka's short fiction often leaves much to be fleshed out in the way of descriptive details, but this piece of prose is replete with minutely observed gestures, details of dress and placement, colors, etc. In the first paragraph, no fewer than ten people — eleven, if one includes the corpse on the bier — are placed in action. In some ways it almost reminds one of a film script:

> Zwei Knaben saßen auf der Quaimauer und spielten Würfel. Ein Mann las eine Zeitung auf den Stufen eines Denkmals im Schatten des säbel-schwingenden Helden. Ein Mädchen am Brunnen füllte Wasser in ihre Bütte. Ein Obstverkäufer lag neben seiner Ware und blickte auf den See hinaus. In der Tiefe einer Kneipe sah man durch die leeren Tür- und Fensterlöcher zwei Männer beim Wein. Der Wirt saß vorn an einem Tisch und schlummerte. Eine Barke schwebte leise, als werde sie über dem Wasser getragen, in den kleinen Hafen. Ein Mann in blauem Kittel stieg ans Land und zog die Seile durch die Ringe. Zwei andere Männer in dunklen Röcken mit Silberknöpfen trugen hinter dem Bootsmann eine Bahre, auf der unter einem großen blumengemusterten, gefransten Seidentuch offenbar ein Mensch lag. (*SE* 328)

> [Two boys were sitting on the harbor wall playing with dice. A man was reading a newspaper on the steps of the monument, resting in the shadow of a hero who was flourishing his sword on high. A girl was filling her bucket at the fountain. A fruitseller was lying beside his wares, gazing at the lake. Through the vacant window and door open-ings of a cafe one could see two men quite at the back drinking their wine. The proprietor was sitting at a table in front and dozing. A bark was silently making for the little harbor, as if borne by invisible means over the water. A man in a blue blouse climbed ashore and drew the rope through a ring. Behind the boatman two other men in dark coats with silver buttons carried a bier, on which, beneath a great flower-patterned fringed silk cloth, a man was apparently lying. (*CS* 226)]

After another very detailed paragraph of the dock setting, an equally detailed passage describing the Mayor's walk to his meeting with Grac-chus follows. The scene for the conversation has been set. Within the next two pages, the conversation hits on many striking images, such as the Hunter's being forever "auf der großen Treppe" ("on the great stair") leading to the other world (*SE* 330; *CS* 228); the Hunter's refer-ring to himself as a butterfly; his shabby condition; and the picture of the bushman with a spear aimed at the Hunter (*SE* 331; *CS* 229), to name a few that have been often commented on by various interpreters of the tale.[2]

When the Mayor identifies himself to Gracchus, it is established that the scene is Riva on Lake Garda, the only geographically specific setting in any of Kafka's short fictions. Indeed, specificity might be said to be the theme of the passage, perhaps even of the story and the fragments. The specific is offered prodigally and with it comes a series of questions.

On the one hand, there are the questions in the text (most prevalent in the "Fragment"), interrogations that might benefit the characters somehow. "Woher stammst du?" (*BK* 335; "Where do you come from?" *CS* 234) asks the interlocutor in the fragment, and the answer to this innocent question marks the conclusion to the tale, rather than its beginning. That is, this basic knowledge (which, perhaps, "everyone knows" *CS* 234), far from leading somewhere, is the proof that "du kennst wirklich gar nichts" (*BK* 335; "you don't really know anything,"*CS* 234). But who does?

The reason that no one seems to know what needs to be known is that there is a second form of specificity: the specific points that we who are not in the story must interrogate as readers, hunting for a sense of the story. Going back to the opening paragraph of the tale, we might ask about the dice that the boys, two of them to be precise, are playing with. Can we allow dice without a wager? Can we allow a wager without involving a whole literary line of gamblers, particularly a gambler who bet his soul to the devil back near the Black Forest? And was not Faust a hunter, who sought knowledge because he "really didn't know anything" but was led astray by illusion, false specificity? If this seems a strained, pointless reading, perhaps a look at the man with the newspaper by the hero's statue will offer more. The emptiness of the popular press matches the transience of fame and conquest. The newspaper offers only "what everyone knows," which is that "old, old story" (*CS* 233) that has the advantage of being coherent ("nun wüsste ich gerne etwas im Zusammenhang über dich," [*BK* 334; "I'd like to know something coherent about you," *CS* 233]), but ultimately leads nowhere. Even the dead man knows nothing of himself and advises his interlocutor to ask the historians.

The two false leads that begin "Der Jäger Gracchus" — and it hardly matters that I have conflated two versions of the Gracchus story, because the false leads, the specificities that will not take us to a plausible conclusion about the meaning of the tales, are everywhere — certainly remind us that we are hunters, seeking our prey everywhere, shooting wildly at the details that come into range. And what will we have when we bag our game, as we always do? A parable. The specific reference to Riva is the smell of red meat for an interpreter. Max Brod and Kafka visited Riva on the northwest end of Lake Garda in September of 1909. There must be meaning here! And Gracchus, the Roman hero (with a sword raised high as in the statue?) is a grackle, the same blackbird that the Czechs called *kavka,* and that Kafka's father had on his letterhead.[3] There must be more meaning here! The scent is too strong. And meaning we shall find, Oedipus in Riva, Gracchus/Kafka as Faust or Flying Dutchman or Ancient Mariner (as Guy Davenport has it [27]), or a thousand more possibilities.

Each of these possibilities may yield a superb reading; I belong to the tribe that hunts these meanings. But the Hunter Gracchus will not be laid to rest. It is his fate, as he puts it, to remain in ignorance, although "tot, tot, tot" (*BK* 335; "dead, dead, dead," *CS* 234), a condition that should provide some understanding. The interlocutor is also ignorant, knowing less than "das kleine Kind des Steuermanns" (*BK* 335; "the helmsman's little child" (*CS* 234). This piece of specificity (which suggests further seductive possibilities — the helmsman must cross the Styx, so the child of death is knowledge itself . . .) brings us to a striking place. Knowledge recedes. We begin with knowledge, and as we learn more we know less. Gracchus tells the interlocutor of the fragment that perhaps ". . . [du] verschweigst . . ., was du von mir weisst" (*BK* 334–35; "you conceal what you know about me" *CS* 233) or ". . . du [verwechselst] meine Geschichte mit einer andern . . ." (*BK* 335; "you confuse my story with someone else's" *CS* 234). And Gracchus himself asks not to be asked. "Weiss nicht warum," he says (*BK* 335; "Don't know why . . .," *CS* 234). Maybe historians can help, he says quite unpersuasively. But this ignorance is not primal or existential. After all, "alles war in Ordnung" ("everything was in order") at one time. The mistake is inexplicable: Gracchus may blame the boatman, but his accusation persuades no one.

Wilhelm Emrich made "Der Jäger Gracchus" the key for his understanding of all of Kafka's works (Emrich 4–78). Despite Erwin Steinberg's critical challenge to Emrich that he failed to take into account all of the fragmentary versions of the work, of which there are actually four (even more than Steinberg writes about), Emrich's discussion claims to offer an understanding of Kafka that transcends interpretation.[4] He sees the text as an expression of a universal theme — that the hunter has dropped out of any classifications of this world or the hereafter and as such "is universally everywhere and nowhere" (Emrich 8).

What Emrich has done is to place "Der Jäger Gracchus" clearly in the realm of enigma. What makes an "enigma" different from a "secret," according to Perniola, is that with a secret *someone* has to be "in the know," but with an enigma nothing is hidden. No one holds the key as with a secret. An enigma is always explicable, but there is always another explanation that undercuts the first, and another, and another. Enigma is capable of explanation on many levels of meaning, all equally valid, and "draws its strength from the questioning tension that it arouses" (Perniola 10). There is no secret in Gracchus's world. No one — not the Mayor, not the boatman, not Gracchus himself — possesses an answer to Gracchus's strange plight, and no one can direct the situation to a logical and satisfying outcome.

Where do all the details lead? Our expectation as readers is that each one may serve as a clue to the all-important meaning of the tale; if it does not, we read it as simply a ruse or an indigestible bit of literary reality. When none of these threads is picked up again, not only are we disappointed, but we feel compelled to hunt more obsessively for their meaning so that we may in some way explain the enigma that the written text presents to us. To be sure, we have been cautioned about this practice by Emrich:

> If Kafka's writing were, as many interpreters assume to be the case, a reflected image, an expression or symbol and allegory for certain religious concepts and matters of faith or for certain social and biographical phenomena . . ., it would be incomprehensible why Kafka enigmatized his works in this way at all. Merely to dupe the reader, or to have his works appear particularly "interesting"? . . . The enigmatic structure of his writing is, on the contrary, an essential expression of the fact that the true universal, which is striving to assume form here, is itself something enigmatic — enigmatic, to be sure, only with regard to the conceptual world of man caught in his own finite categories. In this it differs fundamentally from the true universal of the poetry of the past. (Emrich 16)

Emrich attributes the enigmatic quality in Kafka's writing to the enigma that is the real world and to Kafka's sense that there is no harbor, no security, no hold. Boundaries dissolve — history becomes eternal; but this eternal history, which we are always repeating, does not empower us with its familiarity because it comes to us with a perennial difference, leaving us perennially unequipped. That is the enigma that each of Kafka's protagonists must face. As readers, we understand their fear and relive it. By coming up with interpretations, we ease our own discomfort with the enigmatic, and momentarily dispel it; but as Kafka's readers, we also know that this is only a momentary balm. The fear of that moment of dissolved boundaries will return with each new reading.

There is, however, a real paradox at work here. When any critic approaches one of Kafka's texts, whether for the first time or again, she holds a subtle hope or desire that perhaps, just perhaps, the text is really only secretive rather than enigmatic — that this time, the definitive answer will be discovered, and she, like Detective Columbo, will have finally and neatly solved the puzzle. But, at the same time, she thrives on the enigma, which allows her to indulge in the real pleasure principle of reconfrontation of a text — this time it will be both the same and different, and she both delights in and fears this reality.

What justifies Emrich's confidence that he has put his finger on the source of the Kafkan enigma? Why would a religious, social, or biographical allegory be comprehensible — that is, have no need of enigmatics — when universals, the conceptual world, or finite categories seem to require just this kind of expression for Kafka? In other words, why doesn't Emrich see that his (excellent) reading is just as much a reflected image or allegory as any of those he disputes? And more particularly, how can he claim to know the very terms within which Kafka becomes comprehensible? If, as he suggests, a Kafka who sought to fascinate or fool his readers, to keep them turning the pages, so to speak, is an incomprehensible Kafka, it can only be on the basis of a reading that believes it has already taken into account the duping of past readers and the widespread interest in Kafka's work. Emrich sees "Der Jäger Gracchus" as central to a vision of Kafka that cannot support a center.

We know that Kafka wrote in creative spurts of spontaneous inspiration. Perhaps this explains why commentary responds so readily to the short fictional pieces, even more than to his three novels, all of which remained incomplete. He obviously had great difficulty in sustaining his artistic intensity over long periods of time, and thus the short fiction is not only more representative of Kafka's focused creativity but also benefits from it. The open-endedness of these short texts has made them particularly attractive to interpretation by critics; they seem easy prey for hunters of meaning. Every season these hunters return with a large kill. Because these pieces ultimately resist "correct" readings, they become vehicles for layer upon layer of critical effort. The hunters kill them over and over; they won't stay dead.

Kafka relentlessly poses a problem with parable. And this problem is especially apparent in the short fiction. Parables are the prey of the hunter-readers of Kafka because of the meticulously crafted frustration of resolution that he weaves into his texts. We must ask "what does this mean?" and this leads us to "what could this mean?" and this brings forth endless readings that are either more plausible (if often less interesting because they raise the question whether the meaning is worth the effort) or more far-fetched (but all the more widely admired for that, in many cases, because the reading seems to rival the text in ingenuity and surprise, although only in a secondary way). These meanings, readings, accumulate like barnacles around the texts themselves. We cannot read them innocently, cleanly. Add to this the fact that the readings also live by killing each other or at the least drawing the life's blood from a prior reading, and we see that each text is surrounded by piles of dead, dying, and for the moment triumphant counterversions of it. The text itself, if such there can be, is at the center, but is neither alive nor dead. It cannot remember what it means, but must resignedly defer that task to others, however ignorant they may be. In this sense it resembles what Stanley Fish calls "a self-consuming artifact" (40), but with the following difference. Rather than progressing through a series of projected meanings that lead, like the rungs of a ladder, to a final apotheosis of the experience of reading that text, the accumulated meanings of the enigmatic texts live and die but do not lead to a final stage.

Enigmas proliferate because, as time goes by, knowledge recedes behind the pile of readings. Now one may argue that this is the fate of all literature. Roland Barthes did. We, that is, our entire literary culture, are dirty with meaning and its endless connotations, and we cover art, from which we learn our meanings, with the litter of our work. The dream of a pristine word that will rise perpendicularly and escape the weight of meanings is only a utopian vision. As a rule, though, we overlook this. Narratives, substantial, sequential, time-driven, mimic our illusory sense that we are living a story. The more cues and clues we are offered (and writing itself cannot help but provide these on every line), the more motifs and themes and, with them, meanings. And that satisfies us, even if the meanings are awkward and fail to match our lives. Kafka's short pieces, however, by offering the cues without the massive aggregate of a full story, novella, or novel, foreground the arbitrariness of thematizing. Kafka, I suggest, knew this, and used the short and fragmentary fictions to protest.

The protest, I suggest in this reading, which shall be added to the pile of others, is clear enough in "Von den Gleichnissen" (On Parables). The piece begins with "Viele beklagen sich," and what "many complain" of is the uselessness of the words of the sages in real life. The sage may say, "Gehe hinüber" ("Go over"), but he doesn't mean cross to a real place (nor, we may note, recalling the Hunter Gracchus's predicament, does he mean cross over finally to death itself), but rather to a "sagenhaftes Drüben" ("fabulous yonder"), a yonder that is both unknown to us and that Kafka cannot adequately describe to us in his writing. This last is precisely the romantic definition of metaphor as Coleridge and so many others saw it. Parable is one secondary set of signs standing alongside, but also in place of, another, primary set of signs, in order to bring meaning to them. Whether we accept it as a limited function of interpretation (as Bloomfield has it in "Interpretation as Allegory") or as the general situation of "alles Vergängliche" — might we say, *Dasein* in general — as Goethe puts it at the end of *Faust*, the idea is to add meaning to the world. This is what Kafka does not allow. His own voice takes the place of the "many," and he refuses to accept the vision of a creative outside force, either appealed to by the sage, or brought to life by the readers of the words of the sage. "Alle diese Gleichnisse wollen eigentlich nur sagen, daß das Unfaßbare unfaßbar ist, und das haben wir gewußt" (*SE* 411; "All these parables really set out to say merely that the incomprehensible is incomprehensible, and we know that already," *CS* 457). The reason for this is the absolute difference between life and art. Neither a mirror nor a lamp, so to speak, the words of the wise are gnomic and inert — or so "many complain" — dead but still living because of the foolish curiosity of those who, like the Hunter Gracchus's interlocutor, must know things. "Ask the historians," says the hunter (*CS* 234). All your inquiries make you know less and less. And he, the hunter, has forgotten.

Not everyone, however, has such a pessimistic view of literary interpretation and everyday life. "Darauf sagte einer: 'Warum wehrt ihr euch?'" ("Concerning this a man said: 'Why such reluctance?'"). As the parable tells us, we must follow the parables, become parables, and lose our daily cares. In the perspective of this advice, to follow the lessons of the wise is to lose one's reality. One lives literature then, not life, and lives and dies in a carefree state.

> Ein anderer sagte: "Ich wette, daß auch das ein Gleichnis ist."
> Der erste sagte: "Du hast gewonnen."
> Der zweite sagte: "Aber leider nur im Gleichnis."
> Der erste sagte: "Nein in Wirklichkeit; im Gleichnis hast du
>   verloren." (*SE* 411)

> [Another said: "I bet that is also a parable."
> The first said: "You have won."
> The second said: "But unfortunately only in parable."
> The first said: "No, in reality: in parable you have lost." (*CS* 457)]

So the first laughingly advises the second to give it up, releasing his need for real life and accepting a simulacrum, a parable life. He admits, however, that his advice is only a parable, itself in need of something extra to have force. When the second replies that his victorious interpretation is only a victory in parable, the first points out that victories of this sort only take place in reality. In parable one can never win, because there is always a twist, another reading, endlessly making the possibility of victory more and more remote.

"Von den Gleichnissen," then, ends with a full chiasmus and paralysis. So Kafka's protest, if taken as a protest in parable, is victorious. But this of course cannot be. One cannot successfully protest against the parable by use of parable itself. On the other hand, if his protest is made in reality, he has lost. It is he himself who has crafted the fictions into the enigmatic objects that elicit parables that surround and engulf them. But this is what Kafka, as much as any writer we know, chose to do. It is unthinkable that he was repelled — in reality — by the fascination caused by his work and the renown that this fascination brought him. This is what writers want most of all, and Kafka was above all a writer. It is possible that Emrich, in being right about Kafka, was also wrong about Kafka.

In regard to a story that was first published in 1917 in the monthly magazine *Der Jude,* Kafka specifically wrote Martin Buber, the editor, that his contribution, "Schakale und Araber" (Jackals and Arabs) should not be considered a parable and rather wanted it designated as a "Tiergeschichte," an "animal story." Referring to both "Schakale und Araber" and "Ein Bericht für eine Akademie," which were published together, Kafka wrote: "Gleichnisse bitte ich die Stücke nicht zu nennen, es sind nicht eigentlich Gleichnisse . . ." (I ask you not to call the pieces parables, they are actually not parables . . ., Kauf, 421). It would seem that for Kafka, no moral or lesson should be extracted from "Schakale und Araber," and yet, most of the critics who have written about it read the tale as a parable. They have all created very credible narratives and captured various elements in the text, each accentuating a different aspect of the piece in question. They have each become a hunter and hunted for the meaning of the story.

To Herbert Tauber, "Schakale und Araber" is a story with an existential theme showing the futility of the revolt of humanity against natural law (69–70). William C. Rubinstein understands the tale to contain "specifically" Jewish material, demonstrating its readability as a parable about the coming of the Old Testament Messiah, "who according to the prophets is to appear to kill the enemies of the Jews and restore them to Israel" (13–18). The dramatic quality of the tale is highlighted in Evelyn Beck's analysis, which takes Rubinstein's interpretation a step further, showing that the Hebrew word for jackal could be a pun on the Hebrew word for teachers of Mishna. Walter Sokel's reading elucidates the cohesion of structure and content within the parable, comparing it to "Vor dem Gesetz" (Before the Law) and *Der Proceß,* and at the same time, demonstrating the tale's distinctive Nietzschean perspective. It is Sokel's reading that I would like to use as a basis for discussion here.

In his article "Das Verhältnis der Erzählperspektive zu Erzählgeschehen und Sinngehalt in 'Vor dem Gesetz,' 'Schakale und Araber' und
'Der Prozess,'" Sokel distinguishes three structural figures or figure-
groupings in the tale — the observer (the narrator), the tormentor (the
whip-cracking Arab), and the suffering victims (the jackals) (276). As the
tale is played out, the jackal-victims ask the narrator-observer from the
North to free them from their tormentors, the Arabs, but this request
will go unfulfilled. The jackals believe the visitor from the "hohen Nor-
den," the "far North," where the understanding that is lacking "hier
unter den Arabern" ("here among the Arabs") can be found, is their
salvation — their messiah. The head jackal describes how generations of
jackals have waited for the narrator — "bis hinauf zur Mutter aller Schakale" (*SE* 150; "right back to the first mother of all the jackals," *CS*
408). Sokel points out one of the two basic mistaken assumptions made
by the victims here, in that they equate intelligence or understanding
with those who are revolted by the violent killing of animals for food.
Those who kill animals and consume their flesh have no intelligence —
those who eat carrion do. The observer is quick to distance himself from
the jackals' position, but in so doing distances himself from the other
side as well with his comment: "'Mag sein, mag sein,' sagte ich, 'ich
maße mir kein Urteil an in Dingen, die mir so fern liegen; es scheint ein
sehr alter Streit; liegt also wohl im Blut; wird also vielleicht erst mit dem
Blute enden'" (*SE* 150–51; "'Maybe, maybe,' said I, 'matters so far
outside my province I am not competent to judge; it seems to me a very
old quarrel; I suppose it's in the blood, and perhaps will only end with
it.'" *CS* 408). By denying any judgmental action, the observer has established his objectivity. But his meaning is completely misunderstood by
the jackals.

Using the figure of speech "im Blut liegen" (to lie or be in the
blood), the narrator implies that the struggle between Arab and jackal is
probably innate and will only end with the dying out of one or the other
group; the jackals, however, have taken the phrase to mean a literal
bloodbath. They want the Arabs killed so that they will be rid of their
stench and filth and violent ways. For this to happen, they need an intermediary, for they have no hands, and it is precisely their revulsion at
the Arabs that prevents them from getting close enough to kill them.
The jackals plead with the observer to be their savior:

> "Herr, du sollst den Streit beenden, der die Welt entzweit. So wie du
> bist, haben unsere Alten den beschrieben, der es tun wird. Frieden
> müssen wir haben von den Arabern; atembare Luft; gereinigt von ihnen

den Ausblick rund am Horizont; kein Klagegeschrei eines Hammels, den der Araber absticht; ruhig soll alles Getier krepieren; ungestört soll es von uns leergetrunken und bis auf die Knochen gereinigt werden. Reinheit nichts als Reinheit wollen wir. . . . Darum, o Herr, darum o teuerer Herr, mit Hilfe deiner alles vermögenden Hände schneide ihnen mit dieser Schere die Hälse durch!" Und einem Ruck seines Kopfes folgend kam ein Schakal herbei, der an einem Eckzahn eine kleine, mit altem Rost bedeckte Nähschere trug. (*SE* 151–52)

["Sir, we want you to end this quarrel that divides the world. You are exactly the man whom our ancestors foretold as born to do it. We want to be troubled no more by Arabs; room to breathe; a skyline cleansed of them; no more bleating of sheep knifed by an Arab; every beast to die a natural death; no interference till we have drained the carcass empty and picked its bones clean. Cleanliness, nothing but cleanliness is what we want. . . . And so, sir, and so, dear sir, by means of your all-powerful hands slit their throats through with these scissors!" And in answer to a jerk of his head a jackal came trotting up with a small pair of sewing scissors, covered with ancient rust, dangling from an eyetooth. (*CS* 409–10)]

They need a liberator, because they cannot free themselves, and not simply because they have no hands. Their unconquerable disgust at carnality and the dirt of the Arabs prohibits them from attaining the purity they desire. Their wish to be free of the Arabs cannot overcome their revulsion at them. Drive is stronger than will.

Unwilling to involve himself in this struggle, the narrator is himself "saved" by the whip-cracking Arab who drives back the pack of jackals. The observer is now treated to a "spectacle" staged for the entertainment of the Arabs and his own edification. Calling the jackals "fools," the Arab is ready to show the observer just how nonsensical their hopes for deliverance are. A camel carcass is thrown to the jackals:

Sie hatten die Araber vergessen, den Haß vergessen, die alles auslöschende Gegenwart des stark ausdunstenden Leichnams bezauberte sie. . . . Da strich der Führer kräftig mit der scharfen Peitsche kreuz und quer über sie. Sie hoben die Köpfe; halb in Rausch und Ohnmacht; sahen die Araber vor sich stehen; bekamen jetzt die Peitsche mit den Schnauzen zu fühlen; zogen sich im Sprung zurück und liefen eine Strecke rückwärts. Aber das Blut des Kamels lag schon in Lachen da, rauchte empor, der Körper war an mehreren Stellen weit aufgerissen. Sie konnten nicht widerstehen; wieder waren sie da. . . . (*SE* 152–53)

[They had forgotten the Arabs, forgotten their hatred, the all-obliterating immediate presence of the stinking carrion bewitched them. . . . And now the caravan leader lashed his cutting whip crisscross over their backs. They lifted their heads; half swooning in ecstasy; saw the Arabs standing before them; felt the sting of the whip on their muzzles; leaped and ran backwards a stretch. But the camel's blood was already lying in pools, reeking to heaven, the carcass was torn wide open in many places. They could not resist it; they were back again. . . . (*CS* 410–11)]

Finally, the only salvation of the jackals is carrion. Their own lust for blood makes them into victims of themselves. They are slaves to their enemies because they are parasites, depending on the Arabs to give them what they truly desire. They are no longer the victims of the Arabs but rather victims of their own passions. Sokel's reading, as I have abbreviated it here, also links "Schakale und Araber" with "Vor dem Gesetz" and *Der Proceß* and argues that there are two basic types of narrative in Kafka's mature work — parables and stories.

The guilt and misery of the beasts derives from their own beastliness. Passion prevails over reason and causes their oppression. This morality play could hardly be more parabolic; it retells the tale as a legal case, in which one party is finally revealed as the true culprit in the suit. Sokel thus stands in his reading of the story in a position analogous to the observer in the tale, but he is neither the savior desired by the jackals nor the non-moralizing critic specified by Kafka. He is the adjudicator "from the North," a critic who will decide the ultimate issue of the fiction — that is, what it means. Kafka's parable, in fact, does what any parable will do, namely spawn another parable. The contagion is rampant, and I shall succumb to it and suggest that "Schakale und Araber" is rather the story of this contagion. Sokel's version will serve as the jumping off place.

The person of the narrator offers us the first point of entry. The fact that he comes from a place in which people do not kill animals violently for food, Sokel tells us, makes him a possible messiah for the jackals. And because he can speak and give authoritative reports on the situation, he can accomplish what the jackals can never do: eliminate their enemy through discursive judgment. The jackals are authors, particularly modernist authors. They claim to despise their readers, the Arabs, whose willful commonness — the smell of their endless misconceptions — maddens them. They appeal to the observer-narrator to free them from these oppressors through a higher critical understanding. But where would the observer, whom we now recognize as the critic, obtain such an understanding? Mere observation, it seems, is not enough. Some key must be provided to kill the wildly proliferating interpretive parabolizing of the readers, always in search of meanings in a literary moment (high modernism) that will not reveal itself. The key, of course, is the scissors, a cutting instrument that recalls the etymology of criticism.[5] So the critic will eliminate the reader by providing a discourse that is not dirty, not foul with interpretation and its endless proliferation. The jackal-authors hate their Arab-readers and scorn, as good modernists, the fame, the commercial success, the literary wealth that they provide.

And yet there are two problems, one illustrated by Sokel's interpretation, the second by Sokel's practice. Sokel makes it clear (as, I admit, does Kafka) that the jackals are not sincere in their contempt for what the Arabs provide for them, the red meat they in fact crave and which causes them to lose all perspective on the Arabs, forgetting even their presence. The red meat is popular success, and it is what the jackals really desire, whatever they may tell the critic-observer. The Arab-readers know this and have little respect for the hypocrisy of the so-called literary elite. In my reading of Sokel's reading, the tale is a re-enactment of a critic's encounter with the truth of the matter. But there is a problem (in fact, there are many, but that is another story). The tool that the jackals believe will empower the observer-critic is, I suggest, the method of a non-interpretive, anti-parabolic criticism — a formalism that will build a meaning from within and surround it with defenses against any "message" that may attack it from without. These scissors that should cut so neatly the parts of the literary text(ile) — they are, after all, sewing scissors — are rusty, imperfect. The cleanliness that is so valued by the jackals is not to be found in the tool of critical reading. And Sokel's reading itself, as we have seen and as he himself admits, cannot account for Kafka's decree that "Schakale und Araber" is not a parable.

If it is not a parable, what is it? Is this a simple warning to keep our distance? Past readings, the hermeneutic history, vanish; future possibilities are foreclosed. The story is a frozen present, not exactly dead, but at least not the possession of the dirty, all-powerful Arab-readers, who have no real standards at all. Perniola comments that this seems to be the fate of art in our time, to become like Hegel's description of ancient Egypt, full of mummies, *tableaux vivants*, "little by little becoming space" (46). An *esprit de finesse* pervades the culture, in Perniola's view, so that every event is "so complex that it not only authorizes opposed and contradictory interpretations but also refutes them all" (57). An enigma.

To assert that Perniola's vision describes Kafka, as I believe it does, is to be caught up in the same error with which I have charged Emrich. I have, finally, offered an anti-reading of Kafka's short fictions, and this is itself nothing but a reading, indeed a parable. As a reader, I bag it like an Arab hunter. Must I feel guilt for this? Have I oppressed the poor jackal (grackle)? Emrich says so because he believes that Kafka was above it all. If Franz had been merely a trickster, a magician, as Thomas Mann always confessed to being, then his works would be incomprehensible. Perhaps. But I cannot help thinking that the parable is never closer or more seductive than when Kafka tells us there is none.

Notes

[1] Page references to Kafka's stories are to Kafka, *Sämtliche Erzählungen,* ed. Paul Raabe (Frankfurt am Main: Fischer Verlag, 1981), abbreviated as *SE* or *Beschreibung eines Kampfes: Novellen, Skizzen, Aphorismen aus dem Nachlass* (New York: Schocken Books, 1946), abbreviated as *BK.* Page references to Kafka's stories when quoted in English are from Kafka, *The Complete Stories,* ed. Nahum G. Glatzer (New York: Schocken Books, 1971), abbreviated in text as *CS.*

[2] For some interesting readings of the specific possibilities of interpretation for these images, see the articles of Hartmut Binder, Donald P. Haase, Guy Davenport, Ronald Spiers, and Erwin Steinberg, among others.

[3] Binder and Davenport both speak about the etymology of the Latin *Gracchus* and its relation to the Italian *gracchio,* meaning jackdaw — just as *kavka* means jackdaw in Czech — and the resulting connection and even identification of Kafka with his dark hunter-protagonist.

[4] Steinberg takes exception with Emrich for not examining the implications of the fragments being incomplete, as well as Emrich's dealing with them "pretty much as a single coherent story" (309). For the purpose of my argument, I will follow Emrich's method of conflation rather than specific individualization of each of the fragments.

[5] According to *Der grosse Duden's* volume on etymology, the Greek root of "kritisch" goes back to the verb *krínein* — to split, to separate, to discern, to judge — and belongs to the word family whose radical root "skeri-" relates to the German words *Schere* (scissors), *scheren* (to care about something), *schneiden* (to cut), and *scharf* (sharp), among other word groups. The same root of "criticism" can also be traced in English in *The American Heritage Dictionary.*

Works Cited

Beck, Evelyn Torton. *Kafka and the Yiddish Theatre: Its Impact on His Work.* Madison, Milwaukee, London: U of Wisconsin P, 1971. 179–81.

Binder, Hartmut. "'Der Jäger Gracchus': Zu Kafkas Schaffensweise und poetischer Topographie." *Jahrbuch der deutschen Schillergesellschaft* 15 (1971): 375–440.

———. *Kafka-Kommentar zu sämtlichen Erzählungen.* Munich: Winkler Verlag, 1975.

Bloomfield, Morton W. "Allegory as Interpretation." *New Literary History* 3 (1972): 301–17.

Davenport, Guy. "The Hunter Gracchus." *The New Criterion*. 14 (1996): 27–35.

Der grosse Duden: Band 7, Etymologie, Herkunftswörterbuch der deutschen Sprache. Ed. Drosdowski, Grebe, et al. Mannheim, Vienna, Zurich: Duden, 1963.

Emrich, Wilhelm. "The Universal Thema." *Franz Kafka: A Critical Study of His Writings*. Trans. Sheema Zeben Buehne. New York: Frederick Ungar, 1968. 4–78.

Fish, Stanley. *Is There a Text in This Class?* Cambridge: Harvard UP, 1980.

Haase, Donald P. "Kafka's 'Der Jäger Gracchus': Fragment or Figment of the Imagination?" *Modern Austrian Literature* 11 (1978): 319–31.

Kafka, Franz. *Beschreibung eines Kampfes. Gesammelte Schriften*, vol. 5. New York: Schocken, 1946. (*BK*)

———. *The Complete Stories*. Ed. Nahum G. Glatzer. New York: Schocken Books, 1971. (*CS*)

———. *Sämtliche Erzählungen*. Ed. Paul Raabe. Frankfurt am Main: Fischer Verlag, 1981. (*SE*)

Kauf, Robert. "Verantwortung: The Theme of Kafka's *Landarzt* Cycle." *Modern Language Quarterly* 33 (1972): 420–32. Includes first printing of Kafka's letter to Martin Buber, 12 May 1917.

Nägele, Rainer. "Auf der Suche nach dem verlorenen Paradies." *German Quarterly* 47 (1974): 60–72.

Perniola, Mario. *Enigmas: The Egyptian Moment in Society and Art*. London and New York: Verso, 1995.

Rubinstein, William C. "Kafka's 'Jackals and Arabs.'" *Monatshefte* 59 (1967): 13–18.

Sokel, Walter. "Das Verhältnis der Erzählperspektive zu Erzählgeschehen und Sinngehalt in 'Vor dem Gesetz,' 'Schakale und Araber' und 'Der Prozeß.'" *Zeitschrift für deutsche Philologie* 86 (1967): 267–300.

Spiers, Ronald. "Where There's a Will There's No Way: A Reading of Kafka's 'Der Jäger Gracchus.'" *Oxford German Studies* 14 (1983): 92–110.

Steinberg, Erwin R. "The Three Fragments of Kafka's 'The Hunter Gracchus.'" *Studies in Short Fiction*. 15 (1978): 307–17.

Tauber, Herbert. *Franz Kafka, an Interpretation of His Works*. Trans. G. Humphreys Roberts and R. Senhouse. New Haven: Yale UP, 1948. 69–70.

A Dream of Jewishness Denied: Kafka's Tumor and "Ein Landarzt"

Sander L. Gilman

FRANZ KAFKA KNEW HIS FREUD. In complicated ways he grew up and into the age of Freud. Much as the surrealists such as Max Ernst and André Breton "invented" Freud, finding in Freud "scientific" proof of their own manner of seeing the world, Kafka too created his own Freud. And Freud in his deepest fantasies about the psyche invented the world in which Ernst and Breton and Kafka could be imagined. Like Freud's own "dream book," which Kafka read and annotated, Kafka's diaries are full of real, invented, or desired dreams (see Sokel and Born). Indeed, in complex ways and in spite of his struggle with psychoanalysis, Kafka's fascination with the dream as a key to his own internal life remained consistent over his adult life. But as often as not Kafka's dreams (like that of Gregor Samsa) were waking dreams: "Ich kann nicht schlafen. Nur Träume kein Schlaf" (*T* 567; I can't sleep. Only dreams, no sleep) he wrote on 21 July 1913 (cited in Guidice and Müller 18). These waking dreams are constructed from what Freud calls "day residue," the images left over from daily experience. Kafka knew this category and wrote on 11 February 1914 to Grete Bloch: "Diese Art Schlaf, die ich habe, ist mit oberflächlichen, durchaus nicht phantastischen, sondern das Tagesdenken nur aufgeregter wiederholenden Träumen durchaus wachsamer und anstrengender als das Wachen" (*LFFE* 18; This type of sleep I have is superficial, truly not fantastic, rather constructed from the thoughts of day; they are exciting, repetitious dreams that are more lively and exhausting than being awake). On 22 March 1922 Kafka entered into his diary the following dream: "Nachmittag Traum vom Geschwür an der Wange. Die fortwährend zitternde Grenze zwischen dem gewöhnlichen Leben und dem scheinbar wirklicheren Schrecken" (*T* 913; In the afternoon a dream of a tumor on the cheek. The continually trembling border between the normal life and the seemingly more real horror). Let us imagine with Kafka where such a dream can be located within the world of culture and dreaming of the Austro-Hungarian Empire.

On 7 March 1913, Julius Tandler, the Jewish professor of anatomy and Viennese city councilor, addressed the German Society for Racial

Hygiene (that is, Eugenics — see Tandler). It was Tandler who in 1924 would intercede for the terminally ill Franz Kafka at the behest of Kafka's friend Franz Werfel and enable Kafka to get a bed at the Kierling Sanatorium, where he finally died (Hackermuller 120). In this basic address, Tandler attempts to align a series of concepts that were loosely used at the turn of the century, among them constitution, predisposition, and race. Tandler assumes that these aspects define the human being, and that they are present simultaneously. For him all of these categories are "predetermined at the moment of conception" (13). Anything that can be altered by environment is not constitutional. Constitution is the individual variation that is present in an individual once the qualities of type and race are subtracted. This would include any "inherent relative abilities" such as the specific "disposition" for an illness. Thus there are "tumor races" (20). (There is a slippage from constitution to race in Tandler's argument.) According to Tandler, there are races that develop specific forms of tumors.

Who are the "tumor races" and why are tumors the sign of their racial difference? What was a "tumor" of the cheek for Kafka in 1922? In 1838 Johannes Müller had discovered that the cell structure of a tumor is inherently different from normal cell structure. In Berlin Hermann Lebert then was able to describe in detail the morphology of the cancerous cell. By the 1860s Rudolf Virchow's view that only cells could give rise to other cells (*omnis cellula a cellula*), and therefore, that cancer was not a foreign intrusion into the body was accepted. Cancer was an inherent, degenerative cellular disease, which, by 1886, was believed to be limited by the specific origin of the cell from which the tumor sprang (*omnis cellula e cellula eiusdem naturae*).

But what caused cancer? The views were as diverse as the theories themselves. With the success of Pasteur's view on the bacteriological origin of certain diseases, such as rabies, one focus was on bacteria. The fascination with local inflammation, and the observation that it seemed to produce tumors, gave rise to the alternative view that cancer was a disease resulting from scarring. With the central importance of the science of race in nineteenth-century medicine, it is of little wonder that at the beginning of the twentieth century the focus turned to the question of race and its role in the origin of cancer.

In 1914 Theodor Boveri, professor of zoology at the University of Würzburg, published his study of the origin of malignant tumors, in which he argued that carcinomas had their ultimate origin in an error of the chromosomes, which could be caused through either mechanical or chemical means (see Boveri). This view augmented earlier work by David von Hansemann who saw in the growth of malignant tumors a growth parallel to that of normal cells, that is, he understood cancer as a type of development response to external stimulus (see Hansemann). Cancer was to be understood as a somatic mutation that could, therefore, be inherited, rather than simply being the result of some unknown infectious disease (see de Grouchy). This view had been widely discussed in the course of the late nineteenth century. The rise of greater knowledge about the mode and means of inheritance, following the rediscovery of Mendelian genetics at the beginning of the twentieth century, led to the re-establishment of this view as one of the central theories of the origin of cancer. By the 1930s this view of cancer as a disease of the chromosomes had led it to become one of the cadre of inherited diseases that eugenics claimed could be eliminated by careful breeding (see Fischer-Wasels).

The origin of the debate about who suffered from cancer and the related debate about what causes cancer is an ancient one. During the course of the nineteenth century the question of race became one of the means of distinguishing those at risk from those who were seen to be immune from the disease. In the 1860s Cesare Lombroso had begun to study the question of the comparative mortality of the Jews of Verona and the non-Jewish population. There he observed that Veronese Jews suffered from twice as many cases of cancer as did Veronese Christians (see Lombroso). Lombroso's statistics supported the contention that Jews were a separate and unique race, whose medical anomalies derived from this separateness. They were, to quote a study of the early twentieth century, ". . . a race of considerable purity of stock, [which] . . . by their ubiquitous presence. . . . supply the interesting phenomenon of a racial unit subjected to widely-differing geographical influences" (Sorsby 1). In Berlin during 1905, 8.6 percent of all deaths among Jews were attributed to cancer, compared to 6 percent in the rest of the population (Gutmann 50–51).

British physicians such as James Braithwaite had also made the simple reversal of Lombroso's claim about a Jewish predisposition to cancer at the turn of the century (see Fishberg). This view, that "cancer occurs rarely among Jews," was then refuted by further statistical evidence to the contrary ("Cancer among Jews" 681). But if Jews were neither immune from nor predisposed to cancer, they certainly were seen as a group that presented a very specific manifestation of the disease (see Peller).

By the beginning of the twentieth century the question was no longer whether "Jews" suffered from "cancer" or not, but whether Jews were predisposed to or immune from certain specific types of tumors. There was a growing statistical literature that discussed the Jewish pre-disposition to specific forms of cancer. Jews it seemed had an immunity to certain cancers. In 1890 W. S. Bainbridge could cite the case of a sarcoma in a Jewish woman as a pathological curiosity (Sorsby 77). In Munich Adolf Theilhaber saw the social rather than the racial profile of his patients playing a major role in the frequency with which any group of them developed specific tumors, such as uterine tumors (see Theil-haber, 1909). The religious practices of the Jews, such as circumcision, were felt to play a role in the lower incidents of uterine cancer, as shown in the work of Felix Theilhaber, Adolf Theilhaber's son (see F. Theil-haber 1927). The Jewish neurologist Leopold Löwenfeld reinterpreted Theilhaber's findings in a very different way. He saw the lower incidence of uterine cancer among Jewish women as a reflection of types, rather than of race. The earlier menarche of Jewish women reflected the pre-dominance of a specific type among Jews, which he called the plethoric. This resulted in lower incidences of uterine cancer because of the in-creased amount of blood in the organ (128). As we have seen, the re-placement of racial arguments with typological arguments was common in the fin de siècle. Theilhaber also stressed the greater risk that Jewish men have for cancer of the stomach and of the intestine (Theilhaber and Greischer 548).

Felix Theilhaber began his work on the decline of the Jewish birth-rate with an interest in cancer gained while at his father's proprietary hospital for female diseases in Munich. He documented the complex literature on the relationship of cancer to "race," stressing the much lower rate of cancer of the uterus and cervix for Jewish women and the much higher rate of cancer of the stomach for Jewish men (F. Theilhaber 1910, 11–14). He clearly saw that this was in no way tied to the question of class, as the Jews he examined came from many social classes. He discounted the normal views about the lower rate of uterine and cervical cancer: Jewish women tended to have more children (his figures were from Budapest) so a lower birthrate does not account for the lower rate of cancer, as was frequently claimed; they were admitted to hospitals more frequently (which would tend to provide a higher rather than a lower reporting of incidents); and they were exposed to the same surgical procedures. He noted that the "Jews are a purer race than those people among whom they live" and that they suffered from many fewer cases of cervical cancer (13). Theilhaber left open the cause of the lower rate, but his assumption was that it had to do with the etiology of the tumors.

The Theilhabers make little distinction between "racial," that is, endogenous, and "social," or exogenous causes for cancer and its localization. But certain overall views can be extrapolated from their findings. For the Theilhabers the localization of specific cancers made it possible to speak of a gender-based difference of the types of cancer among Jews. The stated rationale for the lower incidents of uterine and cervical cancer among Jewish women was the sexual practices of the Jews, specifically the "strict observance of the Mosaic Law regarding marital relations" (Vineberg 1224). The laws that govern abstinence among Jewish women during and following their menstrual cycle decreased the amount of "continued irritation," which was seen as "a potent causative factor" in the etiology of cancer. But hidden within this argument is the assumption that one further cause is the ritual circumcision of male Jews as well as their lower incidence of sexually transmitted disease (see Pejovic and Thuaire). For there was a strong assumption in the course of the late nineteenth and early twentieth centuries (which is still held) that cervical or uterine cancer had a parasitical origin that could be sexually transmitted (see Onuigbo). The etiology for the higher incidence of stomach cancer among Jewish men is the pace of life; the lower rate of cervical cancer among women is due to the sexual practices of the Jews. Kafka's contemporaries would have had access to a summary of this debate in Felix Theilhaber's essay on cancer and the Jews in the *Jüdisches Lexikon* (1138–39).

Certainly the central debate about the localization of cancer in both male and female Jews centered about the central biological marker of the Jew, the circumcised penis, and its implications (see Remondino). There is a detailed literature on the relationship between penile cancer and circumcision. Penile cancer accounted for between two and three percent of all cancerous tumors in males during the nineteenth century and was one of the most physically and psychological devastating diseases. As early as 1882 the British surgeon Jonathan Hutchinson related the occurrence of cancer of the penis to the appearance of phimosis, the constriction of the foreskin, in infants. He also encouraged the practice of circumcision as it "must necessarily tend to cleanliness" (*Archives of Surgery* 15, 267–69). The relatively rare anomaly of the constriction of the foreskin became one of the standard rationales for the advocacy of universal male circumcision by the end of the century and its introduction into the United States.

In 1907 J. Dellinger Barney of the Harvard Medical School published a study of one hundred cases of cancer of the penis, in which he noted "that not a single circumcised Jew was found in the hundred cases. This

seems to my mind a most convincing argument in favor of circumcision . . ." (894). Benjamin S. Barringer and Archie Dean added a study
of thirty-six cases to the literature on cancer of the penis in 1923 and
noted, early in their paper, that "no Jews appear in this series" (497).
Abraham Wolbarst of New York asked the most evident question: "Is
circumcision a prophylactic against penis cancer?" His examination of 675
males, all of whom, with few exceptions, were Jews, uncovered "not a
single case of cancer of the penis" (308). The reason that Wolbarst gives
is the "cleanliness" that circumcision affords (302). For the Austrian
situation, the 1926 publication of V. Föderl, at von Hochenegg's surgical
clinic at the University of Vienna, argued precisely the same point: he
reported on forty cases from his clinic over a period of twenty-four years,
of which none were Jews. In addition he accounted for 276 cases of
cancer over 11 years among men from the Viennese Jewish Hospital, in
which again not a single case of penile cancer was recorded (208). Further
studies in Vienna done over the years of 1921 to 1927 recorded 2,252
cases of cancer in males, in which not a single case of cancer of the penis
was found among Jews (Sorsby 65). These statistics implied that circumcision afforded immunity to penile cancer, but, taken together with
Theilhaber's work on cervical cancer, that cancer of the genitalia was
substantially less frequent among Jews than among the general population. Circumcision was a prophylaxis against cancer and was a sign of
sexual hygiene. Here the implications of the debate about Jews and the
transmission of syphilis lurked in the background.

There is a complex interrelationship between many of these views
concerning Jewish immunity to or propensity for specific diseases. Given
the debate about the lower (or higher) incidence of syphilis among Jews,
it is of little wonder that this view is linked to statistics concerning specific forms of cancer. Thus cancer of the mouth was assumed to be the
result of scarring left by syphilis. In the standard nineteenth-century
handbook on syphilis there is an extensive discussion that "in the case of
the tongue, the association of the two [cancer and syphilis] is so common, that it is difficult to avoid an impression, that syphilis must exercise
some degree of predisposing influence . . . In attempting to lay down
rules for the differential diagnosis between cancer and syphilis, I am most
anxious to insist, as already done, on its extreme difficulty. . . . Cancerous
processes may be simulated by syphilis in the closest possible manner"
(Hutchinson 512). In one study, 30 percent of all of the cases of cancer
of the mouth were claimed to have a syphilitic origin (A. and F. Theilhaber 561). Maurice Sorsby used this as an illustration to rebut the
assumption that the Jewish immunity to certain forms of cancer was

hereditary: "A low incidence of [cancer of the tongue] among Jews would lend no support to the suggestion of racial immunity to it among Jews, for it is well known that cancer of the tongue is frequently excited by syphilis, and syphilis is by no means so common among Jews as it is among non-Jews; indeed, in the past it was almost completely absent" (Sorsby 2–3). Indeed, there was an assumption that there was a low incidence of cancer of the buccal cavity (the soft tissues of the mouth and tongue) among Jews (Sorsby 79–80).

For the period from 1924 to 1929 Sigismund Peller documented a greater incidence of death from cancer of the buccal cavity among Jewish men than among Jewish women. (In Peller's sample, 28 Jewish men died as against 9 Jewish women. For every 100 cases of cancer reported, 2.5 Jewish men and .7 Jewish women suffered from buccal cancer as opposed to 3.5 non-Jewish men and .4 non-Jewish women. In the overall statistics 37 Jews and 319 non-Jews died of buccal cancer, a ratio of 1 to 8.5.) Peller notes that Jewish men are much less likely to have cancer of the oral cavity and Jewish women much less likely to have cancer of the genitalia (Peller 139). Later work contrasted cancer of the mouth and cancer of the breast among men and women: cancer of the mouth was five times more frequent among men and cancer of the breast was seventeen times more frequent among women (Auler 395). What cancer of the breast represented for the female, the mouth represented in the male. Except for Jews — Jewish males had a substantially lower rate of buccal tumors than the general population, but higher than Jewish women. Disease was "gendered" as much as it was categorized by race (see, for example, Schachter).

Are tumors of the cheek racial signs or they are signs of syphilitic infection — or both? Are they "male" or "female" illnesses? Following these chains of association leads us toward understanding the day-residue in Kafka's dream. Kafka had been diagnosed with tuberculosis (and not cancer or syphilis) in 1917. Tuberculosis was, however, like syphilis, a "social disease" according to the French physician Jules Héricourt. But it was not considered to be a "Jewish" disease. Indeed Jews were seen in Central Europe as relatively immune to the disease, at least until the horrible winter of 1916–1917 (see Haltrecht). Tuberculosis was already signaled with the signs of disease written on the body. The *habitus physicus,* the tubercular body with its sunken chest and lanky, bony frame, was Kafka's body even before his diagnosis. These stigmata of the *habitus physicus* only revealed the innate tendency of the body. With circular reasoning, tuberculosis is the result of "the privations and the fatigue undergone by men of weakly constitution [that] end by reawakening attenuated or torpid cases of tuberculosis" (viii). These "men of weakly constitution" were understood to be Jews. In 1920 Héricourt's British translator, Bernard Miall, provided the ultimate rationale for a eugenics that would separate the healthy from these sick but hidden bodies, the beautiful from the potentially ugly:

> We need a religion of beauty, of perfection. It would be a simple matter to teach children to worship perfection rather than hate it because it reveals their own imperfection. For we cannot teach what beauty is without making plain the hideousness of egoism. Beauty is the outward and visible sign of health — perfection — virtue. Pleasure is the perception of beauty, or some of its elements. What makes for the fullness and perfection of life, for beauty and happiness, is good; what makes for death, disease, imperfection, suffering, is bad. These things are capable of proof, and a child may understand them. Sin is ugly and painful. Perfection is beautiful and gives us joy. We have appealed to the Hebraic conscience for two thousand years in vain. Let us appeal to the love of life and beauty, which is innate in all of us. A beauty-loving people could not desire to multiply a diseased or degenerate strain, or hate men and women because they were strong and comely and able. . . . The balance of the races is overset, and only the abandonment of voluntary sterility by the fit, and its adoption by the unfit — which is eugenics — can save us. (244–45)

It was the Hebrews (not the Hellenes) whose fantasy of the body had condemned modern man to the world of self-loathing and disease. And yet it was not evident when one looked at the Jew that he was diseased. The reason for this was that Jews had over the years undertaken certain ritual practices that left them unmarked by certain ailments such as tuberculosis:

> All these peculiarities in the comparative pathology of the Jews are not due to any ethnic, "biostatic," or racial characteristics of a purely anatomical or physiological nature in relation to non-Jews. They have their origin in the past history of the Jews, in their habits of life, and in the fact that syphilis and alcoholism have but rarely been seen among them. When the Jew is commingling with his Christian neighbors and adopts their customs and habits of life, he sooner or later loses his "racial characteristics," and his comparative pathology presents no special peculiarities (Fishberg, 1901, 581).

Only in the acculturated Western Jew (read: Franz Kafka) did the signs of disease (read: tumors, cancer, tuberculosis, and syphilis) become immediately evident, for these Jews had shed their supposed immunity as they left ritual behind them.

Kafka began to refer to this notion of a diseased Jewish body that fails when it is acculturated even before his diagnosis with tuberculosis. Kafka's feet increasingly prevented him from undertaking the strenuous physical activity that he needed to reform and transform his body, a hopeless task given the unchangeability of the Jew's body. In early October 1910, he dislocated his big toe (*LFFE* 67). He writes that "the foot in particular is enormously swollen — but it is not very painful. It is well bandaged and will improve" (*LFFE* 67). The physical foot may improve, but Kafka's symbolic foot never will: it will inexorably become the limping foot of Kafka's miracle rabbi. It represents an inability to be a real man. It is a sign of the Jew, the devil, and of the cripple: "Als Hinkender die Gerti; geschreckt, das Schreckliche des Pferdefußes" (*T* 768; I frightened Gerti [Kafka's young niece] by limping; the horror of the club foot). The limping Jew is the evil Jew.

The limping foot is conspicuous in the anti-Semitic discourse of the time. In Oskar Panizza's fin-de-siècle drama *The Council of Love*, the Devil appears as a Jewish male, his corruption written on every aspect of his body including his foot: "The Devil stands before them, leaning on one foot and supporting the other with his hands. He wears a black, close-fitting costume, is very slender, close-shaven with a fine-cut face, but his features wear an expression that is decadent, worn, embittered. He has a yellowish complexion. His manners recall those of a Jew of high breeding. He leans on one foot, the other is drawn up" (79). The "yellowish" skin color, the limping leg, the degeneracy of the Jew form Panizza's image of the seducer of humankind. His limping signifies his Jewish illness and effeminacy.

At the fin de siècle, it was the syphilitic who limped, as the Parisian neurologist Joseph Babinski showed in 1896, when he proved that a diminished plantar reflex was a sign of neurosyphilis. Panizza's Devil's limping reveals him to be a syphilitic Jew. He thus prefigures the central theme of the play — the introduction of syphilis into the Europe of the Renaissance. He is already infected with his "disease," his Jewishness, and he will presumably spread it by using the Jews as intermediaries. Syphilis was actually considered a Jewish disease as early as its first modern outbreak in the fifteenth century, and Panizza also presents it as such, personified in a Jewish, male Devil (see Foa).

But the symbolic association of Jewish or Satanic limping with syphilitic limping was already well established in the culture of the late nineteenth century, by means of the intermediate image of the "yellow" skin of the Jew. His yellow, "Oriental" skin is also part of the standard image of the diseased Jew. For Otto Weininger, the quintessential Jewish self-hater of the turn of the century, had stressed that Jews "possess a certain anthropological relationship with both Negroes and Mongolians" (303). From the former, they get their "readily curling hair," from the latter, their "yellowish complexion." This is an unchanging racial sign. For Kafka this yellow skin color later marks a disease process in the bearded "friend in Russia" in his tale "Das Urteil" (The Judgment, 1912) whose "Gesicht, dessen gelbe Hautfarbe auf eine sich entwickelnde Krankheit hinzudeuten schien" (*L* 39; "skin was growing so yellow as to indicate some latent disease," *CS* 77). He bears the symptoms associated with the diseased Jew, including his skin color. "Schon vor drei Jahren war er gelb zum Wegwerfen" (*L* 52; Even three years ago he was yellow enough to be thrown away," *CS* 87). This "yellowness" suggests the jaundice that signals a number of "Oriental" illnesses such as malaria and thalassemia but is also associated with the skin color of the syphilitic in European popular belief.

Kafka's world is a world of bodies and of images of bodies. Having presented the complexity of the tumor about which Kafka dreamt (and wrote) let us turn to a literary tale in which fragmented aspects of this chain of images is employed. And let us do so using the model that Freud proposed, a model that both revealed underlying fantasies through images and disguised the meaning of the images. Kafka knew this model. Whether he accepted it in its totality is doubtful, but the devices he uses (and that Freud presents) belong to the shared turn-of-the-century notion of hidden meanings in dreams and texts. These are, however, meanings exposed through the verbal account of visual images.

Kafka's "Ein Landarzt" (A Country Doctor) appeared in 1919 but was most probably written during the war winter of 1916–1917, which preceded Kafka's diagnosis of tuberculosis (and saw a spectacular increase of the disease in Prague). It is an account of a failed cure and the meaninglessness of modern Western medicine. To begin at the beginning: One evening the country doctor, actually the regional health officer, is called out on an emergency. He is at a loss as to how he is to get to his patient when a groom suddenly appears. Magic horses also appear out of the doctor's abandoned pigsty to pull his carriage. As he is about to depart the groom suddenly turns on the doctor's maid, Rosa: "Doch kaum war es bei ihm, umfaßt es der Knecht und schlägt sein Gesicht an ihres. Es schreit auf und flüchtet sich zu mir; rot eingedrückt sind zwei Zahnenreihen in des Mädchens Wange" (*L* 201; "Yet hardly was she [Rosa] beside him when the groom clipped hold of her and pushed his face against hers. She screamed and fled back to me; on her cheek stood out in red the marks of two rows of teeth," *CS* 221). The mark on the cheek is the first sign of something wrong with the representations of the characters' bodies in the story, a sign of something being out of joint. It is a visible sign of the destruction presented by the introduction of illness into the tale, for without the call to the patient, who is ill, none of the magic would have been needed. We, through the eyes of the country doctor, see the marks on Rosa's cheek and we know their causation — the bite of the groom. But this is, of course, only the proximate cause, the sign now written on the body. The ultimate cause seems to be the illness of the patient. It is a diagnosis that identifies the cause of the illness that fails at this point.

While the doctor threatens the groom with a beating, he is also made internally aware that the groom has appeared to *help* him to reach the patient and therefore can not be punished, as the patient must (according to the Hippocratic oath) take precedent. We read this in his thoughts as revealed by the narrator. So he is forced to abandon Rosa to the further attacks of the groom as the horses carry him to his patient. The "tumor on the cheek" has begun to appear in the tale. Sexuality, destruction, and illness are all linked in the wound on the maid's cheek. This image is also indicative of the problem of Western medicine in trying to understand its multiple roles in a complex society.

When the doctor magically reaches his patient, he provides us with an account of the visual and tactile nature of the patient's appearance: "Mager, ohne Fieber, nicht kalt, nicht warm, mit leeren Augen, ohne Hemd, hebt sich der Junge unter dem Federbett . . ." (*L* 202; "Gaunt, without any fever, not cold, not warm, with vacant eyes, without a shirt, the youngster heaved himself up from under the feather bedding . . .," *CS* 221). Having given this physical examination, the doctor dismisses the patient as a malingerer until he is forced by the family to examine him further. At that point he discovers the tumor: "In seiner rechten Seite, in der Hüftengegend hat sich eine handtellergroße Wunde aufgetan. Rosa, in vielen Schattierungen, dunkel in der Tiefe, hellwerdend zu den Rändern, zartkörnig, mit ungleichmäßig sich aufsammelndem Blut, offen wie ein Bergwerk obertags" (*L* 204; "In his right side, near the hip, was an open wound as big as the palm of my hand. Rose-red, in many variations of shade, dark in the hallows, lighter at the edges, softly granulated, with irregular clots of blood, open as a surface mine to the daylight," *CS* 223). This is a vision of a cancerous lesion as well as a syphilitic one, at least in its literary provenance. It is the Grail king's wound to be healed by Parsifal (with Richard Wagner's music being quietly hummed in the background). It is the wound in the groin that marks the appearance of illness, sexuality, and destruction. And being *rose*-colored links it to the maid's cheek visually and literally. The visual link is evoked in the color as well as the visualization of the word. And the doctor now feels that he can not act at all. The case is hopeless. When the patient asks to be left alone to die, the doctor is suddenly brought to think about that other hopeless case, Rosa, whom he has abandoned some ten miles away.

But instead of going to Rosa's aid and leaving the patient in peace, the doctor continues to examine the lesion. In it he finds a further proof of the impossibility of cure. The wound is full of "Würmer, an Stärke und Länge meinem kleinen Finger gleich" (*L* 204; "worms, as thick and as long as my little finger," *CS* 223). The maggots in the wound are read by the doctor as a sign of putrefaction, of the inevitability of his patient's death from the now open tumor. He of course is wrong in this reading. He has been led by the magic horses and through the actions of the magic groom not to evoke the powers of Western medicine but to bring his shamanic authority as a healer to the bedside. The medical world into which he has entered is the world of folk medicine. His modern, Western, enlightened skills may well be useless, perhaps more because of his own ambivalence about them than because of any innate problem with the medicine itself. It is the doctor, not the medicine, that is at fault. The model of medicine that he brings into the country house forces him to misconstrue the meaning of the larva. Maggot therapy is an old folk (and present day clinical) remedy precisely for cleaning ulceration. It had been recognized as a successful means for the debridement of wounds in folk medicine for at least four hundred years before Kafka wrote his tale (see Courtney, Church, and Ryan). By the 1920s the use of maggot therapy had even become part of clinical practice (see Baer). The line between folk medicine and clinical practice is always indistinct, but, from the perspective of the clinician, folk medicine needs always to be distinguished from "quackery." The doctor's misdiagnosis of this folk remedy shows him that his only role is to become part of the magical treatment of the child. He is lifted up by the family and laid in the patient's bed magically to warm and cure the child's lesion. When he is laid on the bed, the boy says to him: "Mein Vertrauen zu dir ist sehr gering. Du bist ja auch nur irgendwo abgeschüttelt, kommst nicht auf eigenen Füßen" (*L* 205; "'I have little confidence in you. Why, you were only blown in here, you didn't come on your own feet,'" *CS* 335). The foot suddenly reappears as part of the definition of the doctor.

In this magical world of dreams structured according to Kafka's reading of Freud, dreams reveal as they dissemble. The images are condensed accounts of complex narratives that reach beyond themselves into the past. Kafka knew this. All of the images that Kafka uses deal with a complex of cultural fantasies about Jews. The wounded or diseased bodies of Rosa and the child both represent classical turn-of-the-century anti-Semitic views embedded in the popular (and clinical) medical discourse of the day. Is the wound cancer, or is it syphilis, or is it a cancer caused by syphilis? The doctor too takes on the yellow coloration ascribed to the Jew during the late nineteenth century. His feet reveal him. Standing on one's own feet is impossible for the acculturated Jew suspended between the systems of belief and the fantasies about the diseased Jewish body inherent in the "rational" world of medical science.

Yet it is clear that Kafka did not write "Ein Landarzt" as a tale about Jews (even if his uncle Siegfried Löwy may have served as a model for the protagonist) (Northey 85). But his vocabulary of images that deal with illness and bodily decay is taken from the vocabulary of his own world. How could it be otherwise? What is removed is the literal reference to the Jewish aspect in Kafka's bodies. All else persists. Kafka's dream of the tumor is the dream in which all the qualities of race, so central to the world in which Kafka's lived, vanish. I have argued in my study of Kafka, *Franz Kafka: The Jewish Patient,* that one of the effects of Kafka's universalizing of the literary discourse in his texts was to deracialize it. While some of his contemporaries, such as Richard Beer-Hoffmann and Arnold Zweig, were moving in precisely the opposite direction, by thematizing Jewishness, Kafka was removing the overt references to the Jewish body from his work (see Gilman 1994). What remains, of course, are the images without their racial references. And yet the racial references would have been present in any contemporary reading of the text. The association between sexuality and disease, the association of specific predisposition to specific forms of tumors, were part of the legend of the Jewish body at the turn of the century. One further association that is quite powerful is the image of the Jew as physician that haunts the anti-Semitic literature of the time (as well as being prevalent in the work of Jewish physicians such as Arthur Schnitzler).

In the tale of Kafka's country doctor, the Jewish references are totally missing. Yet their traces, following Kafka's reading of Freud's theory of the dream, are present. Let us imagine that Kafka *consciously* adapted a Freudian model rather than thinking that this is all a process of unconscious forces. Kafka knew clearly that his texts were to be avant-garde; what he strove for was a reading of his texts, not as a Jewish writer with all of the anti-Semitic taints ascribed to that category, but rather as a "modern" writer. The images he drew on are the images from which he wished to distance himself. They are present in a gestural language: the tumors of the cheek, the lesion in the groin mark the presence of disease.

The unsure-footedness ascribed to the physician and his inability to read the folk medicine he sees (and becomes part of) mirror the sense of being caught between rival claims. On the one hand (foot?) was the claim of the Enlightenment on the Jew as rational being, espousing a "scientific" religion that prefigured much of modern medicine. On the other hand was the desire of Central European Jews at the turn of the century to be different, to express their Jewishness in their own manner, even to reveling in the irrational and the magical. Leopold Sacher-Masoch had presented this dichotomy in 1892 in his key text on the nature of Austrian Jews called "Zwei Ärzte" (Two Doctors), contrasting and reconciling the two types. For him, a late Enlightenment (and non-Jewish) writer, "modern" medicine was recognized by the practitioner of folk medicine as preferable and "won" the competition. Jews of Kafka's generation are no longer so secure in this assumption. Perhaps the lost truths of ancient belief and practice were in their particularism more valuable for the modern Jew than acculturation? In "Ein Landarzt" Kafka too uses the physician as the model for the conflict between rationality and irrationality but is quite clear as to which force will win. The forces of the irrational triumph because the doctor cannot understand what he sees through the lens of his rationality. This too was the dilemma seen by Jews of Kafka's generation from Martin Buber to Walter Benjamin, from Georg Lukács to Gershom Scholem. It echoes in their writing and their desire for a place for the irrational, for the messianic, for the transcendental in the world. Kafka's play with this model of Jewish identity is written into the bodies of his characters, as the irrational nature of the meanings attached to their (and our) bodies.

Works Cited

Archives of Surgery (London) 2 (1891).

Auler, Hans. "Rasse und bösartige Gewächse." In Johannes Schottky, ed. *Rasse und Krankheit*. Munich: J. F. Lehmann, 1937. 388–99.

Baer, W. S. "The Treatment of Chronic Osteomyelitis with the Maggot (larva of the blowfly)." *Journal of Bone Joint Surgery* 13 (1931): 438–75.

Barney, J. Dellinger. "Epithelioma of the Penis. An Analysis of One Hundred Cases." *Annals of Surgery* 46 (1907): 890–914.

Barringer, Benjamin S., and Archie Dean. "Epithelioma of the Penis." *Journal of Urology* 11 (1924): 497–514.

Born, Jürgen, ed. *Kafkas Bibliothek: Ein beschreibendes Verzeichnis mit einem Index aller in Kafkas Schriften erwähnten Bücher, Zeitschriften und Zeitschriftenbeitrage.* Frankfurt am Main: Fischer, 1991.

Boveri, Theodor. *Zur Frage der Entstehung malingner Tumoren.* Jena: Gustav Fischer, 1914.

"Cancer among Jews." *The British Medical Journal* (15 March 1902): 681–82.

Courtney, M., J. C. T. Church, and T. J. Ryan. "Larva Therapy in Wound Management." *Journal of the Royal Society of Medicine* 93 (2000): 72–74.

Davidsohn, I. "Cancer among Jews." *Medical Leaves* 2 (1939): 19–27.

Fischer-Wasels, B. *Die Vererbung der Krebskrankheit.* Berlin: Alfred Metzner, 1935.

Fishberg, Maurice. "Cancer." *The Jewish Encyclopedia* 3: 529–31. 1905–1926.

———. "The Comparative Pathology of the Jews." *New York Medical Journal* 73 (1901): 537–43, 576–82.

Foa, Anna. "Il Nuovo e il Vecchio: L'Insorgere della Sifilide (1494–1530)." *Quaderni Storici* 55 (1984): 11–34.

Föderl, V. "Zur Klinik und Statistik des Peniskarzinomes." *Deutsche Zeitschrift für Chirurgie* 198 (1926): 207–230.

Gilman, Sander L. *Franz Kafka: The Jewish Patient.* New York: Routledge, 1995.

———. "Kafka wept." *Modernism/Modernity* 1 (1994): 17–37.

de Grouchy, Jean. "Theodor Bovéri et la théorie chromosomique de la cacerogenèse." *Nouvelle revue: French Hematology and Blood Cells* 18 (1977): 1–4.

Guidice, Gaspare, and Michael Müller, eds. *Franz Kafka: Träume.* Frankfurt am Main: Fischer, 1993.

Gutmann, M. J. *Über den heutigen Stand der Rasse- und Krankheitsfrage der Juden.* Berlin: Rudolph Müller & Steinecke, 1920. Rpt. 1939.

Hackermuller, Rotraut. *Das Leben, das mich stört: Eine Dokumentation zu Kafkas letzten Jahren 1917–1924.* Vienna: Medusa, 1984.

Haltrecht, N. "Das Tuberkuloseproblem bei den Juden: Eine rassen- und sozialpathologische Studie." *Beiträge zur Klinik der Tuberkulose* 62 (1925): 442–80.

Hansemann, David von. *Die mikroskopische Diagnose der bösartigen Geschwülste.* Berlin: Hirschwald, 1897.

Héricourt, J[ules]. *The Social Diseases: Tuberculosis, Syphilis, Alcoholism, Sterility.* Trans. with a final chapter by Bernard Miall. London: George Routledge and Sons, 1920.

Hutchinson, Jonathan. "The Pre-cancerous Stage of Cancer and the Importance of Early Operations." *The British Medical Journal* (1882): 4–7.

———. *Syphilis*. London: Cassell & Co., 1887.

Kafka, Franz. *The Complete Stories*. Ed. Nahum Glatzer. New York: Schocken, 1983. (*CS*)

———. *Ein Landarzt und andere Drucke zu Lebzeiten*. Ed. Hans-Gerd Koch. Frankfurt am Main: S. Fischer, 1994. (*L*)

———. *Letters to Friends, Family, and Editors*. Ed. Max Brod. Trans. Richard and Clara Winston. New York: Schocken, 1977. (*LFFE*)

———. *Tagebücher*. Ed. Hans-Gerd Koch, Michael Müller, and Malcolm Pasley. Frankfurt am Main: S. Fischer, 1990. (*T*)

Lombroso, Cesare. "Sulla mortalità degli Ebrei di Verona nel Decennio 1855–1864." *Rivista Clinica di Bologna* 6 (1867): 3–37.

Löwenfeld, Leopold. *Über die sexuelle Konstitution und andere Sexualprobleme*. Wiesbaden: J. F. Bergmann, 1911.

Northey, Anthony. *Kafka's Relatives: Their Lives and His Writing*. New Haven: Yale UP, 1991.

Onuigbo, Wilson I. B. "Historical Notes on Cancer in Married Couples." *The Netherlands Journal of Surgery* 36 (1984): 112–15.

Panizza, Oskar. *The Council of Love*. Trans. O. F. Pucciani. New York: Viking, 1979.

Peller, Sigismund. "Über Krebssterblichkeit der Juden." *Zeitschrift für Krebsforschung* 34 (1931): 128–147.

Pejovic, M. H., and M. Thuaire. "Étiologie des cancers du col de l'utérus. Le point sur 150 ans de recherche." *Journal de gynécologie, obstétrice, biologie, et réproduction* 15 (1986): 37–43.

Remondino, Peter Charles. *History of Circumcision from the Earliest Times to the Present. Moral and Physical Reasons for its Performance, with a History of Eunuchism, Hermaphrodism, etc., and of the Different Operations Practiced upon the Prepuce*. Philadelphia: F. A. Davis, 1891.

Sacher-Masoch, Leopold von. "Zwei Ärzte." In *Jüdisches Leben*. Mannheim: Bensheimer, 1892. 287–98.

Schachter, M. "Cancer et race: á propos du cancer chez les Juifs." *Le Progrès médical* 50 (5 December 1931): 2213–14.

Sokel, Walter H. "Freud and the Magic of Kafka's Writing." In J. P. Stern, ed. *The World of Franz Kafka*. New York: Holt, Reinhart, and Winston, 1980. 145–58.

Sorsby, Maurice. *Cancer and Race: A Study of the Incidence of Cancer among Jews*. London: John Bale, Sons & Danielsson, 1931.

Tandler, Julius. "Konstitution und Rassenhygiene." *Zeitschrift für angewandte Anatomie und Konstitutionslehre* 1 (1914): 11–26.

Theilhaber, Adolf. "Zur Lehre von der Entstehung der Uterustumoren." *Münchener Medizinische Wochenschrift* 56 (1909): 1272–73.

Theilhaber, A., and S. Greischer. "Zur Aetiologie des Carcinoms." *Zeitschrift für Krebsforschung* 9 (1910): 530–54.

Theilhaber, Adolf, and Felix Theilhaber. "Zur Lehre vom Zusammenhange von Krebs und Narbe." *Zeitschrift für Krebsforschung* 9 (1910): 554–69.

Theilhaber, Felix. *Die Beschneidung.* Berlin: L. Lamm, 1927.

———. "Gesundheitsverhältnisse." In *Jüdisches Lexikon,* ed. Georg Herlitz and Bruno Kirschner. 4 vols. Berlin: Jüdischer Verlag, 1927–30. 2: 1120–41.

———. *Zur Lehre von dem Zusammenhang der sozialen Stellung und der Rasse mit der Entstehung der Uteruscarcinome.* Diss., Munich, 1910.

———. "Zur Lehre von dem Zusammenhang der sozialen Stellung und der Rasse mit der Entstehung der Uteruscarcinome. *Zeitschrift für Krebsforschung* 8 (1909): 466–88.

Theweleit, Klaus. *Male Fantasies.* Trans. Erica Carter and Chris Turner. 2 vols. Minneapolis: U of Minnesota P, 1987–89.

Vanoosthuyse, Michel. "Récits de rêve et fiction chez Kafka." *Cahiers d'Études Germaniques* 33 (1997): 137–46.

Vineberg, H. N. "The Relative Infrequency of Cancer of the Uterus in Women of the Hebrew Race." *Contributions to Medical and Biological Research Dedicated to Sir William Osler.* 2 vols. New York: P. B. Hoeber, 1919. 2: 1217–25.

Weininger, Otto. *Sex & Character.* [1903] London: William Heinemann, 1906.

Wolbarst, Abraham L. "Is Circumcision a Prophylactic Against Penis Cancer?" *Cancer* 3 (1925–26): 301–9.

Surveying The Castle:
Kafka's Colonial Visions

John Zilcosky

> "Ich [bin] ein braves Kind und Liebhaber der Geographie."
> [I am a good boy and a lover of geography.]
> — Franz Kafka (letter to Max Brod, 12 February 1907)[1]

READERS HAVE LONG PUZZLED over the profession of the protagonist of Kafka's *Das Schloß* (The Castle). Why does Kafka choose to make the faceless hero of his most mysterious novel a land surveyor ("Landvermesser")? Since K. never actually does any surveying in the novel (he doesn't even possess any surveying equipment), the choice of profession might seem to be relatively unimportant. But is it? K. is defined throughout by this putative career, which effectively replaces his name. To the other characters (and to the reader), he becomes "Herr Landvermesser," the "ewige [eternal] Landvermesser" or simply "Landvermesser" (thus the capitalization in the English translation).[2] Critics seem to agree on the importance of unraveling K.'s profession, but their efforts have led only to suggestive yet widely differing metaphorical readings. Does surveying signify artistic ambition: observing, writing, and drawing (Robert 18)? The process of reading: delimiting semiotic difference (Bernheimer 198)?[3] Messianic promise: rebuilding Zion (Göhler 52; Robertson 228–35)? Some readers have questioned K.'s profession even further: claiming that he is not a surveyor at all but rather an impostor (Sokel 403–5). As the son of a Castle sub-secretary assumes at the onset, K. could well be a "Landstreicher" (vagabond) and *not* a "Landvermesser." Others point out that the term "Vermesser" is already undermined by a grim Kafkaesque irony: it signifies audacity and hubris ("Vermessenheit") and, most importantly, the possibility of making a mistake while measuring ("sich vermessen"; Heller 70). Thus, if we take K.'s profession seriously — as I propose we do — then we must acknowledge that this designation persists only in the likelihood of its own error. (The "Vermesser" is "vermessen" and therefore possibly "vermisst sich": misestimates himself).

Such metaphorical and etymological interpretations have greatly enriched readings of *Das Schloß* (I will return to the crucial connection between surveying and reading in the final section of this essay). For the moment, however, one cannot help but wonder whether critics, confronted by the opacity of K.'s profession, have missed the trees for the forest. As far as I can tell, only one interpreter has ever attempted to move behind metaphor and search directly for a historical land surveyor figure that might have influenced Kafka. Peter F. Neumeyer argued in 1971 that Kafka could have borrowed his land surveyor from *Der Zukkerbaron* (The Sugar Baron), Oskar Weber's popular 1914 "memoir" about a "Landvermesser" in South America.[4] Although Neumeyer does not go far enough — he merely notices influence and does not attempt a new reading of *Das Schloß* — he does insist on a possible connection between K. and this 1914 land surveyor. As such, Neumeyer's essay serves as a valuable starting point for gaining some historical footing for K.'s rhetorically slippery profession.

Neumeyer's investigation — ignored by thirty years of subsequent scholarship[5] — begins with a strikingly peculiar postcard of 31 October 1916 from Kafka to his then-fiancée Felice Bauer. In the context of recommending books for her to use in her work at a Jewish home for boys, Kafka mentions a popular adventure series, Schaffsteins' *Grüne Bändchen* (Little Green Books), and calls them his "Lieblingsbücher" (favorite books). He goes on to describe one of them, Weber's *Der Zuckerbaron,* in more detail:

> Unter ihnen [den grünen Büchern von Schaffstein] ist z.B. ein Buch, das mir so nahegeht, als handelte es von mir oder als wäre es die Vorschrift meines Lebens, der ich entweiche oder entwichen bin (dieses Gefühl habe ich allerdings oft), das Buch heißt der Zuckerbaron, sein letztes Kapitel ist die Hauptsache. (*F* 738)[6]

> [Among [the *Little Green Books*] is one book that affects me so deeply that I feel it is about me, or as if it were the prescription for my life, a prescription I elude, or have eluded (a feeling I often have, by the way); the book is called *The Sugar Baron,* and its final chapter is the most important.]

Oskar Weber's *Der Zuckerbaron: Schicksale eines ehemaligen deutschen Offiziers in Südamerika* (The Sugar Baron: The Adventures of a Former German Officer in South America) is essentially what its title claims to be. Its eighty-eight pages tell the perhaps apocryphal story of a down-on-his-luck former officer named "Weber" who travels to South America and, after serving for seven years as a "Landvermesser," survives natural disasters and an attempted revolution before eventually making his fortune in sugar. In the "most important" final chapter, the aging Weber climbs a nearby mountain peak in order to survey his plantation. In a moment of Romantic-Teutonic reflection, he contemplates his own death, and voices his desire to be buried on the top of this mountain.

Neumeyer claims that this memoir of a "Landvermesser" could have influenced Kafka precisely at the time he was choosing a profession for the hero of *Das Schloß*. Kafka's very first sketch for the novel ("Verlockung im Dorf," Temptation in the Village, June 1914, *T* 643–56) features a protagonist traveling to a village and staying in an inn, but he is not yet referred to as a "Landvermesser." Only after Kafka's reading of *Der Zuckerbaron* in 1916 does the hero of *Das Schloß* gain a profession (Neumeyer 9–10). Neumeyer buttresses his argument with further cases of apparent borrowing from *Der Zuckerbaron:* in "Ein Bericht für eine Akademie" (A Report to an Academy) and "In der Strafkolonie" (In the Penal Colony). Weber's moving account of shooting an ape that then becomes uncannily human seems to offer a pretext for the former;[7] for the latter, Weber's interest in machineries of torture resembles that of the Officer in Kafka's penal colony.[8]

Jürgen Born, twenty years after Neumeyer, points out Kafka's peculiar passion for Schaffsteins' *Grüne Bändchen,* but he does not investigate this further. He (like other, silent readers of this postcard?) understandably categorizes Kafka's enthusiasm as "highly subjective" and emotional, and does not address a possible connection to Kafka's fiction (228). It is worth noting, however, that Kafka had already used a travelogue, Arthur Holitscher's *Amerika: heute und morgen* (America: Today and Tomorrow) as source material for his first novel, *Der Verschollene* (The Missing Person) (Wirkner 14–40). Here, Kafka's love for "travel books" and his "longing for freedom and faraway lands," as Max Brod put it in his afterword to the first edition of the novel (which he, as editor, titled *Amerika*), indisputably overlapped with his literary production (260). If Holitscher's travelogue served as literary inspiration, then why not the more "volkstümliche" *Zuckerbaron* as well (Born 228)? New evidence further supports Neumeyer's point by demonstrating that Kafka was thinking about *Der Zuckerbaron,* again, precisely in the middle of his work on the ultimate version of *Das Schloß* (February–September 1922). He mailed a catalogue containing the *Grüne Bändchen* to his sister Elli in June 1922 and enclosed the following explanatory note (which remained unpublished until 1987): "Schaffsteins Grüne Bändchen aus dem beiliegenden Katalog [. . .] sind fast alle für Karl [. . .]; ich liebe besonders Nr 50, 54 und 73, habe aber keine von diesen und hätte sie gern" (Schaffsteins' *Little Green Books,* from the enclosed catalogue [. . .] are almost all for Karl [Elli's husband] [. . .]; I especially love numbers 50, 54, and 73, do not own any of them, however, and would very much like to) (Born 180). Number 54 is *Der Zuckerbaron,* and number 50 is another memoir by Weber that includes a land surveyor: *Briefe eines Kaffeepflanzers: Zwei Jahrzehnte deutscher Arbeit in Zentral-Amerika* (1913, Letters of a Coffee-Planter: Two Decades of German Labor in Central America).

Despite this evidence connecting Kafka's readings of the *Grüne Bändchen* with his conception of *Das Schloß,* any such quest for the "real" origin of Kafka's "Landvermesser" remains dubious. The figure of the land surveyor has, as mentioned above, been little researched in positivistic scholarship, but we can nonetheless hardly hope to have located *the* source of K.'s profession — just as critics have been hard-pressed to unearth one correct historical model for the Castle.[9] The connection between Kafka's surveyor and the Hebrew word for Messiah (*mashiah,* almost the same as *mashoah,* "land surveyor"), for instance, cannot be overlooked in a quest for sources (Beck 195). But my interest in this essay moves beyond a debate on sources and toward the *discourse* of surveying at the fin de siècle. This discourse, as we shall see, encourages us to reconsider Kafka's novel as a reaction to turn-of-the-century colonial understandings of vision, language, and territory. Kafka attempts to "elude" a colonial "Vorschrift" with *Das Schloß.* But, as with most of his fictions, this escape is plotted from within — and thus is inextricably bound up with the structures it endeavors to avoid.

* * * * *

Wilhelm Emrich introduced historical-political discourse into the land-surveyor debate in 1957. He argued, to surprisingly little critical echo, that surveying could be viewed as politically subversive (300–303). Emrich correctly claims that the arrival of a land surveyor might signify the redrawing of borders and, therefore, challenge the Castle's authority. (This explains the insurgent Brunswick's interest in hiring a surveyor.) As was the case following the dissolution of the Austrian and German empires in 1918, surveying, for Emrich, meant less territory for the governing powers. New, unfriendly neighbors (e.g., Czechoslovakia) depended on land surveyors to draw up their borders and thus, literally, to define themselves as nations. Although Emrich's larger argument (that K. is a revolutionary) founders on a lack of textual evidence,[10] his insistence on the geo-political significance of land surveying in the 1922 novel remains a provocative opening for considering land surveying's historical-political role.[11]

Within the history of European imperialism, however, as depicted in the *Grüne Bändchen* and elsewhere, surveying generally represented — pace Emrich — the opposite of revolution. In the Austro-Hungarian empire, as Kafka certainly knew, the land surveyor was a high-ranking governmental official — carrying with him the special rights and responsibilities of the notary public. More adventurous imperial governments in Spain, Britain, and France, meanwhile, hired surveyors to draw new borders and thereby to recast and solidify their empires' expanding frontiers. The journey of Alexander von Humboldt — who surveyed Latin America at the beginning of the nineteenth century — was, for example, financed by the Spanish crown, as were the voyages of less famous eighteenth- and nineteenth-century European surveyors. The traveling surveyor was often joined by cartographers, artists, botanists, and zoologists, and their communal goal was to demarcate, map, and classify national boundaries. In the colonized areas, as Mary Louise Pratt has written, Europeans were identified precisely as measurers: with their "oddlooking instruments" and "obsessive measurings" (of "heights and distances, courses of rivers, altitudes," etc.).[12] Such actions were far from benign. Indeed, if we define the modern state as that entity that possesses the exclusive legitimate right to inflict violence within its prescribed borders,[13] then surveying — while itself not a violent act — supplied the geographic parameters for state violence.

This returns us to Kafka's beloved *Grüne Bändchen,* and specifically to the Sugar Baron — who in Oskar Weber's account begins his career in late nineteenth-century South America as a land surveyor and offers no exception to the profession's reactionary tradition. Like other European contemporaries in Latin America, Weber's Sugar Baron begins his adventure employed by a post-imperial government that continues to cater to European interests. He is hired to parcel up "vacant" land that is eventually to be sold to speculators in coffee and sugar. Making use of the rudimentary engineering skills gleaned from his military service in the Franco-Prussian war, Weber spends seven years at this job. He surveys "abandoned" territories (probably populated by indigenous peoples), in order to ready them for sale to entrepreneurs: "since growing coffee was then a very lucrative business, ownerless ["herrenlose"] governmental estates were being bought up everywhere; these estates [. . .] needed to be surveyed" (18). By taking on these jobs, the hero of the memoir Kafka enthusiastically called his "Vorschrift" becomes a vital cog in the machineries of colonial power.

How familiar was Kafka — beyond having read *Der Zuckerbaron* and *Briefe eines Kaffee-Pflanzers* — with the historical figure of the traveling "Landvermesser" and, more importantly, with its reactionary context? Kafka was an avid reader of travel literature of all sorts,[14] and was thus likely familiar with the journeyman surveyor. As Peter Brenner argues, travel literature became more scientific and less personal in the course of the nineteenth century: the figure of the "scientific" traveler began to overshadow that of the touring gentleman (445).[15] Moreover, Kafka's interest in the *Grüne Bändchen* (throughout which, as we shall see, surveyors play important roles) is more sweeping and profound than even Neumeyer acknowledges: Kafka commented on the series five times in the decade from 1912 to 1922 — always favorably, calling it "die große Reiseliteratur" (the great literature of travel) and once even being moved to the point of "schluchzen" (sobbing) — and he acquired at least seven of the volumes (*T* 615, 15 December 1913; Born 144–48, 175). Finally, the connection between surveying and colonialism could also have reached Kafka through his Uncle Josef, who worked in territories exemplary of the fin-de-siècle mania for mapping and re-mapping: Panama and the Congo.[16] Given the above-mentioned reactionary political use of surveying, it is not surprising that, in the fifth chapter of *Das Schloß*, the Chairman explains to K. that the village peasants become "stutzig" (suspicious) when they hear of the Castle's plans to hire a land surveyor: "die Frage der Landvermessung geht einem Bauer nahe, sie witterten irgendwelche geheime Verabredungen und Ungerechtigkeiten" (*S* 107; "Land surveying is an issue that deeply affects peasants, they scented some sort of secret deals and injustice," *C* 66).

The reactionary land surveyor thus coursed through nineteenth-century "scientific" literature and, eventually, appeared in the colonial entertainment literature of the fin de siècle. In my survey of the *Grüne Bändchen* published between their first appearance in 1910 and 1914, I discovered six volumes that feature surveyors or surveying.[17] These stories are embedded in an ideology of exploration and exploitation, and the surveyors in them, by plying their trade, help to consolidate post-imperial power.[18] However, surveying, here, does more than serve colonial power and land-grabbing. More importantly for a study of Kafka's novel, surveying simultaneously corresponds to two important aesthetic aspects. These two formal traits confirm, as we shall see, Edward Said's claim that aesthetics and politics are always intertwined in the colonial arena: that an investment in empire (in this case, the employing of surveyors) is also always an "aesthetic investment" (in bird's-eye perspectives and narratives of self-discovery) (1993, xxi).

The first of these aspects is the typical plot design, which I will refer to as the "business of self-discovery." This "business" — which combines financial gain with psychological stabilization — is prominent in the three volumes by Oskar Weber that Kafka claimed in 1922 to "especially love": the aforementioned *Der Zuckerbaron* and *Briefe eines Kaffee-Planzers*, and a third book, *Der Bananenkönig: Was der Nachkomme eines verkauften Hessen in Amerika schuf* (The Banana King: What the Offspring of an Indentured Hessian Accomplished in America). Each is the story of an impecunious German going to a faraway country and, following various dramatic setbacks — from fires to volcanoes to revolutions — gaining wealth and personal satisfaction.[19] In each case, the protagonist's economic mastery develops simultaneously with his Bildungsroman-like story of self-discovery. This combination of capital gain and psychological progress is, of course, not new to colonial discourse. Nineteenth-century travelers to the Orient, as Said points out, were often more interested in "remaking" themselves than in "seeing what was to be seen" (1979, 193). Richard Hamann and Jost Hermand, similarly, uncover a fin-de-siècle psycho-economic nexus that they refer to as "imperialism of the soul."[20] Furthermore, Wolfgang Reif argues that Kafka's fin de siècle featured recurring narratives about heroes gaining an identity through travel (447–51), pointing out that many popular and literary authors — Waldemar Bonsels, Graf Keyserling, Hermann Hesse — presented alienated Europeans going abroad with the express goal of "Selbstfindung" (finding themselves, 448). As Keyserling writes in the epigraph to his 1919 *Das Reisetagebuch eines Philosophen* (Travel Diaries of a Philosopher), "The shortest path to oneself leads around the world."

This narrative business of self-discovery is, as the Sugar Baron soon discovers, best performed on a blank foreign landscape; that is, on what I call a "negative topos," a place defined by what it is not.[21] The soon-to-be Sugar Baron, for example, remarks at the onset of his narrative that he chooses South America simply because it is *not* New York: "Should I go to New York like so many other ex-lieutenants before me and there begin a dubious career of washing dishes and the like, or should I [. . .] go to South America?" (5). Ten years before writing *Das Schloß*, Kafka similarly constructs Russia as a negative, or blank, landscape for Georg Bendemann's "Russian friend" in "Das Urteil" (The Judgment). Kafka writes to Felice in 1913 that this "friend" is modeled after Kafka's own Uncle Alfred Löwy, the brother of the aforementioned Josef, but only negatively in terms of topography: "[My uncle] is a bachelor, director of railways in Madrid, knows the whole of Europe *with the exception of*

Russia" ("kennt ganz Europa *außer* Rußland," *F* 435, 5 August 1913, Kafka's emphasis). For Kafka, then, Russia is like South America for the Sugar Baron: a space that is not yet over-determined by traveling European predecessors.[22] This discursive blankness is important for the soon-to-be Sugar Baron (as well as for the Russian friend, who yearns for self-reinvention through "exterritorialization") because he wants to redraw himself, as it were, on a clean slate (Neumann 1981, 147–48). Like earlier visitors to the Orient described by Said, Weber imagines this foreign world to be an erasable writing pad — an unadorned stage on which to perform his self-fashioning.[23]

This business of self-discovery congeals in *Der Zuckerbaron,* as elsewhere in *Grüne Bändchen,* specifically around the act of surveying. The soon-to-be Baron, after surveying for the government and getting rich, finally surveys his own vast properties — thereby transforming them from a negative topos into a positive, particular, inscribed one. Now known simply as "El Varon" [*sic*] by the "natives," he demarcates, as surveyor, his space of new, private mastery (87). The hero of *Briefe eines Kaffee-Pflanzers,* similarly, hires a surveyor after he makes enough money to buy an estate. Only after the surveyor measures his land can he become a titled landowner, and only after this can he legally move his Indian workers onto his plantation. He can then observe his workers at all times. This panoptic strategy gives him more control over them and, consequently, more power for himself (54, 61–62). Political and visual power thus coincide. As the coffee planter claims, "Das Auge des Herrn macht [. . .] die Kühe fett" (32–33; the master's eye fattens the cows).

In contemporary English, "to survey" also connotes looking down at something from above ("sur" + "vidēre" = "to over-see"). This double meaning of measuring and over-seeing — which extends throughout the *Grüne Bändchen* — forms the second aesthetic aspect mentioned above. This is the perspectival aspect, and, like the narrative business of self-discovery, it relates surveying directly to power. The Schaffsteinian surveyors are good seers, and this vision corresponds to their perceived authority over the natives. Like Hermann Hesse on the Pedrotagalla and other contemporary travelers to Asia, South America, and Africa, the heroes of the *Grüne Bändchen* attempt to achieve a commanding view of the foreign landscape (Hesse 105–6).[24] This perspective — which Mary Pratt refers to as the "monarch-of-all-I-survey" view — corresponds to the business of self-discovery in the following way: At the outset, the unfortunate European traveler is lost visually, psychologically, and economically — only later gaining a personal and professional identity. Shortly after he acquires this identity, he achieves a singular view from above that confirms both his financial successes and his acquisition of a stable sense of self. The consolidation of his personal and economic "I" thus corresponds with the streamlining of his "eye."

The late nineteenth-century hero of *Briefe eines Kaffee-Pflanzers* purchases a South American plantation eight hundred meters above sea level. This height, he claims, offers him a beautiful view and a divine sense of self. He feels as if he is "in heaven" and enjoys a rare, clear vision of a neighboring mountain range: "When the forest permits a vista, one has a beautiful view of the facing cordillera, whose high summits stand out in relief against the rich blue sky" (57). Adolf Friedrich zu Mecklenburg's 1910 *Im Hinterlande von Deutsch-Ostafrika* (In the Hinterlands of German East Africa) similarly features a hero who gains a sense of himself (as distinct from the natives) by climbing a mountain and looking down (36–7). Once at the summit, he surveys an "overwhelming" landscape, a picture of what he terms "indescribable grandeur." The connection between this visual discovery and the protagonist's consolidation of power is emphasized by the sketch that accompanies the description (fig. 1).

Here, the fearless adventurer stands on the edge of the promontory looking through binoculars; his frightened servants, meanwhile, cringe far from
the edge. The adventurer is depicted as the single, technologically mediated eye — and thus the uncontested profiteer — in the picture's voyeur-
istic economy. Moreover, he is present only in order to see, not to be seen.
His entire body is covered with clothing (even eyes are concealed by the
binoculars). The cowering, unseeing servants, conversely, are nearly naked.
In the end, the narrator is visible only to us, his readers, and only
through the other end of the glass. We readers maintain a perspective
even more encompassing than Mecklenburg's, because *we* see *him*. As I
will discuss in my conclusion, the readers' position beyond this visual
economy renders us the most powerful — but also, paradoxically, the
most impoverished — figures in this technologically mediated colonial
narrative.

The traveler's ability to see but not to be seen gives him power over
both the foreign Other and the foreign landscape. As Pratt argues, the
nineteenth-century traveler's sense of visual mastery emerges in conjunction with his ability to transform the foreign landscape into a painting,
which, in order to empower him, must not include him. He creates this
painting and invisibly views it, so that he is never present inside it. Typical for this "aestheticizing" scene of visual sovereignty is a rhetorical
"density of meaning";[25] that is, an overload of adjectival modifiers, and
as demonstrated in the following example from another of Schaffsteins'
Grüne Bändchen, Max Wiederhold's 1913 *Der Panamakanal,* a veritable
palette of colors. The German narrator of *Der Panamakanal* describes
his adventure: a thrilling 1907 journey across the still new and relatively
untested canal, culminating in his first-ever view of the Pacific Ocean. As
was characteristic for the new century, the setting from which the European directs his gaze is man-made rather than a part of nature: the hotel
balcony replaces the traditional mountain peak (Pratt 1992, 216). The
narrator's panoramic view is of the sun setting on the ocean, and he
aestheticizes this picture through an overload of color-descriptors:

> The *green* of the near mountains and the *blue* of the distant range be-
> come *purple,* which gradually turns into a *violet* and finally transforms
> into a barely perceptible *gray.* A cloud that shines forth in *red* and *gold*
> lies atop the mountains at the sea; this cloud sends humanity the final
> greeting of the sun, which in the meantime has sunk into the ocean.
> Before the night covers the earth with its *black* shadows, a *pale green*
> spreads over the sky, which is then superseded by a shimmer of *gentle*
> *pink.* Then it is night. (Wiederhold 59–60, my emphasis)

The dizzying array of color modifiers aestheticizes the landscape by turning it into a densely-colored painting (as is fitting for the historical time period of impressionism in visual art). This excessive aestheticizing assists the narrator in his striving toward "Selbstfindung." It transforms his environment into a discrete, that is, framed, work of art. Furthermore, by demanding the attention of the suddenly overtaxed reader, this dense modification helps to cover up the central contradiction in the narrator's act of self-creation. Like the fully-clothed and binoculared hero of *Im Hinterlande von Deutsch-Ostafrika,* the narrator describes everything except himself and his standpoint. He is the invisible creator of a landscape that is defined exclusively by his omnipotent yet unseeable eye. He thus paradoxically erases himself in creating the painting that affirms him. As was the case with nineteenth-century colonial postcards of the Orient, the viewer discovers himself by "making" a landscape that cannot include him because — in order to affirm him — it must remain completely Other.[26]

My final example of a European traveler constructing a panoramic view while effacing himself is the most important one for my upcoming discussion of *Das Schloß.* It issues from *Der Zuckerbaron,* and exemplifies the way in which the business of self-discovery coincides with the monarchical view (and to aesthetic density). The hero is, at the beginning, indigent and visually frustrated, sitting in the lower deck of a ship bound for South America. His personal disorientation, therefore, parallels his inability to gain an overview of the Atlantic Ocean for five long weeks. In direct contrast to this dramatization of visual poverty, *Der Zuckerbaron's* final paragraphs (part of what Kafka called the book's "most important" chapter) present a now wealthy and self-confident Baron standing high above his own estate. He surveys the same ocean he once saw at eye-level. Now the ocean forms an aesthetically pleasing backdrop for his prodigious property as well as for his final act of narrative business:

> I am more than fifteen-hundred meters above the level of the ocean that glimmers toward me like a broad, silver ribbon. And between it and my standpoint I see an everlastingly green ocean of brush and trees, in the midst of which are the white structures of my estate [*meiner Besitzungen*], with shining, light gray corrugated roofs, the light green square plots of the sugar cane and corn fields, the darker and more muted meadows, and the small huts of the workers with their brown straw roofs — all lying out there like toys. From this single point the vista encompasses almost 270 degrees [. . .].
>
> When I first coincidentally became acquainted with this place after the surveying of my property [. . .] I brought ten hard working men

with axes and machetes up here, and I marked for them specifically the individual trees they were to cut down in order to clear the view [. . .]. Every year I have to allow myself the luxury of having the path [leading down to the promontory] and the small plateau cleared of the vegetation which has newly sprung up in the course of the year and interfered with the view. (*Z* 87–88; *SB* 18–19)

The connection between panoramic vision and power is explicit. The narrator aestheticizes a realm that clearly belongs to him ("meine Besitzungen"). The meaning that Weber produces so densely — hardly a noun goes unmodified — increases his psychological wealth, just as the density of his crops increases his financial well-being.

Because the Baron's psychological business is also the business of economics, his position is inflected with eighteenth- and nineteenth-century notions of land-ownership and class. As proprietor, painter, and observer of the landscape, he achieves a profit through detachment similar to that of Hegel's "master" in *Die Phänomenologie des Geistes* (1807, The Phenomenology of Spirit). The Baron does not, in Hegel's terminology, work on ("bearbeiten") the objects of his world; his laborers ("Arbeiter") do this. By avoiding proximity to the objects and thus to their threatening otherness — for Hegel, their "independence" — he can enjoy them purely, as "sheer negativity" (*Phänomenologie* 133; *Phenomenology* 116). For instance, the Baron only marks the trees; his servants cut them down. Through the "mediation" of his servants the Baron can "have done with the thing altogether" and, in this way, achieve full "satisfaction in the enjoyment of it" (*Phänomenologie* 133; *Phenomenology* 116). Hegel's notion of pure enjoyment through aristocratic distance invokes, as John Barrell demonstrates, class intonations from the eighteenth-century discourse of "disinterestedness." Barrell associates the "disinterested man" with the "gentleman of landed property"; that is, with the fellow with enough leisure and money to examine the socio-political landscape (because his rental income supposedly frees him from the interestedness of the working world) (33).[27] For Barrell, this man's "elevated viewpoint," his "overview of the whole," signifies class authority because it divides men "into those qualified to observe and those qualified only to be the objects of others' observation" (38, 44, 35). This socio-political privilege is simultaneously an aesthetic license, because the gentleman's "comprehensive" perspective determines the *way* in which society is viewed. He configures society from his superior viewpoint as one would a landscape painting (35, 31). Moreover, through an act of self-effacing legerdemain similar to those of the Schaffstein heroes, the gentleman viewer/painter somehow manages to "occupy, as it were, a position outside the landscape" (31).

The Baron performs precisely such an act of distancing and self-effacement. To borrow Nietzche's 1886 terminology, the Baron achieves a "Pathos der Distanz" (pathos of distance) by surveying the world beneath him: "aus dem beständigen Ausblick und *Herabblick* der herr-schenden Kaste auf Unterthänige und Werkzeuge" (from the perspective of the ruling class's ceaseless *looking down* on subjects and tools).[28] In his 1887 *Zur Genealogie der Moral* (On the Genealogy of Morals), Nietzsche equates this kind of pathos with a view from above: with the "höheren herrschenden Art im Verhältnis zu einer niederen Art, zu einem 'Unten'" (higher ruling order in relation to a lower order, to a "below").[29] This distancing allows — as with the Baron and Hegel's "master" — for the eventual "Erhöhung" (elevation) of the viewing man: he reaches "ever higher," "more comprehensive states."[30] Such an elevation is exactly what the Baron claims for himself, albeit in a far cruder, more personal form. His "eye," that organ of self-distancing, merges with his "I" — a pronoun that appears four times in the second paragraph alone. He organizes the objects on his estate (including his servants' residences) like a collection of "toys" and, at the same time, consolidates his self through a singular, exemplary overview. With his business of personal and professional discovery now complete, the Baron can pronounce, in the final sentences, his readiness to die on this very spot. Again, in this ultimate sense, the narrator's self-creation corresponds to his self-effacement. His absence from the painting develops into absenting himself from life. This final erasure is the ultimate stage of the "master's" figurative blindness and his possible existential bankruptcy — as analyzed by Hegel.[31]

* * * * *

Whether or not Kafka had the "Vorschrift" of *Der Zuckerbaron* in mind at the moment he invented his own "Landvermesser," he certainly knew of the historical construction of surveyors in the Schaffstein books and elsewhere. Moreover, Kafka's *Schloß* suggests that he was also aware of the discursive relationship between "surveying" ("measuring" and "seeing") and identity-construction. As interpreters of *Das Schloß* ranging from New Critics to poststructuralists have claimed, the major goal of Kafka's land surveyor seems to be to gain a sense of identity. Max Brod first made this claim in his 1926 afterword to the first edition of the novel, in which he reported an alleged conversation with Kafka: In the novel's unwritten ending, K. was to locate a sense of personal and professional stability just before his death (347). Later critics tended to position themselves as either agreeing or disagreeing with Brod, but few disputed the general assumption that K.'s business in the village was to discover himself. The first round of critics to challenge Brod (in the fifties and sixties) claimed that K.'s struggle was non-progressive and that *Das Schloß* was an aggressively modernist anti-Bildungsroman; for such readers, K. learns nothing and does not attain to fulfillment.[32] More sanguine critics from the early seventies returned to Brod's line of thinking, arguing that K. develops in the course of the novel, struggling toward self-completion: he successfully learns "humility and love" by the narrative's end.[33] Poststructuralist readings of the eighties and nineties once more took a gloomier view toward K.'s progress, but again they confirmed that K. is pursuing the elusive goal of self-identity. For example, Charles Bernheimer subtly argues that K. desires — in vain — to render the Castle's confusing semiotic order coherent to his "self" through a "totalizing system of signification" (198). Elizabeth Boa, similarly, uses Lacanian tools to argue that K. "desires absolute recognition of self-identity" (253). Gerhard Neumann claims that K.'s goal — which he fails to achieve — is that of the traditional hero of the Bildungsroman: "sich eine Identität zu schaffen" (to create an identity for himself, 1990, 208).

These methodologically diverse readings suggest — and I agree — that K.'s struggle with the Castle is simultaneously a quest for identity. But I prefer to stress the way in which this narrative of self-discovery is conditioned by the tradition of travel literature. Said's point that the Orient was the nineteenth-century traveler's blank slate of self-discovery is especially fitting for K.'s nameless Castle village — with its generic inns, school, houses, streets, and alleys. At only one point in the novel are "real" places named: K.'s lover, Frieda, mentions her desire to go to Spain or the South of France and, in so doing, jars the reader as much as she does K. (*S* 215). These sites puncture the text's otherwise strictly unspecific structure and thereby form the exception that proves the rule: the village is the negative topos *par excellence*.

The village's neutrality opens a space for K.'s business of self-discovery, but at the same time this very blankness thwarts his corresponding desire to order the village and define his position in it. Like many modern travelers, K. wants to locate meaningful patterns in his foreign world. As a surveyor, he longs to map it; that is, to organize its "signs" in a way that can be deciphered. But this village's lack of signs complicates his task. The very negativity that makes the village ideal for self-refashioning renders it nearly impossible to organize and represent as a discrete text. Entangled, extended in space, lacking signposts and maps, K.'s village can be neither framed nor surveyed. As K. remarks disconcertedly, shortly after his arrival, the village's nearly identical little houses extend interminably, as far as the eye can see. The village seems to have no end (*S* 21; *C* 10).

Tim Mitchell, a critic of travel narratives about the Middle East, makes a similar claim concerning foreign cities as perceived by nineteenth-century European travelers. Despite the traveler's desire to order his view of the city, Mitchell claims, he cannot. He can never adequately "aestheticize" the foreign city and, for this reason, can never sufficiently mark its alterity — its separateness from him. Mitchell's description of the uncontainable negative topos of the nineteenth-century Middle Eastern city uncannily characterizes K.'s 1922 frustrations within the geographically obscure village:

> [The traveler] expected there to be something that was somehow set apart from "things themselves" as a guide, a sign, a map, a text, or a set of instructions about how to proceed. But in the Middle Eastern city nothing stood apart and addressed itself in this way to the outsider, to the observing subject. There were no names to the streets and no street signs, no open spaces with imposing facades, and no maps. The city refused to offer itself in this way as a representation of something. [. . .] It had not been arranged [. . .] to effect the presence of some separate plan or meaning. (32–33)

The difference in mood between the traditional nineteenth-century travel narrative and Kafka's literary modernism is, as Mitchell's text suggests, not that great. The desire for containment and organization recurs — along with the frustration of this desire. If there is a difference between the two ways of seeing, it resides, first, in Kafka's refusal (or inability) to map the village and, second, in K.'s eventual acceptance of this disorder. As we shall see, K. accedes to a visual chaos for which the nineteenth-century traveler could never have allowed.[34]

The traditional traveler, in Mitchell's description, never stops attempting to organize the chaotic unrepresentability of the foreign city. To achieve this end, he made extensive use of panoramic views, sketchings, and maps. K. has similar desires and plans at the beginning of *Das Schloß*. We could indeed view K.'s struggle with the Castle as precisely a surveyor's desire to gain visual mastery: K. wants to measure, organize, and map the Castle territories according to his subjective blueprints. As Gerhard Kurz argues, K. longs to repeat a moment of visual sovereignty from his rarely remembered childhood (159–60). K. recalls this scene, in which he scaled a high wall in his home village, shortly after attempting (and failing) to climb the Castle hill for the first and last time:

> An einem Vormittag — der stille leere Platz war von Licht überflutet, wann hatte K. ihn je, früher oder später, so gesehn? — gelang es ihm überraschend leicht; an einer Stelle wo er schon oft abgewiesen worden war, erkletterte er, eine kleine Fahne zwischen den Zähnen, die Mauer im ersten Anlauf. [. . .] Er rammte die Fahne ein, der Wind spannte das Tuch, er blickte hinunter und in die Runde, auch über die Schulter hinweg auf die in der Erde versinkenden Kreuze, niemand war jetzt und hier größer als er. (*S* 49–50)

> [One morning — the calm, empty square was flooded with light, when before or since had K. ever seen it like this? — he succeeded with surprising ease; at a spot where he had been often rebuffed, with a small flag clenched between his teeth, he climbed the wall on the first attempt. [. . .] He rammed in the flag, the wind filled out the cloth, he looked down, all around, even over his shoulder at the crosses sinking into the earth; there was nobody here, now, bigger than he. (*C* 28–29)]

Kurz's argument is that K. wants to repeat this scene as an adult at the Castle and, in so doing, postpone his own death. Indeed, K.'s desire to overcome death (he symbolically "sinks" the graveyard crosses) relates directly to his narcissistic longing to construct an omnipotent self. K. imagines that his identity will persist over time as long as he can visually contain the Other (here, the dead, and, by symbolic extension, death itself). On this extremely bright day (promising a good view), he scales the wall and makes the megalomaniac claim that no one is "größer" (bigger/greater) than he. K.'s climb reminds us of that earlier purveyor of visual domination, Robinson Crusoe, whom Kafka remembered while working on *Das Schloß*. As Kafka remarked in a letter to Brod of 12 July 1922, Crusoe illustriously capped off his own self-discovery narrative by planting his flag "auf dem höchsten Punkt der Insel" (at the highest point of the island, *B* 392).

If K. had repeated this scene of mastery in the Castle village, he would, perhaps, have immediately completed his business of self-discovery.[35] If K. had made it to the top of the Castle hill during his first attempt, he might have (as he later muses) been accepted as the Castle surveyor right away. Furthermore, if this had happened, he would have gained the sense of personal and professional identity that scholars have often cited as his goal. K.'s search (and Kafka's novel) would have ended here — according to the norms of the Bildungsroman-like adventure narrative. But K. famously fails to scale the hill, fails to confront the authorities about his "calling," and fails to accomplish his narrative business.

These failures repeatedly correspond to the inability of "Herr Landvermesser" to see. In the novel's very first paragraph, we learn of the village's darkness, the eternal snow, and the obscurity of the Castle: "vom Schloßberg war nichts zu sehen, Nebel und Finsternis umgaben ihn, auch nicht der schwächste Lichtschein deutete das grosse Schloß an. Lange stand K. [. . .] und blickte in die scheinbare Leere empor" (*S* 7; "There was no sign of the Castle hill, fog and darkness surrounded it, not even the faintest gleam of light suggested the large Castle. K. stood for a long time [. . .] gazing upward into the seeming emptiness," *C* 1.) As the chapter continues, K.'s desire for a clear view is again thwarted — this time not by darkness and fog but rather by his relatively low standpoint: "Hier [im Dorf] reichte der Schnee bis zu den Fenstern der Hütten und lastete gleich wieder auf dem niedrigen Dach, aber oben auf dem Berg ragte alles frei und leicht empor, *wenigstens schien es so von hier aus*" (*S* 17; "Here [in the village] the snow rose to the cottage windows only to weigh down on the low roofs, whereas up there on the hill everything soared, free and light, or *at least seemed to from here*," *C* 7, my emphasis). Because K. is "here" (that is, below) his view remains unclear, as opposed to the omnipotent clarity of the Castle. Everything K. sees and knows from his impoverished standpoint is only appearance and thus must be questioned.

Opposing the land surveyor's view from below is the monarchical perspective of Klamm, a high-level Castle functionary who is also K.'s direct superior. As we learn during K.'s first conversation with the landlady of the Bridge Inn, Klamm has the point of view of an "eagle" (Adler); K., conversely, sees the world as a "Blindschleiche" (*S* 90; blindworm, a small European lizard, *C* 55).[36] The contrast could not be greater: the "Blindschleiche" sees the world from beneath and is popularly thought to be blind, due to its tiny eyes. Klamm's eagle is so visually powerful, conversely, as to be panoptic — like Weber's Coffee Planter. One can hide nothing from Klamm (*S* 182; *C* 115). K. realizes this woeful state of affairs in the chapter immediately following the pivotal "Waiting for Klamm" scene — after which K. seems finally to resign himself to never seeing Klamm. In the wake of this period of Beckettian waiting, in which K. vainly attempts to gain a glimpse of Klamm, he finally accepts the fact that only Klamm has the power to see anything and everything:

einmal hatte die Wirtin Klamm mit einem Adler verglichen und das war K. lächerlich erschienen, jetzt aber nicht mehr, er dachte an seine Ferne, an seine uneinnehmbare Wohnung, . . . an seinen herabdringenden Blick, der sich niemals nachweisen, niemals widerlegen ließ, an seine von K.'s Tiefe her unzerstörbaren Kreise, die er oben nach unverständlichen Gesetzen zog, nur für Augenblicke sichtbar — das alles war Klamm und dem Adler gemeinsam. (*S* 183–84).

[The landlady had once compared Klamm to an eagle and that had seemed ridiculous to K., but no longer, he considered Klamm's remoteness, his impregnable abode, . . . his piercing downturned gaze, which could never be proved, never be refuted, and his, from K.'s position below, indestructible circles, which he was describing up there in accordance with incomprehensible laws, visible only for seconds — all this Klamm and the eagle had in common. (*C* 115–16)]

Here, K. accepts the invidious comparison between himself and Klamm. Klamm is above, K. is below ("K.'s Tiefe"). Klamm is visible only for moments; K., like the natives in Mecklenburg's *Im Hinterlande von Deutsch-Ostafrika*, is always exposed and thus vulnerable. Klamm is the seer, K. the seen.[37] K. is the failed surveyor; Klamm is, for K., the imperial eye/I. (Kafka's certain knowledge of the symbolism of the eagle — as official emblem for the Austro-Hungarian empire — lends historical weight to this connection.)[38]

This brief look at the "Landvermesser's" visual narrative leads us to the following preliminary conclusion: if Kafka wrote *Das Schloß* with discursive constructions of the land surveyor in mind, he invented K. as a caricature of this standard surveyor. Whereas the successful surveyor (e.g., the Sugar Baron) affirms himself and his power by viewing the world from a mountain peak, K. slithers in the village mud. Like the blindworm, named for its tiny, myopic eyes, K. sees the world as looming, larger-than-life figures that perpetually sneak up on him or appear abruptly out of the corners of unlit rooms. Because K. gains no visual high ground throughout the novel, he can never sufficiently organize the village as a view, can never frame or map it. He thus remains inexorably *inside of* what he is trying to measure and describe. He is not a distinct subject (the hero of a narrative of self-discovery detachedly observing objects) but a subject who is also an object among objects. Part of the field he attempts to survey, K. is beginning to grasp, however dimly, that he is both subject and object at once.

In my cultural-historical framework, we might argue that the Castle corresponds, as some scholars have suggested, to an "imperial" power.[39] Brod first claimed in 1958 that Kafka's Castle was modeled after a nineteenth-century Austrian colonial outpost (161–64). According to Brod, Kafka borrowed this Castle from Božena Němcová's realist novel *Babička* (The Grandmother), which portrays nineteenth-century German-speaking nobility living in a Castle high above a subjugated, Czech-speaking village. To support Brod's historical reading, we could point out the three central traits that ally the Castle to the imperial tradition: an overproductive bureaucracy, an omnipresent threat of violence,[40] and an unquestioned *droit du seigneur* that places village women at the mercy of male Castle officials. Although not a straightforward metaphor for empire, the Castle thus bears particular imperial features. But the Castle also lacks the single factor that, in addition to a grand bureaucracy, most clearly defines an imperial power: an army. The Castle does not have any soldiers, nor is it engaged in territorial aggression.

Brod's reading is thus not watertight and has, correspondingly, been subject to critical attacks (cf. Kisch). Whether or not Kafka actually drew his Castle imagery from a realist account of imperial subjugation is, however, less important for my argument than is Kafka's general concern with imperial rhetoric. My point is that Kafka eschews the broad strokes of imperial history in favor of investigating the particular ways in which empire, conquest, and domination inform our modern ways of seeing. It is no accident that Klamm is referred to as an eagle (with its sharp eyes) and not, say, a lion. Klamm is a seer, as are his secretaries, who serve as additional eyes. In the true spirit of a panoptic, imperial bureaucracy, Momus and other secretaries write down everything they see and then pass it on to Klamm (who may or may not read it), thereby multiplying the apparent effect of Klamm's vision (*S* 179–83; *C* 113–15). If Kafka's Castle is an imperial outpost, then, it is so primarily in the sense that it practices this highly visual form of domination.

Now appearing as the fictional configuration of an unsuccessful imperial surveyor, K. finds his vision failing as the novel progresses. Critics such as Sheppard and Winkelman have argued that K. seems less aggressive vis-à-vis the Castle by the end of the novel. But they have failed to relate this to K.'s "Blindschleiche" perspective, which becomes progressively more pronounced. After the first chapter, K. never again makes a sustained attempt to walk up the Castle hill or even to view the Castle from the village. Moreover, he stops trying to gain glimpses of Klamm, the Castle's highest officer. Corresponding to this surrender of visual ambition is K.'s acceptance of an extremely limited perspectival scope. He spends the final chapters trapped in interiors (Barnabas's house, the Herrenhof bar, Bürgel's bedroom) and, moreover, inside a textual blankness created by Kafka's increasing use of description-free monologues. In the late monological scenes with Olga, Pepi, and Bürgel, K. makes little use of his once-strained eyes. When he sees anything at all, he sees it myopically — for instance, the naked foot of the Castle secretary, Bürgel.

The penultimate scene of the novel, with the Herrenhof landlady, is exemplary in this regard. K. stares at her dress, then looks inside a giant, deep wardrobe filled with dresses. K.'s vision zooms in on the dim interior, inspecting the clothing — whose various colors he notes. In the final scene, K. is led by Gerstäcker through the "darkness" into a room which was "nur vom Herdfeuer matt beleuchtet und von einem Kerzenstumpf, bei dessen Licht jemand in einer Nische gebeugt unter den dort vortretenden schiefen Dachbalken in einem Buche las" (*S* 495; "only dimly illuminated by the fire in the hearth and by a candle stump in the light of which someone deep inside an alcove sat bent under the crooked protruding beams, reading a book," *C* 316). This progression toward darkness and myopia in the novel's last pages suggests an unwritten conclusion that could have led — contra Brod (and Goethe, who called for "more light" on his deathbed) — to more darkness: to the end of what is a thoroughly modernist book, and toward the eventual extinguishing of vision through death. By the closing of the extant text, K. has surrendered his traveling surveyor's desire to achieve subjective distance and visual mastery; instead, he begins to dissolve among the objects of his world. He no longer attempts to frame the Other by scaling the church wall or the Castle hill. Rather, he burrows deeper and deeper into a village world whose old and tattered clothing, as W. G. Sebald has convincingly claimed, augur K.'s own coming decay (33–34).

* * * * *

It is instructive to compare this macabre, myopic ending with the final, according to Kafka, "most important" chapter of *Der Zuckerbaron*. In sharp juxtaposition to the myopic K., the sovereign Weber sits on the edge of a ridge and enjoys a panoramic view. He surveys his vast properties and, in the end, contemplates his own death:

> Here, under the protection of this tree, I want to sleep. No man shall bother me; not even the storm that before long will thunder down from the mountains in the night, at the beginning of the dry season, and which once, in one night, destroyed my coffee plantation, and, with it, my fondest hope. But in the daytime, year after year, the sun will shine upon me; and every day, the whole year long, a small, inconspicuous bird will sing for me its short and wonderfully delicate song, which will be more dear to me than any other singing, here under the

powerful vault of the giant trees and in the all-encompassing silence of this spot. (*Z* 88)

The Baron's confident burial wish represents the precise moment in the colonial drama that most attracts *and* repels Kafka. This is the moment of calm finality that Kafka's own forsaken travelers never achieve. Following the death of Bendemann in "Das Urteil," the Russian friend is left forever in fictional limbo, yellowing and destitute in Petersburg. The ailing stationmaster from the 1914 fragment "Erinnerungen an die Kaldabahn" (Memoirs of the Kalda Railway) is likewise eternally *in extremis*, stuck on the unfinished line of an unfinished story. The Sugar Baron, conversely, is able to complete his narrative and even demand that it be read. *Der Zuckerbaron*, one could argue, represents a version of Kafka's own travel novels with a happy ending — not only *Das Schloß* but also *Der Verschollene*. K. and Karl Roßmann both get good jobs, discover a sense of *Heimat*, and hire reliable servants (*not* K.'s assistants!) who will bury them high above their estates after they die; Franz Kafka, thereby, completes his novels. Max Brod, in his afterword to *Das Schloß*, claims that Kafka planned similar endings (347). Why did he never write them?

Neumeyer responds to this question by citing an apparent Oedipal failure now familiar to Kafka scholarship. He claims that Kafka wanted to be like the Sugar Baron (who stands in for Kafka's self-made father, Hermann) but did not have the fortitude to travel to South America, become a land baron, and write his memoirs. *Der Zuckerbaron*, Neumeyer claims, is "literary wish-fulfillment." It satisfies Kafka's "longings for firmness, competence, direction, self assuredness, and mastery" (14). In his own gloss on *Das Schloß*, Neumeyer compares K.'s view of the Castle from below with the Sugar Baron's vision from above and concludes that the Sugar Baron is the "lord of what he (literally) surveys" (15). Neumeyer thus sees *Das Schloß*, as I do, as a narrative of unsatisfied longings for visual heights; but for Neumeyer this failure is indisputably Kafka's (not just K.'s). He suggests that Kafka wanted to end *Das Schloß* triumphantly, with K. on top of the Castle hill.[41] The masterful, "most important" finale of *Der Zuckerbaron*, according to Neumeyer, is thus one that "Kafka himself did not so much (as he says) elude, as it was one that eluded Kafka" (15).

If, as I maintain, Kafka eluded this narrative (not the other way around), then another question becomes central: What could a writer possibly have to gain by creating a failed protagonist? Why would Kafka desire to fail (as Walter Benjamin claimed in his nuanced reading) (Benjamin 88)? Is there not perhaps something to be gained by the creation of an unsuccessful hero? In other words, if K. fails (in his Schaff-

steinian/Crusoean task of defining himself through a monarchical perspective), does Kafka in any way "win"? How might Kafka's creation of
a "blind" surveyor — a loser in the business of self-discovery — result in
his own victory in the business of writing?

My response necessitates revisiting Kafka's claim that *Der Zuckerbaron* functioned as a "Vorschrift": a book of rules, a prescription or, literally, a pre-text. He does not say that it is a pre- (or, source) text for *Das
Schloß*. Rather, it is a prescription for his life ("eine Vorschrift meines
Lebens"). This "Vorschrift" thus extends beyond literature — beyond
Der Zuckerbaron and *Das Schloß*. It is an "ideology," as in Louis Althusser's definition: a linguistic-cultural-political prescription that seems
to direct our lives (to the point that even acts of resistance appear to be
pre-inscribed).[42] In Kafka's fin de siècle, this "Vorschrift" included the
one followed by his maternal uncles and by Weber. It entailed traveling
to a faraway country, attempting to make one's fortune and, simultaneously, locating a solid sense of self. Like many young men of his era,
Kafka felt strongly tempted by this plot. He imagined living and working
in a variety of different places: Spain, South America, the Azores, Ma-
deira, Palestine, and a generic "island" in the south (*B* 37, to Brod, mid-
August 1907; *M* 319, to Milena Jesenská, November 1923; *F* 427, to
Felice Bauer, 13 July 1913). He longed to participate in the business of
self-discovery, complete with its bird's-eye views of sugar cane and its
financial successes — as the following October 1907 letter to Hedwig
Weiler demonstrates: "Ich bin bei der Assicurazioni-Generali [Kafkas
Büro], und habe immerhin Hoffnung, selbst auf den Sesseln sehr ent-
fernter Länder einmal zu sitzen, aus den Bureaufenstern Zuckerrohrfel-
der oder mohammedanische Friedhöfe zu sehen" (*B* 49; "I am in the
Assicurazioni Generali [Kafka's office] and have some hopes of someday
sitting in chairs in very faraway countries, looking out of the office windows at fields of sugar cane or Mohammedan cemeteries," *LFFE* 35).

But Kafka did not travel to "faraway countries," and not because, as
Neumeyer claims, this plot "eludes" him. Rather, according to Kafka, he
eludes or escapes it. The German verb Kafka uses, as noted above, is
"entweichen," which, translated most literally, means "to escape," as in
a "prisoner escaping from a jail" (*Wahrig* 412). In this sense, Kafka
escapes from colonial ideology; *it* does not elude *him*. He escapes from
Der Zuckerbaron's ideological "Vorschrift" by paradoxically not going
anywhere at all: he lies low and writes, and, more importantly, writes in
a certain way. As a writer, he can elude this "Vorschrift" by creating K.
(who fails in the business of self-discovery) and also by undermining this
prescription's *form:* the monarchical perspective and the corresponding

"density" of meaning. This stylistic escape is where Kafka's writerly victory, if there is one, inheres. And, because this is also an escape from ideology, Kafka also eludes in a political sense: both publicly, by resisting imperial aesthetics and traditions, and privately, by resisting a way of life that seems to be thrust upon him.

Kafka escapes the monarchical perspective, first, through the "Blindschleiche" point of view and, second, through the opposite of aesthetic density: what I will term — in the spirit of Gilles Deleuze and Felix Guattari — linguistic sparseness. What is this sparseness and what is its significance? Deleuze and Guattari, following Klaus Wagenbach, argue that Prague German, in Kafka's day, was a "minor" variation on High German. It was linguistically "abstinent," featuring "withered" diction and "sober," "rigid," "dried-up" syntax. Deleuze and Guattari maintain that Kafka elected *not* to enrich this brand of German artificially (as did Brod, Gustav Meyrink, and others from the Prague School), and instead to further "deterritorialize" High German by *increasing* the poverty of this language. They refer to this strategy as a possible "line of *escape*" (my emphasis, 59). Deleuze and Guattari's point is that Kafka subverts the dominant discourse by deliberately surrendering linguistic territory to it — not by co-opting from it. They oppose Kafka and his "willed poverty" to other "minor" writers such as Brod and Meyrink, who attempts to "reterritorialize" German through expansive prose and comprehensive symbolic networks. (Kafka's "minor" strategies, therefore, are closer to Samuel Beckett's than to James Joyce's: although both Beckett and Joyce wrote in the "minor" environment of Ireland, only the former "resisted the temptation to use language to bring about all sorts of worldwide reterritorializations") (19).

Deleuze and Guattari, however, strikingly fail to offer a single example of Kafka's *style* in comparison with a "territorializing" style — thus leaving their readers with little idea of the precise form of Kafka's deterritorializing mode, with its so-called syntactical poverty and withered diction. I have chosen two brief textual comparisons almost at random from *Das Schloß* and from the final chapter of *Der Zuckerbaron* to serve as such examples. First, I refer the reader back to the description of the Sugar Baron's view from atop his plantation and K.'s comparable account of standing atop the church wall. Focusing only on modifiers, we see a distinct sparseness in Kafka's text: ten modifiers in *Der Zuckerbaron* versus one in a passage of comparable length from *Das Schloß*, demonstrating precisely how Weber bloats syntax while Kafka prunes it. I italicize the modifiers from *Der Zuckerbaron* and the unmodified nouns from *Das Schloß*:

Der Zuckerbaron:

[Ich] sehe ein *ewiggrünes* Meer [. . .], in das die *weißen* Gebäude meiner
Besitzungen mit ihren *hellgrauen, glänzenden* Wellblechdächern, die *hell-
grünen quadratischen* Flecke der Zuckerrohr- und Maisfelder, die *dunkle-
ren, matteren* Weiden, die *kleinen* Hütten der Arbeiter mit ihren *braunen*
Strohdächern [. . .] (*Z* 87)

[I see an *everlastingly green* ocean [. . .] in the midst of which are the
white structures of my estate, with *shining, light gray, corrugated* roofs,
the *light green, square* plots of the sugar cane and corn fields, the
darker and *more muted* meadows, the *small* huts of the workers and
their *brown* straw roofs.]

Das Schloß:

Er rammte die *Fahne* ein, der *Wind* spannte das *Tuch,* er blickte hinunter und in die *Runde,* auch über die *Schulter* hinweg auf die in der
Erde versinkenden Kreuze, niemand war jetzt und hier größer als er. (*S*
49–50)

[He rammed in the *flag,* the *wind* filled out the *cloth,* he looked down,
all around [in die *Runde*], even over his *shoulder* at the crosses sinking
into the earth; there was nobody here, now, bigger than he. (*C* 29)].

If the "meaning" produced by the imperial eye is "dense," then Kafka's
meaning, here and elsewhere, is sparse. The distended syntax of the
Weber passage offers little space for readerly cohabitation. Kafka's style,
conversely, produces a series of bare outposts (flag, wind, cloth) that
invite us to journey into the textual space.

Another example comes from the penultimate sentence of *Der Zuckerbaron,* when Weber, still high above his estate, contemplates his own death.
I juxtapose this with the opening chapter of *Das Schloß,* when K., the
blindworm, tries to glimpse the Castle from below. Again, I note the discrepancy in modifiers (nine versus two) in a comparable amount of text,
and I italicize the modifiers and unmodified nouns from *Der Zuckerbaron*
and *Das Schloß,* respectively:

Der Zuckerbaron:

das *ganze* Jahr, wird mir ein *kleiner unscheinbarer* Vogel sein *kurzes,
wunderbar feines* Lied singen, das mir unter der *mächtigen* Wölbung
der Baumriesen und bei der *allgemeinen* Stille jenes Ortes wie kein *anderer* Gesang mir gefällt. (*Z* 88)

[The *whole* year long, a *small, inconspicuous* bird will sing for me its
short and *wonderfully delicate* song, which will be more dear to me than

any *other* singing, under the *powerful* vault of the giant trees and in the *all-encompassing* silence of this spot.]

Das Schloß:

Die *Augen* auf das *Schloß* gerichtet, gieng K. weiter, nichts sonst kümmerte ihn. Aber im *Näherkommen* enttäuschte ihn das *Schloß*, es war doch nur ein recht elendes Städtchen, aus *Dorfshäusern* zusammengetragen, ausgezeichnet nur dadurch, daß vielleicht alles aus *Stein* gebaut war, aber der *Anstrich* war längst abgefallen, und der *Stein* schien abzubröckeln. (*S* 17)

[Keeping his *eyes* fixed on the *Castle,* K. went ahead, nothing else mattered to him. But *as he came closer* he was disappointed in the *Castle,* it was only a rather miserable little town, pieced together from *village-houses,* distinctive only because everything was perhaps built of *stone,* but the *paint* had long since flaked off, and the *stone* seemed to be crumbling. (*C* 8)]

Here again we see Weber's distended syntax — which creates for us, as in Wiederhold's *Der Panamakanal,* an overdetermined picture (bird, song, vault, and even silence are modified, all in one sentence). *Das Schloß,* conversely, exhibits again the "poverty" of Kafka's diction, and also his "thin" (albeit elastic) syntax. Kafka's word-choice is concrete and basic (eyes, Castle, town, houses, stone, paint) and radically limited ("Castle" and "stone" are repeated instead of being replaced by synonyms); these few substantives are stretched sparingly across the length of two sentences. The bird's-eye view thus corresponds to syntactical density; Kafka's "Blindschleiche" perspective, meanwhile, couples with sparseness.

Pratt argues that monarchical views and density of meaning are typical of imperial narration (as they are in *Der Zuckerbaron* and other *Grüne Bändchen*). But does the opposite obtain? Is Kafka's *Schloß,* because it escapes a bloated colonial "Vorschrift," anti-colonial? Does it deterritorialize imperial discourse without attacking it directly? Deleuze and Guattari would say yes and, moreover, argue that the content of *Das Schloß* mirrors its linguistic subversiveness. *Das Schloß,* they claim, is exemplarily deterritorializing, psychologically as well as politically. Indeed, K. arrives in the village without a family, a past, or even a name; he thus appears to represent a subject exemplarily uprooted from tradition, desire, and history. More radically than Josef K. from *Der Proceß* (The Trial), therefore, K. is "nothing but [deterritorialized] desire" (52). Deleuze and Guattari repeatedly return to metaphors of topography and territory (even though they make surprisingly few references to K.'s corresponding profession). The linguistic sobriety of *Das Schloß,* they claim, creates a "new map" on which K. practices a strategy of "deterritorializing" (78). Deleuze and Guattari's anarchic land surveyor is, in this sense, not far from Emrich's 1957 revolutionary one: both are capable of questioning the present distribution and (for Deleuze and Guattari) conceptualization of territory. Kafka's successful "escape" from a colonial "Vorschrift," therefore, appears to take place in terms of both form and content.

Even K.'s more traditional, nostalgic desires seem to threaten the territorial order. From the first chapter onward, nothing is more remarkable than K.'s quest for a home, but this quest is more the nomad's search for refuge than the colonialist's desire for what the Sugar Baron refers to as a "zweite Heimat" (second home, 83). In fact, K.'s always-incomplete nostalgia undermines the very binary of "home" and "away" or of "dwelling" and "traveling" so dear to colonialism (Clifford 1992, 101). K. gets engaged on just his fourth day in the village, and desires a home for himself and his fiancée, but this home is, first, a cramped room in the Bridge Inn and, later, a spot on the schoolhouse floor. One of K.'s first acts in the Inn room is to nail the letter acknowledging his appointment as land surveyor onto the wall above his and Frieda's bed — thereby marking this transitory space as his own (S 43; "in diesem Zimmer würde er wohnen, hier sollte der Brief hängen" [in this room he would be living, so the letter should hang here, C 25]). He is, however, almost immediately threatened with eviction, and decides to leave. Later, K. and Frieda transform the schoolhouse classroom into an uncanny home for their "family": straw becomes a bed; parallel bars and a blanket transform into a partition; the teacher's desk becomes a dinner table (complete with table cloth, coffee pot, flowered cup, box of sardines, bread and sausage). Such deterritorializations of public space abound in Kafka. I also think of Josef K.'s boarding house "home" in *Der Proceß*, Gregor Samsa's hotels and his many-doored bedroom in "Die Verwandlung" (The Metamorphosis), Karl Roßmann's balcony lodging in *Der Verschollene*. The elevators in the latter novel's Hotel Occidental, moreover, serve as homes for the itinerant lift-boys: they reside in the elevators for almost all of their waking hours, eat and make love in them, and proudly and somewhat neurotically (in the case of Karl) polish "their" brass bars.

In all of these cases, transitory spaces serve as homes, thereby questioning the very idea of "home." Kafka's writings, correspondingly, challenge Martin Heidegger's nostalgic distinction between "building" and "dwelling" (a mere "building" being where one spends much of one's time and even sometimes feels "at home" whereas a "dwelling" uniquely offers "shelter" as well as an authentic homeyness) (145–46).

In *Das Schloß,* for example, every building is a potential home, but these homes are subject to the randomness of the world — and thus anathema to the notion of a true shelter. Is Gregor Samsa's flat (and bedroom sofa) a "dwelling" or a "building"? Which is the underground maze in "Der Bau" (The Burrow, 1923–24)? What about the narrator's shop, surrounded by nomads, in "Ein altes Blatt" (An Old Manuscript, 1917)? Kafka's fictions undermine the notion of homeyness and instead maintain that shelter is at once everywhere and nowhere. This diluted concept of dwelling does *not,* as the cultural anthropologist James Clifford points out, "make the margin a new center (e.g., 'we' are all travelers)"; rather, it presents transitory homes (hotel, flop house, airport) as ubiquitous and therefore as threats to all traditional dialectics of domesticity (1992, 101).[43]

Kafka's fictions place colonial binaries under stress, and this kind of stress was of course familiar to Kafka, who lived as a German Jew in Prague. The peculiar nature of Kafka's nationhood placed him somewhere in between the position of the colonizer and the colonized, and deserves a brief word of mention. Pre-war Prague was effectively a foreign — that is, Czech — city, dominated by a small German-speaking ruling class of which Kafka was part. But Kafka's relationship to Czech-speaking Prague was not only that of the perceived Austro-German colonialist. His Prague ruling class was mostly Jewish and, despite this group's cultural and commercial power, it had had its own history of being colonized. Provincial Jews, like Kafka's father (whose own father was a kosher butcher in the Czech village of Wossek), had been brought under the sway of eastward-spreading Austro-German culture. In the process, they had surrendered a sense of Jewish cultural identity that Kafka famously later tried to regain. In this sense, then, Kafka was colonizer and colonized at once. Kafka's liminal position within the imperial economy makes it difficult to understand him solely in terms of the classical colonial binaries offered by J. A. Hobson and, more recently (and with greater nuance), by Edward Said.[44] Kafka appears to be post-colonial *avant la lettre.*

* * * * *

But we cannot place Kafka too cavalierly into the camp of the deterritorializers and post- (or anti-) colonialists. His strongly colonial European moment does not allow for this. Like most Austro-Hungarian Jews (who rightly feared German and Czech nationalism in the event of an Austrian defeat), Kafka supported the Empire and even backed the Austro-

Hungarian war cause with passion: registering "Traurigkeit über die österreichischen Niederlagen" (sorrow over the Austrian defeats), getting angry with the "sinnlose" (foolish) Austrian leadership following the 1914 defeats in Serbia, and feeling himself "unmittelbar am Krieg beteiligt" (directly involved in the war) (*T* 677, 13 September 1914; *T* 710, 15 December 1914; *T* 771, 5 November 1915). Scott Spector has pointed out, moreover, that the territorially embattled German Jews of Kafka's Prague were often staunchly anti-liberal — sometimes choosing to retrench within linguistic Germanness or even to expand this Germanness in order to block insurgent Czech deterritorializations.[45] Within this general culture of territorial anxiety, Kafka's diaries, as was typical for his moment, were not strongly critical of colonialism, whether intra-European (Austrian) or extra-European (French, British, German). He was obsessed with Napoleon as a bold adventurer, not as a colonial oppressor (Kafka compiled an exhaustively detailed list containing seventeen reasons why Napoleon lost the war in Russia [*T* 757–64, 1 October 1915]). Moreover, Kafka never censures the obvious brutalities in *Der Zuckerbaron* and elsewhere in the *Grüne Bändchen* he claims to love. One prominent example of Kafka's uncritical stance is his diary note of 15 December 1913 following his reading of the nationalist and sometimes racist memoir, *Wir Jungen von 1870/71* (We Boys of 1870/71), which recounts the founding narrative of German imperialism (the Franco-Prussian War). When Kafka finishes *Wir Jungen* — not only volume thirty-two of the *Grüne Bändchen* series but also the work of the series' co-publisher, Hermann Schaffstein — he writes: "'Wir Jungen von 1870/71' gelesen. Wieder von den Siegen und begeisterten Szenen mit unterdrücktem Schluchzen gelesen" (Read *We Boys of 1870–1*. Again read with suppressed sobs of the victories and scenes of enthusiasm, *T* 615).

With Kafka's suppressed tears in mind, we see that his escape from "Vorschrift" is not clean. He does refuse to take part in the colonial plot by not traveling to Panama and the Congo like his uncle, and he also reverses some of this plot's traditional aesthetic structures; however, because, as Kafka well knew, ideology often contains its own "negativity," he cannot escape this ideology completely. As Kafka once wrote of his relationship to his era: "I have vigorously absorbed the negative element of the age in which I live [*das Negative meiner Zeit*], an age that is, of course, very close to me, which I have no right ever to fight against, but as it were a right to represent" (*Wedding Preparations* 114; *NSII* 98). Vigorously absorbing his era's *Negative* does not create the possibility of direct resistance ("fighting against"); rather, it means that the writer's literary forms of escape will necessarily remain bound up with that which he is attempting to elude.[46] Such a critical double bind informs all of Kafka's writings and is perhaps constitutive of the "Kafkaesque" — of a general structure of self-indictment, entrapment, and duplicity (of judger and judged, jailer and prisoner). But this double bind is most obvious in Kafka's texts with clear colonial references: "In der Strafkolonie" and "Ein Bericht für eine Akademie" (and, as I have been arguing, *Das Schloß*). On the one hand, Kafka exposes brutal colonial apparatuses (the torture machine and the ape's cage, in "In der Strafkolonie" and "Eine Bericht für eine Akademie," respectively). On the other hand, however, the victim in each case is no longer the victim by the end: the Officer's "perfect" machine impales *him*, not the imprisoned native, who runs free; Red Peter, the trained ape, eventually becomes a cigar-chomping and wine-drinking orator who hires a chimpanzee call-girl. Moreover, Kafka borrows the plots (of torture and exploitation) that power his narratives from the very "enthusiastic" Schaffstein narratives that his fictions, at the same time, resist.

Even Kafka's conception of his own writing is not completely divorced from territorializing impulses. Kafka's "Brief an den Vater" (Letter to His Father), written just three years before *Das Schloß*, demonstrates how his writing is, figuratively, an attempt to grab land from an apparently colonial father. Kafka repeatedly compares his father to a hostile, imperial entity — he is "tyrannisch" (tyrannical), a "König" (king), a one-man "Regierung" (government) with young Franz as his "Sklave" (slave) — and Kafka claims that his father's body is itself like an empire, "stretching out diagonally" across the "map of the world" ("Manchmal stelle ich mir die Erdkarte ausgespannt und Dich quer über sie hin ausgestreckt vor") (*LF/BV* 54, 26, 70, 28, 27, 114). Kafka can only consider living in the "regions" not yet colonized by this body, not yet covered by the father's mass or within reach of its imperial extremities ("es ist mir dann, als kämen für mein Leben nur die Gegenden in Betracht, die Du entweder nicht bedeckst oder die nicht in Deiner Reichweite liegen,"114). These "nicht sehr trostreiche" (not very comforting) regions are where Kafka's writing occurs. Kafka imagines his writing topographically: he gains "some distance" from his father's body (the father does not read the son's books) through writing — even if this distance gained is only that of a worm (!) fleeing a human torturer ("hier war ich tatsächlich ein Stück selbstständig von Dir weggekommen, wenn es auch ein wenig an den Wurm erinnert [. . .]" 84). Writing is thus the site of the son's literary-topographical "Fluchtversuche" (attempts at escape, 116).

Three years later, on 12 July 1922, midway through *Das Schloß*, Kafka claims in a letter to Brod that he is always attempting, through his writing, to locate the geographical space of home: "Ich bin von zuhause fort und muß immerfort nachhause schreiben, auch wenn alles Zuhause längst fortgeschwommen sein sollte in die Ewigkeit" (*B* 392; "I am away from home and must always write home, even if everything home-like has long since floated away into eternity," *LFFE* 340). Kafka had already, years earlier, referred to his writing in terms of topography — as if it were not simply words on a page but also a place that he could inhabit. Like more contemporary exilic writers,[47] Kafka claims in April 1918 in another letter to Brod that his writing *is* his home: through his writing, he creates a "Mondheimat" (homeland on the moon) and, in so doing, remains beyond the father's imperial reach (*B* 241).

How does such a territorial claim relate to Kafka's so-called deterritorializing style? Do the withered diction and dried-up syntax that eventually appear on Kafka's moon-homeland (on his personal "Grenzland" [borderland]) signal a form of re-territorialization (*T* 871)? Does Kafka's deterritorializing style, active in fringe areas, become his "own"? Kafka's 1915 reading of volume eighteen of the *Grüne Bändchen: Förster Flecks Erzählung von seinen Schicksalen auf dem Zuge Napoleons nach Russland* (Forest-Ranger Fleck's Narration of His Fate During Napoleon's March on Russia) helps to elucidate this contradiction. Published exactly one hundred years after the fact (at the climax of Germany's and Austria's own imperial marches), *Förster Fleck* describes Napoleon's advance on Russia. Kafka read and recalled one especially gruesome scene in his diary: Napoleon's imperial army, starving and madly retreating, blows up some of its own injured forces in a monastery — perhaps in order to spare them further misery or perhaps simply to be relieved of the burden of caring for them. Ranger Fleck, a German traveling with Napoleon, remembers that he and his fellow soldiers felt no compassion for their murdered comrades. Fleck expresses this cold scene in the expansive syntax and dense style typical of the *Grüne Bändchen:* "Jedoch waren unsere Gefühle durch den täglichen Anblick des namenlosesten Elends und unseres eigenen Unglücks schon zu sehr abgestumpft, als daß wir uns um das Schicksal anderer noch sonderlich gekümmert hätten" (Our feelings were however already so numbed by the daily spectacle of the most nameless misery and our own misfortunes that we would not have been able to concern ourselves especially with the fate of others, 32).

Kafka, witnessing this scene as a reader, offers the following sober revision in his diary entry of 16 September 1915: "*Förster Fleck in Rußland* gelesen. Napoleons Rückkehr auf das Schlachtfeld von Borodino. Das

Kloster dort. Es wird in die Luft gesprengt" (Read *Förster Fleck in Russia*. Napoleon's retreat through the battlefield at Borodino. The cloister there. It was blown up, *T* 754). Kafka increases the desired effect of narrative numbness by not mentioning the actual event at all. Instead of commenting on Fleck's — or Kafka's own? — incapacity for compassion, he understates the macabre event in dry, unadorned prose. Kafka's revision suggests that he could have used this book, and perhaps other *Grüne Bändchen* as well, to practice his "negative" style; that is, his telltale mode of increasing dramatic effect through understatement and the absence of pathetic utterance. The popular text thus offers up the "thrilling" historical event (Born 229); Kafka, the author of "In der Strafkolonie" and "Ein Bericht für eine Akademie," supplies the chilly, slim staccato. Just as Gregor Samsa never remarks on the cruelty of being assaulted by his father and is, in the end, left to die, Kafka records the heartless explosion at Borodino without affect. Style, here, gains dramatic and also political force. It becomes a private practice of deterritorializing discursive expansion, yet it paradoxically signals the simultaneous appropriation of a writerly home.

If Kafka's spare style is also a form of land grabbing, then it is, to continue with the topographical metaphor, a peculiarly gentle form of colonialism. Kafka occupies a liminal terrain — the moon, the borderlands — that is devoid of inhabitants. Moreover, his writing — unlike the dense, colonial style — does not attempt to mark every bit of the fictional world as its own (and *not* the reader's). Like the Sugar Baron, Kafka conquers new territories. But Kafka's spaces are unwanted, marginal regions. Moreover, because they are always only viewed at "Augenhöhe" (eye-level), and not from the heights that allow for encompassing views, these realms, like the desolate steppes, can never be adequately "represented" (*T* 689 3 November 1914; *T* 727, 14 February 1915). Kafka inscribes them only sparsely: we are left, as in *Das Schloß*, with a faceless hero, an unmapped village, and an only vaguely delineated Castle. Kafka's text is the negative topos revisited, and we readers are challenged the way the colonial traveler is. Kafka creates a terrain that invites readers to project and, through various demarcations, re-fashion themselves. Kafka thus shifts the political question of colonialism onto the act of reading. We are given a relatively unmarked space (a village, a Castle, two inns, a schoolhouse) and are caught between the impulse to impose an overview — *the* interpretation — and to burrow endlessly in the text's details (to become, like K., a subject/object among objects). *Das Schloß* thus avoids repeating the colonial gesture and instead presents the colonial problem. Kafka confronts us with the dilemma: What is a traveler to do? Do we, like K., attempt to gain an overview? Or do we — again like K. — lose ourselves among the clothing of the world?

If my reading of *Das Schloß* is also a form of colonialism — a marking of Kafka's negative topos — then it attempts to be so only in the sense that Kafka imagined all of his readers to be colonialists. In a continuation of the epigraph to this essay, Kafka claims (with his usual mix of truth and irony) that his ideal readers are Germans living abroad, specifically in the pre-war African colonies. He is referring explicitly to Max Brod's mention of him in a journal article (at the end of a list of Prague writers), but Kafka's remarks could just as well relate to his own fictions:

> Mit Deutschland, glaube ich, kann ich hier nur wenig rechnen. Denn wieviele Leute lesen hier eine Kritik mit gleicher Spannung bis in den letzten Absatz hinein? Das ist nicht Berühmtheit. Anders aber ist es bei den Deutschen im Auslande, zum Beispiel in den Ostseeprovinzen, besser noch in Amerika oder gar in den deutschen Kolonien, denn der verlassene Deutsche liest seine Zeitschrift ganz und gar. Mittelpunkte meines Ruhmes sind also Dar-es-Salam, Udschidschi, Windhoek. (*B* 35–36, to Brod, 12 February 1907)

> [I don't think I can count much on Germany. For how many people read a review down to the last paragraph with unslacking eagerness? That is not fame. But it is another matter with Germans abroad, in the Baltic Provinces, for example, or still better in America, or most of all in the German colonies; for the forlorn German reads his magazine through and through. Thus the centers of my fame must be Dar es Salaam, Ujiji, Windhoek. (*LFFE* 23)]

Kafka depends on colonial readers because they, unlike the stay-at-home Germans, will read every bit of Brod's article (and thus make it all the way to Kafka's name). Colonial readers are Kafka's ideal readers — *not* because of their ability to achieve monarchical views but rather because of their (colonial?) penchant for reading to the very last word. Kafka's colonists are, in the end, more like K. than like the Sugar Baron's fantasy of himself. The colonial experience leaves them "forlorn" — neither panoptically nor psychologically empowered — and this forlornness turns them into readers. Perhaps, like the heroes of the *Grüne Bändchen*, these colonists unwittingly fall victim to a process of self-creation that relies on simultaneous self-effacement. And it is this paradoxical scene of origination and obliteration — this failure in surveying that means at once "looking out over" and "overlooking" (*übersehen*)[48] — that finally creates the kind of reader Kafka claims to need. Only the colonialist, he insists, is sufficiently forsaken. Denied a monarchical view, the colonialist, in the end, sees the least. However, in spite of — or because of — this failed attempt at visual mastery, the colonialist becomes Kafka's myopic reader *par excellence.* He learns to read, like the unsuccessful and "blind" land surveyor K., "ganz und gar."

Notes

[1] Unless otherwise noted, translations from German are my own.

[2] "Landvermesser" appears in the text 112 times, almost as often as "Schloß" itself, which appears 189 times (Delfosse and Skrodzki, *Synoptische Konkordanz zu Franz Kafkas Romanen,* vol. 2 [Tübingen: Niemeyer, 1993], 1137).

[3] According to Charles Bernheimer: "[K.] is a land-surveyor in the sense that his vocation is to delimit differences, to map out boundaries, in order to establish the symbolic principle relating possession to authority, ownership to its origin, material presence to an absent but recuperable presence. His ambition is to be a successful reader of the symbolic structure binding Castle and village, and he feels that his very existence depends on this success" (*Flaubert and Kafka: Studies in Psychopoetic Structure* [New Haven: Yale UP, 1982], 198).

[4] Peter F. Neumeyer, "Franz Kafka, Sugar Baron," *Modern Fiction Studies* 17 (Spring 1971): 5–16. Oskar Weber, *Der Zuckerbaron: Schicksale eines ehemaligen deutschen Offiziers in Südamerika* (Cologne: Schaffstein, 1914). References to Weber's work will be designated with the abbreviation *Z* and page number. Weber's memoir could well be fictional, since he wrote another "memoir" about a coffee-planter that tells a completely different life story. The important thing for this essay, however, is not the "truth" of Weber's story and its depiction of land surveying but rather the text's connection to the general turn-of-the-century discourse on that topic.

[5] The only exception is Peter Beicken's thorough 1974 overview of the secondary literature (*Franz Kafka: Eine kritische Einführung in die Forschung* [Frankfurt: Athenaion, 1974], 337).

[6] The important terms here are "Vorschrift" and "entweichen." Possible translations of "Vorschrift," are specification, prescription, direction, instruction, order, precept, rule(s), regulation(s). The English translation in the *Diaries* is "book of rules," and Neumeyer uses "formula." I choose "prescription" because it captures the notion of a pre-writing or pre-text, implied by "Vor-schrift."

"Entweichen" is rendered in the *Diaries* as "to avoid," but "escape" and "elude" (my choice) are more accurate.

[7] Weber writes: "[The ape] I shot [. . .] from a low palm-tree, fell, still alive, and sat exactly like a man with his back against the trunk. He pressed his left hand against the wound on his chest and looked at me almost reproachfully with his big, dark eyes, which protruded from his fear-distorted face; at the same time he screamed and whimpered like a child and searched with his right hand for leaves which he picked up off the ground to staunch his wound" (*Z* 11).

[8] With a pleasure in detail matching that of the penal colony officer, he recounts the intricacies of the old-fashioned machinery used to punish recalcitrant "natives," and

then goes on to describe the twelve-hour torture process (cf. Kafka, "In der Strafkolonie," where the torment also lasts twelve hours [D 218]):

> One folds open the top beams like a scissors, sets the feet of the man-to-be-punished [*des zu Bestrafenden*] in the cut-outs on the lower beam, folds the upper beam closed and fastens the lock and bolt. The man is now trapped [. . .] and is, regardless how drunk and murderous, sober and tame within 12 to 24 hours. I have seen this "stock" occasionally utilized elsewhere, but only by very influential locals; I, as a foreigner, have never placed a man in this "stock." (Z 29)

Neumeyer also points out the connection between the sugar press described by the Baron — which twists and turns a piece of cane until it expels its syrup — and the penal colony apparatus, which causes excessive bleeding. Neumeyer, however, fails to note Kafka's apparent borrowing of the specific theme of "auspressen" ("pressing out" or "crushing") from *Der Zuckerbaron*. The press in Weber's book cannot, according to the narrator, satisfactorily "crush" the syrup out of the cane ("die *Auspressung* [war] ungenügend, Z 17, my emphasis); the penal colony's torture machine, similarly, can no longer adequately "crush" a scream out of its victim ("Heute gelingt es der Maschine nicht mehr, dem Verurteilten ein stärkeres Seufzen *auszupressen*," D 226, my emphasis). *Briefe eines Kaffee-Planzers*, another of Weber's Schaffstein books that Kafka claimed to "especially love" ("ich liebe besonders [. . .]") contains a similar scene (Born 180). Here, the narrator describes, in great detail, a large metal machine that shells and sorts coffee beans. The beans, which the narrator anthropomorphizes, lose their skin ("Häutchen") when they are rolled along a piece of cloth (resembling the penal colony apparatus' vibrating "cotton wool"). The "skinned" beans are then, like the blood of the penal colony victim, steered off into "channels" ("Rinnen") leading away from the machine bed (Weber, *BKP* 36). Similarly, Kafka writes, "Das Blutwasser wird dann hier in kleine *Rinnen* geleitet und fließt endlich in diese Haupt*rinne*" (D 215, my emphasis). For the Coffee Planter's beans, as for the penal colony victim, culpability is never to be doubted ("ist immer zweifellos," D 212). The Coffee Planter, indeed, speaks of the coffee beans as if they were animate forebears of Kafka's human condemned man, predetermined for a technologized death (in *Rinnen*) that, in the end, they can never escape (*entrinnen*): "Not one of them escapes [*entrinnt*] its fate. Is it not the same for all of us?" (*BKP* 37).

[9] For possible historical sources for Kafka's Castle, see Binder 442–43 and Beicken 337.

[10] Walter Sokel and, later, Stephen Dowden correctly argue against Emrich and any such benevolent reading of K. They point out that K. seems to be interested only in his own well-being — not in the needs of the community (Sokel, *Franz Kafka: Tragik und Ironie* [Munich and Vienna: Langen/Müller, 1964], 165, 414, 419 [cited in Binder 462]; Dowden, *Kafka's Castle and the Critical Imagination* [Columbia, SC: Camden House, 1995], 30–31, 34–35).

[11] The more recent readers to address the historical-political framework of *Das Schloß* have focused mainly on Kafka's connection to fin-de-siècle Jewish culture and politics (Zionism, the Yiddish theater, Messianism). See Bloom 1–22, Robertson 218–72, Suchoff 136–77.

[12] Mary Louise Pratt, *Imperial Eyes: Travel Writing and Transculturation* (New York: Routledge, 1992), 17. See Pratt's entire chapter, "Science, planetary consciousness, interiors," on Linnaeus and the general eighteenth- and nineteenth-century European desire to classify the world (15–37).

[13] The state, according to this definition, is a form of power separate from ruler and ruled, and also from the economy. It exists primarily as *territory*, and as the corresponding exclusive right to commit violence. See Quentin Skinner, *Foundations of Modern Political Thought*, 2 Vols. (New York: Cambridge UP, 1978), and Nicos Poulantzas, *State, Power, Socialism* (London: NLB, 1978); both are cited in Mary Louise Pratt, "Scratches on the Face of the Country," *Critical Inquiry* 12 (Autumn 1985): 126n16.

[14] His library and reading notes included works about the North Pole, the South Seas, Greenland, Iceland, Mexico, Italy, Russia, Central and South America, Africa, the United States, England, Scotland, East Prussia, and Germany. All the travel books either owned or mentioned by Kafka are indexed in Born, *Kafkas Bibliothek: Ein beschreibendes Verzeichnis* (Frankfurt am Main: S. Fischer, 1990), 235–55).

[15] Brenner refers to this development in his aptly titled chapter on the early nineteenth-century German travel writers Alexander von Humboldt and Adelbert von Chamisso: "Die Vermessung der Welt" (Surveying the World), in his *Der Reisebericht in der deutschen Literatur* (Tübingen: Niemeyer, 1990), 443–90.

[16] Josef Löwy was active in a commercial venture in Panama, and then held important colonial posts in the Congo for nearly twelve years and later in China (Anthony Northey, *Kafka's Relatives: Their Lives and His Writing* (New Haven: Yale UP, 1991), 9, 15–30). During Löwy's (and Kafka's) lifetime, the Panama Canal region was surveyed, measured, and occupied — first, unsuccessfully, by the French (for whom Josef Löwy likely worked), and later by the Americans. The Congo was assigned to King Léopold of Belgium during the 1885 Berlin conference. One of Léopold's driving desires was to build the Congo Railway, for which Löwy was chief of commercial sections.

[17] Borchgrevink 53, Hedin 96–99, Mecklenburg, 37, Weber, *Z* 55–56, 87, Weber, *BKP* 54, 58, 61–62, Wettstein, 6–7, 29, 48. In Wettstein's *Durch den brasilianischen Urwald: Erlebnisse bei einer Wegerkundung in den deutschvölkischen Kolonien Süd-Brasiliens* (*Through the Brazilian Jungle: Reconnaissance Experiences in the Ethnic German Colonies of Southern Brazil*), the narrator recalls his earlier pleasures of "surveying and hunting" (the opening theme of Kafka's "A Report to an Academy") in colonial German Southwest Africa (48).

[18] Used as "Sachliteratur" in imperial German schools, these books did more than describe surveying: they taught pupils how to plant and harvest coffee beans, sugar cane, and banana trees and, as such, functioned as "how-to" manuals for budding entrepreneurs. The broader program of the *Grüne Bändchen* and of the entire Schaffstein Verlag betrayed its general pro-imperial stance. Titles such as Max Wiederhold's *Im Hinterlande von Deutsch-Ostafrika* (1910), K. A. Wettstein's *Durch den brasilianischen Urwald: Erlebnisse bei einer Wegerkundung in den deutschvölkischen Kolonien Süd-Brasiliens* (1911), M. Bayer's *Im Kampfe gegen die Hereros: Bilder aus dem Feldzug in Südwest* (1911), and, after the outbreak of the First World War, F. Re-

quadt's *Wie wir Ostpreußen befreiten* (1915) exposed the ideological backdrop. Not surprisingly, the imperial government displayed some of the Schaffstein Verlag's books at the 1910 Brussels international "Exhibit on Education" (Cornelia Schneider, "Die Bilderbuch Produktion der Verlage Jos. Scholz (Mainz) und Schaffstein (Köln) in den Jahren 1899 bis 1932," [Diss., U. of Frankfurt, 1984], 66).

[19] In *Der Bananenkönig,* the German protagonist is born in a German settlement in the United States, not in Germany. Except for this difference, however, the plot is the same: the young Samuel Rath heads off to Latin America penniless, looking to get rich.

[20] This term connects psychological colonialism to the burgeoning fin-de-siècle interest in travel and travel writing (Hamann and Hermand, *Impressionismus,* 2nd ed. [Munich: Nymphenburger Verlagshandlung, 1974], 14–30).

[21] Susanne Zantop similarly refers to colonies, in the German imagination, as a "blank space for a new beginning, for the creation of an imaginary national self freed from history and convention — a self that would prove to the world what 'he' could do." *Colonial Fantasies: Conquest, Family, and Nation in Precolonial Germany, 1770–1870* (Durham: Duke UP, 1997), 7.

[22] For Kafka, Latin America is not a blank landscape, because of Josef Löwy's work in Panama. But in a 1912 diary entry, Kafka equates the adjective "Russian" with "ein Erlebnis [. . .] äusserste[r] Einsamkeit" (an experience of extreme solitude) and, three years later, defines Russia as a symbol that is emptied out, a site of eternal erasure: "Die unendliche Anziehungskraft Russlands. Besser als die Troika Gogols erfasst es das Bild eines grossen unübersehbaren Stromes mit gelblichem Wasser, das überall Wellen, aber nicht allzu hohe Wellen wirft. Wüste zerzauste Heide an den Ufern, geknickte Gräser. *Nichts erfasst das, verlöscht vielmehr alles"* (*T* 348, 5 January 1912; *T* 727, 14 February 1915, my emphasis; The infinite attraction of Russia. It is best represented not by Gogol's troika but by the image of a vast river of yellowish water on which waves — but not too high ones — are everywhere tossing. Wild, desolate heaths upon its banks, blighted grass. *But nothing can represent it; everything rather effaces it*). Correspondingly, the Stationmaster in Kafka's 1914 fragment "Erinnerungen an die Kaldabahn" (Memoirs of the Kalda Railway) claims that Russia is the ideal spot for him because of its desolation: "je mehr Einsamkeit mir um die Ohren schlug, desto lieber war es mir" (*T* 549; the more solitude ringing in my ears, the better I liked it, *Diaries* 303).

[23] As Said points out, for many travelers, the Orient is "dead and dry — a mental mummy"; it is something travelers, from Alexander Kinglake to Gustave Flaubert, want to "remake" or "bring to life" (*Orientalism* [New York: Vintage, 1979], 193, 185).

[24] For further examples, see Mary Louise Pratt, *Imperial Eyes,* 201–27.

[25] For Pratt, the "monarch-of-all-I-survey" view has three defining qualities: first, the landscape is "aestheticized"; second, "density of meaning" is sought; and third, a relation of "mastery" is constructed between seer and seen. Aesthetics and ideology thus combine to create what Pratt terms a "rhetoric of presence" (*Imperial Eyes* 204–5).

[26] According to Malek Alloula, in his study of the colonial postcard, *The Colonial Harem*, the representation was never to reveal the voyeur; that is, the embodied eye that made the picture possible (cited in Tim Mitchell, *Colonising Egypt* [New York: Cambridge UP, 1988], 26).

[27] Thanks to David Clark for pointing out this connection with Barrell.

[28] Friedrich Nietzsche, *Jenseits von Gut und Böse: Kritische Gesamtausgabe,* part 6, vol. 2, ed. Giorgio Colli and Mazzino Montinari (Berlin: de Gruyter, 1968), 215; translation from *Beyond Good and Evil,* trans. Walter Kaufmann (New York: Vintage, 1966), 201, my emphasis.

[29] Nietzsche, *Zur Genealogie der Moral: Kritische Gesamtausgabe,* ed. Giorgio Colli and Mazzino Montinari, part 6, vol. 2 (Berlin: de Gruyter, 1968), 273; translation from *On the Genealogy of Morals,* trans. Walter Kaufmann and R. J. Hollingdale (New York: Vintage, 1966), 26.

[30] Nietzsche, *Jenseits,* 215; *Beyond,* 201. Nietzsche claims that the modern notion of being disinterested (*"désintéressé"*) remains within the dominion of the moralizing herd instinct (*Genealogie* 274; *On the Genealogy* 26); however, Nietzsche's assertions regarding the pre-historic nobility nonetheless resemble Barrell's description of the disinterested man of the eighteenth century: both lay claim to a form of suprahuman, in Nietzsche's words, "self-surmounting" point of view that purports to be at once more "distanced" and more "comprehensive" than the commoner's (*Jenseits* 215; *Beyond* 201).

[31] Hegel writes, for example: "[The master's] truth is in reality the unessential consciousness and its unessential action" (*Phänomenologie* 134; *Phenomenology* 117). In other words, the master's "truth" is the slave (and the slave's labor). Alexandre Kojève famously argues that, by the end of the "master/slave" dialectic, the master loses and the slave wins: "In the long run, all slavish work realizes not the Master's will, but the will — at first unconscious — of the Slave, who — finally — succeeds where the Master — necessarily — fails" (*Introduction to the Reading of Hegel,* trans. James H. Nichols [New York: Basic Books, 1969], 30).

[32] These critics include Erich Heller (1952), Heinz Politzer (1962), Marthe Robert (1963), and K.-P. Phillipi (1966). See Binder, *Kafka-Handbuch,* 463.

[33] Richard Sheppard summarizes his own and John Winkelman's positions as follows: "Winkelman and Sheppard claim [. . .] that K. must be liberated from this artificial identity — so that his true self can be revealed, and the power of his proud will can be overcome through humility and love" (Binder, *Kafka-Handbuch* 461).

[34] Mitchell further argues that the traveler desires to re-present the other as an object and, in so doing, to define himself as distinct from it. By making photographs, drawings, and maps, and by situating himself on top of Egypt's pyramids or minarets, the traveler can "organize" an otherwise disorderly view. In so doing, he can see the foreign world "as a picture," an object from which he is distinct. Organizing the "objectness of the other" means here, as in the Schaffstein narratives, putting the other into a frame and thereby containing it. When the other becomes a self-enclosed object or "work," the traveler can confirm his separateness and thereby claim the identity that marks the success of his psychological business (1–33).

[35] K. seems to be on the same trajectory of self-discovery as are the heroes of the three Schaffstein novels Kafka claimed to "especially love." K. begins the novel poor and unemployed (resembling a "Landstreicher" or vagabond more than a "Landvermesser"); he has no friends or family (his rumored wife and child are left at home); and he hopes to gain an identity (both personal and professional) in the foreign land.

[36] In the original English translation, the Muirs chose to translate "Blindschleiche" as "snake in the grass," thus effacing Kafka's deliberately visual opposition.

[37] K.'s only view of Klamm occurs in chapter 3, when the mighty Klamm's body is revealed to be pedestrian and unimposing. But the "reality" of K.'s sighting is later called into question by Olga, the sister of Barnabas (a Castle messenger). Olga claims that people are continually mistaking others for Klamm — confusing him for various Castle officials and village secretaries (such as Momus). Because Klamm functions as a locus for subjective longing, he takes on "a variety of shapes" in different people's "imaginations" — thereby putting K.'s, and any other, "authentic" Klamm-sighting in doubt (C 176–77, 181; "ein so oft ersehnter und so selten erreichter Mann wie es Klamm ist nimmt in der Vorstellung der Menschen leicht verschiedene Gestalten an," S 277–79, 286). Klamm, conversely, claims to be keeping a figurative (and panoptic) "eye" on K. at all times ("Ich behalte Sie im Auge"); he does this perhaps with the metonymic help of his many spying secretaries (S 187; C 118).

[38] I thank Mark Anderson for bringing this connection to my attention.

[39] In addition to Brod, see Sokel, who claims that the Castle resembles an "alliance of the Austrian aristocracy and Austrian bureaucracy, that ruled over the peasants of [Czech] Bohemia." (Sokel, *Tragik und Ironie*, 397 [cited in Suchoff, *Critical Theory and the Novel: Mass Society and Cultural Criticism in Dickens, Melville, and Kafka* (Madison: U of Wisconsin P, 1994), 168]).

[40] Although we never see the police in *Das Schloß*, the schoolmistress suggests calling them to remove K. from the schoolhouse, and before that, K. compares his possible status in the adminstration with that of the "Dorfpolicist" (village policeman) (S 210, 41; C 133, 23). Moreover, the villagers' fears of the Castle may be justified fears of violence: the villagers' deformities (heads flattened at the top, as if they had been "geschlagen" [hit]) suggest some form of violence from above (S 39; C 22).

[41] The final chapter of *Der Zuckerbaron*, Neumeyer claims, is an ending that Kafka longed for but "could never have written" (15).

[42] For Althusser, the subject can never avoid ideology, since "the category of the subject is constitutive of all ideology" and, moreover, all ideology "has the function (which defines it) of 'constituting' concrete individuals as subjects." Within this constricting double constitution, resistance is difficult to imagine. Althusser, however, challenges himself and his readers to attempt to "break" with ideology through a "subject-less" discourse: "while speaking in ideology, and from within ideology we have to outline a discourse which tries to break with ideology, in order to dare to be the beginning of a scientific (i.e. subject-less) discourse on ideology" (171, 173).

[43] A contemporary example of how the borders between "dwelling" and "traveling" blur is the 1993 film by Philippe Lioret, *Tombés du Ciel* (In Transit). The action takes place almost entirely in a Paris airport, in the no-man's land between the runway and the customs gate. People without proper papers, denied admittance to

"France," live for years in an abandoned storage area. Here, they demarcate their own "private" spaces (with curtains and piles of belongings), raise families, and engage in intimate, yet public, dialogue.

[44] In the case of Said, I am referring to *Orientalism* — specifically, to James Clifford's claim that Said sets up an inaccurately rigid binary notion of Orient and Occident (Clifford, "On *Orientalism*," in *The Predicament of Culture: Twentieth-Century Ethnography, Literature, and Art* [Cambridge: Harvard UP, 1988], 255–76). Where, in the context of these observations on Kafka, might Jewish-German Prague fit into a model of an "Occident"?

[45] "Each and every one of the 'humanists' of the Prague circle [of German-Jewish literati], while diverging from one another in every other way conceivable, set himself in opposition to the liberalism he saw to be at the root of his contemporary dilemma" (Spector, *Prague Territories: National Conflict and Cultural Innovation in Franz Kafka's Fin de Siècle* [Berkeley: U of California P, 2000], 34). See also Spector 3–4, 13–16, 33–34.

[46] As Theodor Adorno/Max Horkheimer and Michel Foucault claim, respectively, historical resistances (or, here, "escapes") can only take place within the very sociolinguistic "cultures" or "discourses" that they are working to transform. For Adorno and Horkheimer, the resistant "style" of "great" art is always threatened by the hegemonic "culture" that produces it. Culture attempts to homogenize style and, in so doing, neutralize its critical capacity for "discrepancy" and "self-negation" ("Kulturindustrie, Aufklärung als Massenbetrug," in *Dialektik der Aufklärung: Philosophische Fragmente* [Frankfurt am Main: Fischer, 1969], 139). For Foucault on "discourse," see especially his later works — such as the "Method" chapter of *The History of Sexuality*, vol. 1 (New York: Random House, 1980). Here, Foucault argues that apparent resistances can never function outside of the framework of "power." Power resides in resistance even as it resides in oppression: "Power is everywhere not because it embraces everything but because it comes from everywhere" (93). Resistances occur, in other words, only within power's network. Moreover, such resistances cannot be predicted, categorized, organized, or united in common cause: "instead there is a plurality of resistances, each of them a special case" (96). For an elaboration on this point (in terms of Foucault's "Method" chapter), see Culler, *Framing the Sign: Criticism and Its Institutions* (Norman: U of Oklahoma P, 1988), 57–68.

[47] For emigré accounts of writing "home" (in the work of Theodor Adorno and Edward Said), see Caren Kaplan, *Questions of Travel: Postmodern Discourses of Displacement* (Durham, NC: Duke UP, 1996), 118–22.

[48] Throughout *Das Schloß*, Kafka moves back and forth between the two possible meanings of "übersehen": "to survey/look out over" (*S* 60, 122, 422; *C* 36, 76, 269) and "to overlook" (*S* 10, 388; *C* 3, 247). Thanks to Rebecca Comay for bringing up the importance of "übersehen" and also for encouraging me to consider more carefully the position of the reader.

Works Cited

Adorno, Theodor, and Max Horkheimer. "Kulturindustrie, Aufklärung als Massenbetrug." *Dialektik der Aufklärung: Philosophische Fragmente.* Frankfurt am Main: Fischer, 1969. 128–76.

Alloula, Malek. *The Colonial Harem.* Trans. Myrna and Wlad Godzich. Minneapolis: U of Minnesota P, 1986.

Althusser, Louis. "Ideology and Ideological State Apparatuses." *Lenin and Philosophy.* 1970. Trans. Ben Brewster. New York: Monthly Review Press, 1971. 127–86.

Barrell, John. *English Literature in History 1730–80: An Equal, Wide Survey.* New York: St. Martin's, 1983.

Bayer, M. *Im Kampfe gegen die Hereros: Bilder aus dem Feldzug im Südwest.* Cologne: Hermann & Friedrich Schaffstein, 1911.

Beck, Evelyn Torton. *Kafka and the Yiddish Theater: Its Impact on His Work.* Madison: U of Wisconsin P, 1971.

Beicken, Peter. *Franz Kafka: Eine kritische Einführung in die Forschung.* Frankfurt: Athenaion, 1974.

Benjamin, Walter. *Benjamin über Kafka.* Ed. Hermann Schweppenhäuser. Frankfurt: Suhrkamp, 1981.

Bernheimer, Charles. *Flaubert and Kafka: Studies in Psychopoetic Structure.* New Haven: Yale UP, 1982.

Binder, Hartmut. *Kafka-Handbuch in zwei Bänden.* Vol. 2. Stuttgart: Alfred Kröner, 1979.

Bloom, Harold, ed. *Franz Kafka's "The Castle."* New York: Chelsea House, 1988.

Boa, Elizabeth. *Kafka: Gender, Class, and Race in the Letters and Fictions.* Oxford: Clarendon, 1996.

Borchgrevink, Carsten. *Festes Land am Südpol: Erlebnisse auf der Expedition nach dem Südpolarland 1898–1900.* Cologne: Hermann & Friedrich Schaffstein, 1911.

Born, Jürgen. *Kafkas Bibliothek: Ein beschreibendes Verzeichnis.* Frankfurt am Main: S. Fischer, 1990.

Brenner, Peter J. *Der Reisebericht in der deutschen Literatur: Ein Forschungsüberblick als Vorstudie zu einer Gattungsgeschichte.* Tübingen: Max Niemeyer Verlag, 1990.

Brod, Max. "*The Castle;* Its Genesis." *Franz Kafka Today.* Ed. A. Flores and H. Swander. Madison: U of Wisconsin P, 1958. 161–64.

————. "Nachwort zur ersten Ausgabe." Afterword. Franz Kafka. *Amerika.* 1927. Rpt. Frankfurt am Main: Fischer, 1991. 260–62.

————. "Nachwort zur ersten Ausgabe." Afterword. Franz Kafka. *Das Schloß.* 1926. Rpt. Frankfurt am Main: Fischer, 1968. 347–54.

Clifford, James. "On *Orientalism.*" In *The Predicament of Culture: Twentieth-Century Ethnography, Literature, and Art.* Cambridge: Harvard UP, 1988. 255–76.

————. "Traveling Cultures." *Cultural Studies.* Ed. Laurence Grossberg, Cary Nelson, and Paula Treichler. New York: Routledge, 1992. 96–116.

Culler, Jonathan. *Framing the Sign: Criticism and Its Institutions.* Norman: U of Oklahoma P, 1988.

Deleuze, Gilles, and Félix Guattari. *Kafka: Towards a Minor Literature.* 1975. Minneapolis: U of Minnesota P, 1986.

Delfosse, Heinrich P., and Karl Jürgen Skrodzki. *Synoptische Konkordanz zu Franz Kafkas Romanen.* 3 Vols. Tübingen: Niemeyer, 1993.

Dowden, Stephen. *Kafka's Castle and the Critical Imagination.* Columbia, SC: Camden House, 1995.

Emrich, Wilhelm. *Franz Kafka.* Frankfurt am Main: Athenäum, 1957.

Fleck, Förster. *Förster Flecks Erzählung von seinen Schicksalen auf dem Zuge Napoleons nach Rußland und von seiner Gefangenschaft 1812–1814.* Cologne: Hermann & Friedrich Schaffstein, 1912.

Foucault, Michel. *The History of Sexuality.* Vol. 1. New York: Random House, 1980.

Göhler, Helga. *Franz Kafka: "Das Schloß."* Bonn: Bouvier, 1982.

Hamann, Richard, and Jost Hermand. *Impressionismus.* 2nd ed. Munich: Nymphenburger Verlagshandlung, 1974.

Hedin, Sven. *Über den Transhimalaja.* Cologne: Hermann & Friedrich Schaffstein, 1911.

Hegel, G. W. F. *Die Phänomenologie des Geistes.* Ed. Hans-Friedrich Wessels and Heinrich Clairmont. Hamburg: Meiner, 1988.

————. *The Phenomenology of Spirit.* Trans. A. V. Miller. Oxford: Oxford UP, 1977.

Heidegger, Martin. *Poetry, Language, Thought.* Trans. Albert Hofstadter. New York: Harper and Row, 1975.

Heller, Erich. "The World of Franz Kafka." *Twentieth-Century Interpretations of "The Castle."* Ed. Peter F. Neumeyer. Englewood Cliffs: Prentice Hall, 1969. 57–82.

Hesse, Hermann. *Aus Indien: Aufzeichnungen, Tagebücher, Gedichte, Betrachtungen und Erzählungen.* Frankfurt am Main: Suhrkamp, 1982.

Hobson, J. A. *Imperialism: A Study.* 1902. Ann Arbor: University of Michigan Press, 1965.

Holitscher, Arthur. *Amerika: Heute und morgen.* 2nd ed. Berlin: Fischer, 1912.

Kafka, Franz. *Briefe, 1902–1924.* Ed. Max Brod. Frankfurt am Main: S. Fischer, 1958. (*B*)

———. *Briefe an Felice.* Ed. Erich Heller and Jürgen Born. Frankfurt am Main: S. Fischer, 1967. (*F*)

———. *The Castle.* Trans. Mark Harman. New York: Schocken, 1998. (*C*)

———. *The Diaries.* Trans. Joseph Kresh and Martin Greenberg. New York: Schocken, 1975.

———. *Drucke zu Lebzeiten.* Ed. Wolf Kittler, Hans-Gerd Koch, and Gerhard Neumann. Frankfurt am Main: S. Fischer, 1994. (*D*)

———. *Letter to His Father/Brief an den Vater* (bilingual edition). Trans. Ernst Kaiser and Eithne Wilkins. New York: Schocken, 1966. (*LF/BV*)

———. *Letters to Friends, Family, and Editors.* Trans. Richard and Clara Winston. New York: Schocken, 1977. (*LFFE*)

———. *Nachgelassene Schriften und Fragmente II.* Ed. Jost Schillemeit. Frankfurt am Main: S. Fischer, 1992. (*NS II*)

———. *Das Schloß.* Ed. Malcolm Pasley. Frankfurt am Main: S. Fischer, 1982. (*S*)

———. *Tagebücher.* Ed. Hans-Gerd Koch, Michael Müller, and Malcolm Pasley. Frankfurt am Main: S. Fischer, 1990. (*T*)

———. *Wedding Preparations in the Country.* Trans. Ernst Kaiser and Eithne Wilkins. London: Secker and Warburg, 1973.

Kaplan, Caren. *Questions of Travel: Postmodern Discourses of Displacement.* Durham, NC: Duke UP, 1996.

Keyserling, Graf Hermann. *Das Reisetagebuch eines Philosophen.* 1919. Stuttgart/Berlin: Deutsche Verlag-Anstalt, 1932.

Kisch, Guido. "Kafka-Forschung auf Irrwegen." *Zeitschrift für Religions- und Geistesgeschichte* 23 (1971): 339–50.

Kojéve, Alexandre. *Introduction to the Reading of Hegel.* Trans. James H. Nichols. New York: Basic Books, 1969.

Kurz, Gerhard. *Traum-Schrecken: Kafkas literarische Existenzanalyse.* Stuttgart: J.B. Metzler, 1980.

Mecklenburg, Adolf Friedrich zu. *Im Hinterlande von Deutsch-Ostafrika.* Cologne: Hermann & Friedrich Schaffstein, 1910.

Mitchell, Tim. *Colonising Egypt.* New York: Cambridge UP, 1988.

Neumann, Gerhard. "Kafka's 'Schloß'-Roman: Das parasitäre Spiel der Zeichen." *Franz Kafka: Schriftverkehr.* Ed. Wolf Kittler and Gerhard Neumann. Freiburg i.B.: Rombach, 1990. 199–221.

———. *"Das Urteil": Text, Materialien, Kommentar.* Munich: Carl Hanser, 1981.

Neumeyer, Peter F. "Franz Kafka, Sugar Baron." *Modern Fiction Studies* 17 (Spring 1971): 5–16.

Nietzsche, Friedrich. *Beyond Good and Evil: Prelude to a Philosophy of the Future.* Trans. Walter Kaufmann. New York: Vintage, 1966.

———. *Jenseits von Gut und Böse: Vorspiel einer Philosophie der Zukunft. Kritische Gesamtausgabe.* Ed. Giorgio Colli and Mazzino Montinari. Part 6, vol. 2. Berlin: de Gruyter, 1968.

———. *On the Genealogy of Morals.* Trans. Walter Kaufmann and R. J. Hollingdale. New York: Vintage, 1967.

———. *Zur Genealogie der Moral. Kritische Gesamtausgabe.* Ed. Giorgio Colli and Mazzino Montinari. Part 6, vol. 2. Berlin: de Gruyter, 1968.

Northey, Anthony. *Kafka's Relatives: Their Lives and His Writing.* New Haven: Yale UP, 1991.

Phillipi, K.-P. *Reflexion und Wirklichkeit: Untersuchungen zu Kafkas Roman "Das Schloß."* Tübingen: Niemeyer, 1966.

Politzer, Heinz. *Franz Kafka, der Künstler.* 1962. Frankfurt am Main: Fischer, 1965.

Poulantzas, Nicos. *State, Power, Socialism.* Trans. Patrick Camiller. London: NLB, 1978.

Pratt, Mary Louise. *Imperial Eyes: Travel Writing and Transculturation.* New York: Routledge, 1992.

———. "Scratches on the Face of the Country; or, What Mr. Barrow Saw in the Land of the Bushmen." *Critical Inquiry* 12 (Autumn 1985): 119–43.

Reif, Wolfgang. "Exotismus im Reisebericht des frühen 20. Jahrhunderts." *Der Reisebericht: Die Entwicklung einer Gattung in der deutschen Literatur.* Ed. Peter J. Brenner. Frankfurt am Main: Suhrkamp, 1989. 434–62.

Requadt, F. *Wie wir Ostpreußen befreiten: Aufzeichnungen aus dem Augustfeldzug 1914.* Cologne: Hermann & Friedrich Schaffstein, 1915.

Robert, Marthe. *The Old and the New: From Don Quixote to Kafka.* 1963. Berkeley: U of California P, 1977.

Robertson, Ritchie. *Kafka: Judaism, Politics, Literature.* Oxford: Clarendon, 1985.

Said, Edward. *Culture and Imperialism.* New York: Knopf, 1993.

———. *Orientalism.* New York: Vintage, 1979.

Schaffstein, Hermann. *Wir Jungen von 1870/71: Erinnerungen aus meinen Kinderjahren.* Cologne: Hermann & Friedrich Schaffstein, 1913.

Schneider, Cornelia. "Die Bilderbuchproduktion der Verlage Jos. Scholz (Mainz) und Schaffstein (Köln) in den Jahren 1899 bis 1932." Diss. U Frankfurt am Main, 1984.

Sebald, W. G. "The Undiscover'd Country: The Death Motif in Kafka's *Castle.*" *Journal of European Studies* 2 (1972): 22–34.

Sheppard, Richard. *On Kafka's Castle.* London: Croom Helm, 1973.

Skinner, Quentin. *Foundations of Modern Political Thought.* 2 Vols. New York: Cambridge UP, 1978.

Sokel, Walter. *Franz Kafka: Tragik und Ironie: Zur Struktur seiner Kunst.* Munich and Vienna: Langen and Müller, 1964.

Spector, Scott. *Prague Territories: National Conflict and Cultural Innovation in Franz Kafka's Fin de Siècle.* Berkeley: U of California P, 2000.

Suchoff, David. *Critical Theory and the Novel: Mass Society and Cultural Criticism in Dickens, Melville, and Kafka.* Madison: U of Wisconsin P, 1994.

Wahrig Deutsches Wörterbuch. Munich: Mosaic, 1986.

Weber, Oskar. *Der Bananenkönig: Was der Nachkomme eines verkauften Hessen in Amerika schuf.* Cologne: Hermann & Friedrich Schaffstein, 1918.

———. *Briefe eines Kaffee-Pflanzers: Zwei Jahrzehnte deutscher Arbeit in Zentral-Amerika.* Cologne: Hermann & Friedrich Schaffstein, 1913. (*BKP*)

———. *Der Zuckerbaron: Schicksale eines ehemaligen deutschen Offiziers in Südamerika.* Cologne: Hermann & Friedrich Schaffstein, 1914. (*Z*)

Wettstein, Dr. K. A. *Durch den brasilianischen Urwald: Erlebnisse bei einer Wegerkundung in den deutschvölkischen Kolonien Süd-Brasiliens.* 1911. Cologne: Hermann & Friedrich Schaffstein, 1942 (Feldpostausgabe).

Wiederhold, Max. *Der Panamakanal.* Cologne: Hermann & Friedrich Schaffstein, 1913.

Winkelman, John. "An Interpretation of Kafka's *Das Schloß.*" *Monatshefte* 64 (1972): 115–31.

Wirkner, Alfred. *Kafka und die Außenwelt: Quellenstudien zum 'Amerika'-Fragment.* Stuttgart: Ernst Klett, 1976.

Zantop, Susanne. *Colonial Fantasies: Conquest, Family, and Nation in Precolonial Germany, 1770–1870.* Durham: Duke UP, 1997.

Making Everything "a little uncanny": Kafka's Deletions in the Manuscript of *Das Schloß* and What They Can Tell Us About His Writing Process

Mark Harman

KAFKA'S POWERFUL IMAGINATION was always threatening to run amok, and he himself spoke of writing as though in a tunnel, without knowing how his characters would turn out (Martini 298.) In the manuscript of *Das Schloß* (The Castle) the originally garrulous hero blabs out information that Kafka wished to hide, and develops other traits that are equally uncongenial to his creator. So, like a gardener faced with an unruly shrub, Kafka pruned back his fictional alter ego. His goal throughout the simultaneous process of writing and revising was to preserve an aura of ineffable mystery by making everything sound "ein wenig unheimlich," (a little uncanny, *SA* 275).[1]

While the following close reading of Kafka's deletions in the manuscript of *Das Schloß* will not yield an entirely new interpretation of the novel, it may offer glimpses of the creative decision-making process that shaped it. Surprisingly enough, although scholars such as Hartmut Binder, Karlheinz Fingerhut, and Fritz Martini have explored the variants to other texts of Kafka's, relatively little work has been done on the exceptionally rich cache first published in the 1982 *Apparatband* (variant volume) of the Critical Edition of *Das Schloß*, with the noteworthy exception of some astute commentary by its editor Malcolm Pasley and a lucid 1968 essay by Dorrit Cohn. That is a pity because a close examination of Kafka's writing process in the manuscript of *Das Schloß* can shed light on the workings of his imagination.[2]

In composing *Das Schloß* Kafka appears not to have had any preliminary outline but simply made things up as he went along — a remarkable method of composition given the intricate nature of the novel. According to Pasley, Kafka carried out the vast majority of the revisions and deletions on the spot, immediately after writing a given phrase, sentence, or segment. Yet, as I hope to show, his method of composition is as calculated as it is spontaneous.

Since most of Kafka's cross-outs have never appeared in English translation, and were not included in my translation of the text of the Critical Edition (Schocken Books, 1998), I will quote them liberally, in German followed by my fairly literal translation,[3] while exploring the following topics:

I. Biographical variants: Kafka deletes passages that disclose the intimacy of the relationship between the fictional K. of *Das Schloß* and the biographical Kafka of the diaries and letters.

II. Variants of K.: The paradoxical process through which Kafka deepens the ambiguity of the novel by flattening the hero and reducing his psychological complexity. (For the sake of convenience, I shall sometimes call the hero of the variants Variant K. to distinguish him from Castle K., hero in the text proper.)

III. Narrative variants: Changes — such as a switch from first-person "I" to third-person "K." — that alter the narrative form of the novel.

IV. Self-conscious variants: These deletions, which wittily allude to Kafka's own writing process, show — far more clearly than does the text of *Das Schloß* — that Kafka's final novel belongs in the tradition of the self-conscious European novel.

V. Mystical variants: Kafka eliminates allusions to mystical Jewish beliefs when they seem too obvious for his aesthetics of suggestion.

I. Biographical Variants

As Kafka himself once put it in his inimitable metaphorical language, he wished to free his biographical raw material from its terrestrial origins by transporting it to the lunar landscape of the autonomous work of art (Letter to Max Brod, April 1918, *B* 241). Thanks to the Critical Edition of *Das Schloß*, and in the future also with the help of the eagerly awaited facsimile edition of the novel being prepared by Roland Reuß and Peter Staengle for the Stroemfeld Verlag, we can observe Kafka's attempts to create that lunar landscape by detaching his "Schloß-geschichte" (Castle story) from the terrestrial autobiographical crises that partly triggered it: the storms in his largely epistolary relationship with Milena Jesenská, the memories of his "Kampf" (struggle, battle) to marry Felice Bauer, and a mental breakdown, which, according to diary entries in early January 1922, had brought him to the brink of madness.

As he composed *Das Schloß*, Kafka cut or at least concealed the more obvious links between the metaphors such crises inspired and the imaginary world of the novel. Although it is not possible to ascertain with certainty why he deleted any given variant or set of variants, I would argue that, for Kafka, a considerable number of the passages that he deleted did not qualify for inclusion in a work of art because they are not sufficiently autonomous or, to borrow his metaphor, lunar.

One of the most striking variants — the so-called Fürstenzimmer-fragment or prince's room fragment — occurs in the first couple of pages of the manuscript. Actually, these first few pages are not so much a fragment as Kafka's first run at the novel. By deleting the prince's room variant Kafka severed connecting tissue between the metaphorical Kafka of the autobiographical writings and the fictional alter ego of the novel.

In this variant opening, which is cast in the third person, Kafka has not yet given his hero a name, referring to him simply as the guest. This prototype of K. arrives at a village inn, where he is shown to the prince's room. Belligerent from the outset, he asks sharply why the landlord and the maid are whispering, and claims that they must have been expecting him. He then declares openly, if rather enigmatically, that he has come to carry out an unspecified "Aufgabe" (task) that has consumed him throughout his life:

> "Ich habe eine schwere Aufgabe vor mir und habe ihr mein ganzes Leben gewidmet . . . weil es alles ist was ich habe, diese Aufgabe nämlich unterdrücke ich alles was mich bei ihrer Ausführung stören könnte, rücksichtslos." (*SA* 116)

> [I have a difficult task ahead of me, one to which I have devoted my entire life . . . since it's all I have, this task in other words, I ruthlessly suppress everything that could prevent me from carrying it out.]

The unnamed guest might appear to be making an important disclosure about his motives for coming to the remote village at the foot of the Castle hill when he tells us that he has dedicated his entire life to that mysterious task. Yet he offers no further clues about what this task might be. K.'s murky assertion becomes comprehensible only when one takes into account the meaning of that term in the Zürau aphorisms, in which Kafka uses the term "die große Aufgabe" (the great task) to describe his own self-imposed literary-metaphysical mission. Likewise, K. has a self-imposed task, and his dubious, even fraudulent claim to be a surveyor mirrors Kafka's skeptical attitude toward his literary work, which he had by the early twenties come to regard as a highly suspect activity, as attested by the stories "Ein Hungerkünstler" (A Hunger Artist) and "Josefine, die Sängerin oder Das Volk der Mäuse" (Josephine the Singer, or the Mouse Folk) and, last but not least, by *Das Schloß*.

When Variant K. states that he possesses nothing but his task, he echoes too audibly Kafka's assertion in the letters to Milena Jesenská that he, the most characteristic Western Jew, must struggle for everything: "nichts ist mir geschenkt, alles muß erworben werden, nicht nur die Gegenwart und Zukunft, auch noch die Vergangenheit" (*M* 294; nothing is granted me, everything has to be earned, not only the present and the future, but the past too). Likewise, K. does not have a present or a future, and his conflicting claims about his past suggest that it, too, is shaky.

In *Das Schloß* Kafka invested the autobiographical metaphors of the letters to Milena with new meaning. For instance, though the hero of *Das Schloß* must, like the Kafka of those letters, struggle to gain his past, present, and future, in the novel he also has to struggle to earn his own death. In a variant toward the end of the manuscript K. asserts that "er könnte sich sorglos ins Bett legen" (*SA* 475; he could lie down in bed without a worry). Since K. is portrayed throughout as an extremely driven, restless figure, this admission of his longing to lie down in bed could imply that the days of his relentless striving are over and that death itself is not far off. While Kafka deleted the passage, he did not cross out other recurrent allusions to death, which, as the novelist and scholar W. G. Sebald has shown, becomes an omnipresent if often disguised leitmotif in the novel.

By deleting the prince's room scene Kafka crossed out overt references to the precarious mental state that lurks under the hero's combative exterior. In pursuing the fight or struggle to carry out his task, Variant K. is willing to be ruthless. He even goes so far as to identify stubbornness (*Hartnäckigkeit*) as his best trait. In the prince's room variant he tells the landlord and the chambermaid that this ruthless persistence could lead to madness: "ich kann in dieser Rücksichtslosigkeit wahnsinnig werden" (*SA* 116; In this ruthlessness I can go mad). This theme becomes a leitmotif in seminal diary entries in early January 1922 in which Kafka talks about either going mad or channeling into a literary work the unceasing introspection that threatens his sanity (*T* 887–98). A couple of weeks later he begins work on *Das Schloß*.

Although Kafka deleted the overt references to madness, he did not so much eliminate this theme as push it underground. In the novel K. projects onto others the incipient madness that he refuses to acknowledge in himself. For instance, on first getting a closer view of the Castle he comes to the conclusion that there is "something crazy" about it ("etwas Irrsinniges hatte das," *S* 18). Moreover, he imagines an old man, who ought to have kept himself locked up in a remote room, bursting through the roof of the Castle in a gesture of mad rebellion.

In general, the echoes of the autobiographical writings are more audible in the variants than they are in the novel. Whether by accident or design, Kafka crossed out many passages that echo the language of the diaries and letters. Deleting passages entails losses as well as gains: For instance, if Kafka had decided to let the prince's room scene stand, the disclosure of the hero's existential insecurity would have lent psychological plausibility to his ruthless pursuit of his elusive goal. However, as we shall see, Kafka was not primarily interested in creating a psychologically convincing character.

II. Variants of K.

Kafka's heroes tend to be one-dimensional, and K. is no exception.[4] The variants show the deliberate nature of this effect: As he wrote, Kafka flattened his characters, stripping them of "interesting" traits that a more conventional novelist would choose to emphasize. He deletes all subsequent references to the hero's mysterious task. For instance, on first glimpsing the odd pair who turn out to be his assistants, Variant K. realizes that he will not be able to carry out a decisive deed ("entscheidenden Tat," *SA* 135). Such allusions to K.'s secret plans must be eliminated, since Kafka wants K. to remain enigmatic. Not even the most oblique hint about K.'s plans is allowed to stand, such as his telling the teacher that he is no "Vergnügungsreisender" (pleasure-seeking traveler, *SA* 133).

What is more, in the very first chapter the first-person narrator becomes so discouraged that he already wants to give up his attempt to reach the Castle: "Ich . . . wollte nun nicht mehr zum Schloss hinaufgehn" (Then I . . . no longer wanted to go up to the Castle, *SA* 134). Had Kafka let this variant stand, his Castle story would no doubt have developed very differently from the novel as we know it.

Variant K. is an aggressive and duplicitous character who openly admits his willingness to cheat and lie to gain what he wants. He is clearly spoiling for a fight, and says so quite openly: "Zum Kampf bin ich ja hier" (I am here to fight, *SA* 116). Later he confides to Frieda that the quest on which he is embarked calls for "List, Unnachgiebigkeit, Rücksichtlosigkeit" (deception, intransigence, and ruthlessness, *SA* 331). Moreover, he is not in the least disturbed when others respond aggressively, since that means they are taking up the gauntlet. For instance, when Schwarzer, the son of a Castle official, accuses K. of trespassing in the Castle domain and says he has the manners of a tramp, Kafka cuts the hero's silent admission that he is "pleased to be received in this way" ("Mich aber freute es, so empfangen zu werden," *SA* 123) The hero is delighted because the seeming resistance of the Castle provides him with a firm sense of his own otherwise precarious identity.

Kafka deleted many other passages that show K. in a clearly negative light. For instance, in the variants he is blatantly aggressive toward characters such as Amalia and Olga. He snatches Amalia's knitting out of her hand (*SA* 170), and a variant in the first chapter even has him poised to attack the peasants with his walking stick (*SA* 125). Kafka also camouflaged the hero's obsession with power by cutting variants in which K. makes no secret of his obsession with rank and status. For instance, although intensely curious about his new assistants, he does not ask them any questions since that wouldn't "befit" his "position as master" ("es entsprach nicht meiner Herrenstellung," *SA* 148). He also eliminates obvious references to the hero's mendaciously theatrical behavior, such as a passage where K. implicitly concedes that his calm demeanor is an act: "my composure abandoned me" ("die Besonnenheit verliess mich," *SA* 125).[5]

Kafka repeatedly crossed out passages in which the hero attempts to explain himself in explicitly psychological terms. This ought not to surprise us, since we are after all dealing with a writer who urged himself to abandon psychology: "Zum letztenmal Psychologie!" (Never again psychology! *BB* 244.) As a writer of fiction, Kafka could of course never entirely dispense with psychology. However, in the course of writing he strove to diminish the psychological element in his characterization of K. by repeatedly deleting references to his inner life.

In numerous deleted passages K. displays a knack for introspective scrutiny, such as when he admits that his seeming relentlessness masks an underlying insecurity: "Vor allem aber wollte ich in mir keine Ungewissheit aufkommen lassen" (Above all I did not want to allow any uncertainty to arise in me, *SA* 168). Moreover, unlike Castle K., who might appear to turn his back on his strange little family — consisting of himself, Frieda, and the two childlike assistants — solely because of his obsession with Klamm, Variant K. candidly admits that he does so out of fear that the household that Frieda and he have established in the schoolhouse will not be sufficiently durable, for it is "zu provisorisch" (too provisional, *SA* 263).

In the variants Kafka explores the hero's conflicted inner life at far greater depth than he does in the published text of the novel. In the manuscript he consistently crossed out passages that reveal a K. torn between his ambition to get through to the Castle and his longing to establish a home. This inner conflict emerges most strongly in a deleted passage in which K. compares his odd household with that of the Barnabas family and decides in favor of the latter: "in der Schule erwartete ihn wahrscheinlich auch dies alles. . . . Auch lockte ihn das Ziel nicht genug, denn wenn er sich alles, was er zuhause antreffen konnte, in den schönsten Farben vorstellte, merkte er, dass es ihm heute nicht genügen würde" (in the schoolhouse, too, all this probably awaited him . . . Besides, the goal did not tempt him sufficiently, for if he conjured up in the most beautiful colors everything that he would find at home, he realized that it wouldn't suffice, *SA* 251).

Variant K. comes across as a more sensitive and vulnerable character than Castle K. In the novel K. hides his existential and emotional vulnerability under a show of strength, even to the extent of spuriously claiming to have a wife and children. In the variants the hero freely acknowledges his physical and existential isolation: "K. hatte ein grosses Bedürfnis nach Wärme, nach Licht, nach einem freundlichen Wort" (K. had a great need for warmth, for light, for a friendly word, *SA* 251). He admits that without Frieda he is a nothing, and expresses chagrin that she should have omitted him from an account of her doings: "Meine Frau erzählt mir, wie sie ihr Leben eingerichtet hat und ich komme gar nicht darin vor" (My wife gives me an account of how she has set up her life and I don't figure in it at all, *SA* 413). Of course, these belated expressions of emotional dependency could be less than candid, since K. may simply affect these emotions in order to entice back Frieda, who has already moved in with the assistant Jeremias. Nevertheless, Kafka chose to conceal the inner K. that emerges in these variants.

As Kafka wrote, he consistently crossed out sentences and passages that reveal a high degree of self-awareness on his hero's part. At one point Variant K. intimates that his unrealistic quest is depriving him of a full life in the present: "Kann es mir genügen in der Richtung gegen Klamm hin zu schwärmen . . . und über diesem höchsten Ziel den heutigen Tag zu vergessen" (Can I be satisfied with waxing away in the general direction of Klamm . . . and forget the present day for the sake of that highest goal, *SA* 332). Here K. is openly pondering whether it is worth sacrificing the concrete, physical joys of life in the present for the chimera of reaching Klamm in some remote future. However, as Kafka continued writing and revising, he largely eliminated this Hamlet-like internal debate. As a result, the less self-reflective hero of the novel does not appear to recognize until much too late that he is going round and round in circles.

In the variants K. even has epiphanies. His most remarkable moment of insight occurs in the first chapter, when he realizes that the antagonist he is battling is not the Castle but himself: "Auf solche Weise bekämpfte ich nicht die anderen, sondern mich selbst" (In this way I was fighting not the others but rather myself, *SA* 151).

A comparison with Kafka's "Brief an den Vater" (Letter to his Father) may be instructive here because Variant K.'s self-insight matches Kafka's. Variant K. concedes that his true adversary is not the external Castle but some internal adversary, and Kafka dismisses the father's counter-objections on the grounds that he needn't take them seriously since he has invented the father figure in the letter. Likewise, K. implies that his external adversary, the Castle, is a fiction. Although Kafka and Variant K. project their inner *Kampf* onto their relations with the external Father or Castle, in both cases the true adversary lies within.

Nevertheless, Kafka eliminated this important recognition of K.'s. While K.'s epiphany is acute, it would undermine his quest. After all, if K. were aware of his tendency to project his inner struggles onto an external adversary, would he go on fighting with the same unrelenting intensity? Or, to use a fictional prototype that Kafka cherished, would Don Quixote keep up the struggle if he realized that he was tilting at windmills? Surely not, and that is probably why Kafka eliminates many passages in which K. displays considerable self-insight.

The variants can also tell us something about an issue that has been much debated, namely, the question whether or not K. changes for the better (Sheppard 460–63). Toward the end of the manuscript Kafka deleted a passage about a seemingly trivial but actually revealing subject: the landlady's clothes. K. attributes his dislike of them to the fact that they are made of silk. This represents a significant change because K. has always been beguiled by silk, believing it signifies a special connection to the Castle. That conviction has misled him into putting his faith in Barnabas, his voluntary messenger, whose clothes turned out to be merely silk-like.

Toward the end of the novel K. recognizes, at least in a deleted passage, that he has merely been "staggering behind glowing silky will o' the wisps of the Barnabas variety" ("taumelnd hinter seidenglänzenden Irrlichtern von der Art des Barnabas," *SA* 263). That is no doubt why he experiences a powerfully instinctive aversion to the landlady's clothes: "Und plötzlich überkam ihn . . . etwas wie eine leidenschaftliche Abnei-gung gegen diese Kleider" (And suddenly . . . he was overcome by something like a passionate aversion to these clothes, *SA* 457). This burst of intuitive certainty suggests that K. is able to distance himself from his quest precisely because he is rediscovering his inner life.

To sum up: As a character, Variant K. is more fully developed than Castle K. More aggressive and more calculating, he is also more self-aware and more vulnerable. We can attribute the deletion of many of Variant K.'s traits to Kafka's often-expressed dislike of psychology. However, instead of entirely eliminating psychology, Kafka buried the workings of his hero's psyche in the interstices of his writing.

III. Narrative Variants

In the variants Kafka experiments with three different narrative voices: In the first he resorts to a first-person narrator; in the other two he has different characters present reports about K.

After deleting the prince's room scene, Kafka began again from scratch with a first-person narrator's description of his arrival in a snow-covered village. In the beginning, therefore, there was no K., only an I:

> Es war spät abend als ich ankam. Das Dorf lag in tiefem Schnee. Vom Schloßberg war nichts zu sehn, Nebel und Finsternis umgaben ihn, auch nicht der schwächste Lichtschein deutete das große Schloß an. Lange stand ich auf der Holzbrücke die von der Landstraße zum Dorf führt und blickte in die scheinbare Leere empor. (*SA* 120)

> [It was late evening when I arrived. The village lay under deep snow. There was no sign of the Castle hill, fog and darkness surrounded it, not even the faintest gleam of light suggested the large Castle. I stood a long time on the wooden bridge that leads from the main road to the village, gazing upward into the seeming emptiness.]

Kafka retained this first person narrator until part-way through the third chapter, when he made the switch from first to third person. Then he went back and replaced all previous I's with K.s.

In his volume of *Das Schloß* for the Critical Edition, Malcolm Pasley restored a significant narrative nuance in that first paragraph, namely, Kafka's use of the present tense of the verb "führt" (leads), which Max Brod had changed to the past tense "führte." Whereas Kafka's use of the present tense underlined the reality of the Castle, Brod's introduction of the past tense made the Castle seem less real. The Castle is not some fantasy in the mind of the main character. Just as Kafka underscores the reality of the seemingly surreal transformation in "Die Verwandlung"

(The Metamorphosis) by explicitly stating that it was not a dream, his slightly odd use of the present tense in the opening paragraph of *Das Schloß* suggests that the Castle has an independent existence beyond K.'s often delusional perceptions of it.

In exploring possible technical reasons for the significant narrative switch from first to third-person narrator, Dorrit Cohn argues convincingly that it is odd and also rather illogical for a first-person narrator to "feign ignorance of his own conscious motives and desires," as happens frequently in the first two chapters that Kafka initially wrote in the first person (35). She also points out that Kafka could hardly have ended the novel with the death of the hero, as he envisaged doing in a conversation with Brod, if he had continued narrating the book in the first person. Otherwise K. would have had to speak from his grave, a cheap ploy that Kafka would scarcely have found appealing.

As always, Kafka probably had several reasons for deleting this set of variants, and I would suggest another reason why he made this narrative change. It is surely no coincidence that he switches from I to K. just as he is about to write the famous sex scene amid the puddles of beer. The first such switch occurs immediately before that sex scene, when the hero notices a certain free, uninhibited quality in Frieda: "Etwas Fröhliches, Freies war in ihrem Wesen" (*S* 185). This uninhibited quality in Frieda prompts her to jump down behind the counter and kiss K., even though the landlord, who suspects K.'s illicit presence, is questioning her.

It is understandable that Kafka should have felt uncomfortable using the first person in this sex scene. Although he liked to make a sharp distinction between the earth of biographical experience and the moon of the literary work, he was also sensitive about the autobiographical implications of his fiction. Though he could joke about the thinness of the line between his life and his work, he was less than pleased when others did so. For instance, when "Die Verwandlung" first appeared in a Prague periodical, Kafka approached an acquaintance on the street and asked him tongue-in-cheek whether he had heard of the terrible goings-on in the Kafka family apartment. Yet when his sister claimed that the layout of the apartment in "Das Urteil" (The Judgment) was identical to that of the Kafka family, he reacted defensively. So he could easily have felt apprehensive about writing the following sex scene in the first person. (I shall switch one brief excerpt from third to first person to give an impression of how the description of the encounter would have sounded had Kafka stuck with the first person):

wir umfaßten einander, der kleine Körper brannte in meinen Händen, wir rollten in einer Besinnungslosigkeit, aus der ich mich fortwährend aber vergeblich zu retten suchte . . .

[we embraced each other, her small body was burning in my hands; we rolled a few paces in an unconscious state from which I repeatedly but vainly tried to rescue myself . . .]

Why did Kafka change from first to third person at this point? Although we cannot be certain about his intentions, if he did so in order to tone down this sex scene, then this would not be the only such case in the manuscript. For instance, in this very scene he removed a reference to Frieda and K., who "then lay almost undressed, for each had ripped open the other's clothes with hands and teeth" ("lagen dann fast entkleidet, denn jeder hatte des anderen Kleider mit Händen und Zähnen aufgerissen," *SA* 185).

Kafka also cut passages that lay bare the framework of his narrative, which he prefers to keep hidden. One of the ways in which he hints at matters beyond K.'s limited perspective is by letting other characters comment indirectly on K.'s case. The story told in the final chapter by the spiteful, ambitious chambermaid Pepi is one such tale within a tale. Kafka deleted a passage in which Pepi tells K. that her story was really about him, for "she had wanted to hold up his image to him" ("um K. handle es sich, ihm habe sie sein Bild vorhalten wollen" *SA* 471). In another deleted passage K. sounds, quite uncharacteristically, like an eager schoolboy. All too obviously he underlines the didactic quality of Pepi's tale, reminding her that their mistakes have "eine Art Gemeinsamkeit" (something in common) before dutifully concluding that he, like Pepi, has to learn from those mistakes: "Auch er werde umlernen müssen nicht anders als Pepi" (*SA* 474).

Now I should like to turn to the two reports about K., the deletion of which represents a loss and a gain: a gain in the sense that, like many variants, they are too explicit for Kafka's cunning art; a loss because they contain intriguing reflections about writing and interpreting. The first report showcases the "Protokoll" or deposition being compiled by Momus, Klamm's village secretary. In the novel we do not get to hear much about this odd deposition, over which Momus rather comically scatters pretzel crumbs. In the variants, on the other hand, K. grabs it from the secretary and reads a page from it, which we get to read over his shoulder, as it were.

In the variants, as elsewhere in his writing, Kafka anticipates in the text the reactions that his works elicit from readers and critics outside the text. As noted previously, critics come to very different judgments about K. While some consider him a positive figure, others see him as a schemer. Indeed Secretary Momus could be summarizing the critical debate about K. — much as Richard Sheppard does in that indispensable critical compendium, Hartmut Binder's *Kafka-Handbuch* — when he says that K.'s efforts to establish himself in the world dominated by the Castle could be interpreted in several ways: K. could be seen as "a weak, or a stupid or a noble-minded or a rascally person" ("als ein schwacher, oder ein dummer oder ein edelmütiger oder ein lumpiger Mensch," *SA* 273). All those characterizations of K., and more, can be found in the critical literature about *Das Schloß*.

In placing those alternatives side by side and apparently refusing to choose between them, Momus, and behind him Kafka, might appear to be siding with relativists such as Heinz Politzer, who suggest that Kafka's paradoxical parables are inherently so ambiguous that they preclude all clear-cut interpretation. And if Momus stopped right there, we could certainly call him a relativist. However, he goes on to deliver a ringing denunciation of all such interpretations, and discloses the way to reach the truth about K., which he is pursuing in the so-called deposition: "Zur Wahrheit gelangt man erst, wenn man genau in seinen Spuren, die wir von der Ankunft angefangen, hier aufgezeigt haben, bis zu der Verbindung mit Frieda geht" (The only way to reach the truth is to follow exactly in his tracks, which lead, as we have shown here, from his arrival to the liaison with Frieda, *SA* 273). And the truth that this approach uncovers is "haarsträubend" (hair-raising). K. pursued Frieda "nur aus Berechnung schmutzigster Art" (merely out of the filthiest sort of calculation). He went after her because he believed that by acquiring Klamm's mistress he would gain leverage and "Pfand" (security) in his struggle with the Castle.

Before K. seized the bag with the deposition, the landlady had predicted that, if he did so, the deposition would lose all significance and become as meaningless as "eine Blume, abgeweidet auf der Wiese" (a flower cut off in the meadow," *SA* 272). Her prediction now turns out to be correct, since K. detects in the report nothing but "Klatsch . . . weibischer Klatsch" (gossip . . . female gossip, *SA* 275).

An earlier variant would appear to bear out Momus's verdict that K. pursued Frieda out of filthy calculation. Right before the grotesque sex scene amid the puddles of beer, K.'s mind is focused not so much on Frieda as on Klamm: "K. dachte mehr an Klamm als an sie. Die Eroberung Friedas verlangte eine Änderung seiner Pläne" (K. was thinking more of Klamm than of her. Conquering Frieda called for a change in his plans, *SA* 185). In deleting this sentence, Kafka also removed yet another reference to the hero's secret plans, which he needs to revise because he had not anticipated this early conquest.

Like so many other discarded passages, this variant is too explicit for Kafka's artistic purposes. Although Kafka shares Momus's aim of revealing K.'s immoral calculations, his aesthetics of intimation requires a less direct approach than is evident in this scene. Whereas Momus comes straight out with declarations about "the hair-raising truth," Kafka prefers to suggest that truth through subtle hints.

Kafka also experimented with an alternative narrative approach to K.'s bedside interview with the Castle official Bürgel, in the course of which K. falls asleep at what seems like the most inopportune moment. Kafka tried telling the tale of the Bürgel interview in the voice of a third party, an official or perhaps a well-informed villager, who has heard K. recount the story at the inn. The narrator, who clearly relishes the humorous side of K.'s encounter with Bürgel, begins by injecting a sense of perspective, which K.'s thinking sorely lacks. It is funny, he says, that the interview had to be with Bürgel, one of the lower-ranking secretaries of a rather obscure official called Friedrich (*SA* 421)

This deleted passage is significant because it raises questions about the supposedly unique opportunity that Bürgel dangles before the weary K. We discover that the name of this official, Bürgel — the verb "bürgen" means to vouch for something — is ironic: his stature in the hierarchy is so low that he is incapable of vouching for anything. As usual, everybody understands this, "Jeder, nur nicht K." (everybody, save for K., *SA* 421). Incidentally, this is not the first mention of the word "bürgen." In a variant in a much earlier chapter K. tells Olga that she can vouch for Amalia ("bürgen"). Although Kafka crossed out that word, given the latent economy of his seemingly spendthrift method of composition, the verb he deleted may resurface here in the form of an official called Bürgel.

IV. Self-Conscious Variants

As Marthe Robert has persuasively suggested, *Das Schloß* belongs in the tradition of the self-conscious novel that harks back to Cervantes. The variants highlight Kafka's playful reflections about writing *Das Schloß*. In the Momus scene, for instance, the deposition that Momus is compiling sounds suspiciously like the novel that Kafka is writing. Like *Das Schloß*, Momus's deposition tracks K. from the moment he arrives in the village. Again, like Kafka's narrator, Momus "forces" himself to cling to "K.'s train of thought" ("sich . . . ganz in seinen Gedankengang hineinzwingt" [*SA* 272]). Moreover, as Malcolm Pasley has pointed out, the page of the deposition we get to read in the variants is marked number ten, the same number as the chapter in which it appeared in the manuscript of *Das Schloß*.

When Momus refers to the "Schlingen" of his deposition he could also be talking about Kafka's novel, which contains many such "Schlingen" (loops, nooses, traps, or snares). In another characteristically sly joke Momus smilingly underlines passages in his document with "mit starken Strichen" (strong lines) similar to those Kafka uses in the manuscript to cross out passages, including this one (*SA* 268). Incidentally, Kafka, the chief puppeteer behind Secretary Momus, can jokingly refer to himself in a letter to his parents of 26–27 July 1922 as the "Obersekretär" (Chief Secretary), a title to which he was entitled in real life, having been promoted on the third of February 1922 to that leading position at the Workers' Accident Insurance Company.

The variants allow us to eavesdrop on Kafka thinking aloud, since the characters' reflections about their situation are often intimately related to Kafka's thoughts about his writing. For instance, in the Bürgel variant the unnamed narrator promises to tell the story without skipping any of the circumstantial detail on which K. has dwelled. However, this raises a problem that the narrator — and behind him Kafka — must grapple with. Ideally, the comic nature of the hero's predicament would emerge through the very minuteness of the details: "Das eigentlich Komische ist freilich das Minutiöse" (What's truly comic is the minute detail, *SA* 424). Here Kafka reveals far more explicitly than in the novel the discrepancy between K.'s plodding account of his experiences and the Castle's wry view of them.

Moreover, when the narrator explicitly reflects about the difficulties inherent in this proposal to tell K.'s story in all its tedious detail, he is clearly conveying Kafka's worries about the direction in which his seemingly autonomous pen is leading him. The anonymous narrator — and behind him his creator Kafka — fears that if he goes into such detail the story could easily become "langweilig" (boring). Nevertheless, he decides to give it a try: "Aber wagen wir's" (But let's risk it, *SA* 424.) This anonymous narrator and his creator now begin to think at cross-purposes, for just as the narrator declares himself willing to take the risk, Kafka, who as the writer obviously has the upper hand, decides the opposite. We can tell that this is so, because, immediately after the narrator announces he is willing to take the risk, Kafka silences him for good.

Another example of this kind of Pirandello-like metafictional dispute between the characters and their author occurs when K. announces after a rambling monologue that he intends to dwell on the Barnabas family affair at some length and will do so "ohne grosse Bedenken" (without any great reservations, *SA* 360). This is a piquant observation because, unlike his hero, Kafka clearly does have reservations about extending K.'s already wordy monologue. Again we know that Kafka must be thinking along these lines, since, immediately after putting the phrase "without any great reservations" into his character's mouth, he cuts him off and deletes the entire monologue.

Kafka's tendency to dispense with transitions can be a challenge for the translator, as I found out while preparing my translation of the Critical Edition, and so I should like to comment briefly on the impact of the deleted passages on Kafka's style. In an earlier essay on retranslating Kafka for *New Literary History* I attributed this lack of transitions to Kafka's hybrid style, with its unique mix of conservative and modernist elements. It is now necessary to qualify that argument slightly because, as I discovered to my surprise on reading the variants, these dissonant effects can be an unintentional by-product of Kafka's deletions.

If one reads his sentences slowly, one can still perceive in them traces of the variants that he erased. Two such instances will have to suffice: In the first chapter an eerie voice with a stutter asks the hero on the telephone: "Was willst Du?" (What do you want). In the novel K. responds with the silent thought: "Am liebsten hätte er den Hörer schon wegge-legt" (*S* 38; "Most of all he would have liked to put down the receiver," *C* 21). This cutting from an impatient question in a telephone conversation to a short-tempered response in interior monologue might seem like some avant-garde modernist technique, and that is how I first heard it as I translated the passage. However, this seemingly modernist effect is actually quite fortuitous and results from Kafka's deletion of the first thought K. has on hearing the official's question — namely, his sudden insight, which we examined earlier, that he is not so much battling the Castle as himself. (*SA* 151).

While there is a plethora of examples to choose from, I shall restrict myself to one further instance: During a conversation with the authoritarian teacher in the first chapter, K. resolves not to say anything that might be unwelcome ("Um hier nichts Unwillkommenes zu sagen," *S* 19–20). In translating this otherwise crisp exchange I found the phrase puzzling because it seemed out of place in the dialogue. Only on reading the variants did I realize that it probably refers to a deleted passage. In the variant, K. responds to the teacher's statement that strangers never like the Castle by remarking that the villagers seem to talk a great deal about strangers, since the topic has already surfaced at the inn. Kafka promptly erased that remark, and the reference to an unwelcome comment probably alludes not to the teacher but rather to Kafka, who did not welcome K.'s words.

Finally, Kafka makes a point of avoiding language that — for want of a better phrase — one could call "Kafkaesque." For instance, when the words "impenetrably dark" emerge from his pen he immediately crosses them out. While impenetrable is a word one might be tempted to use in describing the effect of Kafka's texts, it is too explicit for Kafka himself, who promptly replaces the phrase with the simpler expression "völlig finster" (completely dark, *SA* 145).

V. Mystical Variants

Shortly before sitting down to work intensively on *Das Schloß*, Kafka claimed in his diaries that, had Zionism not come and distracted his generation of German-Jewish writers, their writings could easily have developed into "a new esoteric doctrine, a Kabbala" ("hätte sich . . . leicht zu einer neuen Geheimlehre, einer Kabbala entwickeln können"). He even appears to imply that there are "Ansätze" (signs or intimations) of that goal in his own work. (*T* 878). Intimation is a good term to describe both the mystical implications of *Das Schloß* and the intuitive aesthetics that guided Kafka as he made quick decisions about which passages to accept and which to reject.

In the manuscript of *Der Proceß* (The Trial) Kafka deliberately heightened the metaphysical resonance of important passages by adding phrases that suggest a supernatural dimension, as Karlheinz Fingerhut has shown. For instance, in the final pages of that novel Josef K. asks a resonant question, which cannot help but make us think of some ultimate judge: "Wo war der Richter, den er nie gesehen hatte?" (Where was the judge whom he had never seen? *P* 312). The relative clause — which creates the metaphysical resonance — was an addition, since Kafka wrote initially: "Wo war der Richter?" (Where was the judge? Fingerhut 58).

In *Das Schloß*, on the other hand, Kafka weakened the metaphysical undertones by deleting passages that are explicitly religious. He crossed out sentences where the religious meaning of *Herr* (gentleman or Lord) — the word he uses to refer to the Castle officials — can be overheard too distinctly, and also eliminated passages in which Klamm's persona acquires an unmistakably transcendental aura: For instance, in one variant there is a reference to the landlady reading over and over again, as though in prayer, Klamm's "teueren Namen" (precious name, *SA* 223). No wonder she is astounded that Variant K. could even conceive of the idea of Klamm's having a private identity in addition to his official one: "Wer kann sich ihn als Privatmann auch nur denken!" (Who can even imagine him as a private person! *SA* 228).

Kafka also lessened the mystical aura of the scene in which K. enters Klamm's coach. In the variants, when K. penetrates into the courtyard where Klamm's carriage is waiting, he seems clearly aware that he is violating a religious or mystical taboo. Kafka had to delete that particular passage because the occurrence three times in a row of the word *verboten* hints too broadly at the existence of some impenetrable esoteric doctrine.

In the same scene Kafka crossed out two related passages about Klamm, one in which K. insists that Klamm's carriage is surmounted by a golden eagle, and another in which he discovers that it is a commonplace carriage. These two passages anticipate a phase in the subsequent critical reception of *Das Schloß*. Like K. in the variants, Max Brod and his allegorical school of interpretation invested Klamm with a mythological and even divine aura. It is thus important to note that, at least in the variants, Kafka undermines such interpretations by pointedly contrasting the exalted carriage that K. imagines with the utilitarian vehicle that he sees.

In *Das Schloß* Kafka went to even greater pains to conceal the novel's roots in Jewish exegetical and mystical tradition than he did in composing *Der Proceß*, in which a priest rather than a rabbi summarizes the Talmudic body of commentary on the parable before the law. In *Das Schloß* he generally deleted passages that clearly betray their religious provenance. For instance, in the variants the occupants of the remote village can sound oddly bookish, scholarly, even Talmudic. The landlady's profound knowledge of Castle lore makes her, in Frieda's words, "fast ein Gelehrter" (almost a scholar, *SA* 481). The villagers learn the procedures for dealing with strangers from esoteric tomes (*SA* 306). Even K. sounds bookish when he chides Pepi for not backing up her complaints by listing her sources ("Quellen").

The fusion of the erotic, the obscene, and the sacred intimated in Amalia's encounter with Sortini is more clearly apparent in the variants than it is in the novel. Though K. is not physically attracted to Pepi, he admits that if he had encountered her in the taproom he would have attempted to draw "das Geheimnis" (the mystery) to himself "with the same embraces" as he did with Frieda (*SA* 240). It is considered only natural that the village girls should fall for "den hohen, den überaus hohen Beamten," (the high, the exceedingly high official, *SA* 228). Here, incidentally, the potential for wordplay in the term "Parteienverkehr" (the still-current Austrian word for "office hours," which literally means "intercourse with the parties"), inevitably gets lost in translation.

Kafka also deleted a possible sexual undercurrent in the all-male nighttime, sometimes even bedside, encounters between the officials and the parties: "Man . . . wird von ihr [der Partei] gehalten oder ist noch tiefer mit ihr verbunden" (one . . . is held by it [the party] or is bound even more deeply to it, *SA* 435). However, readers inclined to take this variant as evidence for the now fashionable homosexual reading of Kafka would be well-advised to note that the German word for party is, at least grammatically, feminine.

The changes in the manuscript show how determined Kafka was to avoid being obvious. For instance, he crossed out passages that too clearly reveal Amalia to be a parallel figure to K. Her story contains lessons for him, which he of course ignores. Olga makes this explicit by repeatedly linking Amalia and K. The questions K. keeps asking about the Castle remind her of Amalia's questions in the immediate aftermath of the Sortini affair.

Kafka also deleted passages that explicitly reveal K.'s disdain for the mystery around which the novel revolves. In the variants K. regards Momus and the landlady as a void because he has nothing but disdain for their "armseligen Geheimnissen" (wretched mysteries, *SA* 276). Neither in the variants nor in the novel proper is the hero privy to the conviction Kafka expressed in the aphorisms he wrote in 1917 in Zürau that the spiritual world can be grasped only by means of "Andeutung" (suggestion).

The term "Andeutung," a cornerstone of Kafka's skeptical mysticism, recurs repeatedly throughout the novel and the variants, having first surfaced in the opening paragraph, where we learn that "nicht einmal der schwächste Lichtschein deutete das große Schloß an" (not even the faintest gleam of light suggested the large Castle).

The deleted passages can also tell us something about K.'s enigmatic assistants Artur and Jeremias, whom K. harshly insists on calling by the same name. Frieda, who gets her information from the learned landlady, tells K. that the assistants are "Geschenke" (gifts) from the authorities, and that he, a stranger, is dependent on such gifts. Though there is nothing arbitrary about the gifts, it is solely a matter for the authorities, and this means that "die Gründe der Entscheidung verborgen bleiben" (the reasons for the decision remain hidden, *SA* 306). Once K. has accepted these gifts, which at the very least show "eine Spur von Freundlichkeit" (a hint of friendliness), he cannot give them away. It is impossible to shake them off — only the authorities can do so — and anybody who tries to do so merely runs the risk of turning them into "unabschüttelbare Feinde" (unshakeable enemies). That is indeed what K. ends up doing with his odd gifts. Thus, he turns a deaf ear to the hints repeatedly dropped by the

Castle's seemingly buffoonish messengers, namely Artur and Jeremias, to the effect that K. should forget about the elusive Castle and focus on the tangible reality of life in the village.

In *Das Schloß* Kafka takes a strong stand against the interpretative frenzy that grips K., so it is quite ironic that the novel should have become such a battleground for competing armies of interpreters. Interestingly, Kafka deleted a passage that makes K. sound like an ambitious scholar determined to secure "Anerkennung" (recognition) for his interpretation, but let stand another in which K., the champion (over-) interpreter, pleads for an end to the ceaseless interpreting that takes up so much of the novel: "Laß die Deutungen!" (*S* 324; "Stop interpreting everything!" *C* 205). K. is of course chronically unable to heed his own advice.

In a deleted passage Olga affirms the superiority of relationships in the here and now to K.'s lonely speculations: "Nicht Deine Meinungen trösten mich, sondern Deine Gegenwart" (It's not your opinions that comfort me but your presence, *SA* 384). Olga's message is one that reaches K. only when it is too late. His real tragedy is not that he never reaches the Castle but that, as Momus puts it in the deleted deposition: "es ist ihm nicht gegeben, sich hier einzuleben" (it's not within his reach to settle down here. *SA* 421) In the variants Olga, who may have been partly modeled after Kafka's beloved sister Ottla, often sounds like a spokeswoman for Kafka himself. She is clearly speaking for Kafka when she says that when confronted with mystery "Verstand . . . beiweitem nicht ausreicht" (reason is nowhere near sufficient, *SA* 353).

Kafka's style in *Das Schloß* is splendidly oblique, yet there is little doubt about where he himself stands. One can overhear in Olga's rhetorical question Kafka's own impatience with K.'s ceaseless appetite for speculation: "Was helfen solche Fragen?" (What use are questions like that? *SA* 391). This is worthwhile advice for readers approaching *Das Schloß*, especially for those tempted to speculate endlessly about the mysterious Castle, which, as the deleted passages so clearly indicate, is intentionally kept under wraps, much as the mist that enshrouds it in the opening lines never quite lifts.

Notes

[1] In the variants K. ascribes this goal of creating an uncanny effect to Momus, who, as discussed later in this essay, is composing a narrative about K. that bears a striking resemblance to the novel that Kafka is writing. K. accuses Momus of destroying this uncanny effect, and Kafka may well have deleted Momus's account precisely because it makes K.'s story more transparent than uncanny. The word uncanny naturally makes one think of Freud, even though Kafka himself may never have read Freud's seminal piece "On the Uncanny," which first appeared in *Imago* in 1919 (In *On Creativity and the Unconscious: Papers on the Psychology of Art, Literature, Love, Religion* [New York: Harper and Row, 1958], 122–61). As it turns out, the most relevant passage in that famous essay on the "Unheimliche" — for which uncanny is the closest though far from perfect English equivalent — is Freud's paraphrase of Schelling's definition of the uncanny. Of *Das Schloß*, too, one could say that "everything that ought to have remained hidden and secret" becomes uncanny (Freud 129).

A somewhat different version of this essay, initially presented as a lecture at the American Academy in Berlin, appeared in German under the title "Die Ästhetik der Andeutung: Kafkas Streichungen im Schreibprozess" (trans. Reiner Stach) in *Die neue Rundschau* 112:2 (2001): 104–23.

[2] The French scholar and translator Bernard Lotholary has attacked the Critical Edition as a waste of energy and resources. He faults Malcolm Pasley for including lists of purely mechanical emendations and maintains that the second volume with the variants yields only a "maigre récolte" (Lotholary, "À quoi sert l'édition critique du château," *Études Germaniques* 39:2 (1984): 221). I would argue to the contrary that Pasley was right to publish the minor as well as the major deletions as they appear in the manuscript, thereby allowing individual readers to examine the variants and come to their own conclusions.

[3] References to the text of *Das Schloß* in the version of the Critical Edition, edited by Malcolm Pasley, are cited as *S* and page number; references to Pasley's *Apparatband* are cited as *SA* and page number. For the sake of legibility, all editorial marks within the quotations from the *SA* have been omitted.

[4] James Rolleston justly observes that "nothing is harder than to evolve an image of the 'character' of a Kafka hero." Rolleston, *Kafka's Narrative Theater* (University Park, PA: Pennsylvania State UP, 1974), 140.

[5] While Kafka deleted passages in which K. discloses that he is acting, he let stand those in which the hero detects actor-like traits in others. In the first chapter K. notes that Schwarzer has an actor's face, and accuses him of putting on a farce ("Komödie"). The word "Komödie" could be rendered idiomatically as "play-acting" or "carrying on," but in my translation of *Das Schloß* I chose to render it literally as comedy, so as to mimic Kafka's subtle allusion to the comedy underlying K.'s ostensibly grim ordeal. For readers interested in such translation issues, I should like to draw attention to two detailed review-essays on my *Castle* translation, one by Robert Alter in the *New Republic* ("The Old and the New," 4: 343 [April 13, 1998]: 33–37) and the other by J. M. Coetzee in the *New York Review of Books* ("Kafka: Transla-

tors on Trial," XLV: 8 [May 14, 1998]: 14–16). The latter was reprinted, as "Translating Kafka," in Coetzee's collection *Stranger Shores.*

Works Cited

Alter, Robert. "The Old and the New." *New Republic* 4: 343 (April 13, 1998): 33–37.

Binder, Hartmut. "Kafkas Varianten." *Deutsche Vierteljahrsschrift für Literaturwissenschaft und Geistesgeschichte.* 50:4 (1976): 684–719.

Coetzee J. M. "Translating Kafka." *Stranger Shores: Literary Essays, 1986–1999.* New York: Viking, 2001. 74–87.

Cohn, Dorrit. "K. enters *The Castle.* On the Change of Person in Kafka's Manuscript." *Euphorion* 62 (1968): 28–45.

Fingerhut, Karlheinz. "Annäherung an Kafkas Roman '*Der Prozeß*' über die Handschrift und über Schreibexperimente." *Nach erneuter Lektüre: Franz Kafka "Der Prozess."* Ed. Hans Dieter Zimmermann. Würzburg: Koenigshausen & Neumann, 1992.

Freud, Sigmund. "On the Uncanny." *On Creativity and the Unconscious: Papers on the Psychology of Art, Literature, Love, Religion.* New York: Harper & Row, 1958. 122–61.

Harman, Mark. "Approaching K.'s Castle." *Sewanee Review* 55:4 (Fall 1997): 513–23.

———. "'Digging the Pit of Babel': Retranslating Franz Kafka's *Castle.*" *New Literary History* 27 (1996): 291–311.

Kafka, Franz. *Beim Bau der chinesischen Mauer.* Ed. Hans-Gerd Koch. Frankfurt am Main: S. Fischer, 1994. (*BB*)

———. *Briefe 1902–1924.* Ed. Max Brod. Frankfurt am Main: S. Fischer, 1958. (*B*)

———. *Briefe an Milena.* Ed. Jürgen Born and Michael Müller. Frankfurt am Main: S. Fischer, 1983. (*M*)

———. *The Castle: A New Translation, Based on the Restored Text.* Trans. Mark Harman. New York: Schocken Books: 1998. Paperback: 1999. (*C*)

———. *Der Proceß.* Ed. Malcolm Pasley. Frankfurt am Main: S. Fischer, 1990. (*P*)

———. *Das Schloß: Apparatband.* Ed. Malcolm Pasley. Frankfurt am Main: S. Fischer, 1982. (*SA*)

———. *Das Schloß: Kritische Ausgabe.* Ed. Malcolm Pasley. Frankfurt am Main: S. Fischer, 1982. (*S*)

———. *Tagebücher.* Ed. Hans-Gerd Koch, Michael Müller, and Malcolm Pasley. Frankfurt am Main: S. Fischer, 1990. (*T*)

Lotholary, Bernard. "À quoi sert l'édition critique du château." *Études Germaniques* 39:2 (1984): 220–26.

Martini, Fritz. "Ein Manuskript Kafkas: 'Der Dorfschullehrer.'" *Jahrbuch der deutschen Schillergesellschaft* 2 (1958): 266–300.

Pasley, Malcolm. *Die Schrift ist Unveränderlich . . .: Essays zu Kafka.* Frankfurt am Main: S. Fischer, 1995.

———. "Zu Kafkas Interpunktion." *Euphorion* 75 (1981): 474–90.

Politzer, Heinz. *Franz Kafka: Parable and Paradox.* Ithaca: Cornell UP, 1966.

Robert, Marthe. *The Old and the New: From Don Quixote to Kafka.* Trans. Carol Cosman. Berkeley: U of California P, 1977.

Rolleston, James. *Kafka's Narrative Theater.* University Park: Pennsylvania State UP, 1974.

Sebald, W. G. "The Undiscover'd Country: The Death Motif in Kafka's *Castle.*" *Journal of European Studies* 2 (1972): 22–34.

Sheppard, Richard. "Das Schloß." *Kafka-Handbuch,* vol. 2. Ed. Hartmut Binder. Stuttgart: Kröner, 1979.

Kafka Imagines His Readers:
The Rhetoric of "Josefine die Sängerin" and "Der Bau"

Clayton Koelb

KAFKA'S LAST STORIES, written in the knowledge that his life was not likely to last much longer, reflect an artist's last attempts to come to grips with the question of the place of art in a world that by and large has other things to worry about. Even artists themselves have other things to worry about, and sometimes those things — things like dying — are extremely urgent. In the case of these late stories the urgency of the situation shows up not so much in the pace of the narratives, which are for the most part leisurely and even contemplative, as in their subject matter and narrative style. Subject matter and style actually merge here, for Kafka creates narrators whose apparently trivial discourse examines obsessively other trivial discourse which might, on second thought, be the most important thing in the world.

Both stories are first-person narratives, and though they were not Kafka's first attempts at this mode of storytelling, they are nonetheless atypical of his usual practice. Normally he tended to adhere as much as possible to the *erlebte Rede* technique, the "free indirect style" made famous by Flaubert. This is the style of all the novels, of "Die Verwand-lung" (The Metamorphosis), "Das Urteil" (The Judgment), "In der Strafkolonie" (In the Penal Colony), and indeed most of the classics of the Kafka canon. But such a style, though it looks initially very different, is in one regard not necessarily a very far step from the first-person narra-tive. *Erlebte Rede,* as has long been recognized, may have the form of a third-person narrative with an omniscient narrator, but its perspective is normally limited to the point of view of a single character (see, for exam-ple, Cohn). It is clear that, for Kafka at least, the boundary between the two was not very strong, as is evident from the manuscript of *Das Schloß* (The Castle). The opening of the novel was originally composed in the first-person, but Kafka changed his mind. He crossed out the first-person pronouns and inserted the familiar and personally resonant letter K. in their place, thus converting his novel to the *erlebte Rede* style with a few strokes of the pen.

In *Das Schloß*, Kafka evidently did not wish to foreground the first-person perspective, though he wanted on the whole to maintain it. In the last stories, on the other hand, he clearly did wish to draw attention to the involvement of the narrators in the narratives. These stories are personal. That they were intensely personal for Kafka himself is evidenced by the fact that "Josefine die Sängerin" and "Der Bau" present as their central characters artists who are animals with a human consciousness. This amalgam of the animal and human is one of Kafka's most frequent themes, and it is also one of his most personal concerns. The very idea of the animal-human combination arises from the circumstances of Kafka's personal life, the linguistic accident that made the name of an avian animal (the crow or jackdaw — Czech *kavka*) the name of his family. On top of this was the peculiar fact that his parents had given him the Hebrew name Amschel, a word commonly associated among Central European Jews with another black bird, the *Amsel* ("blackbird"). Franz/Amschel Kafka, a person highly sensitive to language, could not avoid noticing that language had dubbed him an animal, and this not once but twice. It was an essential element of his being, and it is hardly surprising that it ends up a leading motif in his fiction (see Koelb 18–20).

Nor is it surprising that this motif comes into particular prominence at the end of Kafka's career. While contemplating what it meant to be who he was, he could hardly have come up with a more fitting fictional image than the insecure animal-artist living on the edge of oblivion, a description that fits both Josephine, the mouse-singer, and the builder of the burrow. Well aware that he was himself near the edge of the abyss, Kafka felt the need to consider what it was about his work that kept him so immersed in it even under such grim circumstances.

The story Max Brod published as "Der Bau" (The Burrow) appears as a long untitled fragment in Kafka's notebooks. In its original context it follows a paragraph featuring a protagonist called K. — probably a different K. from the figures we are familiar with from the *Proceß* and *Schloß* manuscripts, but possibly not — which begins "Dann lag die Ebene vor K. . . ." (*EP* 165; Then the plain lay before K. . . .). The use of the letter K. to signify an important fictional character is a noteworthy feature of Kafka's rhetorical strategy. While on the one hand it clearly refers back to the author's own surname, on the other it conveys a sense of mystery and openness, as the missing letters tantalizingly call on the reader to fill them in. This deliberate omission of important or even crucial information is one of the most typical and most effective of

Kafka's rhetorical strategies. It engages the reader in a potentially endless act of trying to complete the text, to supply the missing context, and to find a significance appropriate to the clues that the text actually offers.

The paragraph that precedes the "Der Bau" fragment may in fact bear an interesting relation to the quite different material that follows. It concerns K.'s arrival at a house that he assumes to be his. The house is very dilapidated, and at first it seems to have been long uninhabited. But, as he enters, two distressing things happen: first, he disturbs a cat, which in response makes a distinctly un-catlike noise — "so schreien Katzen sonst nicht"; and second, he hears from upstairs "eine zitternde fast röchelnde Stimme" (a quavering, almost wheezing voice) asking who's there (*EP* 165). We cannot know for sure just how quickly Kafka moved from this K.-related material to the "Der Bau" fragment that follows, but there does seem to be at least one noteworthy connection: the "K." fragment, like the other, is concerned with a dwelling that is supposed to belong to the central character but which turns out to contain a mysterious other, known only by the unpleasant noise it makes. This idea may have set Kafka to thinking about elaborating the idea of such a dwelling in other terms. In any case, he did in fact stop working on the "K." fragment and turned to the much more substantial project beginning "Ich habe den Bau eingerichtet" (I have completed the construction of my burrow).

Although Kafka never finished the work and never gave it a title, one has to think that Kafka's literary executor Max Brod was following a basically sound instinct in his edition of Kafka's manuscript, not only because he decided to go ahead and publish the piece, fragment though it was, but also because he supplied the very appropriate title "Der Bau." (For reasons that will be explained shortly, the English title "The Burrow" is not quite so appropriate.) Perhaps Brod had noticed that the German word "Bau," along with related words, has a special importance in the notebooks from this period in Kafka's life. An especially telling entry expressing Kafka's frustration — almost despair — over his difficulties with writing occurs earlier in the same larger set of documents containing "Der Bau." He speaks of a plan to move away from fiction to a kind of biographical writing:

> Daraus will ich mich dann aufbauen so wie einer, dessen Haus unsicher ist, daneben ein sicheres aufbauen will, womöglich aus dem Material des alten. Schlimm ist es allerdings wenn mitten im Bau seine Kraft aufhört und er jetzt statt eines zwar unsicheren aber doch vollständigen Hauses, ein halbzerstörtes und ein halbfertiges hat, also nichts. (*EP* 10)

[I plan to develop ["aufbauen"] myself out of this material, rather like someone with an unsteady dwelling who wants to build ["aufbauen"] a more secure one nearby, if possible out of the materials of the old one. Of course things could go badly if his strength gives out in the midst of construction ["Bau"], and now instead of an insecure but nonetheless complete house he has one half destroyed and one half completed — in other words, nothing (trans. mine).]

The German word "bauen" brings together a set of senses combined in no single English word, for it means both "to dig or delve in the earth" (a farmer is called a *Bauer* in German) and, more generally, "to build, construct," with the extended metaphorical sense of "develop." Beyond these conventional senses, the word had an additional, very personal significance for Kafka, since the surname of his longtime friend and sometime fiancée Felice Bauer contained the very same root. Just as the paragraph quoted above links the issue of autobiographical material with the notion of "bauen," so does Kafka's life experience link the possibility of personal development, in particular the founding of a family, with an alliance to a Bauer. The name Bauer thus has nearly the same depth of resonance for Kafka as his own; and just as we find numerous crows, jackdaws, and all sorts of human-like animals in his stories, so do we find here a protagonist who is precisely a "Bauer" (builder, burrower) in the most fundamental, literal sense. Of course he is also an animal-human amalgam, so that there is an element of the "kavka" in him as well. The narrator of "Der Bau" is thus, in literature, a sort of offspring of a marriage between a Kafka and a Bauer that almost, but never quite, took place in real life.

We can also see in the house-building fragment a link between the construction ("aufbauen") of a text and the development ("aufbauen") of a human self. This is once again a very common Kafkan theme, one that is investigated in the fragment in an atmosphere of the direst anxiety. The burrow-builder, in spite of the self-satisfaction he expresses in his opening statement, is filled with nagging fears that at times reach the level of pure dread (e.g. "bleibt nur die Annahme der Existenz des großen Tieres" [*EP* 201; "it only remains for me to assume the existence of a great beast," *CS* 353]). What is at stake is the very existence of the builder, not only because the strange noises he hears might signal the presence of a dangerous predator, but because, if the integrity of the construction is compromised, the meaning of its constructor's existence is put into question. There is, after all, little more to the life of this creature than its building activity. The story is exclusively concerned with the burrow, its construction, and its properties. We know nothing about the narrator apart from stray hints that come in the course of his discussion of the structure.

This is quite in keeping with Kafka's sense of himself as having practically no existence apart from literature. What Kafka was making when he wrote was nothing less than himself, a self that was for him a kind of house that was constantly under construction and reconstruction. It is quite logical, even inevitable, under such circumstances that in the story the burrow-builder's anxiety about his building should escalate almost immediately to a terror of physical violence. The burrow is in effect an extension of his body, and harm to it is indistinguishable from a wound. The narrator is quite explicit: "die Empfindlichkeit des Baues hat mich empfindlich gemacht, seine Verletzungen schmerzen mich als wären es die meinen" (*EP* 203; "the vulnerability of the burrow has made me vulnerable; any wound to it hurts me as if I myself were hit," *CS* 355). And paradoxically, the more he extends and refines this burrow-body, the more vulnerable he becomes, because "Eben als Besitzer dieses großen empfindlichen Werkes bin ich wohlverstanden gegenüber jedem ernsteren Angriff wehrlos" (*EP* 203; "simply by virtue of being owner of this great vulnerable edifice I am obviously defenseless against any serious attack," *CS* 355).

The exact nature of the threat to the builder's vulnerable structure is not known to him; he can only make anxious guesses. He is by nature trepidatious, and he believes in the existence of enemies: "es gibt auch solche [Feinde] im Innern der Erde, ich habe sie noch nie gesehen, aber die Sagen erzählen von ihnen und ich glaube fest an sie" (*EP* 167; "enemies in the bowels of the earth. I have never seen them, but legend tells of them and I firmly believe in them," *CS* 326). Such enemies cannot be seen, and even "selbst wer ihr Opfer ist hat sie kaum gesehen, sie kommen, man hört das Kratzen ihrer Krallen knapp unter sich in der Erde, die ihr Element ist, und schon ist man verloren" (*EP* 167; "their very victims can scarcely have seen them; they come, you hear the scratching of their claws just under you in the ground, which is their element, and already you are lost," *CS* 326). Thus only a noise indicates the presence of such a terrifying danger. No wonder, then, that any unidentified noise causes the burrower to worry, and no wonder, too, that the most wonderful experience he knows is the total silence of his burrow. When that silence is broken, even if only by a barely perceptible whistling noise ("Zischen oder Pfeifen," *EP* 200), there can be no peace for the burrower.

The noise that bothers him at first seems to be the work of the little creatures he calls "Kleinzeug" ("small fry," *EP* 193 *et passim*), very possibly the mice he mentions early in the narrative and allows to share his dwelling because they serve as a ready source of food (*CS* 327). But this reassuring explanation doesn't satisfy, for the noise — if indeed there really is a noise — can be heard all over the burrow, even in its innermost core. The very ubiquity of the frightening sound occasionally affords a temporary reassurance: perhaps it means that the great beast is still very far away. But the narrator's imagination will not be satisfied with such explanations, and he continues to fear the worst.

Indeed the narrator's power of imagination ("Einbildungskraft"), specifically mentioned as the source of his notion of a great beast (*EP* 201), is surely as much the source of his problem as is the noise itself. The alien whistler with its terrible claws and jaws is just as much a construction of the narrator as is his beloved burrow. He has built the one by zealous digging, the other by obsessive acts of imagination. Both are aspects of the narrator's self, perhaps equally valid expressions of that self. We can see how deeply the burrower identifies himself with the burrow in his apostrophe to it:

> Euretwegen Ihr Gänge und Plätze, und Du vor allem Burgplatz, bin ich ja gekommen, habe mein Leben für nichts geachtet nachdem ich lange Zeit die Dummheit hatte seinetwegen zu zittern und die Rückkehr zu Euch zu verzögern. Was kümmert mich die Gefahr jetzt, da ich bei Euch bin. Ihr gehört zu mir, ich zu Euch, verbunden sind wir, was kann uns geschehen." (*EP* 187).

> [It is for your sake, ye passages and rooms, and you Castle Keep, above all, that I have come back, counting my life as nothing in the balance, after stupidly trembling for so long, and postponing my return to you. What do I care for danger now that I am with you? You belong to me, and I to you, we are united; what can harm us? (*CS* 342)]

Here is rhetoric of a very specific sort, in the form of a series of "rhetorical" questions. Such questions are called rhetorical because they appear not to seek an answer but rather to deny the existence of the thing put into question. "What do I care?" means "I don't care," and "what can harm us?" means "nothing can harm us." The possibility that these particular questions are rhetorical seems even stronger in Kafka's manuscript, where there are no question marks.

But of course one cannot be certain that the questions really are "rhetorical" in this way. Kafka writes in such a way as to prevent us from being absolutely sure that his questions do not expect an answer. As the narrative continues, it becomes clear that the burrower does indeed care and that he believes he can be harmed. So these could be genuine questions, and they could have very unpleasant answers. "What can harm us?" "What do I care?" In fact, the narrative goes into a great deal of detail about what could harm the burrower, and how he could be harmed, and why he should care. Even if the danger exists only in his imagination, it remains a powerful force in a world that is entirely constructed by the narrator. Since so much of the burrower's world is the product of his imagination to begin with, that world is particularly vulnerable to enemies that exist inside that same imaginative space.

The imagined enemy communicates its presence by a discourse of piping or whistling that may itself be another product of the imagination. He admits that the noise that bothers him is almost inaudible and that nobody but himself would hear it. But in effect it makes no difference whether the noise comes from the external world of the "earth" or the internal world of the burrower's psyche, since it is not so much the noise itself as what is made of it that matters. The sound becomes important only in the construction of the narrator, where we understand "construction" both as a thing built and a thing interpreted (construed). Even if the noise is trivial, faint, hardly perceptible, perhaps not really there at all, its significance is at least potentially profound. This little tiny noise might be the most important thing in the burrower's universe, and within the space of the story it indeed becomes so, no matter what uncertainties remain about its exact nature. Indeed, shortly before the fragment breaks off, the burrower confesses: "Ich bin so weit, daß ich Gewißheit gar nicht haben will" (*EP* 206; "I have reached the stage where I no longer wish to have certainty," *CS* 358).

Certainty of any kind also eludes the narrator of Kafka's very last story, "Josefine die Sängerin, oder oder Das Volk der Mäuse" (Josephine the Singer, or the Mouse Folk). He, too, urgently wants to know the meaning of a piping or whistling sound ("Pfeifen") made by an enigmatic and possibly dangerous creature, and ultimately he, too, must be content with guesses.

Of course there are a number of significant differences between the "Der Bau" fragment and "Josefine." For one thing, Kafka completed the latter text and published it during his lifetime, so we have what we can consider an "authorized" text to work with. For another, the narrator of "Josefine" is not also the central figure in the tale but rather an observer with only limited direct participation in the events narrated. This distance between the teller of the story and its leading characters complicates the tale's rhetorical structure, for there is an additional layer of language that lies between the reader and the voice of the protagonist. When we hear the voice of the burrower, we hear it directly; but when we hear Josephine, we hear her as she is heard and understood by someone else. We can be very sure that Kafka made a deliberate decision to insert this interpreting other between us and the heroine, for it is precisely the problem of what to make of her singing — if it is indeed "singing" that she does — that stands at the heart of the fiction.

Still, despite these and other differences, it is difficult indeed not to see a strong resemblance between these two stories so urgently concerned with a noise described by the German word *Pfeifen* ("whistling" or "piping"). One is tempted to believe that Kafka has moved from one part of the burrower's world to another, one only hinted at near the beginning of the burrower's narrative when he mentions the field mice who dig certain holes he finds useful. Perhaps the piping "Mouse Folk" of this last story are not-so-distant relatives of these little burrowers. And it is difficult, too, not to see the work of the burrow-builder, an activity that lies somewhere between inborn instinct and highly conscious art, reflected in the activity of a mouse-singer whose song is hardly distinguishable from the natural piping sounds made by all mice.

Readers of Kafka have long since noticed that many of his later fictions deal either explicitly or implicitly with art, artists, artworks, and audiences, and that he is particularly concerned with forms of art that border on or curiously merge with ordinary, non-artistic pursuits. In addition to "Der Bau" and "Josefine" there is the famous and much interpreted tale of "Ein Hungerkünstler" (A Hunger Artist), in which the art practiced — abstention from food and drink — is presented as the sole possible lifestyle for an artist who has never found any food he could stomach. Is this art? Should we admire it and reward it? Should we pay any attention to it at all? Very similar questions arise in the case of Josephine's singing, and it is quite clear that Kafka wanted his readers to share his urgent interest in them.

"Ich habe oft darüber nachgedacht, wie es sich eigentlich mit dieser Musik verhält," says the narrator early on in his exposition (*D* 350; "I have often thought about what this music of hers really means," *CS* 360). In a more literal translation, the narrator is wondering "how matters really stand with this music." In other words, he is not so much concerned with how to interpret any particular performance of hers as with the question of what place her singing has in the larger scheme of things. The question comes up because no one, including the narrator, is exactly sure what Josephine does, if anything, that deserves any special notice:

> Ist es denn überhaupt Gesang? Ist es vielleicht doch nur ein Pfeifen?
> Und Pfeifen allerdings kennen wir alle, es ist die eigentliche Kunstfer-

tigkeit unseres Volkes, oder vielmehr gar keine Fertigkeit, sondern eine charakeristische Lebensäußerung. Alle pfeifen wir, aber freilich denkt niemand daran, das als Kunst auszugeben, wir pfeifen, ohne darauf zu achten. . . . (*D* 351–52)

[So is it singing at all? Is it not perhaps just a piping? And piping is something we all know about, it is the real artistic accomplishment of our people, or rather no mere accomplishment but a characteristic expression of our life. We all pipe, but of course no one dreams of making out that our piping is an art, we pipe without thinking of it. . . . (*CS* 361)]

The problem becomes complicated by two curious facts: first, Josephine's piping, ordinary though it may be, draws eager, receptive, and enthusiastic audiences; and second, Josephine, ordinary though she may be, demands for herself special privileges on account of the status she claims as a unique artist.

One thing, at least, about Josephine's piping appears clear: it has a profound effect on those who listen to it. The narrator confesses that, no matter how ordinary her vocalizing may be, "dringt doch — das ist nicht zu leugnen — etwas von ihrem Pfeifen unweigerlich auch zu uns" (*D* 362; "there is yet something — it cannot be denied — that irresistibly makes its way into us from Josephine's piping," *CS* 367). For a moment her singing becomes the most important thing in the world, a kind of "Botschaft des Volkes zu dem Einzelnen" (*D* 362; "message from the whole people to each individual," *CS* 367). In this way the otherwise unremarkable little singer becomes the voice of the entire community and thus, in some sense, as valuable as the whole community. That, at least, is the claim she wants to press.

Josephine's ability to hold and affect her audience may serve as evidence that her piping is really a form of art; but not everyone believes it, particularly because this very ability is also a significant problem for the community. From time to time "such large gatherings have been unexpectedly flushed by the enemy, and many of our people left lying for dead" very possibly because Josephine "attracted the enemy by her piping" (*CS* 371; "solche Versammlungen unerwartet vom Feind gesprengt wurden, und mancher der unsrigen dabei sein Leben lassen mußte . . . durch ihr Pfeifen den Feind vielleicht angelockt hatte," *D* 367). The consequences of this "art" can be nothing short of disastrous for its adherents, and yet the audiences continue to assemble. Is this evidence that Josephine's singing is remarkable, or does it only prove that her audience is courageous, foolhardy, or perhaps some bizarre combination of both?

In fact the narrator pays nearly as much attention to the nature of Josephine's audience as he does to Josephine herself. Kafka clearly meant to keep both artist and public firmly in focus when he gave his story a double title, the first half naming the singer and the second specifying the community that forms her audience. And he connected the two with the rhetorically complex little word "or." The complexity arises from the fact that "or" can be used in either an exclusive or inclusive way. "Give me liberty or give me death!" is a forceful use of the exclusive "or," since the speaker clearly considers the two possibilities mutually incompatible. But one can also use "or" in circumstances where one thing can readily substitute for another. "In this recipe you may use butter or margarine": the implication is that it doesn't much matter which. You could presumably even use a combination of both butter and margarine if you didn't have quite enough of either to do the whole job. The German word "oder" behaves in exactly the same way. In the case of Kafka's title, though, it is impossible to say whether the reader is supposed to understand the "oder" as an inclusive or exclusive "or." Are we supposed to make a choice between Josephine and the Mouse Folk, or are we to believe that one can take the place of the other?

The issue is far from trivial. It is a frequent claim of the artist — an artist such as Thomas Mann, to name one prominent example that Kafka knew well — that the artist can indeed "take the place" of the group by serving as its collective voice. The individual represents the whole people. At times, so the narrator reports, just such a thing seems to happen when Josephine sings. But at other times, as in the passage quoted above in which Josephine's singing puts the group in deadly danger, it appears that artist and community are at odds, that the welfare of one is harmful to the other. Kafka's story does not attempt to resolve this question; rather it seeks to pose it in the most forceful way possible.

Josephine herself makes the whole matter more difficult by drawing herself apart from the group that nurtures and protects her. She even scoffs at the very idea of obtaining protection from the community: "Ich pfeife auf euren Schutz," she says (*D* 359), which literally means "I whistle (or pipe) on your protection." The desperate translator grasps at straws and comes up with "Your protection isn't worth an old song" (*CS* 365–66). The locution that Josephine employs turns the word used for her artistic activity, piping ("Pfeifen"), into a vulgar gesture of rejection. It also forces the reader to reconsider the whole question of what it is that Josephine does when she sings: *sie pfeift auf das Volk,* to express it in the terms the story presents. The German pun tacitly proposes that when Josephine pipes for the people, she also "pipes on" (that is, rejects) the people. The people, however, placidly disregard this rejection and continue to listen to her piping in rapt silence, "mäuschenstill" ("quiet as a mouse"). Now perhaps this is no great feat for people who really are mice, but still it bespeaks respect — a respect that Josephine, for her part, does not reciprocate.

She separates herself even further from the people by demanding special treatment:

Schon seit langer Zeit, vielleicht schon seit Beginn ihrer Künstlerlauf-bahn, kämpft Josefine darum, daß sie mit Rücksicht auf ihren Gesang von jeder Arbeit befreit werde; man solle ihr also die Sorge um das täg-liche Brot und alles, was sonst mit unserem Existenzkampf verbunden ist, abnehmen und es — wahrscheinlich — auf das Volk als Ganzes überwälzen. (*D* 368–69)

[For a long time, perhaps since the very beginning of her artistic career, Josephine has been fighting for exemption from all daily work on ac-count of her singing; she should be relieved of all responsibility for earning her daily bread and being involved in the general struggle for existence, which — apparently — should be transferred on her behalf to the people as a whole. (*CS* 371)]

Kafka had a very personal stake in this claim for exemption from daily work. He had in fact actually achieved something like the dispensa-tion Josephine desires, though not because of his art. He had been pen-sioned off from his job at the Workers' Accident Insurance Company because of his illness, and this respite from the need to earn a living allowed him — for a short time — to devote himself entirely to his writ-ing. Josephine, however, has no success in persuading the community to approve her request. In marked contrast to her singing, her rhetoric falls on deaf ears: "Das Volk hört sie an und geht darüber hinweg. Dieses so leicht zu rührende Volk ist manchmal gar nicht zu rühren" (*D* 369; "The people listen to her arguments and pay no attention. Our people, so easily moved, sometimes cannot be moved at all," (*CS* 372).

But Josephine persists: "hat sie ihn [den Kampf] bisher nur durch Worte geführt, fängt sie jetzt an, andere Mittel auszuwenden" (*D* 372; "hitherto she has used only words as her weapons but now she is begin-ning to have recourse to other means," *CS* 373). These other means include a claim of injury, a threat to alter her performance by cutting the embellishments ("Koloraturen" — the translation has "grace notes"), and a protestation that she is too exhausted to perform. None is effective. Finally Josephine plays what she must believe is her trump card: she disappears. Surely her complete absence, the utter loss of her song, will persuade the Mouse Folk of her unique value.

Of course even this ultimate gesture is futile. The community finds that the absence of her singing is not detectably different from its presence. With a gentle, excruciatingly candid simplicity, the narrator asks a set of devastating rhetorical questions:

> War ihr wirkliches Pfeifen nennenswert lauter und lebendiger, als die Erinnerung daran sein wird? War es denn noch bei ihren Lebzeiten mehr als eine bloße Erinnerung? Hat nicht vielleicht vielmehr das Volk in seiner Weisheit Josefinens Gesang, eben deshalb, weil er in dieser Art unverlierbar war, so hochgestellt? (*D* 376–77)

> [Was her actual piping notably louder and more alive than the memory of it will be? Was it even in her lifetime more than a simple memory? Was it not rather because Josephine's singing was already past losing in this way that our people in their wisdom prized it so highly? (*CS* 376)]

The power of Josephine's art is by no means denied; what is denied is only that Josephine is needed for that power to find expression. The memory of her singing might actually be even more powerful than its physical presence, since the process of imagination that makes memory possible need not be constrained by the rough contingencies of the real world. It can let the imagined song soar higher, farther, and purer than any real-life song ever could.

The lines that close "Josefine die Sängerin" were the last Kafka ever wrote. When he speaks of the little mouse singer in the final words of the text as being "vergessen . . . wie alle ihre Brüder" (*D* 377; "forgotten like all her brothers," *CS* 376), he was certainly thinking of his own future. We would be mistaken, though, to assume that Kafka saw his story's end, or the end of its heroine, as a melancholy one. The forgetting that is to befall the singer is placed in sharp contrast to the remembering of the song. Indeed, the community's forgetting of Josephine is possible and even likely precisely because the memory of her song is so secure. The artist may disappear forever, but the art remains intact and alive in the imagination of the audience.

Kafka believed in, and wanted us to believe in, the power of imagined discourse. This power could be corrosive and even lethal, as it seems to be in the "Der Bau" fragment, or it could be healing and revivifying, as it is in "Josefine." In either case, the locus of that power is not in its producer, whether the terrifying piping beast or the fragile piping mouse, but in those who hear the piping and make something of it. Kafka believed that those who imagine might make something of his often tentative, often incomplete, sometimes barely comprehensible art and turn it into a force far more powerful than his failing presence could ever be. In that way he, like Josephine, could attain the "gesteigerte Erlösung" (*D* 377; "heights of redemption," *CS* 376) and join the vast and peaceful community of the forgotten.

Works Cited

Cohn, Dorrit. "Erlebte Rede im Ich-Roman," *Germanisch-Romanische Monatsschrift* 19 (1969): 305–13.

Kafka, Franz. *The Complete Stories*. Ed. Nahum Glatzer. New York: Schocken Books, 1971. (*CS*)

———. "Der Bau." *Das Ehepaar und andere Schriften aus dem Nachlaß*. Ed. Hans-Gerd Koch. Frankfurt am Main: S. Fischer Verlag, 1994. (*EP*)

———. *Drucke zu Lebzeiten*. Ed. Wolf Kittler, Hans-Gerd Koch, Gerhard Neumann. Frankfurt am Main: S. Fischer Verlag, 1994. (*D*)

Koelb, Clayton. *Kafka's Rhetoric: The Passion of Reading*. Ithaca and London: Cornell UP, 1989.

Notes on the Contributors

RUSSELL A. BERMAN is the Walter A. Haas Professor in the Humanities at Stanford University, where he has been a member of the faculty since 1979. His books include: *The Rise of the Modern German Novel* (1986); *Modern Culture and Critical Theory* (1989); *Cultural Studies of Modern Germany* (1993); and *Enlightenment or Empire: Colonial Discourse in German Culture* (1998). He is currently working on a book on literary history.

STANLEY CORNGOLD is Professor of German and Comparative Literature at Princeton University. He is the author of *The Fate of the Self: German Writers and French Theory* (1986); *Borrowed Lives, a novel* (with Irene Giersing, 1991); and *Complex Pleasure: Forms of Feeling in German Literature* (1998). In addition to an earlier study of Kafka titled *The Commentators' Despair: The Interpretation of Kafka's "Metamorphosis"* (1973), he has written *Franz Kafka: The Necessity of Form* (Cornell UP, 1988) and a new book on Kafka tentatively titled "Lambent Traces."

SANDER L. GILMAN is a distinguished professor of the Liberal Arts and Medicine at the University of Illinois, Chicago. A cultural and literary historian, he is the author of a study of Franz Kafka, *The Jewish Patient* (1995). His other books include a study of the visual stereotyping of the mentally ill, *Seeing the Insane* (1982), as well as *Jewish Self-Hatred* (1986).

ROLF J. GOEBEL is Professor of German at the University of Alabama in Huntsville. He is the author of two books on Kafka: *Kritik und Revision: Kafkas Rezeption mythologischer, biblischer und historischer Traditionen* (1986), and *Constructing China: Kafka's Orientalist Discourse* (1997), as well as numerous articles on Kafka, Benjamin, and other, mostly modernist writers. He is co-editor of the *Franz Kafka Encyclopedia* (forthcoming, Greenwood Press).

RICHARD GRAY is Professor of German at the University of Washington and the author of *Constructive Destruction: Kafka's Aphorisms, Literary Tradition and Literary Transformation* (1987) as well as *Stations of the Divided Subject: Contestation and Ideological Legitimation in German Bourgeois Literature, 1770–1914* (1995). He is editor of the MLA volume *Approaches to Teaching Kafka's Short Fiction* (1995), as well as one of the editors of the *Franz Kafka Encyclopedia* currently in preparation for Greenwood Press.

RUTH V. GROSS is Professor of German at the University of Texas, Arlington, where she has served as Dean of the College of Liberal Arts. She is the author of *PLAN and the Austrian Rebirth* (1982) and editor of *Critical Essays on Franz Kafka* (1990), as well as a co-editor of the *Franz Kafka Encyclopedia* (Greenwood Press, forthcoming).

MARK HARMAN is Associate Professor of Modern Languages at Elizabethtown College. He is the translator of Kafka's *The Castle* (1998) and author of articles on Kleist, Joyce, Beckett, Kafka, and Robert Walser, as well as the theory and practice of translation.

CLAYTON KOELB is the Guy B. Johnson Professor of German and Comparative Literature at the University of North Carolina, Chapel Hill. He is the author of *Kafka's Rhetoric: The Passion of Reading* (1989) and is co-editor (with Richard Gray, Ruth Gross, and Rolf Goebel) of the forthcoming *Franz Kafka Encyclopedia*.

RITCHIE ROBERTSON is Professor of German, University of Oxford, and Fellow and Tutor of St. John's College, Oxford. His main publications include: *Kafka: Judaism, Politics, and Literature* (1985); *Heine*, in the series Jewish Thinkers (1988); and *The 'Jewish Question' in German Literature, 1749–1939: Emancipation and its Discontents* (1999). He is editor of *The Cambridge Companion to Thomas Mann*, forthcoming 2002.

JAMES L. ROLLESTON is Professor of German and Literature at Duke University and author of *Rilke in Transition* (1970), *Kafka's Narrative Theater* (1974), and *Narratives of Ecstasy: Romantic Theory and Modern German Poetry* (1985). His translation of Bernd Witte's *Walter Benjamin* won the literary prize of the American Translators Association in 1993. He has also translated Peter Weiss's last play *The New Trial* (2001).

JUDITH RYAN is Professor of German and Comparative Literature at Harvard University. Her books include *The Uncompleted Past: Post-War German Novels and the Third Reich* (1983); *The Vanishing Subject: Early Psychology and Literary Modernism* (1991); and *Rilke, Modernism and Poetic Tradition* (1999).

WALTER H. SOKEL is Professor of German, Emeritus, at the University of Virginia. His books include *The Writer in Extremis: Expressionism in 20th Century German Literature* (1959*); Franz Kafka: Tragik und Ironie* (1964); and *The Myth of Power and the Self: Essays on Franz Kafka* (2002). He is now working on a study of Nietzsche.

HENRY SUSSMAN is Professor of Comparative Literature at the State University of New York, Buffalo. His interests include psychoanalysis, critical theory, and modernism/postmodernism. He has written *Franz Kafka: Geometrician of Metaphor* (1979); *Hegelian Aftermath* (1982); and *Afterimages of Modernity* (1990).

BIANCA THEISEN is Associate Professor of German at The Johns Hopkins University. She is author of *Bogenschluß: Kleists Formalisierung des Lesens* (1996), and has published articles on Romanticism, Nietzsche, Thomas Bernhard, and on literary theory. Currently she is completing a book on contemporary Austrian Literature.

JOHN ZILCOSKY is an Assistant Professor of German and Associate Member of the Centre for Comparative Literature at the University of Toronto. His first book, *Kafka's Travels: Exoticism, Colonialism, and the Traffic of Writing* (New York: St. Martin's/Palgrave), is forthcoming in December 2002. He has published essays on travel writing, colonialism, and literary theory, as well as on Arthur Schopenhauer, Botho Strauss, and Paul Auster.

Index